THE WORLD'S WISDOM

The World's Wisdom

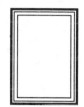

SACRED TEXTS

OF THE

WORLD'S RELIGIONS

PHILIP NOVAK

HarperSanFrancisco
A Division of HarperCollins*Publishers*

Library of Congress Cataloging-in-Publication Data:
The world's wisdom : sacred texts of the world's religions /
Philip Novak. — 1st ed.
        p.   cm.
Includes bibliographic references and index.

1. Sacred books.   I. Title.
BL70.N68   1994   93–43995
291.8'2–dc20   CIP

TO HUSTON

One should follow the wise, the intelligent,
the learned, the much enduring, the dutiful,
the noble; one should follow a good and wise
man, as the moon follows the path of the stars.
(Dhammapada, 208)

Contents

Foreword

HUSTON SMITH

Because this anthology of sacred texts is linked to my own *The World's Religions*, it could be predicted that I would speak well of it. My response, however, is more than perfunctory. The reasons lie with the book's subject, its approach to that subject, and its craftsmanship.

Because his book presents (rather than discusses) religious material, Philip Novak does not mention revelation, but that is essentially what his book is about. This sets the stage for the book's importance, for revelation has shaped human history more than any other force besides technology. Whether revelation issues from God or from the deepest unconscious of spiritual geniuses can be debated, but its signature is invariably power. The periodic incursions—explosions, we might call them—of this power in history are what created the world's great religions, and by extension, the civilizations they have bodied forth. Its dynamite is its news of another world. Revelation invariably tells us of a separate (though not removed) order of existence that simultaneously relativizes and exalts the one we normally know. It relativizes the everyday world by showing it to be less than the "all" that we unthinkingly take it to be, and that demotion turns out to be exhilarating. By placing the quotidian world in a vastly more meaningful context, revelation dignifies it the way a worthy setting enhances the beauty of a precious stone. People respond to this news of life's larger meaning because they hear in it the final warrant for their existence.

If revelation thus understood provides Novak with a worthy subject, how does he approach it? Through its primary sources.

The subtitle of this book announces that it will consist almost entirely of sacred texts, which (in being the earliest reports of the revelations they register) take us as close to their original scenes as we can possibly get. In translation, they provide us with either the actual words through which the world-transfiguring "news" broke into human consciousness, or with eyewitness accounts of revelatory events. Firsthand accounts carry authority in themselves, but in the case of sacred texts, the diction in which they are couched augments that authority. For one thing, it attests to the impact the events had on their reporters; but more important, revelatory accounts are like Rorschach blots in the wealth of interpretations they allow. Commentators never tire of going back to comb them for ever subtler meanings: it is said that every verse of the Qur'an contains a minimum of seven inner significances, and the number can reach to seventy. We hear that "the medium is the message," and with sacred texts this is substantially the case. In favoring direct accounts of revelation—its aftershocks as well as its original earthquakes—Novak honors it in ways that secondary sources cannot.

Every anthology of sacred texts can claim these two virtues, but that is not the case with this book's third virtue.

Revelations are not mere assemblages. They are organisms and works of art, where presiding forms and controlling ideas count for everything. This presents a challenge for those who would anthologize them, for texts are not like pictures that can be reduced without losing anything but scale. Reducing a sacred text requires choosing at every point between what must be sacrificed (to keep the book within bounds) and what must be retained to preserve the revelation's integrity. In addition, thin explanatory tightwires must be stretched across the chasms that deletions create. Enter all the insight, talent, and gifts of discernment that an anthologizer can muster and pray for. It is a daunting project. In the end success turns on spiritual artistry, and the plainest compliment I can pay this book is to say that nowhere else in its genre have I found Novak's artistry equaled.

A word about the book's title. When I first learned that it was to be *The World's Wisdom*, I feared pretension, but I have come to accept it as accurate. Traditional cosmologies do not figure in Novak's texts, modern science having retired them. Nor are social mores (gender relationships and the like) his concern, for these too need to be rethought in our changed world. What remains is the vision of ultimate reality and the way human life can best be comported in its context. That is what Novak fixes on, and I do not know where I could turn to find a richer harvest.

Preface

This book springs from fifteen years of teaching the world's religions at the college level and from an ingrained habit of seasoning lectures with illustrative quotations from foundational texts. The search for a one-volume anthology to replace my own increasingly unmanageable sheaf of papers had long been futile. Few scriptural anthologies covered the ground in one volume; those that did either proffered a format that I found disagreeable or tried to be so inclusive that they became prohibitively bulky. When offered the opportunity to create this new anthology, I eagerly embraced it.

Three criteria governed the composition of the present text: inspirational power, instructional value, and linkage. A word about each.

Inspirational power. Especially when the intended audiences are the beginning student and the general reader, it is easily as important for a text to inspire as to instruct. For it is often upon an initial opening of the heart in wonder and delight that all further study depends. I have therefore taken pains to choose passages that I believe will edify, exalt, and refresh. And in each chapter's concluding "Grace Notes" I roam beyond the scriptural boundaries of the earlier sections to present the brightest gems I could find, many of which reflect the universal character and transcendent unity of these wisdom traditions. The text's power to inspire is also the criterion that counted most when I was faced with a difficult choice among translations. Accustomed to reading aloud to students, I gave the nod to renditions that I felt stood the best chance of quivering a listener's viscera.

Instructional value. Religions share profound family resemblances, but each is also unique. I have tried in every chapter to reveal a tradition's crucial mythic or historical moments, its central doctrines and practices, its distinctive vision, and its characteristic moods. Almost every passage has been pedagogically helpful to me in presenting the uniqueness of these traditions. Teachers will chart their own courses through the chapters, but I have composed each with the hope that any reader, moving attentively from beginning to end, will be rewarded with a vivid sense of a tradition's distinctive personality. To reduce clutter I have kept introductory and explanatory comments to a minimum; enough remains, I believe, to guide solo readers to happy discoveries. In all but the final Grace Notes section of each chapter, I have confined myself almost entirely to selections from foundational scriptures. Only two liberties were taken with them: occasional alteration for inclusive language and frequent minor abridgement—without rewording—in order to include a larger number of selections in the space I allowed myself.

Linkage. Anticipating its use in academic settings, I have linked *The World's Wisdom* to Huston Smith's acclaimed expository text, *The World's Religions* (formerly *The Religions of Man*), a favorite among instructors for almost forty years. The aims of that book— to focus on core ideas and values and to treat the world's religions at their best (as opposed to examining their historical vicissitudes and all-too-human vagaries)—are echoed here. The structure of Smith's book has also been mirrored, thus limiting the number of traditions covered to eight: Hinduism, Buddhism, Confucianism, Taoism, Judaism, Christianity, Islam, and Primal Religions as a category. By virtue of their longevity, historical impact, and/or numbers of current adherents, these are undeniably major traditions. They also seem to be those most often surveyed in introductory courses. Other traditions that could justifiably claim longevity or impact—Zoroastrianism, Jainism, Sikhism, Shinto, the Latter Day Saints—are not included here, not because of any inherent defect or unworthiness, but simply because that inclusion would have caused the length of the current volume to swell unacceptably. Though the linkage to Professor Smith's work is deliberate, it is certainly neither slavish nor obtrusive. Nothing prevents the current volume from being used in tandem with a different covering text or indeed from being enjoyed in and for itself. Every effort has been taken to make it meaningful for the general reader.

Religion shows an ugly face to many contemporary eyes. In-group prejudice, violence perpetrated in its name, sexism, commercialism, and quackery—these crude surfaces often blind us to the liberating wisdom that courses far below. Let us readily admit that not all aspects of these wisdom traditions are enduringly wise.[1] Their cosmologies have been overtaken by modern science, and their social blueprints, drawn for times now gone, need revision in the light of changed circumstances and the continuing quest for social justice. But while jettisoning their chaff, we should continue to sift for wheat. "The telling question of a person's life," Carl Jung once wrote, "is whether or not [she or] he is related to the infinite."[2] The animating conviction of this book is that these great wisdom traditions remain our most resourceful guides to the Infinite—to that "Beauty so ancient and so new,"[3] "Eternal"[4] yet "closer to us than our jugular veins,"[5] vouchsafing the "unshakeable deliverance of the heart"[6] and the "End of all love-longing."[7]

Let me take this opportunity to thank: at Harper San Francisco, John Loudon for his encouragement and savvy, Priscilla Stuckey for her magnificent editorial work, Mimi Kusch for an angel's aid in the home stretch, and Karen Levine for her patience and help; Mark and Amy Brokering and Paula and Jim Karman for their moral support; my friends and professional colleagues Rabbi Einat Ramon, Rabbi Arik Ascherman, the Reverend Raymond Gawronski, S.J., Dr. Alan Godlas, Dr. Scott Sinclair, and Dr.

---

1. Cf. Huston Smith, *The World's Religions* (San Francisco: HarperSanFrancisco, 1991), 387.
2. Carl Jung, *Memories, Dreams, Reflections* (New York: Pantheon, 1963), 325.
3. Christianity (Augustine).
4. Judaism.
5. Islam (Qur'an).
6. Buddhism.
7. Hinduism (Upanishads).

Kendra Smith for incisive critiques of portions of the text; Katie Field for researching some elusive facts; the students of Dominican College who have explored the wisdom traditions with me; Bridgett Novak for helping me regain balance and perspective when they slipped away (and for some serious typing too); and, finally, Huston Smith, to whom this book is dedicated and without whom it would not be. What is of worth here belongs to him—and the traditions; the rest is mine.

CHAPTER ONE

Hinduism

S*ome four thousand years ago pastoral nomads whose ancestors had sprung from the soil of northeastern Europe entered the Indus Valley of ancient India. They called themselves Aryans, or Noble Ones, and the religion they brought with them comprised the first evolutionary layer of Hinduism. The ritual centerpiece of Aryan religion was a fire sacrifice, a burnt offering to the gods, performed by priests specially trained to chant sacred hymns. The hymns themselves were known as Vedas or "sacred knowledge." The Vedas are the scriptural bedrock of the Hindu tradition.*

The aim of the Vedic fire sacrifice, indeed of Aryan religion in general, was to ensure well-being and prosperity in this life. The early Vedas, the focus of the first section, contain little evidence of sustained thought about human destiny beyond this life. The doctrines most of us associate with Hinduism—the cycle of reincarnations driven by karma and the liberation from this bondage by means of yogic discipline—were to be reflected only a thousand years later in the most recent layers of Vedic literature, called the Upanishads. Selections from the Upanishads comprise the second section of this chapter. The third section focuses on the scripture called the Bhagavad Gita and has its own introduction.

THE EARLY VEDAS

1. He, O Men, Is Indra

Of the four collections of Vedas, the Rig-Veda is the most important and foundational. The most popular god of the Rig-Veda is the expansive and dynamic Indra. He is said to have surpassed the other gods in power as soon as he was born (v. 1), and he is credited both with having created the world by slaying a cosmic serpent and thus releasing the life-giving, monsoon-bringing waters (v. 3), and with helping the Aryans overcome the non-Aryan populations they encountered.

> The chief wise god who as soon as born
>   surpassed the gods in power;
> Before whose vehemence the two worlds trembled by reason
>   of the greatness of his valor: he, O men, is Indra.
>
> Who made firm the quaking earth
>   who set at rest the agitated mountains;
> Who measures out the air more widely,
>   who supported heaven: he, O men, is Indra.
>
> Who having slain the serpent released the seven streams . . .
> Who has made subject the Dasa colour [the non-Aryan
>   population] and has made it disappear . . .
>
> The terrible one of whom they ask "where is he,"
>   of whom they also say "he is not";
> He diminishes the possessions of the foe like the stakes
>   of gamblers. Believe in him: he, O men, is Indra . . .
>
> Even Heaven and Earth bow down before him;
>   before his vehemence even the mountains are afraid.
> Who is known as the Soma-drinker,[1] holding the bolt
>   in his . . . hand: he, O men, is Indra.

---

1. See selection no. 3, below.

2. O Agni, Dispeller of the Night

Because of his role in the all-important fire sacrifice, Agni, the god of fire, is perhaps second only to Indra in popularity, with over one thousand hymns dedicated to him in the Vedas. Here is a brief selection from a few.

a. From Rig-Veda I

I praise Agni, domestic priest, divine minister of sacrifice,
Invoker, greatest bestower of wealth . . .

To thee, dispeller of the night, O Agni, day by day with prayer,
Bringing thee reverence, we come;

Ruler of sacrifices, guard of Law eternal [Rta], radiant one,
Increasing in thine own abode.

Be to us easy of approach, even as a father to his son:
Agni, be with us for our weal.

b. From Rig-Veda II

Thou, Agni, shining in thy glory through the days, art
brought to life from out the waters, from the stone;
From out the forest trees and herbs that grow on ground, thou,
sovereign lord of men, art generated pure.

By thee, O Agni, all the immortal guileless gods eat with thy
mouth the oblation that is offered them.
By thee do mortal men give sweetness to their drink.
Pure art thou born, the embryo of the plants of earth.

c. From Rig-Veda VII

I have begotten this new hymn for Agni, falcon of the sky:
will he not give us of his wealth?

Bright, purifier, meet for praise,
Immortal with refulgent glow,
Agni drives Rakshasas [demons] away.

Agni, preserve us from distress:
consume our enemies, O God Eternal,
with thy hottest flames.

3. We Have Drunk Soma and Become Immortal

*All one hundred and fourteen hymns of the ninth book of the Rig-Veda
are addressed to Soma, the god who inhabits a mysterious psychotropic
beverage, said in the Vedas to be the food of the gods. Soma probably
ranks behind only Indra and Agni in Vedic popularity.*

Of the sweet food I have partaken wisely,
That stirs the good thoughts, best banisher of trouble,
On which to feast, all gods as well as mortals,
Naming the sweet food "honey," come together. . . .

We have drunk Soma, have become immortal,
Gone to the light have we, the gods discovered.
What can hostility do against us?
What, O Immortal, mortal man's fell purpose?

Joy to our heart be thou, when drunk, O Indu,
Like father to a son, most kind, O Soma;
Thoughtful like friend to friend, O thou of wide fame,
Prolong our years that we may live, O Soma.

These glorious freedom-giving drops by me imbibed
Have knit my joints together as straps a chariot;
From broken legs may Soma drops protect me,
May they from every illness keep me far removed. . . .

Be gracious unto us for good, King Soma;
We are thy devotees; of that be certain.
When might and wrath display themselves, O Indu,
Do not abandon us, as wished by foemen.

Protector of our body art thou, Soma,
In every limb hast settled man-beholding:
If we infringe thine ordinances be gracious
As our good friend, O god, for higher welfare. . . .

Ailments have fled away, diseases vanished,
The powers of darkness have become afrighted.
With might hath Soma mounted up within us;
The dawn we've reached, where men renew existence. . . .

4. Varuna, The All-Knowing Guardian of the Cosmic Order (*Rta*)

In these hymns to Varuna, omniscient God and protector of the moral order of the world, we glimpse an early Indian intuition of God's immanence. For transcendent Varuna is also "hidden in this small drop of water."

a. From Rig-Veda I

To gain thy mercy, Varuna, with hymns we bind thy heart,
    as binds
The charioteer his tethered horse . . .

[Varuna] knows the path of birds that fly through heaven, and,
    sovereign of the sea,
He knows the ships that are thereon . . .

He knows the pathway of the wind, the spreading, high and
    mighty wind;
He knows the gods who dwell above.

Varuna, true to holy law, sits down among his people; he,
Most wise, sits there to govern all.

From thence perceiving he beholds all wondrous things, both
    what hath been,
And what hereafter will be done.

b. From Atharva-Veda IV

If a man stands, walks, or sneaks about, if he goes slinking away, if he goes into his hiding-place; if two persons sit together and scheme, King Varuna is there as a third, and knows it.

Both this earth here belongs to King Varuna, and also yonder broad sky whose boundaries are far away. Moreover these two oceans are the loins of Varuna; yea, he is hidden in this small (drop of) water.

He that should flee beyond the heaven far away would not be free from King Varuna. His spies[2] come hither from heaven, with a thousand eyes do they watch over the earth.

King Varuna sees through all that is between heaven and earth, and all that is beyond. He has counted the winkings of men's eyes. As a (winning) gamester puts down his dice, thus does he establish these (laws).

5. Who Can Say How Creation Happened? That One

Though early Vedic religion was blatantly polytheistic, the notion of an underlying and all-encompassing metaphysical unity, so important in the later Upanishads, made an occasional appearance. The following creation hymn marks a level of maturity in Vedic philosophical speculation. In a reflection on origins the author ignores personal names of gods and opts for more abstract concepts like existence and nonexistence (sat and asat). Pondering the possibility that That One (tad ekam) is the ultimate origin of things, the hymn dissolves into total Mystery as its author boldly wonders whether perhaps even That One knows not the Source.

Then even nothingness was not, nor existence.
There was no air then, nor the heavens beyond it.
What covered it? Where was it? In whose keeping?
Was there then a cosmic water, in depths unfathomed?

Then there were neither death nor immortality,
nor was there then the torch of night and day.
The One breathed windlessly and self-sustaining.
There was that One then, and there was no other.

At first there was only darkness wrapped in darkness.
All this was only unillumined water.

---

2. That is, the stars.

That One which came to be, enclosed in nothing,
    arose at last, born of the power of heat.

In the beginning desire descended on it—
    that was the primal seed, born of the mind.
The sages who have searched their hearts with wisdom
    know that which is, is kin to that which is not.

. . . But, after all, who knows, and who can say
    whence it all came, and how creation happened?
The gods themselves are later than creation,
    so who knows truly whence it has arisen?

Whence all creation had its origin,
    he, whether he fashioned it or whether he did not,
he, who surveys it all from highest heaven,
    he knows—or maybe even he does not know.

6. Creation as Cosmic Sacrifice: *The Myth of Divine Self-Immolation and Its Sanction of the Caste System*

A quite different Vedic creation hymn conceives the world's origin as a divine being's (Purusha's) self-sacrifice. Here we confront not only an echo of the theme of many-from-One but also the mythic rationale for the fire sacrifice: since the world began with a divine sacrifice, it is the priestly reenactment of sacrifice that sustains it.

Also important here is the reference to the four social groups (the only such reference in the Rig-Veda) that have constituted the Indian caste system. The Aryan social structure featured a broad occupational division of clans into a priestly caste (Brahmins), a military and political caste (Kshatriyas), and an artisan caste (Vaishyas). Non-Aryan populations were incorporated into this structure mainly as a fourth caste of laborers (Shudras) to serve the other three. Here these social divisions are given a transcendent sanction.

A thousand heads had Purusha, a thousand eyes, a thousand
    feet.
He covered earth on every side, and spread ten fingers' breadth
    beyond.

This Purusha is all that yet hath been and all that is to be;
The Lord of Immortality which waxes greater still by food.

So mighty is his greatness; yea, greater than this is Purusha.
All creatures are one-fourth of him, three-fourths eternal life
in heaven . . .

When gods prepared the sacrifice with Purusha as their
offering,
Its oil was spring, the holy gift was autumn; summer was the
wood. . .

From that great general sacrifice the dripping fat was gathered
up.
He formed the creatures of air, and animals both wild and
tame.

From that great general sacrifice . . . hymns were born;
Therefrom the metres were produced . . .

From it were horses born, from it all creatures with two rows of
teeth;
From it were generated kine, from it the goats and sheep were
born.

When they divided Purusha how many portions did they
make?
What do they call his mouth, his arms? What do they call his
thighs and feet?

The Brahman[3] was his mouth, of both his arms was the
Rajanya [Kshatriya] made.
His thighs became the Vaishya, from his feet the Shudra
was produced.

The moon was gendered from his mind, and from his eye the
sun had birth;
Indra and Agni from his mouth were born, and Vayu from his
breath.

---

3. Variant spelling of Brahmin, the priestly caste.

Forth from his navel came mid-air; the sky was fashioned from
his head;
Earth from his feet, and from his ear the regions. Thus they
formed the worlds.

THE UPANISHADS

*"In the whole world, there is no study so beautiful and so elevating as
the Upanishads. It has been the solace of my life and will be the solace
of my death."*[4] *This is the way that the great nineteenth-century
German philosopher Arthur Schopenhauer paid homage to the sublime
ideas that have been animating the Hindu tradition for almost three
millennia. In the Upanishads, those majestic "Himalayas of the Soul,"
we discover the pan-Indian diagnosis of the human condition as trapped
in a ceaseless round of death and rebirth* (samsara), *due to the consequences of actions* (karma) *performed in ignorance of the divine ground
of all life* (Brahman). *We also hear of the prescription for liberation*
(moksha) *from this confining ignorance through each individual's realization of his or her inner spiritual nature, the Universal Self or
Atman, which is none other than Brahman.*

7. Isa Upanishad: *See All Beings in Your Own Self and Your Self in All Beings*

Behold the universe in the glory of God: and all that lives and
moves on earth. Leaving the transient, find joy in the Eternal: set
not your heart on another's possessions. . . .

The Spirit, without moving, is swifter than the mind; the senses
cannot reach him: He is ever beyond them. Standing still, he overtakes those who run. To the ocean of his being, the spirit of life
leads the streams of action.

. . . Who sees all beings in his own Self, and his own Self in all
beings, loses all fear.

---

4. I have been unable to trace this particular quotation, but Schopenhauer's profound debt to and respect for the Upanishads is well known.

. . . When a sage sees this great Unity and his Self has become all beings, what delusion and what sorrow can ever be near him?

. . . May life go to immortal life, and the body go to ashes, OM.[5] Oh my soul, remember past strivings, remember! O my soul, remember past strivings, remember!

8. Kena Upanishad: *Brahman, the Spirit: Not What People Here Adore*

What cannot be spoken with words, but that whereby words are spoken: Know that alone to be Brahman, the Spirit; and not what people here adore.

What cannot be thought with the mind, but that whereby the mind can think . . .

What cannot be seen with the eye, but that whereby the eye can see . . .

What cannot be heard with the ear, but that whereby the ear can hear . . .

What cannot be indrawn with breath, but that whereby breath is indrawn: Know that alone to be Brahman, the Spirit; and not what people here adore.

9. Katha Upanishad

a. Nachiketas Seeks Wisdom from the King of Death

The Katha Upanishad contains the famous story of Nachiketas, an earnest young yogi who ventures to the abode of Yama, the God of Death, in order to wrest from him the wisdom of life. Nachiketas arrives while Death is away on business and spends three nights alone in his dwelling. Upon returning, Yama apologizes for the inconvenience and offers Nachiketas three compensatory boons. Nachiketas's first

---

5. OM is a sacred syllable, the fundamental sound that the Upanishads mysteriously identify with reality itself. See selection no. 11, this chapter.

wish is that his father suffer no anxiety about him and recognize him upon his return. His second wish is to know the secrets of the fire sacrifice. Then Yama tells Nachiketas, "Choose now thy third boon." Nachiketas replies,

When a man dies, this doubt arises: some say "he is" and some say "he is not." Teach me the truth.

Death. Even the gods had this doubt in times of old; for mysterious is the law of life and death. Ask for another boon. Release me from this.

Nachiketas. This doubt indeed arose even to the gods, and you say, O Death, that it is difficult to understand; but no greater teacher than you can explain it, and there is no other boon so great as this.

Death. Take horses and gold and cattle and elephants; choose sons and grandsons that shall live a hundred years. Have vast expanses of land, and live as many years as you desire. Or choose another gift that you think equal to this, and enjoy it with wealth and long life. Be a ruler of this vast earth. I will grant you all your desires.

Ask for any wishes in the world of mortals, however hard to obtain. To attend on you I will give you fair maidens with chariots and musical instruments. But ask me not, Nachiketas, the secrets of death.

Nachiketas. All these pleasures pass away, O End of all! They weaken the power of life. And indeed how short is all life! Keep thy horses and dancing and singing.

Man cannot be satisfied with wealth. Shall we enjoy wealth with you in sight? Shall we live whilst you are in power? I can only ask for the boon I have asked.

When a mortal here on earth has felt his own immortality, could he wish for a long life of pleasures, for the lust of deceitful beauty?

Solve then the doubt as to the great beyond. Grant me the gift that unveils the mystery. This is the only gift Nachiketas can ask. . . .

Death. There is the path of joy, and there is the path of pleasure. Both attract the soul. Who follows the first comes to good; who follows pleasure reaches not the End.

The two paths lie in front of man. Pondering on them, the wise man chooses the path of joy; the fool takes the path of pleasure.

You have pondered, Nachiketas, on pleasures, and you have rejected them. You have not accepted that chain of possessions wherewith men bind themselves and beneath which they sink.

There is the path of wisdom and the path of ignorance. They are far apart and lead to different ends. You are, Nachiketas, a follower of the path of wisdom: many pleasures tempt you not.

Abiding in the midst of ignorance, thinking themselves wise and learned, fools go aimlessly hither and thither, like blind led by the blind.

What lies beyond life shines not to those who are childish, or careless, or deluded by wealth. "This is the only world: there is no other," they say; and thus they go from death to death.

Not many hear of him; and of those not many reach him. Wonderful is he who can teach about him; and wise is he who can be taught. Wonderful is he who knows him when taught.

He cannot be taught by one who has not reached him; and he cannot be reached by much thinking. The way to him is through a Teacher who has seen him: He is higher than the highest thoughts, in truth above all thought.

This sacred knowledge is not attained by reasoning; but it can be given by a true Teacher. As your purpose is steady you have found him. May I find another pupil like you![6]

b. Atman: The Universal Self

In sections b through g Death is the speaker, continuing his teaching to Nachiketas.

Death. Atman, the Spirit of vision, is never born and never dies. Before him there was nothing, and he is ONE for evermore. Never-

---

6. Some translations suggest "may I *never* find another pupil like you." That is, if all were as wise as Nachiketas, Death would lose its power over human beings.

born and eternal, beyond times gone or to come, he does not die when the body dies.

If the slayer thinks that he kills, and if the slain thinks that he dies, neither knows the ways of truth. The Eternal in man cannot kill: the Eternal in man cannot die.

Concealed in the heart of all beings is the Atman, the Spirit, the Self; smaller than the smallest atom, greater than the vast spaces. The man who surrenders his human will leaves sorrows behind, and beholds the glory of the Atman by the grace of the Creator. . . . Not even through deep knowledge can the Atman be reached, unless evil ways are abandoned, and there is rest in the senses, concentration in the mind and peace in one's heart.

c. The Path to Liberation Is as Narrow as a Razor's Edge

Awake, arise! Strive for the Highest, and be in the Light! Sages say the path is narrow and difficult to tread, narrow as the edge of a razor.

The Atman is beyond sound and form, without touch and taste and perfume. It is eternal, unchangeable, without beginning or end: indeed above reasoning. When consciousness of the Atman manifests itself, man becomes free from the jaws of death.

d. Who Sees the Many and Not the One Wanders On from Death to Death

Who sees the many and not the ONE, wanders on from death to death.

Even by the mind this truth is to be learned: there are not many but only ONE. Who sees variety and not the unity wanders on from death to death. . . .

As water raining on a mountain-ridge runs down the rocks on all sides, so the man who sees variety of things runs after them on all sides.

But as pure water raining on pure water becomes one and the same, so becomes, O Nachiketas, the soul of the sage who knows.

e. Eternal Brahman: Unmanifest Source of All Manifestation

As fire, though one, takes new forms in all things that burn, the Spirit, though one, takes new forms in all things that live. He is within all, and is also outside.

As the wind, though one, takes new forms in whatever it enters, the Spirit, though one, takes new forms in all things that live. He is within all, and is also outside.

As the sun that beholds the world is untouched by earthly impurities, so the Spirit that is in all things is untouched by external sufferings.

There is one Ruler, the Spirit that is in all things, who transforms his own form into many. Only the wise who see him in their souls attain the joy eternal.

He is the Eternal among things that pass away, pure Consciousness of conscious beings, the ONE who fulfills the prayers of the many. Only the wise who see him in their souls attain the peace eternal.

f. Roots Above, Branches Below

The Tree of Eternity has its roots in heaven above and its branches reach down to earth. It is Brahman, pure Spirit, who in truth is called the Immortal. All the worlds rest on that Spirit and beyond him no one can go.

g. Yoga and Immortality

When the five senses and the mind are still, and reason rests in silence, then begins the Path supreme.

This calm steadiness of the senses is called Yoga. Then one should become watchful, because Yoga comes and goes. . . .

When all desires that cling to the heart are surrendered, then a mortal becomes immortal, and even in this world he is one with Brahman.

When all the ties that bind the heart are unloosened, then a mortal becomes immortal. This is the sacred teaching.

. . . And Nachiketas learnt the supreme wisdom, taught by the god of after-life, and he learnt the whole teaching of inner-union, of Yoga. Then he reached Brahman, the Spirit Supreme, and became immortal and pure. So in truth will anyone who knows his Atman, his higher self.

10. Mundaka Upanishad

a. Brahman, the Source and End of All

This is the truth: As from a fire aflame thousands of sparks come forth, even so from the Creator an infinity of beings have life and to him return again.

b. Brahman, the Infinite, Hidden in the Heart

Radiant in his light, yet invisible in the secret place of the heart, the Spirit is the supreme abode wherein dwells all that moves and breathes and sees. Know him as all that is, and all that is not, the end of love-longing beyond understanding, the highest in all beings.

c. Attain That Goal, O My Child!

He is self luminous and more subtle than the smallest; but in him rest all the worlds and their beings. He is the everlasting Brahman, and he is life and word and mind. He is truth and life immortal. He is the goal to be aimed at: attain that goal, O my son!

Take the great bow of the Upanishads and place in it an arrow sharp with devotion. Draw the bow with concentration on him and hit the center of the mark, the same everlasting spirit.

The bow is the sacred OM,[7] and the arrow is our own soul. Brahman is the mark of the arrow, the aim of the soul. Even as an arrow becomes one with its mark, let the watchful soul be one in him.

---

7. See note 5 above and selection 11, this chapter.

In him are woven the sky and the earth and all the regions of the air, and in him rest the mind and all the powers of life. Know him as the ONE and leave aside all other words. He is the bridge of immortality.

Where all the subtle channels of the body meet, like spokes in the center of the wheel, there he moves in the heart and transforms his one form unto many. Upon OM, Atman, your Self, place your meditation. Glory unto you in your far-away journey beyond darkness!

. . . And when he is seen in his immanence and transcendence, then the ties that have bound the heart are unloosened, the doubts of the mind vanish, and the law of Karma works no more.

In the supreme golden chamber is Brahman indivisible and pure. He is the radiant light of all lights, and this knows he who knows Brahman.

There the sun shines not, nor the moon, nor the stars; lightnings shine not there and much less earthly fire. From his light all these give light; and his radiance illumines all creation.

Far spreading before and behind and right and left, and above and below, is Brahman, the Spirit eternal. In truth, Brahman is all.

d. Two Sweet Friends: Individual Soul and Universal Spirit

There are two birds, two sweet friends, who dwell on the self-same tree. The one eats the fruits thereof, and the other looks on in silence.

The first is the human soul who, resting on that tree, though active, feels sad in his unwisdom. But on beholding the power and glory of the higher Spirit [Atman], he becomes free from sorrow.

e. Who Knows Brahman Becomes Brahman

A man whose mind wanders among desires, and is longing for objects of desire, goes again to life and death according to his desires. But he who possesses the End of all longing, and whose self has found fulfillment, even in this life his desires will fade away.

As rivers flowing into the ocean find their final peace and their name and form disappear, even so the wise become free from name and form and enter into the radiance of the Supreme Spirit who is greater than all greatness.

In truth, who knows Brahman becomes Brahman.

11. OM: *The Sound of the Real*

a. From the Katha

I will tell you the Word that all the Vedas glorify, all self-sacrifice expresses, all sacred studies and holy life seek. That word is OM.

That Word is the everlasting Brahman: that Word is the highest End. When that sacred Word is known, all longings are fulfilled.

It is the supreme means of salvation: it is the help supreme.

b. From the Maitri

There are two ways of contemplation of Brahman: in sound and in silence. By sound we go to silence. The sound of Brahman is OM. With OM we go to the End: the silence of Brahman. The End is immortality, union and peace.

Even as a spider reaches the liberty of space by means of its own thread, the man of contemplation by means of OM reaches freedom.

c. From the Chandogya

Even as all leaves come from a stem, all words come from the sound OM. OM is the whole universe. OM is in truth the whole universe.

d. From the Mandukya

OM. This eternal Word is all: what was, what is and what shall be, and what beyond is in eternity. All is OM.

Brahman is all and Atman is Brahman. Atman, the Self, has four conditions.

The first condition is the waking life of outward-moving consciousness, enjoying the seven outer gross elements.

The second condition is the dreaming life of inter-moving consciousness, enjoying the seven subtle inner elements in its own light and solitude.

The third condition is the sleeping life of silent consciousness when a person has no desires and beholds no dreams. That condition of deep sleep is one of oneness, a mass of silent consciousness made of peace and enjoying peace.

. . . The fourth condition is Atman in his own pure state: the awakened life of supreme consciousness. . . .

This Atman is the eternal Word OM. Its three sounds, A, U, and M, are the first three states of consciousness, and these three states are the three sounds.

The first sound A is the first state of waking consciousness, common to all men. . . .

The second sound U is the second state of dreaming consciousness. . . .

The third sound M is the third state of sleeping consciousness.

The word OM as one sound is the fourth state of supreme consciousness. It is beyond the senses and is the end of evolution. It is non-duality and love. He goes with his self to the supreme Self who knows this, who knows this.

12. Svetesvatara Upanishad

a. The Practice of Yoga

With upright body, head, and neck lead the mind and its powers into thy heart; and the OM of Brahman will then be thy boat with which to cross the rivers of fear.

And when the body is in silent steadiness, breathe rhythmically through the nostrils with a peaceful ebbing and flowing of breath. The chariot of mind is drawn by wild horses, and those wild horses have to be tamed.

Find a quiet retreat for the practice of Yoga, sheltered from the wind, level and clean, free from rubbish, smoldering fires, and ugliness, and where the sound of waters and the beauty of the place help thought and contemplation. . . .

The first fruits of the practice of Yoga are: health, little waste matter, and a clear complexion; lightness of the body, a pleasant scent, and a sweet voice; and an absence of greedy desires.

Even as a mirror of gold, covered by dust, when cleaned well shines again in full splendor, when a man has seen the Truth of the Spirit he is one with him, the aim of his life is fulfilled and he is ever beyond sorrow.

Then the soul of man becomes a lamp by which he finds the Truth of Brahman. Then he sees God, pure, never-born, everlasting; and when he sees God he is free from all bondage.

b. The Transmigration of the Soul

The soul is born and unfolds in a body, with dreams and desires and the food of life. And then it is reborn in new bodies, in accordance with its former works.

The quality of the soul determines its future body: earthly or airy, heavy or light. Its thoughts and its actions can lead it to freedom, or lead it to bondage, in life after life.

But there is the God of forms Infinite, and when a man knows God he is free from all bondage. . . .

He is an incorporeal Spirit, but he can be seen by a heart which is pure. . . . He is God, the God of love, and when a man knows him then he leaves behind his bodies of transmigration.

c. Refuge in the Silence of Eternity

He is the never-created Creator of all: he knows all, He is pure consciousness, the creator of all time. . . . From him comes the transmigration of life and liberation: bondage in time and freedom in Eternity.

. . . I go for refuge to God who is ONE in the silence of Eternity, pure radiance of beauty and perfection, in whom we find our peace. He is the bridge supreme which leads to immortality, and the Spirit of fire which burns the dross of lower life.

If ever for man it were possible to fold the tent of the sky, in that day he might be able to end his sorrow without the help of God.

13. Maitri Upanishad: *Aphorisms on the Transformation of Mind*

Even as fire without fuel finds peace in its resting-place, when thoughts become silence the soul finds peace in its own source.

And when a mind which longs for truth finds the peace of its own source, then those false inclinations cease which were the result of former actions done in the delusion of the senses.

Samsara, the transmigration of life, takes place in one's own mind. Let one therefore keep the mind pure, for what a man thinks that he becomes: this is a mystery of Eternity.

If men thought of God as much as they think of the world, who would not attain liberation?

When the mind is silent, beyond weakness or non-concentration, then it can enter into a world which is far beyond the mind: the highest End.

The mind should be kept in the heart as long as it has not reached the Highest End. This is wisdom, and this is liberation. Everything else is only words.

Words cannot describe the joy of the soul whose impurities are cleansed in deep contemplation—who is one with his Atman, his own Spirit. Only those who feel this joy know what it is.

Even as water becomes one with water, fire with fire, and air with air, so the mind becomes one with the Infinite Mind and thus attains final freedom.

Mind is indeed the source of bondage and also the source of liberation. To be bound to things of this world: this is bondage. To be free from them: this is liberation.

14. Taittiriya Upanishad

a. From Joy All Beings Have Come, Unto Joy They All Return

Joy comes from God. Who could live and who could breathe if the joy of Brahman filled not the universe?

Once Bhrigu Baruni went to his father Varuna and said: "Father, explain to me the mystery of Brahman."

Then his father spoke to him of the food of the earth, of the breath of life, of the one who sees, of the one who hears, of the mind that knows, and of the one who speaks. And he further said to him, "seek to know him from whom all beings have come, by whom they all live, and unto whom they all return. He is Brahman."

So Bhrigu went and practiced *tapas*, spiritual prayer.

Then he thought that Brahman was the food of the earth. . . .

Then he thought that Brahman was life. . . .

Then he thought that Brahman was mind. . . .

Then he thought that Brahman was reason. . . .

Then he saw that Brahman is joy: for FROM JOY ALL BEINGS HAVE COME, BY JOY THEY ALL LIVE, AND UNTO JOY THEY ALL RETURN.

b. I Am Food!

Oh, the wonder of joy!

I am the food of life, and I am he who eats the food of life: I am the two in ONE.

I am the first-born of the world of truth, born before the gods, born in the center of immortality.

He who gives me is my salvation.

I am that food which eats the eater of food.

15. Chandogya Upanishad: Thou Art That

There is a light that shines beyond all things on earth, beyond us all, beyond the heavens, beyond the highest, the very highest heavens. This is the Light that shines in our heart.

OM. There lived once a boy, Svetaketu Aruneya by name. One day his father spoke to him in this way: "Svetaketu, go and become a student of sacred wisdom. There is no one in our family who has not studied the holy Vedas and who might only be given the name of Brahman[8] by courtesy."

The boy left at the age of twelve, and, having learnt the Vedas, he returned home at the age of twenty-four, very proud of his learning and having a great opinion of himself.

His father, observing this, said to him: "Svetaketu, my boy, you seem to have a great opinion of yourself, you think you are learned, and you are proud. Have you asked for that knowledge whereby what is not heard is heard, what is not thought is thought, and what is not known is known?"

"What is that knowledge, father?" asked Svetaketu.

"[By] knowing a lump of clay, my son, all that is clay can be known, since any differences are only words and the reality is clay;

"[And] by knowing a piece of gold all that is gold can be known, since any differences are only words and the reality is only gold. . . ."

Svetaketu said: "Certainly my honored masters knew not this themselves. If they had known, why would they not have told me? Explain this to me, father."

"So be it, my child. Bring me a fruit from this banyan tree."

"Here it is, father."

"Break it."

"It is broken, Sir."

"What do you see in it?"

"Very small seeds, Sir."

"Break one of them, my son."

"It is broken, Sir."

"What do you see in it?"

"Nothing at all, Sir."

Then his father spoke to him: "My son, from the very essence in the seed which you cannot see comes in truth this vast banyan tree.

"Believe me, my son, an invisible and subtle essence is the Spirit of the whole universe. That is reality. That is Atman. THOU ART THAT."

---

8. The priestly caste.

"Explain more to me, father," said Svetaketu.

"So be it, my son. Place this salt in water and come to me tomorrow morning."

Svetaketu did as he was commanded, and in the morning his father said to him: "Bring me the salt you put into the water last night."

Svetaketu looked into the water, but could not find it, for it had dissolved.

His father then said, "Taste the water from this side. How is it?"

"It is salt."

"Taste it from the middle. How is it?"

"It is salt."

"Taste it from that side. How is it?"

"It is salt."

"Look for the salt and come again to me."

The son did so, saying: "I cannot see the salt. I only see the water."

His father then said: "In the same way, O my son, you cannot see the Spirit. But in truth he is here.

"An invisible but subtle essence is the Spirit of the whole universe. That is Reality. That is Truth. THOU ART THAT."

16. Brihadaranyaka Upanishad: *How Can the Knower Be Known?*

"As when a lump of salt is thrown into water and therein being dissolved it cannot be grasped again, but wherever the water is taken it is found salt, in the same way, O Maitreyi, the supreme Spirit is an ocean of pure consciousness boundless and infinite. Arising out of the elements, into them it returns again: there is no consciousness after death." Thus spoke Yajnavalkya.

Thereupon Maitreyi said: "I am amazed, O my Lord, to hear that after death there is no consciousness."

To this Yajnavalkya replied: "I am not speaking words of amazement; but sufficient for wisdom is what I say.

"For where there seems to be a duality, there one sees another, one hears another, one feels another's perfume, one thinks of another, one knows another. But when all has become Spirit, one's own Self, how and whom could one see? How and whom could one hear? How and whom could one know? How can one know him who knows all? How can the Knower be known?"

. . . This is the great never-born Spirit of man, never old and immortal. This is the Spirit of the universe, a refuge from all fear.

THE BHAGAVAD GITA

It is difficult to overestimate the esteem in which Hindus hold the Bhagavad Gita. It has been called "the most important, the most influential, the most luminous of all the Hindu scriptures,"[9] "the most popular book in Hindu religious literature,"[10] and the one that "most Hindus regard as containing the essence of the Vedas and the Upanishads."[11]

The message of the Bhagavad Gita is that each human life has but one ultimate end and purpose: to realize the Eternal Self within and thus to know, finally and fully, the joy of union with God, the Divine Ground of Being (Brahman). Whereas such knowledge was traditionally sought in retreat from the world, the Gita, without omitting that option, teaches that it may be attained in the midst of the world through nonattached action in the context of devotion (bhakti) to God.

The setting of the Gita reinforces its message. The Gita forms a minute portion of the longest epic poem in the world, the Mahabharata, which took shape in the centuries between 400 B.C.E. and 400 C.E. The Mahabharata is an account of the origins, the actual course, and the aftermath of a great war between two clans, the Pandavas, on the one side, and their cousins, the evil sons of Dhritarashtra, on the other. The Gita opens on the battlefield where the two vast and powerful armies are arrayed. There is no doubt that it is going to be a bloodbath and, worse, among blood relatives. Profoundly disturbed by this prospect is the saintly warrior Arjuna, whose task it is to lead the righteous Pandava clan into battle. Tormented, Arjuna begs help from the Divine Lord, Krishna, who, in human form, stands beside Arjuna in his char-

---

9. R. C. Zaehner, *Hinduism* (London: Oxford Univ. Press, 1962), 10.
10. Swami Prabhavananda and Christopher Isherwood, trans., *The Song of God: Bhagavad Gita* (New York: New American Library, 1944), 28.
11. John Koller, *The Indian Way* (New York: Macmillan, 1982), 188.

iot. Faced on the one hand with social duty as a warrior to protect his family from evil aggression, and on the other hand with the spiritual duty of nonviolence, Arjuna confesses his confusion to Lord Krishna:

17. Arjuna's Distress

Krishna, Krishna,
Now as I look on
These my kinsmen
Arrayed for battle,
My limbs are weakened,
My mouth is parching,
My body trembles,
My hair stands upright,
My skin seems burning,
The bow Gandiva
Slips from my hand,
My brain is whirling
Round and round,
I can stand no longer:
Krishna, I see such
Omens of evil!
What can we hope from
This killing of kinsmen?

. . . Knower of all things,
Though they should slay me
How could I harm them?
I cannot wish it:
Never, never,
Not though it won me
The throne of the three worlds;
How much the less for
Earthly lordship!

Krishna, hearing
The prayers of all men,
Tell me how can

We hope to be happy
Slaying the sons
Of Dhritarashtra?
Evil they may be,
Worst of the wicked,
Yet if we kill them
Our sin is greater.
How could we dare spill
The blood that unites us?
Where is the joy in
The killing of kinsmen?

Foul their hearts are
With greed, and blinded:
They see no evil
In breaking of blood-bonds,
See no sin
In treason to comrades.
But we, clear-sighted,
Scanning the ruin
Of families scattered,
Should we not shun
This crime, O Krishna?

. . . What is this crime
I am planning, O Krishna?
Murder most hateful,
Murder of brothers! Am I indeed
So greedy for greatness?

Rather than this
Let the evil children
of Dhritarashtra
Come with their weapons
Against me in battle:
I shall not struggle,
I shall not strike them.

Now let them kill me,
That will be better.

18. Krishna's Response: *Understand the True Nature of Existence*

a. Shake Off This Cowardice!

Krishna begins his response to Arjuna with a surprising rebuke:

Arjuna, is this hour of battle the time for scruples and fancies? Are they worthy of you, who seek enlightenment? Any brave man who merely hopes for fame or heaven would despise them.

What is this weakness? It is beneath you. Is it for nothing men call you the foe-consumer? Shake off this cowardice, Arjuna. Stand up.

b. The Real Cannot Suffer Death

Krishna continues:

Your words are wise, Arjuna, but your sorrow is for nothing. The truly wise mourn neither for the living nor for the dead.

There never was a time when I did not exist, nor you, nor any of these kings. Nor is there any future in which we shall cease to be.

Just as the dweller in this body passes through childhood, youth and old age, so at death he merely passes into another kind of body. The wise are not deceived by that.

Feelings of heat and cold, pleasure and pain, are caused by the contact of the senses with their objects. They come and they go, never lasting long. You must accept them.

A serene spirit accepts pleasure and pain with an even mind, and is unmoved by either. He alone is worthy of immortality.

That which is non-existent can never come into being, and that which is can never cease to be. Those who have known the inmost Reality know also the nature of *is* and *is not*.

That Reality which pervades the universe is indestructible. No one has power to change the Changeless.

Bodies are said to die, but That which possesses the body is eternal. It cannot be limited, or destroyed. Therefore you must fight.

c. Krishna Teaches About the Atman, the Universal Self

Some say this Atman
Is slain, and others
Call It the slayer:
They know nothing.
How can It slay
Or who shall slay it?

Know this Atman
Unborn, undying,
Never ceasing,
Never beginning,
Deathless, birthless,
Unchanging for ever.
How can it die
The death of the body?

Knowing it birthless,
Knowing it deathless,
Knowing it endless,
For ever unchanging,
Dream not the power
Is yours to command it.

Worn-out garments
Are shed by the body:
Worn-out bodies
Are shed by the dweller
Within the body.
New bodies are donned
By the dweller, like garments.

. . . Death is certain for the born. Rebirth is certain for the dead. You should not grieve for what is unavoidable.

Before birth, beings are not manifest to our human senses. In the interim between birth and death, they are manifest. At death they return to the unmanifest again. What is there in all this to grieve over?

19. The Illumined Person

Arjuna now asks Krishna to describe those who know. "In what manner does an illumined soul live in the world?" he asks. Krishna replies:

Not shaken by adversity,
Not hankering after happiness:
Free from fear, free from anger,
Free from the things of desire.
I call him a seer, and illumined.

The bonds of his flesh are broken.
He is lucky, and does not rejoice:
He is unlucky, and does not weep.
I call him illumined.

The tortoise can draw in his legs:
The seer can draw in his senses.
I call him illumined.

The abstinent run away from what they desire
But carry their desires with them:
When a man enters Reality,
He leaves his desires behind him.

Even a mind that knows the path
Can be dragged from the path:
The senses are so unruly.
But he controls the senses
And recollects the mind
And fixes it on me.
I call him illumined.

Thinking about sense-objects
Will attach you to sense-objects;
Grow attached, and you become addicted;
Thwart your addiction, it turns to anger;

Be angry, and you confuse your mind;
Confuse your mind, you forget the lesson of experience;
Forget experience, you lose discrimination;
Lose discrimination, and you miss life's
only purpose.

When he has no lust, no hatred,
A man walks safely among the things of lust and hatred.
To obey the Atman
Is his peaceful joy:
Sorrow melts
Into that clear peace:
His quiet mind
Is soon established in peace.

The uncontrolled mind
Does not guess that the Atman is present:
How can it meditate?
Without meditation, where is peace?
Without peace, where is happiness?

. . . Water flows continually into the ocean
But the ocean is never disturbed:
Desire flows into the mind of the seer
But he is never disturbed.
The seer knows peace:
The man who stirs up his own lusts
Can never know peace.
He knows peace who has forgotten desire.
He lives without craving:
Free from ego, free from pride.

This is a statement of enlightenment in Brahman:
A man does not fall back from it
Into delusion.
Even at the moment of death
He is alive in that enlightenment:
Brahman and he are one.

20. Karma Yoga: *The Great Teaching on Nonattached Action*

Arjuna remains confused. Krishna has told him to act, *but according to traditional wisdom,* action (karma) *only begets more of the same, leading to further bondage. Now Krishna explains* karma yoga, *the yoga whereby, in the very midst of action, one may be free from further bondage to its consequences. For the spiritual problem—as Krishna points out in the first verses below—is not action itself. Rather it is how one acts, the quality of mind with which one acts. If one identifies with one's actions, desiring certain results, one is bound to that action-pattern and doomed to rebirth. However, if one acts earnestly but without attachment to results, performing every action as an offering to God, knowing that God alone is the only Actor, one proceeds on the path to liberation. Karma yoga is perhaps the central teaching of the Bhagavad Gita.*

a. Act Without Seeking the Fruits of Action

[Krishna:]

You have the right to work, but for the work's sake only. You have no right to the fruits of work. Desire for the fruits of work must never be your motive in working. Never give way to laziness, either.

Perform every action with your heart fixed on the Supreme Lord. Renounce attachment to the fruits. Be even-tempered in success and failure; for it is this evenness of temper which is meant by yoga.

Work done with anxiety about results is far inferior to work done without such anxiety, in the calm of self-surrender. Seek refuge in the knowledge of Brahman. They who work selfishly for results are miserable.

In the calm of self-surrender you can free yourself from the bondage of virtue and vice during this very life. Devote yourself to Brahman. To unite the heart with Brahman and then to act: that is the secret of non-attached work. In the calm of self-surrender, the seers renounce the fruits of their actions, and so reach enlightenment. Then they are free from the bondage of rebirth, and pass to that state which is beyond all evil.

When your intellect has cleared itself of its delusions, you will become indifferent to the results of all action, present or future. At present, your intellect is bewildered by conflicting interpretations of the scriptures. When it can rest, steady and undistracted, in contemplation of the Atman, then you will reach union with the Atman.

b. Inaction Is Impossible: Act Without Anxiety About Results

[Krishna continues:]

I have already told you that, in this world, aspirants may find enlightenment by two different paths. For the contemplative is the path of knowledge: for the active is the path of selfless action.

Freedom of activity is never achieved by abstaining from action. Nobody can become perfect by merely ceasing to act. In fact, nobody can ever rest from his activity even for a moment. . . . The world is imprisoned in its own activity, except where actions are performed as worship of God. Therefore you must perform every action sacramentally, and be free from all attachments to results.

c. Do Your Duty Always but Without Attachment

Do your duty, always; but without attachment. That is how a man reaches the ultimate Truth: by working without anxiety about results.

d. Without Devotion to God, Human Beings Are Enslaved by Their Own Actions

When the heart is made pure by that yoga,
When the body is obedient,
When the senses are mastered,
When man knows that his Atman
Is the Atman in all creatures,
Then let him act,
Untainted by action.

The illumined soul
Whose heart is Brahman's heart

Thinks always: "I am doing nothing."
No matter what he sees,
Hears, touches, smells, eats;
No matter whether he is moving,
Sleeping, breathing, speaking,
Excreting or grasping something with his hand,
Or opening his eyes,
Or closing his eyes:
This he knows always:
"I am not seeing, I am not hearing:
It is the senses that see and hear
And touch the things of the senses."

He puts aside desire,
Offering the act to Brahman.
The lotus leaf rests unwetted on water:
He rests on action, untouched by action.

To the follower of the yoga of action,
The body and the mind,
The sense-organs and the intellect
Are instruments only:
He knows himself other than the instrument.
And thus his heart grows pure.

United with Brahman,
Cut free from the fruit of the act,
A man finds peace
In the work of the spirit.
Without Brahman,
Man is a prisoner,
Enslaved by action,
Dragged onward by desire.

e. The Human Will Is the Atman's Friend . . . and Its Enemy

Man's will is the only
Friend of the Atman:

His will is also
The Atman's enemy.

f. Slash Delusion to Pieces: Take Your Stand in Karma Yoga

When a man can act without desire,
Through practice of yoga;
When his doubts are torn to shreds
Because he knows Brahman;
When his heart is poised
In the being of the Atman
No bonds can bind him.

Still I can see it:
A doubt that lingers
Deep in your heart
Brought forth by delusion.
You doubt the truth
Of the living Atman.

Where is your sword
Discrimination?
Draw it and slash
Delusion to pieces.
Then arise
O son of Bharata:
Take your stand
In Karma Yoga.

21. Taming the Mind: *The Yoga of Meditation*

Hinduism recognizes four classes of yoga or methods of self-transformation: the yoga of action (karma), the yoga of devotion (bhakti), the yoga of knowledge (jnana), and the yoga of meditation (raja yoga). Here Krishna teaches Arjuna about the taming of the mind through meditation. The original order of the verses has been transposed.

a. The Wind Is No Wilder

[Arjuna speaks:]

Krishna, you describe this yoga as a life of union with Brahman. But I do not see how this can be permanent. The mind is so very restless.

Restless man's mind is,
So strongly shaken
In the grip of the senses:
Gross and grown hard
With stubborn desire
For what is worldly.
How shall he tame it?
Truly, I think
The wind is no wilder.

b. Concentration

The yogi should retire into a solitary place. . . .

The place where he sits should be firm, neither too high nor too low, and situated in a clean spot. . . .

His posture will be motionless, with the body, head and neck held erect, and the vision indrawn. . . .

Yoga is not for the man who overeats, or for him who fasts excessively. It is not for him who sleeps too much, or for the keeper of exaggerated vigils. Let a man be moderate in his eating and his recreation, moderately active, moderate in sleep and in wakefulness. He will find that yoga takes away all his unhappiness.

When can a man be said to have achieved union with Brahman? When his mind is under perfect control and freed from all desires, so that he becomes absorbed in the Atman, and nothing else. "The light of a lamp does not flicker in a windless place": that is the simile which describes a yogi of one-pointed mind, who meditates upon the Atman.

c. The Fruit of Meditation

Utterly quiet,
Made clean of passion,

The mind of the yogi
Knows that Brahman,
His bliss is the highest.

. . . His heart is with Brahman,
His eye in all things
Sees only Brahman
Equally present,
Knows his own Atman
In every creature,
And all creation
Within that Atman.

. . . Who burns with the bliss
And suffers every sorrow
Of every creature
Within his own heart,
Making his own
Each bliss and each sorrow:
Him I hold highest
Of all the yogis.

22. Krishna Reveals His Divine Form

In chapter eleven of the Gita, Arjuna asks Krishna, who has been standing beside him in human form during this teaching, to reveal himself in his true divine nature. Arjuna is not prepared for the awesome cosmic spectacle that unfolds. It is one of the great theophanies in world religious literature:

a. The Theophany: "Fiery-Faced You Blast the World to Ashes"

[Krishna to Arjuna:]

O conqueror of sloth, this very day you shall behold the whole universe with all things animate and inert made one within this body of mine. And whatever else you desire to see, that you shall see also.

But you cannot see me thus with those human eyes. Therefore, I give you divine sight.

Behold—this is my yoga power.

[Sanjaya, the narrator:]

. . . When he had spoken these words, Sri Krishna, master of all yogis, revealed to Arjuna his transcendent, divine Form, speaking from innumerable mouths, seeing with myriad eyes, of many marvelous aspects, adorned with countless divine ornaments, brandishing all kinds of heavenly weapons, wearing celestial garlands and the raiment of paradise, anointed with perfumes of heavenly fragrance, full of revelations, resplendent, boundless, of ubiquitous regard.

Suppose a thousand suns should rise together into the sky: such is the glory of the Shape of Infinite God.

Then the son of Pandu [Arjuna] beheld the entire universe, in all its multitudinous diversity, lodged as one being within the body of the God of gods.

And then was Arjuna, that lord of mighty riches, overcome with wonder. His hair stood erect. He bowed low before God in adoration, and clasped his hands, and spoke:

[Arjuna:]

Ah, my God, I see all gods within your body;
Each in his degree, the multitude of creatures;
See Lord Brahma throned upon the lotus;
See all the sages, and the holy serpents.

Universal Form, I see you without limit,
Infinite of arms, eyes, mouths and bellies—
See, and find no end, midst, or beginning.

Crowned with diadems, you wield the mace and discus,
Shining every way—the eyes shrink from your splendor
Brilliant like the sun; like fire, blazing, boundless.

You are all we know, supreme, beyond man's measure,
This world's sure-set plinth and refuge never shaken,
Guardian of eternal law, life's Soul undying.
Birthless, deathless; yours the strength titanic,
Million-armed, the sun and moon your eyeballs,
Fiery-faced, you blast the world to ashes. . . .

b. Krishna: "I Am Come as Time"

I am come as Time, the waster of the peoples,
Ready for that hour that ripens to their ruin.

All these hosts must die; strike, stay your hand
   —no matter.
Therefore strike. Win kingdom, wealth and glory.
Arjuna, arise, O ambidextrous bowman.
Seem to slay. By me these men are slain already.

c. Arjuna Awed

Well it is the world delights to do you honor!
At the sight of you, O master of the senses,
Demons scatter every way in terror,
And the hosts of the Siddhas bow adoring.

Mightiest, how should they indeed withhold their homage?
O Prime Cause of all, even Brahman the Beginner—
Deathless, word's abode, the Lord of devas,
You are what is not, what is, and what transcends them.

You are first and highest in heaven, O ancient Spirit.
It is within you the cosmos rests in safety.
You are known and knower, goal of all our striving.
Endless in your change, you body forth creation.

d. Krishna Calms Arjuna

[Arjuna:]
   I have seen what no man ever saw before me:
   Deep is my delight, but still my dread is greater.
   Show me now your other Form, O Lord, be gracious. . . .

[Sanjaya, the narrator:] Having spoken thus to Arjuna, Krishna appeared in his own shape. The Great-Souled One, assuming once more his mild and pleasing form, brought peace to him in his terror.

[Arjuna:] O Krishna, now I see you in your pleasant human form, I am myself again.

e. The Importance of Devotion (Bhakti) to God

[Krishna:] That Shape of mine which you have seen is very difficult to behold. Even the devas themselves are always longing to see it. Neither by study of the Vedas, nor by austerities, nor by alms-giving, nor by rituals can I be seen as you have seen me. But by single-minded and intense devotion, that form of mine may be completely known, and seen, and entered into, O Consumer of the foe.

Whosoever works for me alone, makes me his only goal and is devoted to me, free from attachment, and without hatred toward any creature—that man, O Prince, shall enter into me.

23. "Dear to Me"

Krishna tells Arjuna what manner of person is especially dear to him:

A man should not hate any living creature. Let him be friendly and compassionate to all. He must free himself from the delusion of "I" and "mine." He must accept pleasure and pain with equal tran-quillity. He must be forgiving, ever-contented, self-controlled, united constantly with me in his meditation. His resolve must be unshakable. He must be dedicated to me in intellect and in mind. Such a devotee is dear to me.

He neither molests his fellow men, nor allows himself to be-come disturbed by the world. He is no longer swayed by joy and envy, anxiety and fear. Therefore he is dear to me.

He is pure, and independent of the body's desire. He is able to deal with the unexpected: prepared for everything, unperturbed by anything. He is neither vain nor anxious about the results of his ac-tions. Such a devotee is dear to me.

He does not desire or rejoice in what is pleasant. He does not dread what is unpleasant, or grieve over it. He remains unmoved by good or evil fortune. Such a devotee is dear to me.

His attitude is the same toward friend and foe. He is indifferent to honor and insult, heat and cold, pleasure and pain. He is free from attachment. He values praise and blame equally. He can con-trol his speech. He is content with whatever he gets. His home is everywhere and nowhere. His mind is fixed upon me, and his heart is full of devotion. He is dear to me.

This true wisdom I have taught will lead you to immortality. The faithful practice it with devotion, taking me for their highest aim. To me they surrender heart and mind. They are exceedingly dear to me.

GRACE NOTES: SAYINGS OF SHANKARA, RAMAKRISHNA, AND RAMANA MAHARSHI

Shankara (686–718), Ramakrishna (1836–1886), and Ramana Maharshi (1879–1950), are three of the greatest mystic-sages of the Hindu tradition. They are widely considered to have been jivanmukti, liberated souls. Of Ramakrishna, who has been given the lion's share of space in this section, Mahatma Gandhi once said, "Ramakrishna's life enables one to see God face to face."[12]

24. Shankara

a. On The Nonduality of the Real: All of This Really Isn't

Both bondage and liberation are the fictions of our ignorance. They do not really exist in the Atman. Just as a piece of rope remains rope, whether or not we mistake it for a snake. The imagined snake does not really exist in the rope. The Atman is infinite, without parts, beyond action. . . . There is neither birth nor death, neither bound nor aspiring soul, neither liberated soul nor seeker after liberation—this is the ultimate and absolute truth.

b. A Garland of Questions and Answers

Who, in this world, can be called pure?
  He whose mind is pure.

Who can be called wise?
  He who can discriminate between the real and the unreal.

Who is the greatest hero?
  The person who is not terror-stricken by the arrows which
    shoot from the eyes of a beauty.[13]

---

12. Quoted in Les Hixon, *Great Swan* (Boston: Shambhala, 1992), vii.
13. Adapted for gender neutrality.

Who is poor?
>He who is not contented.

What rolls quickly away, like drops of water from a lotus leaf?
>Youth, wealth and the years of a person's life.

What is hell?
>To live in slavery to others.

How is heaven attained?
>The attainment of heaven is the freedom from cravings.

What is a person's duty?
>To do good to all beings.

What are worthless as soon as they are won?
>Honor and fame.

What brings happiness?
>The friendship of the holy.

What destroys craving?
>Realization of one's true self.

Who are our enemies?
>Our sense-organs, when they are uncontrolled.

Who are our friends?
>Our sense organs, when they are controlled.

Who has overcome the world?
>He who has conquered his own mind.

25. Ramakrishna

a. Grace

The Winds of God's Grace Are Always Blowing

The winds of God's grace are always blowing; it is for us to raise
our sails.[14]

---

14. Commonly ascribed to Ramakrishna. I have not been able to locate the direct
quotation.

Grace Rains Down Ceaselessly

. . . Awakening is not possible so long as the mind is constantly distracted from Truth by remaining habitually egocentric, by instinctively seeking personal gratification. Divine Grace, the healing and illuminating energy that rains down ceaselessly upon the human mind, heart, and soul, cannot be absorbed or assimilated by the high, rocky hill of personal interest and personal importance. This precious, life-giving water runs off the high ground of ego, without ever penetrating its hard, barren soil.

b. On Truth in the Religions

Insanity: "My Religion Alone Is True"

Mother, Mother, Mother![15] Everyone foolishly assumes that his clock alone tells correct time. Christians claim to possess exclusive truth. . . . Countless varieties of Hindus insist that their sect, no matter how small and insignificant, expresses the ultimate position. Devout Muslims maintain that Koranic revelation supersedes all others. The entire world is being driven insane by this single phrase: "My religion alone is true." O Mother, you have shown me that no clock is entirely accurate. Only the transcendent sun of knowledge remains on time. Who can make a system from Divine Mystery? But if any sincere practitioner, within whatever culture or religion, prays and meditates with great devotion and commitment to Truth alone, Your Grace will flood his mind and heart, O Mother. His particular sacred tradition will be opened and illuminated. He will reach the one goal of spiritual evolution. Mother, Mother, Mother! How I long to pray with sincere Christians in their churches and to bow and prostrate with devoted Muslims in their mosques! All religions are glorious!

Single Obstacle, Single Aim, Many Paths

Obsessive self-awareness, whether collective or individual, is a mere machine, an automatic function. God is the only living presence within us, our only true bliss and freedom. Divine Nature,

---

15. Ramakrishna often invoked Divine Reality as Mother.

which alone is our ultimate being, has nothing to do with narrow self-interest or limited self-consciousness. Divine Nature can be realized and fully actualized in daily life by sincerely following any number of revealed paths. All the integral transmissions of sacred wisdom and contemplative practice that survive the test of time are true—true in the sense that they function authentically and bear the sweet fruit of sanctity.

All Spiritual Invitations Come from the Same Host

Place your devotion whole-heartedly at the service of the ideal most natural to your being, but know with unwavering certainty that all spiritual ideals are expressions of the same supreme Presence. Do not allow the slightest trace of malice to enter your mind toward any manifestation of God or toward any practitioner who attempts to live in harmony with that Divine Manifestation. Kali, Krishna, Buddha, Christ, Allah—these are all full expressions of the same indivisible Consciousness and Bliss. These are revelatory initiatives of Divine Reality, not manmade notions. Blessed is the soul who has known that all is one, that all jackals howl essentially alike.

c. On Awakening

The Process of Awakening

My dear friend, when you hear one of the glorious Divine Names— be it Allah, Tara, Krishna, or whichever revealed Name is closest to your heart—if tears of ecstasy come spontaneously to your eyes or if the sensation of weeping springs forth secretly in your heart . . . this is authentic confirmation that you are awakening. . . . You will not have to renounce the formalities of religion. Formalities of every kind will simply disappear from your being. . . . Even the Divine Names most intimate to you will eventually disappear, and you will commune directly with the One Reality, which precedes and which emanates all names and forms. You will experience then only a subtle resonance or a delicate radiance.

. . . Gradually yet inexorably, one is drawn into the living heart of worship. Simplification and intensification occur. Finally, the practice of religion merges into the source of religion. One abides blissfully in the supreme Source, even as this infinite fountain continues to flow with all the precious sacraments, all the powerful forms of worship and meditation ever revealed to humankind.

No Premature Presumption

Yet the authentic practitioner never renounces prematurely the precious disciplines of his tradition—daily prayers, ceremonial worship, study and chanting of scriptures, silent meditation, and selfless service to fulfill the physical and spiritual needs of conscious beings. The genuine aspirant remains in a constant state of inward and outward pilgrimage until actually reaching the one goal of true pilgrims—complete God-consciousness, full awakening as Truth.

Overcoming the Craving for Personal Immortality

The only true sacrifice to offer God, O lovers of God, the only authentic renunciation that can clear away obstacles to spiritual progress, is to abandon once and for all this constant drive for self-perpetuation, this instinctive urge to survive and dominate which manifests in so many subtle and obvious forms—including the obsession with becoming holy or elevated.

Seeing Through the World's Madness

Many people cannot begin to feel the life-giving attraction for Divine Reality until they pass through the painful experiences associated with grasping at habitual enjoyment. This desperate grasping includes selfishly accumulating material wealth, arrogantly cultivating power over others, and welcoming flattery, as well as enjoying absurdly refined comforts and ever more bizarre diversions. We must unequivocally see through this deceptive surface in order to enter the depth of ecstatic Divine Enjoyment.

Recharging Your Battery

To cultivate love for Truth one must occasionally come forth from the conventional environment into spaciousness and clarity. To retire now and then into blessed seclusion, even in one's own house or heart, is necessary—for several hours, for several days, for a month, for a year. Swim peacefully through clear waters of solitude, illuminated by the sunlight of Truth. Then you can return compassionately to the denser, more obscure realms of social responsibility, without becoming disoriented by them.

Spiritual Maturity

The mature spiritual person, one who is truly awakened, need not remain involved in social responsibilities or religious observances. The sense that one must, or even can, initiate any action begins to disappear as one realizes that only God acts. This realization is the final fruition of all aspirations and disciplines.

Everyone Will Arrive

Everyone will attain God-consciousness and be liberated. Some receive their meal early in the morning, others at noon, still others not until evening. But none will go hungry. Without any exception, all living beings will eventually know their own true nature to be timeless awareness.

d. On the Nonduality of the Real

Absolutely Not Two

My dear formless and nameless friend, the omnipresent process of creation and dissolution, the sheer dynamism of Divine Power, is your blissful Mother. The nameless, formless Reality . . . is precisely the same Reality that you perceive blossoming around you. Brahman is not different from shakti. The perfectly peaceful Absolute is not different from the playful relative universe. They are simply not two realities. Nor are they two dimensions of the same reality. They are not even two perspectives. Not two! Absolutely not two!

What Is Simply Is!

Brahman is a shoreless ocean. Shakti is the omnipresent, interdependent action of its waves. . . . As long as Her inscrutable Will keeps consciousness manifest through the human form, one is tempted to think that there are two realities—the formless God and these confusing mirror images called the universe. But no, my friend, there is no such twoness whatsoever. There is no superknowledge separate from or opposed to ordinary ignorance. There is not day as a reality apart from night. There is only wholeness or completeness—beyond night or day, beyond ignorance or knowledge, yet containing both, manifesting both. How to describe this dynamic plenitude? Not with words from any scripture or philosophy. What is simply is!

A Case of Mistaken Identity

. . . This same Truth holds for every conscious being. There never is any duality. The principle of awareness, atman, never engages in any activity, although from this pure principle alone, the luminous, transparent, insubstantial universe spontaneously unfolds. When the practitioner is consciously identified, not with any expression of awareness but with the living principle of awareness. . . there remains no sense of intrinsic involvement with polarities such as good and evil, virtue and vice, self and other, existence and nonexistence. However, when one identifies with activity rather than with principle, manifesting an ego that claims to generate various chains of events, then the tensions between polar opposites split that person's consciousness, creating various forms of obvious and subtle suffering.

Nondual Knowledge: Like Calmly Falling from a Tree

Your very life-breath must become the conscious, timeless affirmation of Reality by Reality. SOHAM, SOHAM, I am It, It is I. Only the dualistic imagination perceives some separate practitioner who makes this primordial affirmation. . . . The actual state of nondual knowledge is comparable to falling from a high tree and remaining clearly aware, without tensing a single muscle or feeling the slightest anxiety.

Seeing God Everywhere

After God-realization, which is the conscious union of the manifest with the Unmanifest, the same Reality is experienced as all dimensions of being and also as the dimensionless Ground or Source of Being—the open space of unconditioned awareness. Every conscious being we gaze upon is then perceived to be God. Inanimate structures as well are God. . . . But the most complete Divine Manifestation, surprising as it may seem, is this human reality, this subtle nervous system—a potential expanse of illumination greater than the physical cosmos and greater then the eternal heavenly realms.

e. The Mystery of Evil

You may ask: "How, then, can we arrive at any explanation of naturally caused misery, human viciousness, pervasive unhappiness?" The answer is that these forms of suffering, which one sincerely struggles to overcome, are experienced by individual awareness but not by the very principle of awareness, which remains ever-free, ever-blissful. There is venom in the snake that may cause others to die or which may be used as a healing medicine, but this substance is neither poison nor medicine to the snake.

26. Ramana Maharshi

a. Why Cover the World with Leather When You Can Wear Shoes?

If the mind is happy, not only the body but the whole world will be happy. So one must find out how to become happy oneself. Wanting to reform the world without discovering one's true self is like trying to cover the whole world with leather to avoid the pain of walking on stones and thorns. It is much simpler to wear shoes.

b. The Point of Religious Practices

We loosely talk of Self-realization, for lack of a better term. But how can one realize that which alone is real? All we need to do is to give up our habit of regarding as real that which is unreal. All religious practices are meant solely to help us do this.

c. On the Nonduality of the Real

Reality Is Always Already Here and Now

There is no greater mystery than this, that we keep seeking reality though in fact we *are* reality. We think that there is something hiding reality and that this must be destroyed before reality is gained. How ridiculous! A day will dawn when you will laugh at all your past efforts. That which will be on the day you laugh is also here and now.

Nothing but Grace

God's grace is the beginning, the middle and the end. When you pray for God's grace, you are like someone standing neck-deep in water and yet crying for water. It is like saying that someone neck-deep in water feels thirsty, or that a fish in water feels thirsty, or that water feels thirsty.

CHAPTER TWO

Buddhism

*B*uddhism has been called the
Light of Asia. In the 2600
years since that light was kindled in ancient India, it has suffused a
wide array of cultures and has been refracted by their palette of indigenous beliefs. Through its many forms the Buddhist tradition has had
an incalculably vast influence on the metaphysical imagination, the
moral bearing, and the aesthetic sensibility of the diverse peoples of
Asia, and in the last hundred years it has shown itself to be potentially
as fecund for the West. For two and a half millennia Buddhism has illumined the minds and lightened the hearts of the world's peoples, the
sophisticated and simple alike. The source of this remarkable irradia-
tion was a man, Siddhartha Gotama, called the Buddha or Awakened
One. There is no better way to begin an understanding of the Buddha
and the Dharma (Way of Truth) he taught than with the instructive
legend of his life.

THE INSTRUCTIVE LEGEND OF THE BUDDHA'S LIFE

1. His Miraculous Birth

There lived once upon a time a king of the Shakyas, a scion of the solar race, whose name was Shuddhodana. . . . He had a wife . . . who was called Great Maya. These two tasted of love's delights, and one day she conceived the fruit of her womb, but without any defilement. . . . Just before her conception she had a dream. A white elephant seemed to enter her body, but without causing her any pain. . . .

She set her heart on going to Lumbini, a delightful grove. [The newborn babe] came out of his mother's side, without causing her pain or injury. . . . And since he had for many aeons been engaged in the practice of meditation, he now was born in full awareness, and not thoughtless and bewildered as other people are. [He] spoke these words full of meaning for the future: "For enlightenment I was born, for the good of all that lives. This is the last time that I have been born into this world of becoming."

2. The Visit of the Wise Man

Then Asita, the great seer, came to the palace. . . . He knew of the birth of [the Buddha]. . . for in his trance he had perceived the miraculous signs which had attended it. With tears flickering on his eyelashes the seer . . . explained his agitation to the king in these words: "It is not for him that I am perturbed, but I am . . . disappointed for myself. For the time has come when I must pass away, just when he is born who shall discover the extinction of birth, which is so hard to win. Uninterested in worldly affairs he will give up his kingdom. By strenuous efforts he will win that which is truly real. . . . To those who are tormented with pains and hemmed in by their worldly concerns, who are lost in the desert tracks of Samsara, he shall proclaim the path which leads to salvation, as to travellers who have lost their way. Creatures are scorched by the fire of greed. . . . He will refresh them with the rain of the Dharma, which is copious like the rain from a mighty cloud when the summer's burning heat is over."

3. The Prisoner of Pleasure

Since the king . . . had . . . heard from Asita that the supreme beatitude would be the prince's future goal, he tried to tie him down by sensual pleasures, so that he might not go away into the forest. He selected for him . . . a maiden, Yasodhara by name, chaste and outstanding for her beauty. . . .

The monarch decided that his son must never see anything that could perturb his mind, and he arranged for him to live in the upper storeys of the palace, which was . . . brilliantly white. . . . It contained rooms suited to each season, and the melodious music of the female attendants could be heard in them. . . . Soft music came from gold-edged tambourines which the women tapped with their finger-tips, and they danced as beautifully as the choicest heavenly nymphs. They entertained him with soft words, wanton swayings, sweet laughter, butterfly kisses, and seductive glances. Thus he became a captive of these women who were well versed in the subject of sensuous enjoyment and indefatigable in sexual pleasure. And it did not occur to him to come down. . . .

Yasodhara bore . . . a son, who was named Rahula. . . .

4. The First Three Passing Sights: *Old Age, Disease, and Death*

a. The Prince Ventures Out

In the course of time, . . . feeling like an elephant locked up inside a house, [Siddhartha] set his heart on making a journey outside the palace. The king heard of his plans and arranged a pleasure excursion. . . . He gave orders that all the common folk with any kind of affliction should be kept away from the royal road, because he feared that they might agitate the prince's sensitive mind. Very gently all cripples were driven away, and all those who were crazy, aged, ailing, and the like, and also all wretched beggars. So the royal highway was supremely magnificent.

b. He Confronts the Inevitability of Decay

But as fate would have it, a bent, toothless, and haggard old man appears on the roadside. Stunned by the sight, Prince Siddhartha asks his charioteer to explain this oddity. The charioteer responds:

"Sweet Prince!
This is no other than an aged man.
Some fourscore years ago his back was straight,
His eye bright, and his body goodly: now
The thievish years have sucked his sap away,
Pillaged his strength and filched his will and wit;
His lamp has lost its oil, the wick burns black;
What life he keeps is one poor lingering spark
Which flickers for the finish: such is age."
. . . Then spake the Prince—
"But shall this come to others, or to all,
Or is it rare that one should be as he?"
"Most noble," answered Channa, "even as he,
Will all these grow if they shall live so long."
"But," quoth the Prince, "if I shall live as long
Shall I be thus; and if Yasodhara
Live fourscore years, is this old age for her. . . ?"
. . . "Yea, great Sir!"
The charioteer replied.

c. The Prince Responds

[The prince:] "So that is how old age destroys indiscriminately the memory, beauty and strength of all! And yet with such a sight before it the world goes on quite unperturbed. Turn round the horses and travel back quickly to our palace! How can I delight to walk about in parks when my heart is full of fear of ageing?" . . . And the prince went back into his palace which now seemed empty to him. . . .

On a second pleasure excursion [he saw] *a man with a diseased body*. When this fact was explained to him, [he] was dismayed and in his compassion he uttered these words in a low voice: "This then is the calamity of disease, which afflicts people! . . . Since I have learnt of the danger of illness, my heart is repelled by pleasures and seems to shrink into itself."

On a third excursion [he saw] a *corpse*. . . . Leaning his shoulder against the top of the chariot rail, he spoke these words in a forceful voice: "This is the end which has been fixed for all, and yet the world forgets its fears and takes no heed! The hearts of men are surely hardened to fears, for they feel quite at ease even while travelling along the road to the next life. Turn back the chariot! This is no time or place for pleasure excursions. . . ."

5. A World on Fire

From then onwards the prince withdrew from contact with the women in the palace, and in answer to the reproaches of Udayin, the king's counsellor, he explained his new attitude in the following words: "It is not that I despise the objects of sense, and I know full well that they make up what we call the 'world,' but when I consider the impermanence of everything in this world, then I can find no delight in it. Yes, if this triad of old age, illness, and death did not exist, then all this loveliness would surely give me great pleasure. [But] the world looks to me as if ablaze with an all-consuming fire. . . ."

6. The Discovery of Meditative Insight

In the hope that a visit to the forest might bring him some peace, he left his palace with the king's consent. . . . His longing . . . carried him deep into the countryside. There he saw soil being plowed. The plows had torn up the sprouting grass . . . and the land was littered with tiny creatures who had been killed. . . . The sight of all this grieved the prince. . . . He observed the plowmen, saw how they suffered from the wind, sun, and dust and how the oxen were worn down by the labour of drawing. . . . He reflected on the generation and the passing of all living things, and in his distress he said to himself: "How pitiful all this!"

His mind longed for solitude. He withdrew . . . to a solitary spot at the foot of a rose-apple tree. . . . There he sat down, reflected on the origination and passing away of all that lives, and then he worked on his mind in such a way . . . that it became stable and concentrated. When he had won through to mental stability, he was suddenly freed from all desire for sense-objects and from cares of any kind. He had reached the first stage of [absorption], which is calm amidst applied and discursive thinking. . . .

When he thus gained insight . . . he lost at the same moment all self-intoxication, which normally arises from pride in one's own strength, youth, and vitality. He now was neither glad nor grieved; all doubt, lassitude, and sleepiness disappeared; sensuous excitements could no longer influence him; and hatred and contempt for others were far from his mind.

7. The Fourth Passing Sight: *The Religious Mendicant*

. . . He saw . . . a *religious mendicant* [and] asked him: "Tell me who you are," and the answer was: "I am a recluse who has adopted a homeless life to win salvation. . . . I search for that most blessed state in which extinction is unknown. Possessions I have none, no expectations either. Intent on the supreme goal I wander about, accepting alms I may receive."

8. The Great Going Forth

There and then [Siddhartha] made plans to leave his palace for the homeless life. . . . He decided to escape during the night. . . . He descended from the upper part of the palace, looked . . . upon the women lying about in all kinds of disorderly positions, and unhesitatingly went to the stables in the outermost courtyard. He roused Chandaka, the groom, and ordered him to bring the horse Kanthaka.

They rode off, till they came to a hermitage, where the prince took off his jewels, gave them to Chandaka, and dismissed him with this message to his father . . . : "So that my father's grief may be dispelled, tell him that I have gone to this penance grove for the purpose of putting an end to old age and death, and by no means because I yearn for Paradise, or because I feel no affection for him, or from moody resentment. . . . There is no reason why he should grieve for me. . . . My father will perhaps say that it was too early for me to leave for the forest. But . . . even if affection should prevent me from leaving my kinsfolk just now of my own accord, in due course death would tear us apart, and in that we would have no say. . . . Birds settle on a tree for a while, and then go their separate ways again. The meeting of all living beings must likewise inevitably end in their parting. This world passes away and disappoints the hopes of everlasting attachment. It is therefore unwise to have a sense of ownership for people who are united with us as in a dream—for a short while only and not in fact."

Siddhartha now studies under two of the greatest yogis of the time, Alara Kalama and Uddalaka Ramaputta. But even after mastering the highest contemplative states that they teach, he finds that the spiritual liberation he senses is possible has not yet been attained. He then turns to bodily mortification.

9. The Rejection of Self-Torture as a Way to Liberation

He . . . embarked upon further austerities, and particularly on starvation. In his desire for quietude he emaciated his body for six years and carried out a number of strict methods of fasting. The bulk of his body was greatly reduced by this self-torture, but by way of compensation his psychic powers grew correspondingly more and more. . . .

After a time, however, it became clear to him that . . . self-torture merely wore out his body without any useful result. . . . He reasoned as follows: . . . That method which some time ago I found under the rose-apple tree,[1] that was more certain in its results. But

---

1. See selection no. 6, above.

those meditations cannot be carried out in this weakened condition; therefore I must take steps to increase again the strength of this body. . . .

Inward calm is needed for success! Inward calm cannot be maintained unless physical strength is constantly and intelligently replenished. Only if the body is reasonably nourished can undue strain on the mind be avoided.

10. The Vow Beneath the Tree

From a compassionate cowherd woman, Siddhartha receives a meal of rice-milk, much offending five companion ascetics who depart in disgust. But Siddhartha, now nourished, positions himself at the foot of a tree, which is soon to become the bodhi tree or tree of enlightenment.

He then adopted the cross-legged posture, which is the best of all because so immovable. . . . And he said to himself: "I shall not change this position so long as I have not done what I set out to do!"

11. The Defeat of Mara

Because the great Sage . . . had made his vow to win emancipation . . . Mara . . . shook with fright. [Mara is] the one who rules events connected with a life of passion . . . who hates the very thought of freedom. He had with him his three sons—Agitation, Mania, and Sullen Pride—and his three daughters—Discontent, Excitement, and Craving. These asked him why he was so disconcerted in his mind. And he replied to them in these words: "Look over there at that sage, clad in the armor of determination. He has sat down with the firm intention of conquering my realm. . . ."

Mara's sons and daughters invade Siddhartha's mind, attempting to move him to terror or lust, but he remains calm, unshaken by fear or desire.

Mara could achieve nothing against the Bodhisattva,[2] and he and his army were defeated, . . . their elation gone, their toil ren-

---

2. Literally, "wisdom-being," the term refers to one who is on the way to becoming a Buddha. See selection 39, below.

dered fruitless. . . . The great seer, free from the dust of passion, victorious over darkness' gloom, had vanquished him.

12. The Realization of Nibbana (Nirvana)

Nibbana is often considered the ultimate goal of Buddhist endeavor. Its attainment removes the mind's last traces of craving and aversion and frees it fully and finally from the round of rebirth. See selection 34, this chapter.

a. The Progress of Insight

Now that he had defeated Mara's violence by his firmness and calm, the Bodhisattva . . . put himself into trance, intent on discerning both the ultimate reality of things and the final goal of existence. . . .

In the *first watch* of the night he recollected the successive series of his former births. "There was I so and so; that was my name; deceased from there I came here."—in this way he remembered thousands of births, as though living them over again. When he had recalled his own births and deaths . . . the Sage turned his compassionate mind towards other living beings, and he thought to himself: "Again and again they must leave the people they regard as their own, and must go elsewhere, and that without ever stopping. Surely this world is unprotected and helpless, and like a wheel it turns round and round."

. . . In the *second watch* of the night . . . he looked upon the entire world as though reflected in a spotless mirror. He saw that the decease and rebirth of beings depend on whether they have done superior and inferior deeds. . . .

Then as the *third watch* of that night drew on [hc] turned his meditation to the real and essential nature of this world: "Alas, living beings wear themselves out in vain! Over and over again they are born, they age, die, pass on to a new life, and are reborn!" He then surveyed the twelve links of conditioned co-production.[3]

---

3. Or "dependent origination." See 29, below.

When the great seer had comprehended that where there is no ignorance whatever, there also the karma-formations are stopped —then he had achieved a correct knowledge of all there is to be known, and he stood out in the world as a Buddha. He passed through the eight stages of transic insight, and quickly reached their highest point. From the summit of the world downwards he could detect no self anywhere. Like the fire, when its fuel is burnt up, he became tranquil. He had reached perfection, and he thought to himself: "This is the authentic Way on which in the past so many great seers . . . have travelled on to ultimate and real truth. And now I have obtained it!"

At that moment, in the *fourth watch* of the night . . . pleasant breezes blew softly, rain fell from a cloudless sky, flowers and fruits dropped from the trees out of season—in an effort, as it were, to show reverence for him.

b. The Buddha Rejoices

It is said that at this moment the Buddha uttered the following paean of joy:

> Through many a birth I wandered in this world,
> Seeking in vain the builder of this house.
> Unfulfilling it is to be born again and again.
> O housemaker! Now I have seen you!
> You shall build no more houses for me!
> All your beams are broken,
> Your ridgepole is shattered.
> My mind is freed from all past conditionings,
> And craves the future no longer.

c. In Praise of Liberty

> I, Buddha, who wept with all my brother's tears,
>   Whose heart was broken by a whole world's woe,
> Laugh and am glad, for there is Liberty!
>   Ho! ye who suffer! know
> Ye suffer from yourselves. None else compels
>   None other holds you that ye live and die,

And whirl upon the wheel, and hug and kiss
Its spokes of agony.

13. After Hesitating, the Buddha Decides to Teach

a. The Hesitation

For seven days he dwelt there—his body gave him no trouble, his eyes never closed, and he looked into his own mind. He thought: "Here I have found freedom," and he knew that the longings of his heart had at last come to fulfillment. . . . He surveyed the world with his Buddha-eye, intent on giving it peace. When, however, he saw on the one side the world lost in low views and confused efforts, thickly covered with the dirt of passions, and saw on the other side the exceeding subtlety of the Dharma of emancipation, he felt inclined to take no action. But when he weighed up the significance of the pledge to enlighten all beings he had taken in the past, he became again more favorable to the idea of proclaiming the path to Peace.

b. The Buddha's Decision

[And he resolved:] Yet there are beings whose eyes are only a little covered with dust: they will understand the truth.

14. The Buddha's First Encounter

He had fulfilled his task, and now, calm and majestic, went on alone. . . . A mendicant . . . saw him on the road and in wonderment . . . said to him: "The senses of others are restless like horses, but yours have been tamed. Who then is your teacher?". . . But he replied: "No teacher have I. . . . Quite by myself, you see, have I the Dharma won. . . . That is the reason I am a Buddha. . . . I am now on my way to Varanasi. . . . There shall I beat the deathless Dharma's drum, unmoved by pride, untempted by renown. Having myself crossed the ocean of suffering, I must help others to cross it. Freed myself, I must set others free. . . ."

Thus begun, the Buddha's teaching career spans the next forty-five years. The content of that teaching will be outlined below, under "Core Doctrines." We close this section with accounts of the Buddha's final hours and last words.

15. "My Death Is an Occasion for Joy"

He then went to Kushinagara, bathed in the river, and gave this order to Ānanda: "Arrange a couch for me between those twin Sal trees! In the course of the night the Tathāgata[4] will enter [final] Nirvana!" . . . Go and tell the Mallas [a clan of that vicinity] about it. For they will regret it later on if they did not now witness the [final] Nirvana. . . ."

The Mallas, their faces covered with tears, came along to see the Sage. They paid homage to Him, and then, anguish in their mind, stood around Him. And the Sage spoke to them as follows: "In the hour of joy it is not proper to grieve. Your despair is quite inappropriate, and you should regain your composure! The goal, so hard to win . . . now at last is no longer far away. When that is won . . . how is there room for grief then in your minds? . . . At the time I won enlightenment, I got rid of the causes of becoming. . . . Now the hour comes near when I get rid also of this body, the dwelling place of the acts accumulated in the past. Now at last this body, which harbours so much ill, is on its way out. . . . Now that at last I emerge from the vast and endless suffering—is that the time for you to grieve?

"It is indeed a fact that salvation cannot come from the mere sight of Me. It demands strenuous efforts in the practice of Yoga. . . . A man must take medicine to be cured; the mere sight of the physician is not enough. . . . Therefore be energetic, persevere, and try to control your minds! Do good deeds, and try to win mindfulness!"

. . . But still the tears continued to pour from their eyes. . . .

---

4. Another name for the Buddha, meaning "one who has thus gone."

16. The Buddha's Final Instructions

a. Nothing Held Back

The Venerable Ānanda went up to him, paid his respects, sat down to one side and spoke to the Lord thus: "[I am] a little comforted by the thought that the Lord would not pass away until he had left his instructions concerning the Order."

"What, Ānanda! Does the Order expect that of me? I have taught the truth without making any distinction between exoteric and esoteric doctrines; for with the Tathāgata there is no such thing as the closed fist of the teacher who keeps some things back."

b. Let My Teaching Be Your Refuge

You might think: "Gone is the doctrine of our master. We have Master no more." But thus you should not think; for the Law (*dhamma*) and the Discipline which I have taught you will after my death be your master.

The Law be your isle,
The Law be your refuge
Look for no other refuge!

c. "Be Your Own Lamps"

So, Ananda, you must be your own lamps, be your own refuges. . . . Hold firm to the truth as a lamp and a refuge and do not look for refuge to anything besides yourselves. A monk becomes his own lamp by continually looking on his body, feelings, perceptions, moods and ideas in such a manner that he conquers the cravings and depressions of ordinary persons and is always diligent, self-possessed and collected in mind. Whoever among my monks does this, either now or when I am dead, if he is anxious to learn, will reach the summit.

d. The Mission: For the Happiness of Many

Go your ways, oh monks, for the benefit of many, for the happiness of many, out of compassion for the world, for the good, benefit and happiness of gods and men. Now two should go in the same direction. Teach the Dhamma which is beneficent in the beginning, in the middle, and in the end—both the spirit and the letter of it. Make known your own pure way of life.

17. The Last Words of the Buddha

Impermanent are all formations.
Observe this carefully, constantly.

THE REBEL SAINT: The Buddha's Attitude Toward Authority, Ritual, and Moot Points

The Buddha's pragmatic concern to relieve suffering and his psychological emphasis on self-transformation made him pointedly critical of certain common aspects of religion, including blind reliance on authority, belief in the efficacy of ritual, and windy debate about unanswerable questions.

18. It Is Proper to Doubt: *See for Yourselves*

It is proper . . . to doubt, to be uncertain. . . . Do not go upon what has been acquired by repeated hearing; nor upon tradition; nor upon rumour; nor upon what is in a scripture; . . . nor upon the consideration, "The monk is our teacher." [Rather] when you yourselves know: "These things are bad; [when] undertaken and observed, these things lead to harm and ill," abandon them. [Likewise] when you yourselves know: "These things are good; [when] undertaken and observed, these things lead to benefit and happiness," enter on and abide in them.

19. Against Ritual

a. Dubious Efficacy

To seek to win peace through others, as priests or sacrificers, is the same as if a stone were thrown into deep water, and now people, praying and imploring and folding their hands, came and knelt down all around saying: "Rise, O dear stone! Come to the surface, O dear stone!" But the stone remains at the bottom.

b. Right Action, Not Ritual, Ennobles

If this river . . . were full of water . . . and a man with business on the other side . . . standing on this bank, should invoke the further bank, and say, "Come hither, O further bank! come over to this side!"

Now what think you? Would the further bank . . . by reason of that man's invoking and praying and hoping and praising, come over to this side?

. . . In just the same way . . . do the Brahmans [priestly caste], omitting the practice of those qualities which really make a person [noble] and adopting the practice of those qualities which really make people [ignoble], say thus: "Indra we call upon . . . Brahma we call upon!" [The thought that] they, by reason of their invoking and praying and hoping and praising, would, after death . . . become united with Brahma—verily such a condition of things can in no wise be.

20. Against Wasting Precious Time on Ineluctably Moot Points

a. The Ten Unanswered Questions and the Parable of the Arrow

Now it happened to the venerable Malunkyaputta, being in seclusion and plunged in meditation, that a consideration presented itself to his mind, as follows: "These theories . . . the Blessed One has left unexplained, has set aside and rejected:

that the world is eternal or not
that the world is finite or not
that the soul is one thing and the body another, or not
that the person who has achieved Nirvana exists after death, or
     does not exist after death, or both, or neither.

... And the fact that the Blessed One does not explain them to me does not please me or suit me.

So Malunkyaputta takes himself to the Buddha and addresses these issues to him. The Buddha replies:

It is as if ... a man had been wounded by an arrow thickly smeared with poison, and his friends and companions, his relatives and kinsfolk, were to procure for him a physician ... and the sick man were to say, "I will not have this arrow taken out until I have learnt whether the man who wounded me belonged to the warrior caste, or to the Brahmin caste, or to the agricultural caste or to the menial caste."

Or again he were to say, "I will not have this arrow taken out until I have learnt the name of the man who wounded me, and to what clan he belongs."

Or again he were to say, "I will not have this arrow taken out until I have learnt whether the man who wounded me was tall, or short, or of the middle height."

Or again he were to say, "I will not have this arrow taken out until I have learnt whether the man who wounded me was black, or dusky or of a yellow skin."

Or again he were to say, "I will not have this arrow taken out until I have learnt whether the man who wounded me was from this or that village, or town, or city."

Many other possibilities are mentioned.

That man would die, Malunkyaputta, without ever having learned [all] this. . . .

The religious life . . . does not depend on [the answer to these questions].

Accordingly . . . bear always in mind what it is that I have not explained and what it is that I have explained. I have not explained [any of the aforementioned issues].

And what . . . *have* I explained? Misery have I explained; the origin of misery, the cessation of misery, and the path leading to the cessation of misery have I explained.

b. Other Unwise Considerations

And unwisely [an aspirant] considers thus: "Have I been in the past? Or, have I not been in the past? What have I been in the past? How have I been in the past? From what state into what state did I change in the past? —Shall I be in the future? Or shall I not be in the future? What shall I be in the future? How shall I be in the future?. . ."

CORE DOCTRINES: The Four Noble Truths, the Eightfold Path, and Other Basic Buddhist Concepts

21. The Four Noble Truths and the Eightfold Path

From the Buddha's first sermon, "Setting Rolling the Wheel of Truth."

a. The Four Truths

Suffering, as a noble truth, is this: Birth is suffering, ageing is suffering, sickness is suffering, death is suffering, sorrow and . . . pain . . . and despair are suffering, association with the loathed is suffering, dissociation from the loved is suffering, not to get what one wants is suffering—in short suffering is the five [groups] of clinging's objects.[5]

Thus *the origin of suffering,* as a noble truth, is this: It is the craving that produces renewal of being, accompanied by enjoyment and lust—in other words, craving for sensual desires, craving for being, craving for non-being.

Cessation of suffering, as a noble truth, is this: It is remainderless fading and ceasing, . . . letting go and rejecting, of that same craving.

---

5. The five *skandhas,* or "groups of existence" that make up a human individual. See no. 27, below.

The way leading to the cessation of suffering, as a noble truth is this: It is simply *the eightfold noble path* [of] *right view, right intention, right speech, right action, right livelihood, right effort, right mindfulness, right concentration.*

b. Their Centrality

As long as the . . . true knowledge and insight as regards these Four Noble Truths was not quite clear in me, so long was I not sure that I had won that supreme Enlightenment. . . . But as soon as the true knowledge and insight as regards these Four Noble Truths had become perfectly clear in me, there arose in me the assurance that I had won that supreme Enlightenment unsurpassed.

22. The Eightfold Path as the Middle Way

Also from the Buddha's first sermon, "Setting Rolling the Wheel of Truth":

Monks, these two extremes ought not to be cultivated by one gone-forth from the home-life. What are the two? There is . . . indulgence . . . in the objects of sensual desire, which is inferior, low, vulgar, ignoble, and leads to no good; and there is devotion to self-torment, which is painful, ignoble, and leads to no good.

The middle way . . . avoids both these extremes; it gives vision, it gives knowledge, and it leads to peace, to direct acquaintance to nibbāna. And what is that middle way? It is simply the noble eight-fold path. . . . [See 21a.]

23. Karma

a. Volition

It is volition that I call "karma." Having willed, one [then] acts by body, speech, and mind.

b. Deeds

All beings are the owners of their deeds (karma), the heirs of their deeds; their deeds are the womb from which they sprang. . . . Whatever deeds they do—good or evil—of such they will be the heirs.

c. Ignorance and Craving

Truly, because beings, obstructed by ignorance and ensnared by craving, seek ever fresh delight, fresh rebirth continually comes to be.

24. The Three Poisons: *Greed, Hatred, Delusion*

And the action . . . that is done out of greed, hatred and delusion, . . . wherever this action ripens there one experiences the fruits of this action, be it in this life, or the next life, or in some future life. . . .

25. Samsara

a. Its Inconceivable Beginnings

Inconceivable is the beginning of this Samsara; not to be discovered is any first beginning of beings, who obstructed by ignorance and ensnared by craving, are hurrying and hastening through this round of rebirths.

b. The Tears Shed on This Long Way

Which do you think is more: the flood of tears, which weeping and wailing you have shed upon this long way—hurrying and hastening through this round of rebirths, united with the undesired, separated from the desired—this, or the waters of the four oceans?

Long have you suffered the death of father and mother, of sons, daughters, brothers and sisters. And whilst you were thus suffering, you have indeed shed more tears upon this long way than there is water in the four oceans.

26. The Three Marks of Existence

All formations are impermanent [*anicca*]; all formations are subject to suffering [*dukkha*]; all formations are "without a self" [*anatta*].

27. The Five *Skandhas* or Groups of Existence

The skandhas *are the Buddha's fivefold classification of the physical and mental factors comprising reality; unreflective persons mistake the local interaction of these factors for an ego or personality.*

And what, in brief, are the Five Groups of Existence? They are materiality, sensation, perception, moods and thoughts.[6]

28. *Anatta* or Without-a-Self

Anatta *is a fundamental Buddhist doctrine. It suggests that just as what we designate by the name* car *has no existence apart from axle, wheels, shaft, motor, and so on, that which we conventionally designate* person *or "I" is nothing but a continually shifting combination of impersonal physical and mental phenomena.*

Suppose a person who was not blind beheld the many bubbles on the Ganges as they drove along. . . . After he had carefully watched them and examined them they would appear to him empty, unreal and unsubstantial. In exactly the same way does the student of the Buddha behold all corporeal phenomena, sensations, perceptions, moods, and thoughts. . . . He watches them, examines them care-

---

6. Adapted; my source uses the terms *corporeality, feeling, perception, mental formations,* and *consciousness.*

fully; and, after carefully examining them, they appear to him empty, void and without a self.

29. Dependent Origination

The doctrine of dependent origination is the counterpart of the anatta doctrine. Because all processes are empty-of-self, they cocondition and codetermine each other. Accordingly, reality is a vast field of mutually conditioning events.

a. The Buddha on the Centrality of Dependent Origination

Who sees Dependent Origination sees the Dhamma[7]; who sees the Dhamma sees Dependent Origination.

b. The Basic Formula

This body, monks, is not yours, nor does it belong to others. It should be regarded [as the product of] former karma, effected through what has been willed and felt. In regard to it, the [wise person] reflects on Dependent Origination itself: If this is, that comes to be; from the arising of this, that arises; if this is not, that does not come to be; from the stopping of this, that is stopped.

c. The Twelve Links of the Chain of Dependent Origination

Conditioned by ignorance are the karma-formations; conditioned by the karma-formations is consciousness; conditioned by consciousness is mind-and-body; conditioned by mind-and-body are the six sense-fields[8]; conditioned by the six sense-fields is sense impression; conditioned by sense-impression is feeling; conditioned by feeling is craving; conditioned by craving is grasping; conditioned by grasping is becoming; conditioned by becoming is

---

7. Or Dharma (Sanskrit); that is, the Way of Truth.
8. In Buddhism, mind is the sixth sense. It "senses" thoughts in the same way a tongue senses tastes.

birth; conditioned by birth there come into being ageing and dying, grief, sorrow, suffering, lamentation and despair. This is the origin of the whole mass of suffering.

And now the reversal of this process:

But from the stopping of ignorance is the stopping of the karma-formations [and so on until we come to] the stopping of the whole mass of suffering.

d. The Image of Dependent Origination: Indra's Net

This great imaginary net . . . is to be visualized . . . as stretching throughout the entire universe: its vertical extension representing time; its horizontal, space. At every point where the net's threads interconnect [every point-instant of existence], one imagines a crystal bead symbolizing an individual existence. Each one of these innumerable crystal beads reflects on its surfaces not only every other bead in the net but every reflection of every other bead, thus creating numberless, endless reflections of each other while forming one complete and total *whole.*

30. The Five Precepts

I undertake to observe the precept to abstain from killing living beings . . . to abstain from taking things not given . . . to abstain from sexual misconduct[9]. . . . to abstain from false speech . . . to abstain from intoxicating drinks and drugs causing heedlessness.

31. The Nature of Right Speech

Right speech covers more than abstention from lying. Because how and what we speak influence the way we think, attention to how we speak is essential to transforming what we speak.

---

9. The meaning of sexual misconduct is subject to interpretation. An ancient canonical gloss prescribes "no intercourse with such persons as are still under the protection of father, mother, brother, sister or relatives, nor with married women, nor female convicts, nor lastly, with betrothed girls." *Anguttara Nikāya* 10.176.

He avoids tale-bearing. . . . What he has heard here, he does not repeat there so as to cause dissension; . . . thus he unites those that are divided; and those that are united, he encourages. Concord gladdens him . . . and it is concord that he spreads by his words.

He avoids harsh language. . . . He speaks such words as are gentle, soothing to the ear, loving, such words as go to the heart, and are courteous, friendly, and agreeable to many.

He avoids vain talk. . . . He speaks at the right time, in accordance with facts, speaks what is useful, speaks of the law and the discipline: his speech is like a treasure, uttered at the right moment, accompanied by arguments, moderate and full of sense.

32. Right Mindfulness and the Transformation of Consciousness

The Satipatthāna Sutta (The Foundations of Mindfulness) is one of Buddhism's most important teachings on the practice of meditation. It is difficult to appreciate as a text, for it yields its treasures only in the context of sustained practice under the guidance of a teacher. It may be compared to a computer manual: hard to read for pleasure but indispensable when coping with a complex circuitry. A sutta *(Sanskrit,* sutra*) is a Buddhist text that claims to have been uttered by the Buddha himself.*

The Four Foundations of Mindfulness

The only way that leads to the . . . end of pain and grief, to the entering of the right path and the realization of Nibbana, is by the Four Foundations of Mindfulness. And which are these four?

Herein the disciple dwells in sustained awareness[10] of the Body, in sustained awareness of Sensation,[11] in sustained awareness of the Mind, in sustained awareness of the Mind-Objects; ardent,

---

10. Throughout this passage I am using *sustained awareness* where my source uses *contemplation.*

11. I have substituted the word *sensation* where my source used the word *feeling,* in order to underscore the bodily basis of this exercise. Feeling *qua* emotion can be misconstrued as a purely mental phenomenon.

clearly comprehending them and mindful, after putting away worldly greed and grief.

1. Sustained Awareness of the Body

But how does the disciple dwell in sustained awareness of the body? [There are five basic ways:]

Watching over in-and-out-breathing. Herein the disciple retires to a solitary place, seats himself with legs crossed, body erect, and mindfully he breathes in, mindfully he breathes out. . . .

The four postures. And further, while [walking], standing, sitting, or lying down, the disciple [is clearly aware of] any position of the body. . . .

Mindfulness and clear comprehension of bodily acts. And further, the disciple acts with clear comprehension in going and coming; eating, drinking, chewing, and tasting; in discharging excrement and urine; acts with clear comprehension in walking, standing, sitting, falling asleep, awakening; in speaking and keeping silent.

Contemplation of loathsomeness. And further, the disciple contemplates this body from the sole of the foot upward, and from the top of the hair downward, with a skin stretched over it, and filled with manifold impurities: "This body has hairs of the head and of the body, nails, teeth, skin, flesh, sinews, bones, marrow, kidneys, heart, liver, diaphragm, spleen, lungs, stomach, bowels, mesentery, and excrement; bile, phlegm, pus, blood, sweat, lymph, tears, skin-grease, saliva, nasal mucous, oil of the joints, and urine."

Just as if there were a sack, with openings at both ends, filled with various kinds of grain, . . . just so does the disciple investigate this body. . . .

Cemetery meditations. And further, just as if the disciple were looking at a corpse thrown on a charnel-ground, eaten by crows, hawks, or vultures, by dogs or jackals, or devoured by all kinds of worms, so he regards his own body: "This body of mine also has this nature, has this destiny, and cannot escape it. . . ."

2. Sustained Awareness of Sensations

But how does the disciple dwell in contemplation of the sensations? . . . In experiencing sensation, the disciple knows: "I have an agreeable sensation"; or "I have a disagreeable sensation"; or "I have an indifferent sensation. . . ."

3. Sustained Awareness of the Mind

One attempts sustained awareness of one's changing moods or states of mind.

Herein the disciple knows the greedy mind as greedy, and the not greedy mind as not greedy; knows the hating mind as hating, and the not hating mind as not hating; knows the deluded mind as deluded and the undeluded mind as undeluded. He knows the cramped mind as cramped, and the scattered mind as scattered, knows the concentrated mind as concentrated. . . .

4. Sustained Awareness of the Mind-Objects

One attempts sustained awareness of fluxing mental experience through the lens of basic Buddhist formulae.

The Five Hindrances. He knows when there is lust in him; . . . knows when there is anger in him; . . . knows when there is torpor and sloth in him; . . . knows when there is restlessness and mental worry in him; . . . knows when there are doubts in him; . . . he knows [too] when these hindrances are not in him. . . . She knows how they come to arise; knows how, once arisen, they are overcome; and she knows how they do not rise again in the future.

The Five Groups of Existence [Skandhas]. And further: the disciple dwells in sustained awareness of the . . . five groups of Existence. . . . [See no. 27, above.]

The Six Sense-Bases. And further: the disciple dwells in sustained awareness of the six . . . sense-bases. He knows the eye and visual objects, ear and sound, nose and odours, tongue and tastes, body and bodily impressions, mind and mind-objects. . . .

The Seven Factors of Enlightenment. He knows when there is in him "Mindfulness," "Investigation of the Law," "Energy," "Enthusiasm," "Tranquility," "Concentration," and "Equanimity." He knows when [these are] not in him, knows how [they come] to arise, and how [they are] fully developed.

The Four Noble Truths. And further: the disciple dwells in sustained awareness of the Four Noble Truths. [See no. 21, above.]

[Conclusion]

The only way that leads to the attainment of purity, to the overcoming of sorrow and lamentation, to the end of pain and grief, to the entering upon the right path, and the realization of Nibbana [Nirvana], is by these four foundations of mindfulness.

33. The Cultivation of Loving-Kindness (*Metta*)

Buddhist practice includes the cultivation of four qualities said to be divine conditions of the mind. They are: compassion, loving-kindness, sympathetic joy, and equanimity. Here is a scriptural passage on loving-kindness:

METTA SUTTA

In safety and in bliss
May all creatures be of a blissful heart.
Whatever breathing beings there may be,
No matter whether they are frail or firm,
With none excepted, be they long or big
Or middle-sized, or be they short or small
Or thick, as well as those seen or unseen,
Or whether they are far or near,
Existing or yet seeking to exist,
May all creatures be of a blissful heart.
Let no one work another one's undoing
Or even slight him at all anywhere;
And never let them wish each other ill
Through provocation or resentful thought.

And just as might a mother with her life
Protect the son that was her only child,
So let him then for every living thing
Maintain unbounded consciousness in being,
And let him too with love for all the world
Maintain unbounded consciousness in being
Above, below, and all round in between,
Untroubled, with no enemy or foe.

And while he stands or walks, or while he sits
Or while he lies down, free from drowsiness,
Let him resolve upon this mindfulness:
This is Divine Abiding here, they say.

34. Nibbana (Nirvana)

a. End of Karma

This, truly, is Peace, this is the Highest, namely the end of all karma formations, the forsaking of every substratum of rebirth, the fading away of craving, detachment. . . .

b. Eradication of the Three Poisons

The extinction of greed, the extinction of hate, the extinction of delusion: this indeed is called Nibbana.

c. Deliverance of the Heart

The purpose of the Holy Life does not consist in acquiring alms [or] honour, . . . nor in gaining morality [or] concentration. . . . That unshakeable deliverance of the heart: that indeed, is the object of the Holy Life, that is its essence, that is its goal.

d. End of Old Age and Death

For those who in mid-stream stay, in great peril in the flood, . . . do I proclaim the Isle . . . of No-beyond. Nirvana do I call it—the utter extinction of ageing and dying.

e. It Is Real

There is an Unborn, Unoriginated, Uncreated, Unformed. If there were not [then] escape from the world of the born, the originated, the created, the formed, would not be possible.

But since there is an Unborn, Unoriginated, Uncreated, Unformed, therefore, escape is possible from the world of the born, the originated, the created, the formed.

35. The Arahant (Arhat)

The Arahant (literally, "noble person") is one who has traversed the Buddhist path to its end and realized Nibbana. Sapientially and ethically there is no difference between an Arahant and a Buddha; the latter title is simply reserved for one who has rediscovered the path without the help of another.

a. Finished

And for a disciple thus freed, in whose heart dwells peace, there is nothing to be added to what has been done, and naught more remains for him to do. Just as a rock of one solid mass remains unshaken by the wind, even so, . . . neither the desired nor the undesired can cause such a one to waver. Steadfast is his mind, gained is deliverance.

b. Happy Indeed

Ah, happy indeed the Arahants! In them no craving's found. The "I am" conceit is rooted out; confusion's net is burst. Lust-free they have attained; translucent is the mind of them. Unspotted in the world are they, . . . with outflows none. . . . They roar the lion's roar: "Incomparable are Buddhas in the world."

36. The Three Jewels

The Buddha (the Awakened One), Dharma (the way of truth he taught), and Sangha (the community of those who live by that teaching) are called the Triple Gem because of their purity and inestimable value. A triple recitation of the following formula is a basic Buddhist act of piety.

I go for refuge to the Buddha. (*Buddham saranam gacchami*)

I go for refuge to the Dharma. (*Dhammam saranam gacchami*)
I go for refuge to the Sangha. (*Sangham saranam gacchami*)

37. The Buddha Summarizes the Teaching of the Awakened

To refrain from evil,
To achieve the good,
To purify one's own mind
This is the teaching of all Awakened Ones.

MAHAYANA BUDDHISM

Religions, like organisms, mutate and evolve. Buddhist innovation was fueled by disagreements over the spirit and letter of the master's message, and by the adaptive pressures of new environments. By the first or second century C.E. a family of sects calling itself the Mahayana *or "Greater Vehicle" had appeared. While affirming the core doctrines of Buddhism, Mahayanists claimed that these teachings were in some ways preliminary. They undertook to write new scriptures that, in their eyes, not only represented the ultimate message of the Buddha but that also allowed wider popular access to the Buddha's saving power. Three key Mahayana innovations are singled out for attention below: (1) the idea of emptiness; (2) the bodhisattva ideal; and (3) devotional Buddhism, which is based on the belief that the term* Buddha *names not only the historical Indian sage but also a grace-bestowing cosmic principle, a divine being who responds to the prayers and devotions of the faithful.*

38. Emptiness

The idea of emptiness can be viewed as the result of a relentless extrapolation of the doctrine of dependent origination (no. 29 above). The doctrine of dependent origination teaches that because every thing or event arises from the interplay of countless factors, no thing or event can be

said to bring itself into being, and therefore every thing/event is empty
of own-being. *The Mahayana applied this insight even to the Buddha
and his teachings. Because the Buddha's career itself was dependently
originated, even the Buddha, the four noble truths, and the eightfold
path are all* empty of own-being. *This does not mean they are worthless; it means that because they have been conditioned by various circumstances, they are not truly* ultimate. *What, then, is* ultimate?

*The answer is: emptiness itself. To those of inferior understanding
the Buddha taught that we are lost in samsara and that we must struggle to win nirvana. But, says the Mahayanist, to the enlightened who
see that both samsara and nirvana (like all else) are empty, these two
relative realities "collapse" into the ultimate reality of emptiness. But
emptiness is not somewhere else; it is here and now, all-embracing, and
inalienable; it is a perfect, unimpeded Total Field of Enlightenment or
Suchness—and it is what we are! We are all already Buddha-Nature,
if only we would realize it. There is ultimately no problem (suffering, samsara) and no solution (nirvana), because "everything" and
"everyone" is always-already enlightened. A final twist: emptiness too
is empty. It is not an ultimately "correct" concept but rather a lever to
extricate ourselves from the delusion that any concept, including
Buddhist concepts, are ultimate. The really Real can be known only by
intuitive realization, never by discursive conceptualizing.*

a. "Those Who Seek Nirvana Are to Be Laughed At"

That which the Lord revealed in his perfect enlightenment was not
[any of the five skandhas] for none of these five components come
into being, neither does the supreme wisdom come into being. . . .
And how can that which does not come into being know that which
also does not come into being? Since nothing can be grasped, what
is the Buddha, what is wisdom, what is the bodhisattva, what is
revelation? All the components are by nature empty—just convention, just names, agreed tokens, coverings. . . . Thus all things are
the perfection of being, infinite perfection, unobscured perfection,
unconditioned perfection. All things are enlightenment, for they
must be recognized as without essential nature—even the five
greatest sins are enlightenment, for enlightenment has no essential
nature and neither have the five greatest sins. Thus those who seek
for Nirvana are to be laughed at. . . .

b. The Heart Sutra

This sutra, the full title of which is The Great Heart of Perfect Wisdom, is perhaps the densest expression of the Mahayana idea of emptiness.

Homage to the Perfection of Wisdom, the lovely, the holy!

Avalokita, the holy Lord and Bodhisattva, was moving in the deep course of the wisdom that has gone beyond. He looked down from on high, he beheld but five [skandhas], and he saw that in their own-being they were empty.

Here, O Sariputra, form is emptiness and the very emptiness is form; emptiness does not differ from form, form does not differ from emptiness; whatever is form, that is emptiness, whatever is emptiness, that is form. . . .

Here, O Sariputra, all dharmas are marked with emptiness; they are not produced or stopped, not defiled or immaculate, not deficient or complete.

Therefore, O Sariputra, in emptiness there is no form, nor feeling, nor perception, nor impulse, nor consciousness; no eye, ear, nose, tongue, body, mind, no forms, sounds, smells, tastes, touchables or objects of mind; no sight-organ element, and so forth, until we come to: no mind-consciousness-element; there is no ignorance, no extinction of ignorance, and so forth, until we come to: there is no decay and death, no extinction of decay and death; there is no suffering, no origination, no stopping, no path; there is no cognition, no attainment, and no non-attainment.

Therefore, O Sariputra, it is because of his indifference to any kind of personal attainment that a Bodhisattva . . . dwells without thought-coverings . . . and in the end he attains to Nirvana.

All those who appear as Buddhas in the three periods of time fully awake to the utmost, right and perfect enlightenment because they have relied on the perfection of wisdom.

Therefore, one should know the Prajnaparamita [Perfection of Wisdom] as the great mantra,[12] the mantra of great knowledge, the

---

12. A mantra is a sound or a word, or a series of these, the sacred import of which lies not only in its semantic meaning (if it has one), but also in its power to tap, as if by resonance, other orders of reality.

utmost mantra, the unequalled mantra, allayer of all suffering, in truth—for what could go wrong?

. . . [The] mantra. . . runs like this:

Gone, Gone, Gone Beyond, Gone Altogether Beyond, O What an Awakening! All Hail!

This completes the Heart of Perfect Wisdom.

39. The Bodhisattva

The bodhisattva (literally, "wisdom-being") is the spiritual hero of Mahayana tradition. A bodhisattva is a person who, out of compassion, renounces his or her own entry into nirvana in order to be reborn repeatedly to undertake this infinite work of saving all sentient beings. Amidst this work, however, the bodhisattva is aware that there are ultimately no beings to save and no one to do the saving. Without this wisdom, the bodhisattva is not a bodhisattva.

a. From the Diamond Sutra

The Lord said: . . . Someone who has set out in the vehicle of a Bodhisattva should think in this manner: "As many beings as there are in the universe of beings—egg-born, born from a womb, moisture-born, or miraculously born—all these must I lead into that Realm of Nirvana which leaves nothing behind. And yet, although innumerable beings have thus been led to Nirvana, in fact no being at all has been led to Nirvana." And why? If in a Bodhisattva the notion of a "being" should take place, he could not be called a "Wisdom-being." And why? He is not to be called a Wisdom-being in whom the notion of a self or of a being should take place, or the notion of a living soul or a person. . . .

b. The Infinite Compassion of the Bodhisattva

The bodhisattva's wisdom consists in knowing that even the "I" who takes a vow to save others is an illusion. Nevertheless she or he compassionately adopts the illusion of selfhood in order to liberate those still confounded by it.

A Bodhisattva resolves: I take upon myself the burden of all suffering. . . . I do not turn or run away, do not tremble, am not terrified, . . . do not turn back or despond.

And why? . . . I have made the vow to save all beings. . . . The whole world of living beings I must rescue, from the terrors of birth-and-death, from the jungle of false views. . . . My endeavors do not merely aim at my own deliverance. . . . I must rescue all these beings from the stream of Samsara. . . . And I must not cheat beings out of my store of merit. I am resolved to abide in each single state of woe for numberless aeons; and so I will help all beings to freedom, in all the states of woe that may be found in any world system whatsoever.

And why? Because it is surely better that I alone should be in pain than that all these beings should fall into states of woe.

c. The Difference Between Bodhisattvas and Other (Non-Mahayana) Buddhists

It is claimed that non-Mahayanists neglect to radiate their enlightenment to others because they mistakenly feel that this would be as futile as a glowworm trying to illuminate India. Bodhisattvas, however, rightly confident of the cosmic implications of their enlightenment—for since all is emptiness there are no obstructions in the Infinite Field—radiate their enlightenment like the rising sun lights up the earth. The following passage also makes the important point that bodhisattvas do not postpone their enlightenment, only their entry into final nirvana, that is, death without rebirth.

The Lord [said]: . . . Does it occur to any of the [non-Mahayanists] to think "after we have known full enlightenment, we should lead all beings to Nirvana, into the realm of Nirvana which leaves nothing behind"?

Sariputra: No indeed, O Lord. . . .

The Lord: But such are the intentions of a bodhisattva. A glowworm, or some other luminous animal, does not think that its light could illuminate the Continent of [India] or radiate over it. Just so the [non-Mahayanists] do not think that they should, after winning full enlightenment, lead all beings to Nirvana. But the sun, when it has risen, radiates its light over the whole of [India]. Just so a bodhisattva, after he has accomplished the practices which lead to the full enlightenment of Buddhahood, leads countless beings to Nirvana.

40. Devotional Buddhism

Believing that differences among beings require a variety of skillful means (upaya) *to save them, Mahayanists produced new scriptures to spread their good news. The justification for this practice is rooted in the belief that the ultimate source of Buddha's saving power is not his historical person but the absolute reality called emptiness or* dharmakaya. *Since all points in time are equidistant from the dharmakaya's timeless infinitude, the latter can express its saving power at any time.*

Some of these new scriptures, as we have seen, were expositions of key ideas like emptiness and the bodhisattva. Others, however, accommodated the devotional impulse in human beings and the needs of a Buddhist laity who could not be expected to engage in meditation practices or master the subtleties of emptiness thinking. Buddhist devotional literature presupposes that because Buddha *names an omnipresent reality, there are actually countless Buddhas and bodhisattvas ready to lend a helping hand to those who call upon them in prayer, faith, and devotion. In the sections below we glimpse but a tiny fraction of the immense devotional literature of Buddhism.*

a. From the Lotus Sutra: The Buddha as a Rain Cloud of Universal Grace

. . . I refresh this entire world
Like a cloud which releases its rain evenly for all;
Equal is enlightenment for noble and mean alike,
For those who are immoral and for moral ones . . .

I preach the Dharma to beings whether their intellect
Be inferior or superior, and their faculties weak or strong.
Setting aside all tiredness,
I rain down the rain of the Dharma . . .

So the nature of the Dharma always exists for the weal of the
    world,
And it refreshes by the Dharma the entire world.

And then, refreshed, just like the plants,
The world will burst forth into blossoms.

b. The Buddha Saves All Beings and They Reach Salvation in Many Ways

The Buddha himself abides in the Great Vehicle [Maha-Yana],
And . . . He saves all beings . . .
If men turn in faith to the Buddha, [He] will not deceive
them . . .

[Those] who have come into contact with former Buddhas,
[Who] have learned the Law and practiced charity. . .
All of these people have reached the level of Buddhahood.

Those people who, for the sake of the Buddha,
Installed images, or had them carved,
Have reached the level of Buddhahood.

Those who with a happy frame of mind
Have sung the glory of the Buddha, even with a very small
sound,
Or have worshipped, or have merely folded their hands,
Or have uttered one "Namo" [Praise be],
All have reached the level of Buddhahood.

. . . the Buddhas of the past . . . the Buddhas of the future,
Their number will be infinite . . .
All these Buddhas, with an infinite number of suitable means,
Will save all living beings,
And enable them to dwell in the Pure Wisdom of the
Buddha . . .

c. Rewards for Devotion to the Buddha

Verily, for countless aeons [one] is not reborn blind or lame
If, after he has decided to win enlightenment, he venerates a
Stupa[13] of the [Buddha] . . .

---

13. A stupa is a Buddhist reliquary mound, a dome built on a low square or circular base and containing relics of the Buddha. Clockwise circumambulation of a stupa is a traditional act of Buddhist piety.

One who does worship to [the Buddha] has the best and
unequalled reward.
Deceased here . . . he goes to the Heavens of the Thirty-Three,
And there he obtains a brilliant palace made of jewels . . .
And there he gets a celestial lotus-pond . . .
With a floor of golden sand . . .
In hundreds of thousands of . . . births he will everywhere
Be honored after he has placed a garland on a shrine.

d. The Pure Land (*Sukhavati*) of Amitabha, the Buddha of Infinite Light

*For millions, Buddhism means invoking the name of a Buddha called
Amitabha in the following words:* A'-mi-t'o-fo *(in Chinese) or* Namo
Amida Butsu *(in Japanese). They can thereby be confident of their salvation into Amitabha's Pure Land, a paradise to which the faithful go
after death and from which the final journey to nirvana is made easier.*

This . . . world system of the Lord Amitabha is rich and prosperous, comfortable, fertile, delightful. And in this world system . . .
there are no hells . . . and none of the unauspicious places of rebirth. . . .

And that world system . . . emits many fragrant odors, it is rich
in a great variety of flowers and fruits, adorned with jewel trees,
which are frequented by flocks of various birds with sweet
voices. . . .

On all sides it is surrounded with golden nets, and all round
covered with lotus flowers made of all the precious things. Some of
the lotus flowers are half a mile in circumference, others up to ten
miles. And from each jewel lotus issues thirty-six hundred thousand kotis [a koti is "a huge number"] of rays. And at the end of
each ray there issue thirty-six hundred thousand kotis of Buddhas,
with golden-colored bodies. . . .

And many kinds of rivers flow along in this world system, up to
fifty miles broad and twelve miles deep. . . .

And . . . both the banks of those great rivers are lined with vari-
ously scented jewel trees. . . . And those rivers flow along with
golden sand at the bottom. And all the wishes those beings may
think of, they all will be fulfilled, as long as they are rightful.

And . . . everyone hears the pleasant sound he wishes to hear, i.e., he hears of the Buddha, the Dharma, the Sangha. . . . And, hearing this . . . brings about the state of mind which leads to the accomplishment of enlightenment. . . .

And that . . . is the reason why this world-system is called the "Happy Land.". . .

And the beings . . . do not eat gross food, like soup or raw sugar; but whatever food they may wish for, that they perceive as eaten, and they become gratified in body and mind, without there being any further need to throw the food into the body.

. . . And the beings who are touched by the winds, which are pervaded with various perfumes, are filled with a happiness as great as that of a monk who has achieved the cessation of suffering. . . .

And all the beings who have been born, who are born, who will be born in this Buddha-field, they all are fixed on the right method of salvation, until they have won Nirvana. . . . And if any beings . . . plant a large and immeasurable root of good, having raised their hearts to enlightenment, and if they vow to be reborn in that world system, then, when the hour of their death approaches, . . . Amitabha . . . will stand before them, surrounded by hosts of monks. Then, having seen that Lord, and having died with hearts serene, they will be reborn in just that world-system. . . .

e. Hōnen's Teaching on the *Nembutsu*

Hōnen (1133–1212) was a Japanese Buddhist who preached the saving power of invoking the name of Amida (Amitabha) Buddha, a practice called nembutsu. *Here he counsels one of his followers:*

I am delighted to know that you are invoking the sacred name. Indeed the practice of the Nembutsu is the best of all for bringing us to *ōjō* [rebirth in the Pure Land]. . . . This Nembutsu . . . has the endorsement of all the Buddhas of the six quarters; and, while the disciples of [other] schools . . . are indeed most excellent, the Buddhas do not give them final approval. And so, although there are many kinds of religious exercise, the Nembutsu far excels them all. . . . And so you should now cease from all other religious practices, apply yourself to Nembutsu alone, and in this it is all-important to do it with undivided attention. . . . Is there anything anywhere that is superior to it for bringing happiness in the present or the future life?

f. Nichiren on Faith in the Buddha and the Lotus Sutra

Nichiren (1222–1282) was a Japanese Buddhist prophet who held that one particular scripture, the Lotus Sutra, represents the final and supreme teaching of the Buddha. For him, it is the name of the Lotus Sutra, not the name of Amida Buddha, which should be on the lips of every Buddhist.

When you fall into an abyss and someone has lowered a rope to pull you out, should you hesitate to grasp the rope because you doubt the power of the helper? Has not the Buddha declared, "I alone am the protector and saviour"? There is the power! Is it not taught that faith is the only entrance [to salvation]? There is the rope! . . . Our hearts ache and our sleeves are wet [with tears], until we see face to face the tender figure of the One, who says to us, "I am thy Father.". . . Should any season be passed without thinking of the compassionate promise, "Constantly I am thinking of you"? Should any month or day be spent without revering the teaching that there is none who cannot attain Buddhahood? . . . Devote yourself wholeheartedly to the "Adoration to the Lotus of the Perfect Truth," and utter it yourself as well as admonish others to do the same. Such is your task in this human life.

A. TIBETAN BUDDHISM

Tibetan Buddhism accepts the cardinal notions of Buddhism and, in its Mahayana way, embraces not only the strategic concept of emptiness and the ideal of the bodhisattva, but also honors the transformative possibilities of devotionalism. Its uniqueness lies more in its methods than in its doctrine, in its ways of deploying the full complement of human faculties in the work of enlightenment. Its spiritual repertoire includes: mantra, *the ritual and meditative use of sacred sounds or phrases;* mudra, *ritual gestures and postures for worship or meditation; the painting and contemplation of* mandala *or sacred, symbolic diagrams; and the disciplined use of the eidetic or visual imagination in meditative* visualization. *Other unique threads in Tibet's otherwise traditional Buddhist quilt derive from its history. The northern-Indian Buddhism that reached Tibet in about the eighth century C.E. had already been influenced by an outlook called Tantrism that involved secret initiatic teachings, ritual cultivation of magical powers, the invocation of female counterparts to Buddhas and bodhisattvas called* Taras, *and, in certain lineages, the use of ritualized sex as a yoga. Also sewn into this complex fabric was the indigenous shamanic tradition,* Bön.

In an anthology such as this, it is impossible even to hint at the full range of a subtradition such as Tibetan Buddhism. In the four selections below I have included only an excerpt from the well known Tibetan Book of the Dead (41), examples of Tantric teachings that are not necessarily representative of the Tibetan tradition as a whole (42 and 43), and a description and short interpretation of the Wheel of Life (44).

41. The Tibetan Book of the Dead: *Instructions to the Dying*

This is how the Lama [monk] instructs the dying person:

Preamble

I now transmit to you the profound teachings which I have myself received from my Teacher. . . . Pay attention to it now, and do not allow yourself to be distracted by other thoughts! Remain lucid and calm, and bear in mind what you hear! If you suffer, do not give in to the pain! If restful numbness overtakes you, . . . do not surrender yourself to that! Remain watchful and alert!

The factors which made up the person known as [you] are about to disperse. Your mental activities are separating themselves from your body, and they are about to enter the intermediary state. Rouse your energy so that you may enter this state self-possessed and in full consciousness!

I. The Moment of Death, and the Clear Light of Pure Reality

First of all there will appear to you, swifter than lightning, the luminous splendor of the colorless light of Emptiness, and that will surround you on all sides. Terrified, you will want to flee from the radiance, and you may well lose consciousness. Try to submerge yourself in that light, giving up all belief in a separate self, all attachment to your illusory ego. Recognize that the boundless Light of this true Reality is your own true self, and you shall be saved!

Few, however, are those who, having missed salvation during their life on earth, can attain it during this brief instant which passes so quickly. The overwhelming majority are shocked into unconsciousness by the terror they feel.

The emergence of a subtle body. If you miss salvation at that moment, you will be forced to have a number of further dreams, both pleasant and unpleasant. Even they offer you a chance to gain understanding, as long as you remain vigilant and alert. A few days after death there emerges a subtle illusory dream-body, [or] "mental body." It is impregnated with the after-effects of your past desires, endowed with all sense and faculties, and has the power of unimpeded motion. It can go right through . . . hills, boulders, and walls, and in an instant it can traverse any distance. Even after the physical sense-organs are dissolved, sights, sounds, smells, tastes and touches will be perceived and ideas will be formed. These are . . . the after-effects of what you did with your body and mind in the past. But you must know that all you perceive is a . . . mere illusion, and does not reflect any really existing objects. Have no fear and form no attachment! View it all evenmindedly, without like or dislike!

II. The Experience of the Spiritual Realities

Three and a half days after your death, Buddhas and Bodhisattvas will for seven days appear to you in their benign and peaceful aspect. Their light will shine upon you, but it will be so radiant that you will scarcely be able to look at it. Wonderful and delightful though they are, the Buddhas may nevertheless frighten you. Do not give in to your fright! Do not run away! Serenely contemplate the spectacle before you! Overcome your fear, and feel no desire! Realize that these are the rays of the grace of the Buddhas, who come to receive you into their Buddha-realms. Pray to them with intense faith and humility, and, in a halo of rainbow light, you will merge into the heart of the divine Father-Mother, and take up your abode in one of the realms of the Buddhas. Thereby you may still at this moment win your salvation.

But if you miss it, you will next, for another seven days, be confronted with the angry deities, and the Guardians of the Faith, surrounded by their followers in tumultuous array, many of them in the form of animals which you have never seen in the life you left. Bathed in multicolored light they stand before you, threatening you and barring your passage. Loud are their voices, with which they shout, "Hit him! Hit him! Kill him! Kill him!" This is what you have to hear, because you turned a deaf ear to the saving truths of religion! All these forms are strange to you, . . . they terrify you, . . . and yet it is you who have created them. Do not give in to your fright, resist your mental confusion! All this is unreal, and what you see are the contents of your own mind in conflict with itself. All these terrifying deities, witches and demons around you— fear them not, flee them not! They are but . . . the contents of your own mind in the mirror of the Void. If at this point you should manage to understand that, the shock of this insight will stun you, your subtle body will disperse into a rainbow, and you will find yourself in a paradise among the angels.

III. Seeking Rebirth

But if you fail to grasp the meaning of what you were taught, if you still continue to feel a desire to exist as an individual, then you are now doomed to again re-enter the wheel of becoming.

The judgment. You are now before Yama, King of the Dead. In vain will you try to . . . deny or conceal the evil deeds you have done. The Judge holds up before you the shining mirror of Karma, wherein all your deeds are reflected. . . . The mirror in which Yama seems to read your past is your own memory, and also his judgement is your own. It is you yourself who pronounce your own judgement, which in its turn determines your next rebirth. No terrible God pushes you into it. . . . The shapes of the frightening monsters who take hold of you, place a rope round your neck and drag you along, are just an illusion which you create from the forces within you. Know that apart from these karmic forces there is no Judge of the Dead, no gods, and no demons. Knowing that, you will be free!

The desire for rebirth. At this juncture you will realize you are dead. You will think, "I am dead! What shall I do?" and you will feel as miserable as a fish out of water on red-hot embers. Your consciousness, having no object on which to rest, will be like a feather tossed about by the wind, riding on the horse of breath. At about that time the fierce wind of karma, terrific and hard to bear, will drive you onwards, from behind, in dreadful gusts. And after a while the thought will occur to you, "O what would I not give to possess a body!" But because you can at first find no place for you to enter into, you will be dissatisfied and have the sensation of being squeezed into cracks and crevices amidst rocks and boulders.

The dawning of the lights and the six places of rebirth. Then there will shine upon you the lights of the six places of rebirth. The light of the place in which you will be reborn will shine most prominently, but it is your own karmic disposition which decides about your choice. . . .

If you have deserved it by your good deeds, a white light will guide you into one of the heavens, and for a while you will have some happiness among the gods. Habits of envy and ambition will attract you to the red light, which leads to rebirth among the warlike Asuras, forever agitated by anger and envy. If you feel drawn to a blue light, you will find yourself again a human being, and well you remember how little happiness that brought you! If you had a heavy and dull mind, you will choose the green light, which leads you to the world of animals, unhappy because insecure and excluded from the knowledge which brings salvation. A ray of dull yellow will lead you to the world of the ghosts, and, finally, a ray of the color of darkish smoke into the hells. Try to desist, if you can! Think of the Buddhas and Bodhisattvas! Recall that all these visions are unreal, control your mind, feel amity towards all that lives! And do not be afraid! You alone are the source of all these different rays. In you alone they exist, and so do the worlds to which they lead. Feel not attracted or repelled, but remain evenminded and calm!

Reincarnation. If so far you have been deaf to the teaching, listen to it now! An overpowering craving will come over you for the sense-experiences which you remember having had in the past, and which through your lack of sense-organs you cannot now have. Your desire for rebirth becomes more and more urgent. . . . This desire now racks you; you do not, however, experience it for what it is, but feel it as a deep thirst which parches you as you wander along, harassed, among deserts of burning sands. . . . Greatly anxious, you will look for a safe place of refuge.

Everywhere around you, you will see animals and humans in the act of sexual intercourse. You envy them, and the sight attracts you. If your karmic coefficients destine you to become a male, you feel attracted to the females and you hate the males you see. If you are destined to become a female, you will feel love for the males and hatred for the females you see. Do not go near the couples you see, do not try to interpose yourself between them, do not try to take the place of one of them! The feeling which you would then experience would make you faint away, just at the moment when egg and sperm are about to unite. And afterwards you will find that you have been conceived as a human being or as an animal.

42. With Impurity the Wise Make Themselves Pure

Seeming to echo William Blake's dictum that "the road of excess leads to the palace of wisdom," Tibetan Tantrism, grounded in the philosophy of emptiness, sometimes teaches that the way to freedom lies, paradoxically, in total indulgence.

They who do not see the truth
Think of birth-and-death as distinct from Nirvana . . .

This discrimination is the demon
Who produces the ocean of transmigration.
Freed from it the great ones are released
From the bonds of becoming . . .

The mystics, pure of mind,
Dally with lovely girls,
Infatuated with the poisonous flames of passion,
That they may be set free from desire

He is not Buddha, he is not set free,
If he does not see the world
As originally pure, unoriginated,
Impersonal and immaculate . . .

Water in the ear is removed by more water,
A thorn [in the skin] by another thorn.
So wise men rid themselves of passion
By yet more passion.

As a washerman uses dirt
To wash clean a garment,
So, with impurity,
The wise man makes himself pure.

43. Of What Use Is Meditation?

Perhaps to free listeners from spiritual greed, the author of the text below chooses the wisdom of emptiness in order to debunk traditional wisdom and orthodox religious practice. This author's ultimate message, though, is that the heart of the spiritual life is the service of others.

. . . Will one gain release, abiding in meditation?
. . . What's to be done by reliance on mantras?

What is the use of austerities?
What is the use of going on pilgrimage?. . .

Abandon such false attachments and renounce such
    illusion! . . .

Without meditating, without renouncing the world,
One may stay at home in the company of one's wife.
Can [it] be called perfect knowledge . . .
If one is not released while enjoying the pleasures of sense?

Mantras and tantras, meditation and concentration,
They are all a cause of self-deception.

. . . Eat, drink, indulge the senses,
Fill the mandala (with offerings) again and again,
By things like these you'll gain the world beyond.
Tread upon the head of the foolish worldling and proceed!

As is Nirvana, so is Samsara.
Do not think there is any distinction.

Do not sit at home, do not go to the forest,
But recognize mind wherever you are.
When one abides in complete and perfect enlightenment,
Where is Samsara and where is Nirvana?

Do not err in this matter of self and other.
Everything is Buddha without exception . . .

The fair tree of thought that knows no duality,
Spreads through the triple world.
It bears the flower and fruit of compassion,
And its name is service of others.

. . . He who clings to the void
And neglects Compassion,
Does not reach the highest stage.
But he who practices only Compassion,
Does not gain release from toils of existence.
He, however, who is strong in practice of both,
Remains neither in Samsara nor in Nirvana.

44. The Wheel of Life

The following description refers to the figure on page 94.

The picture shows a hideous demon holding a large circle divided
into six wedge-shaped sections. The demon is Yama, the judge of
the dead, and each section represents a different realm of life—the
realm of gods [who are blissful but dangerously complacent], the
realm of titans or demigods [who are powerful and wealthy but in-
fected with envy, jealousy, and greed for more], the realm of
human beings, the realm of animals [who are driven by instincts
and have little freedom], the realm of hungry ghosts [whose huge
bellies but pinpoint mouths and eyes suggest insatiable craving],
and the realm of hell beings [who are consumed with relentless
rage]. At the center or hub of the circle is a smaller circle containing a rooster, a pig, and a snake, chasing one another around and
around. They symbolize the forces that keep people caught up in
the samsaric round of existence: the rooster stands for greed, the
pig for ignorance, and the snake for hatred.

You can read the wheel's symbols exoterically, as a diagram of six
different kinds of existence into which one my be born in the endless round of reincarnation. . . . You can also read the symbolism

TIBETAN WHEEL OF LIFE
(Tracing of a Tibetan temple-fresco of Sankar Gompa, Leh)

esoterically (on at least two different levels) as psychology. One way
is to view each of the realms as a different type of human existence ... lived out by certain kinds of people according to their
karmic fortunes of personality type and socioeconomic status. . . .
[Another way to view it is] as a description of *situations* or states of
consciousness that everybody passes through again and again in the
course of a day.

B. ZEN BUDDHISM

Some thirteen centuries ago in China the commingling of Mahayana Buddhism and Taoism produced a species of Buddhism called Ch'an *by its Chinese progenitors and* Zen *by its Japanese inheritors. Because contemporary Buddhism had in their eyes become overscholasticized and largely a matter of scriptural mastery, they reemphasized the practice of meditation (which is roughly what* Ch'an *and* Zen *mean) as the indispensable heart of the Buddha's way. According to the Zen school, every being has Buddha-nature. Sitting meditation actualizes our inalienable Buddha-nature; the insight it fosters bestows true freedom. Though Zen claimed to be a teaching "outside the scriptures," its philosophical roots lie in Mahayana emptiness and scriptures like the Heart and Diamond sutras.*

45. Bodhidharma Defines Zen

The following description of Zen Buddhism is attributed to Bodhidharma (ca. 500 C.E.), the sage reputed to have brought Zen mind from India to China. Actually it was formulated during the T'ang dynasty when Zen was at its apogee (ca. 700–800 C.E.).

A special tradition outside the scriptures;
No dependence upon words and letters;
Direct pointing at the mind;
Seeing into one's own nature, and the attainment of
    Buddhahood.

46. The Secret of the Flower

Zen Buddhists believe that their tradition stretches back to the Buddha, who himself initiated the practice of "no dependence on words and letters" and "direct pointing to mind" as related in the following story of the monk Kashapa.

One day when a large assembly of his monks was waiting for the Buddha to begin an address, the Buddha surprised them all by remaining silent. Smiling, he then turned a flower in his fingers and held it silently before his listeners. Only one monk, Kashapa, smiled in full recognition. The Buddha said: "I have the Dharma-eye which is not expressed in words, but specially transmitted from mind to mind. This teaching I have given to the great Kashapa."

47. The Marrow of Zen

Toward the end of his life Bodhidharma addressed his most advanced disciples:

"Let each of you say what you have attained.". . . Tao-fu replied: "As I see it [the truth] neither adheres to words or letters, nor is it separate from them. Yet it functions as the Way."

The Master said: "You have attained my skin."

Then a nun, Tsung-chih spoke: "As I understand it, [the truth] is like the auspicious glimpse of the Buddha Land. . . . It is seen once, but not a second time."

The Master replied: "You have attained my flesh."

Tao-yü said: "The four great elements are originally empty; the five skandhas have no existence. According to my belief there is no [truth] to be grasped."

To him the Master replied: "You have attained my bones."

Finally there was Hui-k'o. He bowed respectfully and stood silent.

The Master said: "You have attained my marrow."

48. On Trust in the Heart

This brief excerpt is from a writing attributed to the third Chinese patri-arch, Seng-Ts'an (died 606 C.E.). The Chinese word hsin, *translated as "heart" in the title above, could just as well be translated "mind."*

The Perfect Way is difficult only for those who pick and
    choose;
Do not like, do not dislike; all will then be clear.
Make a hairbreadth difference, and Heaven and Earth are set
    apart;
If you want the truth to stand clear before you, never be for or
    against.

The struggle between "for" and "against" is the mind's worst
    disease . . .

The more you talk about It, and the more you think about It,
    the further from It you go;
Stop talking, stop thinking, and there is nothing you will not
    understand . . .

There is no need to seek Truth; only stop having views . . .
The ultimate Truth about both Extremes is that they are One
    Emptiness . . .

. . . Whether we see it or fail to see it, it is manifest always and
    everywhere . . .
Take your stand on this, and the rest will follow of its own
    accord;
To trust in the Heart is the Not Two, the Not Two is to trust in
    the Heart.

I have spoken in vain; for what can words tell
Of things that have no yesterday, tomorrow or today?

49. Dharma Combat: *Shên-hsiu and Hui-nêng on Zen Mind*

The following verses are the centerpieces in a story of how in seventh-century China the Zen school split into northern and southern sects, which respectively favored gradual and sudden approaches to awakening. Wherever the philosophy of emptiness alights, there is bound to be tension between the commonsense way of steady practice toward the goal (the "gradual" approach), on the one hand, and the emptiness-generated intuition that nothing can separate us from our always-already originally awakened natures (the "sudden" approach), on the other. In a poetry contest to determine who had the greater awakening, Shên-hsiu and Hui-nêng represented these two perspectives:

[Shên-hsiu:]
    The body is a Bodhi tree,
    The mind a mirror bright;

Take care to clean it carefully
And let no dust alight.

[Hui-nêng:]
The Bodhi tree does not exist
Nor does the mirror bright.
Since everything is empty
Where can dust alight?

50. Ma-tsu and the Polished Tile

To guard against clinging to meditation and to lever practitioners into new frames of mind, Zen, the meditation school, sometimes mocked the practice of meditation.

Ma-tsu was then residing in the monastery continuously absorbed in meditation. His master, aware of his outstanding ability, . . . asked him: "For what purpose are you sitting in meditation?" Ma-tsu answered: "I want to become a Buddha." Thereupon the Master picked up a tile and started rubbing it on a stone. Ma-Tsu asked, "What are you doing, Master?" "I am polishing this tile to make a mirror," Huai-jang replied. "How can you make a mirror by rubbing a tile?" exclaimed Ma-tsu. "How can one become a Buddha by sitting in meditation?" countered the Master.

51. Zen Kōan

A unique aspect of Zen is its use of kōan, pithy enigmas upon which students are told to meditate and to which they are required to find "answers"—however cognitively impossible that may seem.

a. The Dog

A monk once asked Master Joshu, "Has a dog the Buddha Nature or not?" Joshu said, "Mu!"

b. Wash Your Bowls

Once a monk made a request of [Master] Joshu: "I have just entered the monastery," he said, "please give me instructions,

Master." Joshu said: "Have you had your breakfast?" "Yes I have," replied the monk. "Then," said Joshu, "wash your bowls." The monk had an insight.

c. The Oak Tree

A monk asked Joshu, "What is the meaning of the Patriarch's coming from the West?" Joshu answered, "The oak tree in the front garden."

d. Three Pounds of Flax

A monk asked Master Tozan, "What is the Buddha?" Tozan said, "Three pounds of flax."

e. Why Practice?

Ummon said, "Look! This world is vast and wide. Why do you put on your priest's robe at the sound of the bell?"

f. Shit-Stick

A monk asked Ummon, "What is Buddha?" Ummon said: "A shit-stick!"

g. Master Gutei Raises a Finger

Gutei raised his finger whenever he was asked a question about Zen. A boy attendant began to imitate him in this way. When anyone asked the boy what his master preached about, the boy would raise his finger.

Gutei heard about the boy's mischief. He seized him and cut off his finger. The boy cried and ran away. Gutei called and stopped him. When the boy turned his head to Gutei, Gutei raised up his own finger. In that instant the boy was enlightened.

h. Flapping Mind

Two monks were arguing about a flag. "The flag is flapping," said one. "No," said the other; "the wind is flapping." The argument went back and forth. The Master happened to be passing by. He told them: "Not the wind, not the flag; your minds are flapping."

52. Zen Master Dōgen (1200–1253) on the Importance of *Zazen* (Sitting Meditation)

a. The Merit Lies in Sitting

In the pursuit of the Way the prime essential is zazen. . . . By reflecting on kōan . . . one may perhaps get a sense of them but it will only result in one's being led astray from the way. . . . Just to pass the time in sitting straight, without any thought of acquisition, without any sense of achieving enlightenment—this is the way of the patriarchs. It is true that our predecessors recommended both the kōan and sitting, but it was the sitting that they particularly insisted upon. There have been some who attained enlightenment through the . . . kōan, but the true cause of their enlightenment was the merit and effectiveness of sitting. Truly the merit lies in the sitting.

b. Attainment Through the Body

. . . To do away with mental deliberation and cognition, and simply to go on sitting, is the method by which the Way is made an intimate part of our lives. . . . Thus the attainment of the Way becomes truly attainment through the body. That is why I put exclusive emphasis upon sitting.

53. Zen Master Dōgen on the Oneness of Practice and Enlightenment

Though Dōgen stressed the importance of practice, he also understood that enlightenment was an inalienable possession, always already here and now. This is Dōgen's stunning doctrine of the oneness of practice and enlightenment:

In Buddhism, practice and enlightenment are one and the same. Since practice has its basis in enlightenment, the practice of even the beginner contains the whole of original enlightenment. Thus while giving directions as to the exercise [the Zen Master] warns him not to await enlightenment apart from the exercise, because this [the exercise] points directly to the original enlightenment.

Since enlightenment is already contained in the exercise, there is no end to enlightenment, and since it is the exercise of enlightenment, it has no beginning.

54. Hakuin on Zen Enlightenment

Zen Master Hakuin (1686–1769) adopted Buddhism at the age of eight upon hearing of the tortures that awaited the faithless in Buddhist hells. A period of intense devotion was followed by one of total cynicism when "staring at Buddhist images and sutras was like staring at mud." Later, Hakuin resumed Buddhist practice. The passage below tells of Hakuin's first enlightenment experience (satori) and provides an amusing example of interchanges between Zen students and their masters.

In the spring of my twenty-fourth year, I was . . . struggling at the Eiganji [temple]. . . . I slept neither day nor night. . . . A great doubt suddenly possessed me, and I felt as if frozen to death in the midst of an icy field extending thousands of *li* . . , [14] I could not move. I was virtually senseless. What remained was only [the kōan] *Mu*. . . . This condition lasted for several days until one night I heard the striking of a temple bell. All at once a transformation came over me, as though a layer of ice were smashed. . . . Instantly I came to my senses. . . . Former doubt had completely dissolved, like ice which had melted away. "How marvelous! How marvelous!" I cried aloud. There was no cycle of birth and death from which I had to escape, no enlightenment for which I had to seek. There was no point even in devoting time to the seventeen hundred kōan. . . . My pride soared like a mountain. . . . Shouldering this experience, I . . . set out on the road to . . Shinano.

I interviewed Master Shōju and presented in verse my insight on enlightenment. The master took the verse in his left hand, saying, "This is what you have understood through your brain." Holding out his right hand, he said, "Now show me your intuitive insight."

---

14. A li is a Chinese measure of linear distance equivalent to 2.44 miles.

"If there is anything at all to present to the master, it should be vomited away," I said, and made a vomiting sound.

The Master asked, "What is your understanding of . . . *Mu?*"

I replied, "How can *Mu* be attached to the hands and legs?"

The Master twisted my nose and said, "It is still attached to your hands and legs." I was about to ask what he meant, when the master burst out laughing and said, "This is a poor devil attached to the scriptures.". . . From that time on whenever the master saw me he called me "a poor devil attached to the scriptures."

One evening the master sat cooling himself on the veranda. I again presented him with my verse on enlightenment. The master said, "Delusions and fancies!" I shot back, "Delusions and fancies!" Grabbing me, the master showered me with twenty or thirty blows of his fists and finally threw me off the veranda. . . . I lay in the mud as if dead, unconscious, breathless and unable to move. The master was on the veranda laughing aloud. After a little while I regained my senses. I rose and bowed to him. . . . The master shouted, "Here is a poor devil attached to the scriptures!" From then on I took up serious study . . . , not stopping to eat or sleep.

Hakuin then describes, dryly and briefly, a series of other satoris he has had. After one of them, his master ceases calling him "a poor devil attached to the scriptures," but Hakuin's story ends like this:

. . . One night I took up the *Lotus Sutra,* and read it again. Immediately I perceived the perfect, true, and ultimate significance of the *Lotus* and all my initial doubts cleared away. I recognized the many errors I had made in some of my earlier understandings of enlightenment. I found myself in tears. The practice of Zen, one must realize, is by no means simple. . . .

55. The Wisdom of Zen Masters

a. Stinking of Zen

On his death-bed a Master was asked by his disciple and Dharma-heir: "Master, is there anything else that I need to know?" "No," said the Master, "I am quite satisfied by and large. But there is one thing that still worries me." "What is it?" asked the heir. "Please tell me so I can set it right." "Well," said the Master, "the trouble is you still stink of Zen."

b. What Is Lacking?

Master Rinzai was fond of asking: "What, at this moment, is lacking?"

c. Is That All?

Master Baso asked Master Hyakujo what truth he taught. Master Hyakujo raised his fly-whisk. Baso said: "Is that all? Nothing else?" Master Hyakujo lowered his fly-whisk.

d. When Hungry, I Eat

Master Rinzai said: "When hungry, I eat; when tired, I sleep. Fools laugh at me. The wise understand."

e. Sick from the Medicine

The Heart is Buddha: this is medicine for sick people.
No Heart, No Buddha: this is for people who are sick because
    of the medicine

f. Knowing the Buddha

There is Buddha
    for those who don't know what he is, really.
There is no Buddha,
    for those who know what he is, really.

GRACE NOTES

56. Selections from the Dhammapada

The Dhammapada is a collection of some four hundred brief verses attributed to the Buddha.

a. An Ecology of Mind

All that we are is a result of what we have thought: it is founded on our thoughts, it is made up of our thoughts. If a man speaks or acts with an evil thought, pain follows him, as the wheel follows the foot of the ox that draws the wagon.

All that we are is a result of what we have thought: it is founded on our thoughts, it is made up of our thoughts. If a man speaks or acts with a pure thought, happiness follows him, like a shadow that never leaves him.

Mindfulness is the way to the deathless, inattentiveness the way to death. Those who are diligently attentive do not die, those who are thoughtless are as if dead already.

As a fletcher makes straight his arrow, a wise man makes straight his trembling and unsteady mind, which is difficult to guard, difficult to hold back.

It is good to tame the mind, which is difficult to hold in and flighty, rushing [about]; a tamed mind brings happiness.

b. The Purification of Emotions

"He abused me, he beat me, he defeated me, he robbed me,"— in those who harbour such thoughts hatred will never cease. "He abused me, he beat me, he defeated me, he robbed me,"—in those who do not harbour such thoughts hatred will cease.

For never does hatred by hatred cease: hatred ceases by love alone: this is an old law.

The world does not know that we must all come to an end here; but those who know, their quarrels cease at once.

Victory breeds hatred, for the conquered is unhappy. He who has given up both victory and defeat, he, the contented, is happy.

c. The Intelligent and the Foolish

When the learned man drives away vanity by earnestness, he, the wise, climbing the terraced heights of wisdom, looks down upon the fools, free from sorrow he looks upon the sorrowing crowd, as one that stands upon a mountain looks down upon them that stand upon the plain.

Long is the night to him who is restless; long is a league to him who is tired; long is the round of rebirth to the foolish who do not know the true Law.

If a traveller does not meet with one who is his better or his equal, let him keep firmly to his solitary journey; there is no companionship with a fool.

"These sons belong to me, and this wealth belongs to me"; with such thoughts a fool is tormented. He himself does not belong to himself; how much less sons and wealth?

If a fool be associated with a wise man even all his life, he will perceive the truth as little as a spoon perceives the taste of soup.

If an intelligent man be associated for one minute only with a wise man, he will soon perceive the truth, as the tongue perceives the taste of the soup.

Fools of little understanding are their own greatest enemies, for they do evil deeds which must bear bitter fruits.

Those who are immersed in craving run down the stream (of desires) as a spider runs down the web which he himself has spun; having cut this (bond), the steadfast retire from the world, with no backward glance, leaving all sorrow behind.

He who has tasted the sweetness of solitude and tranquillity, is free from fear and sin, while he drinks in the nectar of the Law.

d. Human Birth, Hard to Obtain

Difficult it is to obtain birth as a human being, difficult is the life of mortals, difficult is the hearing of the true Law, difficult is the rise of the Awakened Ones.

e. Happily We Live

Let us live happily then, not hating those who hate us! Among men who hate us, let us dwell free from hatred!

Let us live happily then, free from ailments among the ailing! Among men who are ailing, let us dwell free from ailments!

Let us live happily then, free from greed among the greedy! Among men who are greedy let us dwell free from greed!

Let us live happily then, though we call nothing our own! We shall be like the bright gods feeding on happiness.

f. The Doorway to Freedom

When with deep and even-minded awareness one sees only the in-cessant arising and fading of body- and mind-states, one knows utter bliss. The discerning thus apprehend the Deathless.

57. The Parable of Me and Mine

Some children were playing beside a river. They made castles of sand, and each child defended his castle and said, "This one is mine." They kept their castles separate and would not allow any mistakes about which was whose. When the castles were all fin-ished, one child kicked over someone's else's castle and completely destroyed it. The owner of the castle flew into a rage, pulled the other child's hair, struck him with his fist and bawled out, "He has spoilt my castle! Come along all of you and help me to punish him as he deserves." The others all came to his help. They beat the child with a stick and then stamped on him as he lay on the ground. . . . Then they went on playing in their sand-castles, each saying, "This is mine; no one else may have it. Keep away! Don't touch my castle!" But evening came; it was getting dark and they all thought they ought to be going home. No one now cared what became of his castle. One child stamped on his, another pushed his over with both his hands. Then they turned away and went back, each to his home.

58. The Bracelets

There was a king of Benares. One summer when the weather was very hot he lay down in an upper room on a couch adorned with gold, silver and many precious stones, and made a servant massage him with ointment of sandalwood from the Bull's Head Mountain. The servant was wearing a great many bracelets on her arms, and they jangled together while she massaged the king. The sound irritated him and he asked her to take one of the bracelets off. She did so, and there was a little less noise. She took off another, and there was less noise still. He made her go on taking them off till there was only one left, and then there was no jangling at all. When the noise stopped the king had a sudden awakening. "That is just what I ought to do with my kingdom, my ministers, subjects, concubines, and attendants," he said to himself. "In fact, with all business and bother." From that moment onward he had no further worldly desires, but spent his time meditating in complete seclusion, and became a solitary (*Pratyeka*) Buddha.

59. Carrying a Girl

Two monks on pilgrimage came to the ford of a river. There they saw a girl dressed in all her finery and obviously not knowing what to do, for the river was high and she did not want her clothes spoilt. Without more ado, one of the monks took her on his back, carried her across, and put her down on dry ground. Then the monks continued on their way. But the other monk started complaining: "Surely it is not right to touch a woman; it is against the commandments to have close contact with women; how can you go against the rules for monks!" and so on in a steady stream. The monk who had carried the girl walked along silently, but finally he remarked: "I set her down by the river. But you are still carrying her."

60. Dōgen Near Death

To what indeed shall I liken
The world and the life of man?
Ah, the reflection of the moon
In the dewdrop
On the beak of the waterfowl.

61. A Lesson for Kisa Gotami

When Kisa Gotami grew up, she married, going to the house of her husband's family to live. There, because she was the daughter of a poverty-stricken house, they treated her with contempt. After a time she gave birth to a son. Then they accorded her respect.

. . . But when that boy of hers was old enough to play and run about, he died. Inconsolable sorrow sprang up within her. . . . Taking her son on her hip, she went about from one house door to another, saying: "Give me medicine for my son!"

Wherever people encountered her, they . . . laughed in derision. She had not the slightest idea what they meant.

Now a certain wise man saw her and thought: this woman must have been driven out of her mind by sorrow for her son. But medicine for her, no one else is likely to know. So he said to her: ". . . Go to the Buddha and ask for help."

. . . Taking her son on her hip, she took her stand in the outer circle of the congregation and said: "O Exalted One, give me medicine for my son!"

The Buddha . . . said: "You did well, Gotami, in coming hither for medicine. Go enter the city, make the rounds of the entire city, beginning at the beginning, and in whatever house no one has ever died, from that house fetch tiny grains of mustard seed."

"Very well, reverend sir," said she. Delighted in heart that the Buddha might bring her son back to life, she entered within the city, and at the very first house said: "[The Buddha] bids me fetch tiny grains of mustard seed for medicine for my son, . . . but I cannot take it if someone has died herein.". . .

"What say you, Gotami!" said the person at the door. "Many have died in this house.". . .

In this same way she went to the second house, and to the third. She realized: at every house in the entire city this must be the case! This the Buddha, full of compassion for the welfare of mankind, must have seen! Overcome with emotion, she went outside of the city, carried her son to the burning ground, and, holding him in her arms, said: "Dear little son, I thought that you alone had been overtaken by this thing which men call death. But you are not the only one death has overtaken. This is a law common to all mankind." So saying, she cast her son away in the burning ground.

CHAPTER THREE

Confucianism

*W*hatever else religion does, it relates a view of the ultimate nature of reality to a set of ideas of how man is well advised. . . to live."[1] *Thus reminded by anthropologist Clifford Geertz, we can promptly shelve the old debate about whether the Confucian social ethic amounts to a religion. For although Confucius may spend more time examining "how we are advised to live" than probing "the ultimate nature of reality," he nevertheless assumes that the right and good life depends utterly upon its harmony with reality's larger patterns. His explicit conviction that human affairs can prosper only when they are moral derives from the implicit assumption that the cosmos itself is a moral order.*

No student of our planetary religious heritage, therefore, can afford to ignore Confucius. The great body of thought linked to his name has profoundly and continuously influenced about one-fifth of the world's

---

1. Clifford Geertz, "Religion," in Arthur C. Lehmann and James E. Myers, *Magic, Witchcraft and Religion*, 2d. ed. (Mountain View, CA: Mayfield Publishing, 1985), 15.

population for two and a half thousand years. Although the Chinese mind has also been shaped by folk religion, Taoism, Buddhism, and in this century by communism, Confucianism remains, by any historical measure, its chief mentor.

What are the primary sources of this vast influence? The core Confucian canon consists of ten titles. The first six are the Ancient Classics, four of which were already venerable by the time of Confucius's birth in 551 B.C.E. Confucius is credited with having saved them from eclipse by assiduous redaction. These four are the Book of History (Shu Ching), the Book of Poetry (Shih Ching), the Book of Change (I Ching), and the Book of Rites (Li Chi). The other two classics are the Spring and Autumn Annals (Chun Chiu), a local history that Confucius himself wrote, and the Book of Filial Piety (Hsiao Ching), attributed to Confucius.

Four other titles, called the Four Books of Confucius, complete the Confucian canon. These are The Great Learning (Ta Hsüeh), The Doctrine of the Great Harmony[2] *(Chung Yung),*[3] *the Mencius (Meng Tzu), which records the teaching of Confucius's great disciple, Mencius, born a century after him, and the Analects (Lun Yü), sayings of and observations about the master collected posthumously by devoted disciples. Most of the selections in this thematically arranged chapter will be from the latter four Confucian books and a few from the above-mentioned Book of Rites and Book of Filial Piety.*

If Confucius the humanist were alive today I feel certain that, despite his traditionalism, he would understand that the social transformation for which he longed depends fundamentally upon speaking to both halves of humanity. In the spirit of his own principle of the "Rectification of the Names" (no. 9, below), I have taken the liberty of recasting his sayings in inclusive language wherever I felt this was feasible.

A final introductory word: Confucius is a different kind of sage. Unlike the great spiritual personages of the Western traditions, he is not a prophet crying out in the wilderness, proclaiming the revelation of God and railing against human indifference. Nor does Confucius fit the

---

2. Often translated as "Doctrine of the Mean."
3. These first two books of Confucius, however, are collected as chapters in the above-mentioned Book of Rites.

profile of the classic spiritual hero of India, the yogi, who through as-
cetic withdrawal from the world and sustained psychophysical discipline
taps suprahuman reservoirs of wisdom. Rather, Confucius is, un-
abashedly, an educator. He is a learner and a teacher, a person-in-
community who encourages nothing less than the full moral maturity of
the entire body politic. Words once used by a Chinese scholar to intro-
duce the Confucian sayings are well worth keeping in mind for the en-
tirety of this chapter:

> For 2,500 years, they have always exasperated the young in-
> quiring mind, looking for exciting truths and brilliant intel-
> lectual sorties, and always won over the mind when it grows
> older and matures . . . . There they stand, so deep in wisdom
> and so mellow in tone, a tribute to the nation which worships
> them. Like mellow old masters, and unlike magazine covers,
> these sayings . . . are for the connoisseurs, i.e., the moral
> connoisseurs. The gentleness of touch, the softness of tone,
> the skill coming from mastery are best appreciated by those
> who have thought deeply about human problems. . . .
> This accounts for [their] classic, immortal influence on
> generations. . . .[4]

CONFUCIUS THE MAN

1. The Learner

a. Learning as Pleasure

The Master said, To learn and at due times to repeat what one has
learnt, is that not after all a pleasure?

b. Mellowing in the Way

The Master said, At fifteen I set my heart upon learning. At thirty,
I had planted my feet firm upon the ground. At forty, I no longer

---

4. Lin Yutang, ed., *The Wisdom of India and China* (New York: Random House,
1942), 812–13. I have rearranged the sentences to suit my purposes here.

suffered from perplexities. At fifty, I knew what were the biddings of Heaven. At sixty, I heard them with a docile ear. At seventy, I could follow the dictates of my own heart; for what I desired no longer overstepped the boundaries of right.

c. Still Learning

The Master said, Give me a few more years, so that I may have spent a whole fifty in study, and I believe that after all I should be fairly free from error.

2. A Lover of the Ancients

Confucian thought is characterized by profound regard for a golden past. Confucius was shaped by, and in turn helped to shape, the renowned Chinese respect for age.

a. A Transmitter, Not an Originator

The Master said, I have transmitted what was taught to me without making up anything of my own. I have been faithful to and loved the Ancients.

b. The Great Way of the Past

Once, Confucius was taking part in the winter sacrifice. After the ceremony was over, he went for a stroll along the top of the city gate and sighed mournfully. He sighed for the state of Lu.

His disciple . . . asked: "Why should the gentleman sigh?"

Confucius replied: "The practice of the Great Way, the illustrious people of the Three Dynasties—these I shall never know in person. And yet they inspire my ambition! When the Great Way was practiced, the world was shared by all alike. The worthy and the able were promoted to office and people practiced good faith and lived in affection. Therefore they did not regard as parents only their own parents, or as children only their own children. . . . The young were provided with an upbringing and the widow and the widower, the orphaned and the sick, with proper care. Men . . . and women . . . disliked the thought that their energies were not fully used, yet they used them not for private ends. Therefore all evil plotting was prevented and thieves and rebels did not arise, so that people could leave their outer gates unbolted. This was the age of the Grand Unity.

"Now the Great Way has become hid and the world is in possession of private families. Each regards as parents only his own parents, as children only his children; goods and labor are employed for selfish ends. . . ."

3. The Teacher

The Master said, He who by reanimating the Old can gain knowledge of the New is fit to be a teacher.

The Master said, I have listened in silence and noted what was said, I have never grown tired of learning nor wearied of teaching others what I have learnt. These at least are merits which I can confidently claim.

The Master said, From the very poorest upwards—beginning even with the student who could bring no better present than a bundle of dried flesh—none has ever come to me without receiving instruction.

The Master said, Only one who bursts with eagerness do I instruct; only one who bubbles with excitement, do I enlighten. If I hold up one corner and a student cannot come back to me with the other three, I do not continue the lesson.

The Duke of Shê asked Tzu-lu about Master K'ung [Confucius]. Tzu-lu did not reply. The Master said, Why did you not say "This is the character of the man: so intent upon enlightening the eager that he forgets his hunger, and so happy in doing so, that he forgets the bitterness of his lot and does not realize that old age is at hand. That is what he is."

The Master said, As to being a Divine Sage or even a Good Man, far be it from me to make any such claim. As for unwearying effort to learn and unflagging patience in teaching others, those are merits I do not hesitate to claim.

4. Glimpses of His Character

a. Warmth

That friends should come to one from afar, is this not after all delightful?

b. Forbearance

To remain unsoured even though one's merits are unrecognized by others, is that not after all what is expected of a noble person?

c. Humility and Candor

The Master said, In vain I have looked for a single person capable of seeing his own faults and bringing the charge home against himself.

The Master said, Yu, shall I teach you what knowledge is? When you know a thing, to recognize that you know it, and when you do not know a thing, to recognize that you do not know it. That is knowledge.

The Master said, I would much rather not have to talk. Tzu-kung said, If our Master did not talk, what should we little ones have to hand down about him? The Master said, Heaven does not speak; yet the four seasons run their course thereby, the hundred creatures each after its kind, are born thereby. Heaven does no speaking!

d. Earnestness and Perseverance

The Master said, The thought that "I have left my moral power (*te*) untended, my learning unperfected, that I have heard of righteous men, but been unable to go to them; have heard of evil men, but been unable to reform them"—it is these thoughts that disquiet me.

The Master said, If a man does not continually ask himself "What am I to do about this, what am I to do about this?" there is no possibility of my doing anything about him.

In the discharge of the ordinary duties of life and in the exercise of care in ordinary conversation, whenever there is shortcoming, never fail to strive for improvement, and when there is much to be said, always say less than what is necessary. . . .

e. Integrity

The Master said, Those who seek only coarse food to eat, water to drink and bent arm for pillow, will without looking for it find happiness to boot. Any thought of accepting wealth and rank by means that I know to be wrong is as remote from me as the clouds that float above.

f. Sympathy

If at a meal the Master found himself seated next to someone who was in mourning, he did not eat his fill. When he had wailed at a funeral, during the rest of the day he did not sing.

g. Humanism

Tzu-lu asked how one should serve ghosts and spirits. The Master said, Till you have learnt to serve people, how can you serve ghosts? Tzu-lu then ventured upon a question about the dead. The Master said, Till you know about the living, how are you to know about the dead?

h. Metaphysical Sensibility

When the Master was very ill, Tzu-lu asked leave to perform the rite of Expiation. The Master said, Is there such a thing? Tzu-lu answered saying, There is. In one of the Dirges it says, "We performed rites of expiation for you calling upon the sky-spirits above and the earth-spirits below." The Master said, My expiation began long ago!

Confucius remarked: The power of spiritual forces in the Universe—how active it is everywhere! Invisible to the eyes, and impalpable to the senses, it is inherent in all things, and nothing can escape its operation.

5. His Demeanor

In his leisure hours the Master's manner was very free-and-easy, and his expression alert and cheerful.

The Master's manner was affable yet firm, commanding but not harsh, polite but easy.

There were four things that the Master wholly eschewed: he took nothing for granted, he was never over-positive, never obstinate, never egotistic.

The Master fished with a line but not with a net; when fowling he did not aim at a roosting bird.

When in the Master's presence anyone sang a song that he liked, he did not join in at once, but asked for it to be repeated and then joined in.

Once when Tzu-lu, Tseng-Hsi, Jan Ch'iu and Kung-shi Hua were seated in attendance upon him, Confucius said . . . "Now suppose some prince were to recognize your merits, what would be your wishes?" Tzu-lu without hesitation replied: "Take a kingdom [beset with difficulties, and] in three years' time I could make it brave and make it understand the right course to pursue." Confucius smiled at him.

"And how about you, Ch'iu?" [Ch'iu said:] "Take a district [and] in three years' time I could make its people live in abundance. . . ."

". . . And how about you, Tien [Tseng-Hsi]?"

Tseng Hsi paused in the playing of the zither. [He said:] "In the latter days of spring, when the light spring garments are made, I would like to take along five or six grown-ups and six or seven youths to bathe in the River Yi, and after the bath to go to enjoy the breeze in the woods among the altars of Wu-yi, and then return home, loitering and singing on our way."

Confucius heaved a deep sigh and said: "You are the man after my own heart."

THE CONFUCIAN PROJECT

The Confucian project is nothing less than the task of becoming a fully human community. Like its fellow wisdom traditions, Confucianism understands that authentic humanity evolves to the extent that blind egoism erodes. To expand the heart and mind in ever-wider circles of empathy so that, starting with oneself, those circles embrace one's family, one's community, one's nation, and finally all humanity—this is the Confucian aim. Yet this great and never-ending work of personal and social transformation involves many constituent efforts. Below are selections arranged thematically around key Confucian virtues and ideals that, taken together, constitute the great work.

6. Harmony with the Universal Order

What is God-Given[5] is what we call human nature. To fulfill the law of our human nature is what we call the moral law [Tao]. The cultivation of the moral law is what we call culture.

The moral law is a law from whose operation we cannot for one instant in our existence escape. . . .

Our central self or moral being is the great basis of existence, and *harmony* or moral order is the universal law in the world. . . .

Confucius remarked: "The life of the moral person is an exemplification of the universal moral order. . . . The life of the vulgar person, on the other hand, is a contradiction of the universal moral order."

Confucius remarked: "To find the central clue to our moral being which unites us to the universal order, that indeed is the highest human attainment. . . ."

Confucius remarked: "There are people who seek for the abstruse and strange and live a singular life in order that they may

---

5. Given by *T'ien* or "heaven."

leave a name to posterity. This is what I never would do. There are again good people who try to live in conformity with the moral law, but who, when they have gone half way, throw it up. I never could give it up. Lastly, there are truly moral people who unconsciously live a life in entire harmony with the universal moral order and who live unknown to the world and unnoticed by others without any concern. It is only people of holy, divine natures who are capable of this. . . ."

The Master said, In the morning hear the Way; in the evening, die content!

7. *Li*, Proper Comportment

Li *is a most important notion for understanding the Confucian way. It has two overlapping meanings: proper comportment and ritual. It was not lost on sages like Confucius that habits determine character. The repeating patterns of what we say, what we do, and how we think determine what we become and what we are. As our habits go, so go we. In Confucius's view, attentive performance of social ritual and everyday etiquette shapes human character in accordance with archetypal patterns. We thereby make our own the wise ways of the ancients, which are also heaven's ways. Because it is often difficult for the contemporary student to imagine the meticulous detail with which ancient Chinese society was choreographed, I begin with passages from the pre-Confucian* Book of Li. *If the reader will pause to consider that this sort of detail, covering the myriad situations of life, is recorded for* hundreds *of pages, she or he will, in addition to being duly amazed, gain some idea of the li tradition on which Confucius draws and to which the Confucian writings make frequent reference.*

a. Li: A Miscellany of Specifics

In going to take counsel with an elder, one must carry a stool and a staff (for the elder's use). When an elder asks a question, to reply without acknowledging one's incompetency and (trying to) decline answering, is contrary to propriety [li].

For all children it is the rule:—in winter to warm (the bed for their parents), and to cool it in the summer; in the evening to adjust everything (for their repose), and to inquire (about their health) in the morning. . . .

A son, when he is going abroad, must inform (his parents where he is going); when he returns, he must present himself (before them). . . . In ordinary conversation (with his parents) he does not use the term *old* (with reference to them). . . .

When five are sitting together, the eldest must have a different mat (by himself). . . .

A son should not occupy the southwest corner of the apartment, nor sit in the middle of the mat (which he occupies alone), nor walk in the middle of the road, nor stand in the middle of the doorway. . . .

A boy should never be allowed to see an instance of deceit. . . . He must stand straight and square, and not incline his head in hearing. When an elder is holding him with the hand, he should hold the elder's hand with both his hands. When the elder has shifted his sword to his back and is speaking to him with the side of his face bent down, he should cover his mouth with his hand in answering. . . . When he meets his teacher on the road, he should hasten forward to meet him, and stand with his hands joined across his breast. If the teacher speaks to him, he will answer; if he does not, he will retire with hasty steps. When, following an elder, they ascend a level height, he must keep his face towards the quarter to which the elder is looking. . . .

Whenever (a host has received and) is entering with a guest, at every door he should give place to him. When the guest arrives at the innermost door . . . the host will ask to be allowed to enter first and arrange the mats. Having done this, he will come out to receive the guest, who will refuse firmly (to enter first). The host having made a low bow to him, they will enter (together). When they have entered the door, the host moves to the right, and the guest to the left. . . . Then they offer to each other the precedence in going up (stairs), but the host commences first, followed (immediately) by the other. They bring their feet together on every step, thus ascending by successive paces. He who ascends by the steps on the east should move his right foot first, and the other at the western steps his left foot. . . .

When two people are sitting or standing together, do not join them as a third. When two are standing together, another should not pass between them. Male and female should not sit together (in the same apartment), nor have the same stand or rack for their clothes, nor use the same towel or comb, nor let their hands touch in giving and receiving. A sister-in-law and brother-in-law do not interchange inquiries (about each other). . . .

Do not roll rice into a ball; do not bolt down the various dishes; do not swill down (the soup). Do not make a noise in eating; do not crunch bones with the teeth; do not put back fish you have been eating; do not throw the bones to the dogs; do not snatch (at what you want). . . .

When they have done eating, the guests will kneel in front (of the mat) and (begin to) remove the (dishes) of rice and sauces to give them to the attendants. The host will then rise and decline this service from the guests, who will resume their seats. . . .

b. Li: General Principles

The Summary of the Rules of Propriety [li] says:—Always and in everything let there be reverence; with the deportment grave as when one is thinking (deeply), and with speech composed and definite. This will make the people tranquil.

Pride should not be allowed to grow; the desires should not be indulged; the will should not be gratified to the full; pleasure should not be carried to excess. . . .

When you find wealth within your reach, do not (try to) get it by improper means; when you meet with calamity, do not (try to) escape from it by improper means. Do not seek for victory in small contentions; do not seek for more than your proper share. Do not positively affirm what you have doubts about; and (when you have no doubts) do not let what you say appear (simply) as your own view. . . .

. . . One should not (seek to) please others in an improper way, not be lavish of his words. . . . To cultivate one's person and fulfill one's words is called good conduct. When the conduct is (thus) ordered, and the words are accordant with the (right) course, we have the substance of the rules of propriety. . . . The course (of duty), virtue, benevolence, and righteousness cannot be fully carried out without the rules of propriety; . . . nor can the clearing up of quarrels and discriminating in disputes be accomplished; nor can (the duties between) ruler and minister, high and low, father and son, elder brother and younger, be determined; . . . nor can majesty and dignity be shown in assigning different places at court, in the government of armies, and in discharging the duties of office so as to secure the operation of the laws; nor can there be the (proper) sincerity and gravity in presenting the offerings to spiritual Beings on occasions of supplication, thanksgiving and the various sacrifices. . . .

The parrot can speak, and yet is nothing more than a bird; the ape can speak, and yet is nothing more than a beast. Here now is a man who observes no rules of propriety [li]; is not his heart that of a beast? . . .

c. Confucius on Li

Yen Hui asked about Goodness. The Master said [quoting another text], "He who can himself submit to ritual [li] is Good." If a ruler could for one day "submit himself to ritual," everyone under Heaven would respond to his Goodness. . . . Yen Hui . . . ask[ed] for . . . more detail. . . . The Master said, To look at nothing in defiance of ritual, to speak of nothing in defiance of ritual, never to stir hand or foot in defiance of ritual.

The Master said, Courtesy not bounded by the prescriptions of ritual becomes tiresome. Caution not bounded by the prescriptions of ritual becomes timidity, daring becomes turbulence, inflexibility becomes harshness.

If one only understood the meaning of the sacrifices to Heaven and Earth, and the significance of the services in ancestral worship in summer and autumn, it would be as easy to govern a nation as to point a finger at the palm.

The Master said, If it is really possible to govern countries by ritual and yielding, there is no more to be said. But if it is not really possible, of what use is ritual?

d. Hsün-Tzu on Li

Hsün-Tzu, a Confucian philosopher who lived about 200 years after the master, provides us with an excellent general description of li.

Rites [li] rest on three bases: Heaven and earth, which are the source of all life; the ancestors, who are the source of the human race; [and] sovereigns and teachers, who are the source of government. . . . Should any of the three be missing, either there would be no people or people would be without peace. Hence rites are to serve Heaven on high and earth below, and to honor the ancestors and elevate the sovereigns and teachers. . . . Who holds to the rites is never confused in the midst of multifarious change; who deviates therefrom is lost. Rites—are they not the culmination of culture?. . .

. . . Pairs of opposites are in the rites equally utilized and alternately brought into play. Beautiful adornment, music and rejoicing are appropriate on occasions of felicity; coarse sackcloth, weeping and sorrow are appropriate on occasions of ill-fortune. Rites make room for beautiful adornment but not to the point of being fascinating, for coarse sackcloth but not to the point of deprivation or self-injury, for music and rejoicing but not to the point of being lewd or indolent, for weeping and sorrow but not to the point of being depressing and injurious. Such is the middle path of rites. . . .

Sacrifice is to express a person's feeling of remembrance and longing. . . . If such feelings are not given proper expression, then . . . emotions and memories are disappointed and not satisfied. . . . Thereupon the ancient kings instituted rites, and henceforth the principle of expressing honors to the honored and love to the beloved is fully realized. . . . Among the cultivated it is considered the fully human way; among the uncultivated it is considered having to do with spirits.

8. *Hsiao* (Filiality): *Being Good Sons and Daughters*

If li covers all proper comportment, hsiao *is a crucial aspect of li. Veneration of departed ancestors and profound respect for one's living elders are etched deeply into the Chinese character, so deeply, in fact, that some say the real religion of China is the family. While Confucius himself placed more emphasis on this-worldly conduct rather than on the veneration of ancestral spirits, he certainly saw the traditional practice of the latter as an important manifestation of and a way to inculcate the former. Hsiao, the virtue of filiality, is foundational for the Confucian project.*

The Master said: . . . The ancient kings had a perfect virtue and all-embracing rule of conduct, through which they were in accord with all under heaven. By the practice of it the people were brought to live in peace and harmony, and there was no ill-will between superiors and inferiors. . . . Filial piety [*hsiao*] is the root of (all) virtue, and (the stem) out of which grows (all moral) teaching. . . .

The Master said, For teaching people to be affectionate and loving there is nothing better than Filial Piety. . . .

The Master said, The service which filial children do to their parents is as follows:—In their general conduct to them, they manifest the utmost reverence; in their nourishing of them, their endeavor is to give them the utmost pleasure; when they are ill, they feel the greatest anxiety; in mourning for them (dead), they exhibit every demonstration of grief; in sacrificing to them, they display the utmost solemnity. When children are complete in these five things (they may be pronounced) able to serve their parents.

They who (thus) serve their parents, in a high situation, will be free from pride; in a low situation, will be free from insubordination; and among their equals, will not be quarrelsome. . . . If those three things be not put away, though children every day contribute beef, mutton and pork to nourish their parents, they are not filial.

The Master said, In serving his father and mother a man may gently remonstrate with them. But if he sees that he has failed to change their opinion, he should resume an attitude of deference and not thwart them; may feel discouraged, but not resentful.

... To gather in the same places where our fathers before us have gathered; to perform the same ceremonies which they before us have performed; to play the same music which they before us have played; to pay respect to those whom they honored; to love those who were dear to them—in fact, to serve those now dead as if they were living, and now departed as if they were still with us: this is the highest achievement of true filial piety.

9. The Rectification of Names

Li cannot flourish if people misuse language.

If terms be not correct, language is not in accordance with the truth of things. If language is not in accordance with the truth of things, affairs cannot be carried out to success. . . . Therefore a superior person considers it necessary that the names he uses be spoken appropriately. What the superior person requires is that in his words there be nothing that is incorrect.

10. The Five Constant Relationships

Human individuals are cells in the social organism. Confucius empha-sized attention to the five relationships and their concomitant duties as a way of underscoring this fact and of promoting shared participation in li.

a. The Five Duties

The duties of universal obligation are five, and the moral qualities by which they are carried out are three. The duties are those be-tween ruler and subject, between parents and children, between husband and wife, between elder sibling and younger, and those in the intercourse between friends. These are the five duties of uni-versal obligation. Wisdom, compassion and courage—these are the three universally recognized moral qualities of human beings. It matters not in what way people come to the exercise of these moral qualities, the result is one and the same. . . .

b. The Master Measures Himself

And with characteristic candor and humility about his own inability to reach the ideal of behaving with perfect li within the five relationships, Confucius says:

There are four things in the moral life of a person, not one of which I have been able to carry out in my life. To serve my parents as I would expect my children to serve me: that I have not been able to do. To serve my sovereign as I would expect a minister under me to serve me: that I have not been able to do. To act towards my elder siblings as I would expect my younger siblings to act towards me: that I have not been able to do. To be the first to behave towards friends as I would expect them to behave towards me: that I have not been able to do.

11. The Spirit of Li: *Reciprocity, Loyalty, and the Golden Rule*

a. The Single Thread

The Master said, Shen! My Way has one (thread) that runs right through it. . . . When the Master had gone out the disciples asked, . . . What did he mean? Master Tseng said, Our Master's way is simply this: Loyalty [to superiors], consideration [for the feelings of others].

b. Confucius's Golden Rule

Tzu-kung asked saying, Is there any single saying that one can act upon all day and every day? The Master said, Perhaps the saying about consideration: Never do to others what you would not like them to do to you.

12. The Master Virtue, *Jen: Goodness or Human-Heartedness*

Jen, here rendered "good" or "goodness," is the master Confucian virtue. It may be thought of as the end to which li and its constitutive virtues are the means.

One who is free to choose, yet does not prefer to dwell among the Good—how can he be accorded the name wise?

The Master said,

Without Goodness a person
Cannot for long endure adversity,
Cannot for long enjoy prosperity,

The Master said, In the presence of a good person, think all the time how you may learn to equal her. In the presence of a bad person, turn your gaze within!

The Master said, When it comes to Goodness one need not avoid competing with one's teacher.

The Master said, Is Goodness indeed so far away? If we really wanted Goodness, we should find that it was at our very side.

Wealth and rank are what every person desires; but if they can only be retained to the detriment of the Way he professes, he must relinquish them. Poverty and obscurity are what every person detests; but if they can only be avoided to the detriment of the Way she professes, he must accept them. The noble person who ever parts company with Goodness does not fulfill that name. Never for a moment does a noble person quit the way of Goodness. . . .

The Master said, I for my part have never yet seen one who really cared for Goodness, nor one who really abhorred wickedness. One who really cared for Goodness would never let any other consideration come first. . . . Has anyone ever managed to do Good with his whole might even as long as the space of a single day? I think not. . . . It may well have happened, but I for my part have never seen it.

13. The *Chun-Tzu: The Noble Person or Fully Human Being*

The chun-tzu *is Confucius's term for the person of fully evolved character, one who manifests human-heartedness.*

The Master said, [the good person] does not grieve that other people do not recognize her merits. Her only anxiety is lest she should fail to recognize theirs.

Tzu-kung asked about the truly human being. The Master said, He does not preach what he practices till he has practiced what he preaches.

The Master said, A noble person takes as much trouble to discover what is right as lesser people take to discover what will pay.

The Master said, A noble person covets the reputation of being slow in word but prompt in deed.

The Master said,

A noble person does not
Accept people because of what they say,
Nor reject sayings, because the speaker is what he is.

The Master said, A noble person who never goes on eating till he is sated, who does not demand comfort in his home, who is diligent in business and cautious in speech, who associates with those that possess the Way and thereby corrects his own faults—such a one may indeed by said to have a taste for learning.

The Master said, A noble person is ashamed to let her words outrun her deeds.

The Master said, A noble mind can see a question from all sides without bias. Small minds are biased and see a question only from one side.

The Master said, A truly human being is calm and at ease; the small person is fretful and ill at ease.

The Master said, The noble person can influence those who are above her; the small person can only influence those who are below her.

The Master said, A noble person is distressed by his own lack of capacity; he is never distressed at the failure of others to recognize his merits.

The Master said, The demands that a noble person makes are upon himself; those that a small person makes are upon others.

The Master said, The noble person calls attention to the good points in others; he does not call attention to their defects. The small person does just the reverse of this.

The Master said, When natural substance prevails over ornamentation, you get the boorishness of the rustic. When ornamentation prevails over natural substance, you get the pedantry of the scribe. Only when ornament and substance are duly blended do you get the truly noble person.

The Master said, The Ways of the true human being are three. I myself have met with success in none of them. For he that is really Good is never unhappy, he that is really wise is never perplexed, he that is really brave is never afraid. Tzu-kung said, That, Master, is your own Way [Tao]!

14. *Te: Moral Force*

Confucius believed that the only influence one really has on others flows directly from the moral fiber of one's character. Authority or force can achieve results but not without a leaving a toxic residue. Moral energy, by contrast, burns clean.

The Master said, In vain have I looked for those whose desire to build up their moral power [te] was as strong as their sexual desire.

The Master said, they who rule by moral force are like the polestar, which remains in its place while all the lesser stars do homage to it.

The Master said, Govern the people by regulations, keep order among them by chastisements, and they will flee from you, and lose all self-respect. Govern them by moral force, keep order among them by ritual [li], and they will keep their self-respect and come to you of their own accord.

The Master said, If the ruler himself is upright, all will go well even though he does not give orders. But if he himself is not upright, even though he gives orders, they will not be obeyed.

Chi K'ang-tzu asked Master K'ung about government. . . . Master K'ung replied, . . . If you desire what is good, the people will at once be good. The essence of the noble person is that of the wind; the essence of lesser persons is that of grass. And when a wind passes over the grass, it cannot choose but bend.

The Master said, Moral force never dwells in solitude; it will always bring neighbors.

Tzu-kung asked about government. The Master said, sufficient food, sufficient weapons, and the confidence of the common people. Tzu-kung said, Suppose you had no choice but to dispense with one of these three, which would you forgo? The Master said, Weapons. Tzu-kung said, Suppose you were forced to dispense with one of the two that were left, which would you forgo? The Master said, Food. For from of old death has been the lot of all men; but a people that no longer trusts its rulers is lost indeed.

15. *Wen*, the Arts: *Music, Poetry, Literature, and Dance*

Long before Shakespeare, Confucius understood that music soothes the savage beast. Indeed, for Confucius music and the other arts are not only therapy but essential ingredients in the work of transforming human nature toward the good.

a. Music, Harmony, and Virtue

Music rises from the human heart when the human heart is touched by the external world. . . .

   Therefore the ancient kings were ever careful about things that affected the human heart. They tried therefore to guide the people's ideals and aspirations by means of li, establish harmony in sounds by means of music, regulate conduct by means of government, and prevent immorality by means of punishments. Li, music, punishments and government have a common goal, which is to bring about unity in the people's hearts and carry out the principles of political order.

. . . Who understands music comes very near to understanding li, and if they have mastered both li and music, we call them virtuous, because virtue is fulfillment. . . .

Music expresses the harmony of the universe, while rituals express the order of the universe. Through harmony all things are influenced, and through order all things have a proper place. . . . When rituals and music are well established, we have the Heaven and Earth functioning in perfect order. . . .

Music illustrates the primordial forces of nature, while li reflects the products of the creation. Heaven represents the principle of eternal motion, while Earth represents the principle of remaining still, and these two principles of motion and rest permeate life between Heaven and Earth. Therefore, the Sage talks about rituals and music. . . .

Therefore, the noble person tries to create harmony in the human heart by a rediscovery of human nature, and tries to promote music as a means to the perfection of human culture. When such music prevails and the people's minds are led toward the right ideals and aspirations, we may see the appearance of a great nation.

Character is the backbone of our human nature, and music is the flowering of character. . . . The poem gives expression to our heart, the song gives expression to our voice, and the dance gives expression to our movements. These three arts take their rise from the human soul, and then are given further expressions by means of the musical instruments.

b. Transformative Music

The Master said, For teaching people to be affectionate and loving there is nothing better than Filial Piety; . . . for changing their manners and altering their customs there is nothing better than Music. . . .

c. Music and Goodness

The Master said, A person who is not Good, what can she or he have to do with ritual? A person who is not Good, what can she or he have to do with music?

THE GREAT LEARNING: A Summation

16. The Great Learning

Ta Hsüeh, literally, "Education for the True Adult," is one of the Four Books of Confucius. Its brevity allows us to reproduce it here in full. It may be read as a summary of the Confucian project. Its core idea is that the work of transforming the world requires one's own self-transformation.

[The Great Learning] consists in manifesting the clear character, loving the people, and abiding in the highest good.

Only after knowing what to abide in can one be calm. Only after having been calm can one be tranquil. Only after having achieved tranquillity can one have peaceful repose. Only after having peaceful repose can one begin to deliberate. Only after deliberation can the end be attained. Things have their roots and branches. Affairs have their beginnings and their ends. To know what is first and what is last will lead one near the Way.

The ancients who wished to manifest their clear character to the world would first bring order to their states. Those who wished to bring order to their states would first regulate their families. Those who wished to regulate their families would first cultivate their personal lives. Those who wished to cultivate their personal lives would first rectify their minds. Those who wished to rectify their minds would first make their wills sincere. Those who wished to make their wills sincere would first extend their knowledge. The extension of knowledge consists in the investigation of things.

When things are investigated, knowledge is extended; when knowledge is extended, the will becomes sincere; when the will is sincere, the mind is rectified; when the mind is rectified, the personal life is cultivated; when the personal life is cultivated, the family will be regulated; when the family is regulated, the state will be in order; and when the state is in order, there will be peace throughout the world.

From the Son of Heaven down to the common people, all must regard cultivation of the personal life as the root or foundation. There is never a case when the root is in disorder and yet the branches are in order. There has never been a case when what is treated with great importance becomes a matter of slight importance or what is treated with slight importance becomes a matter of great importance.

MENCIUS

The last of the Four Books of Confucius takes its name from the second most influential philosopher in the Confucian tradition, Meng Tzu or Mencius, who flourished about a hundred years after his master. Like Confucius's Analects, the Mencius was probably compiled by disciples.

Mencius, like his mentor, revered the wisdom of the past, urged the cultivation of jen or human goodness, and, in the realm of politics, insisted that wise rulers govern more by the power of their moral character than by force.

Mencius also stressed i, or "righteousness," an ideal whose meaning and function was not absolute but relative to its social context. Resisting the views of his philosophical rival, Mo Tzu, who preached an equal and universal love for all humanity, Mencius, following the more realistic dicta of Confucius, argued that right conduct toward others could not help but be expressed in varying degrees depending on the degree of personal relationship involved.

Mencius is well known for his doctrine of human nature: people tend by their nature toward goodness, and it is only the adverse circum-

stances of their nurture that erode goodness and engender evil. Our individual task, then, is to discover and express our innate goodness, while our collective task is to establish the just social order that makes that discovery and that expression possible for all.

17. Our Original Capability Is Goodness

The disciple Kung-tu Tzu said: "Kao Tzu [a philosophical rival of Mencius] says that human nature is neither good nor bad. Some say that human nature can be turned to be good or bad. Thus when [sage-kings] Wen and Wu were in power the people loved virtue; when [wicked kings] were in power the people indulged in violence. Some say that some natures are good and some natures are bad. . . . Now you say that human nature is good. Are the others then all wrong?"

Mencius replied: "When left to follow its natural feelings human nature will do good. This is why I say it is good. If it becomes evil, it is not the fault of our original capability. The sense of mercy is found in all people; the sense of shame is found in all people; the sense of respect is found in all people; the sense of right and wrong is found in all people. . . . Only we give them no thought. Therefore, it is said: 'Seek and you will find them, neglect and you will lose them.' Some have these virtues to a much greater degree than others—twice, five times, and incalculably more—and that is because those others have not developed to the fullest extent their original capability."

18. Our Natural Tendency Is Goodness

Kao Tzu [a rival] said: "The nature of humanity may be likened to a swift current of water: you lead it eastward and it will flow to the east; you lead it westward and it will flow to the west. Human nature is neither disposed to good nor to evil, just as water is neither disposed to east nor west."

Mencius replied: "It is true that water is neither disposed to east nor west, but is it neither disposed to flowing upward nor downward? The tendency of human nature to do good is like that of water to flow downward. There is no person who does not tend to do good; there is no water that does not flow downward. Now you may strike water and make it splash over your forehead, or you may even force it up the hills. But is this the nature of water? It is of course due to the force of circumstances. Similarly, persons may be brought to do evil, and that is because the same is done to their nature."

19. Our Compassionate Core

Mencius said: "All people have a sense of commiseration. . . . Why I say [this] is this: Here is a person who suddenly notices a child about to fall into a well. Invariably she or he will feel a sense of alarm and compassion. And this is not for the purpose of gaining the favor of the child's parents, or seeking the approbation of its neighbors and friends, or for fear of the blame should he fail to rescue it. Thus we see that no person is without a sense of compassion, or a sense of shame, or a sense of courtesy, or a sense of right and wrong. The sense of compassion is the beginning of humanity; the sense of shame is the beginning of righteousness; the sense of courtesy is the beginning of decorum [li]; the sense of right and wrong is the beginning of wisdom. Every person has within himself these four beginnings; just as he has four limbs. . . . The person who considers himself incapable of exercising them is destroying himself. . . . Let every person but attend to expanding and developing these four beginnings that are in our very being, and they will issue forth like a conflagration being kindled and a spirit being opened up. . . .

20. Goodness Does Not Require Repression

Kao Tzu said: "The nature of humanity may be likened to the willow tree, whereas righteousness may be likened to wooden cups and wicker baskets. To turn human nature into goodness and righteousness [i] is like turning a willow tree into cups and baskets."

Mencius replied: "Sir, can you follow the nature of the willow tree, and [still] make cups and baskets? Or must you violate its nature to make cups and baskets? . . . Your words, alas, would incite everyone in the world to regard humanity and righteousness as a curse!"

21. How Can People Be Good if They Are Hungry?

Mencius said: . . . "Only the true scholar is capable of maintaining, without certain means of livelihood, a steadfast heart. As for the multitude, if they have no certain means of livelihood, they surely cannot maintain a steadfast heart. Without a steadfast heart they are likely to abandon themselves and fall prey to all manner of depravity. If you wait till they have lapsed into crime and then mete out punishment, it is like placing traps for the people. If a human ruler is on the throne how can she permit such a thing as placing traps for the people? Therefore, when an intelligent ruler regulates the livelihood of the people, she makes sure that they will have enough to serve their parents on the one hand and to support their families on the other, so that in good years all may eat their fill and in bad years no one need die of starvation. Thus only will she urge them to walk the path of virtue, and the people will follow her effortlessly."

22. The Political Importance of Moral Force (Te)

Mencius said: "It was because Chieh and Chou lost the people that they lost the empire, and it was because they lost the hearts of the people that they lost the people. Here is the way to win the empire: win the people. . . . Here is the way to win the people: win their hearts. . . . Here is the way to win their hearts: give them and share with them what they like, and do not do to them what they do not like. The people turn to a humane ruler as water flows downward or beasts take to wilderness."

23. The Root of Social Transformation Is Self-Transformation

Mencius said: "People are in the habit of speaking of the world, the state. As a matter of fact, the foundation of the world lies in the state, the foundation of the state lies in the family, and the foundation of the family lies in the individual."

24. Having Children

Mencius said: "There are three things that are unfilial, and the greatest of them is to have no posterity."

GRACE NOTES

Some of the most poignant indications of Confucian influence on the Chinese mind occur not within explicitly philosophical treatises but in such quotidian sources as family letters or popular proverbs. The first few selections below are from the family letters of Cheng Panch'iao (1693–1765), a scholar and artist. According to Lin Yutang, a noted interpreter of China to the West who translated these letters, they serve "better than anything else to show the kindly temper of the Chinese people and the typical spirit of Chinese culture at its best."[6]

The concluding selections are proverbs taken from a handbook written in the seventeenth century. Again, while not explicitly or exclusively Confucian, they shed light on the spirit of the Chinese mind.

25. From the Letters of Cheng Panch'iao to His Brother Mo, in the Mid-1700s

a. Generosity of Spirit: Against Legalism

. . . After I, your foolish brother, became a government graduate,[7] whenever I found in the old trunks at our home some deed of a slave sold into our family in the former generation, I at once burned it over the oil lamp. I did not even return it to the person concerned, for I felt if I did, it would be an obvious act and in-

---

6. Lin Yutang, ed., *The Wisdom of India and China* (New York: Random House, 1942), 1068.

7. One who passed the civil service examinations, the doorway to a prestigious career.

crease the man's embarrassment. Since I began to employ people, I have never required contracts. If we can get along with the servant, we keep him; and if not, we send him away. Why keep such a piece of paper to provide a pretext for our next generations to use it as a claim or a means of extortion? To act with such a heart is to have consideration for others, which is to have consideration for ourselves. If we try always to obtain a legal hold, once we get into the meshes of legality, we shall never be able to get out again. We shall only become poor more quickly and disaster will follow immediately. . . . You just look at the people of the world who are shrewd at calculations; do they ever succeed in overcoming others by their shrewd calculations? They are only calculating toward their own ruin. What a pity! Remember this, my younger brother.

b. On Tolerance: Don't Blame the Buddha and Confucius for the Follies of Buddhists and Confucians

The world is filled with [Buddhist] monks. But they are not sent here from Tibet, but are fathers and brothers of China who have no home to go to or who have entered the faith. When we shave, we become monks, and when they let their hair grow again, they become ourselves. It would be a mistake to look at them with anger, call them heretics and treat them with hatred and disgust. . . . Besides . . . Confucianism has come back into its own, and the Buddhist religion is gradually on the wane. The rulers have followed the Six Classics and the Four Books as the means of regulating family life and governing the Empire. To denounce Buddhism at this late hour would be as meaningless as chewing candle-wax. The monks are sinners against the Buddha. They rob and kill and seek after women and are greedy and snobbish, for they have not followed the doctrines of purifying their hearts and seeking their original nature. The government graduates are also sinners against Confucius, for they are neither kind nor wise, and devoid of courtesy or justice. They are no longer concerned with the keeping of the ancient tradition and of Confucian teachings. The government graduates love to abuse the monks and the monks love to abuse the government graduates. The proverb says, "Let each one sweep off the snow at his door-step, and not interfere with frost on the neighbors' roof." What do you think of this? . . . I have also shown this to Monk Wufang and it gave him a good laugh.

c. Forgiveness and Forbearance

If one loves other people, he himself becomes worthy of love; if one hates other people, he himself deserves hatred. . . . I always love criticizing people, particularly the government graduates. But come to think about it, the trouble with the graduates is that they are so bound up with themselves. On the other hand, if they were not so bound up with themselves, they wouldn't be graduates. But I think it is unfair to criticize the graduates alone—who nowadays are not bound up with themselves? I am an old man now and living alone. I must watch out for this habit of mine. It is good to love people, and a bad habit to criticize people. . . . You must also often remind me of this point, old brother.

d. Sharing Wealth

. . . For several years now I have occupied an official post without any mishap, which means that I have robbed [our] clan of its luck and monopolized it all myself. Can my heart feel at ease? It is pitiful to see our relatives at the East Gate catch fish and shrimps . . . living in huts and eating chaffs and wheat gruel. They pick floating heart, radish and water-bamboo and boil them and if they have buckwheat cakes to go along with them, they consider them delicacies and the young children fight for them. Whenever I think of them, tears fill my eyes. When you bring money from my salary home you should distribute it from house to house. Although the six families at the South Gate, the eighteen families at Chuhuengchiang and the lone family at Hsiat'ien are more distant relatives, they are of the same blood, and should be given something also. . . . Hsü Tsungyü and Lu Poyi are my college friends, and we used to go about daily together. I still remember discussing ancient literatures with them in an old temple deep into the night with the falling leaves flying about. Sometimes we sat on the stone lions and discussed ancient warfare and all topics in the universe. They have been unfortunate, and must also be given a share of my money for old friendship's sake. People usually think a great deal of their own writings and scholarship and believe that getting degrees is an easy matter for them, but do not realize that it is all due to luck. . . . This is therefore not something to make one conceited toward friends. The principal thing is to cement good-will among relatives and members of the clan and remember old friends; for the rest, you can do what you think fit in the way of helping the neighbors and people of the village. Spend it all; I shall spare the details.

e. Fellow-Feeling Toward Nonhuman Beings

My only son was born to me in my fifty-second year. Of course, I love him, but there is a correct way of loving one's children. Even in games, he should be taught to show the heart of mercy and generosity, and avoid cruelty. What I hate most is to have caged birds; we enjoy them while they are shut up in prison. What justification is there that we are entitled to thwart the instincts of animals to please our own nature? As for tying up a dragon-fly by the hair or tying a crab with a piece of string, it affords the children some fun only for a little while, and soon the little thing is dead. Now nature creates all things and nourishes them all. Even an ant or an insect comes from the combination of forces of the *yin* and *yang* and the five elements. God also loves them dearly in his heart, and we who are supposed to be the crown of all creation cannot even sympathize with God's heart. How then is the animal world going to have a place of refuge? Snakes, and centipedes, tigers, leopards and wolves are most dangerous animals. But since Heaven has given birth to them, what right have we to take their lives? If they were all meant to be killed, then why in the first place did Heaven give them life? All we can do is to drive them far away so that they shall not harm us. What wrong has the spider committed by spinning its web? Some kill them without mercy on the fairy-tale that they curse the moon or that they may make the walls crumble down. On what authority is such a statement based. . . ? Will this do? Will this do?. . .

Postscript. Regarding what I have just said about not keeping birds in cages, I must say that I always love birds, but that there is a proper way of doing it. One who loves birds should plant trees, so that the house shall be surrounded with hundreds of shady branches and be a country and a home for birds. Thus, at dawn, when we wake up from sleep and are still tossing about in bed, we hear a chorus of chirping voices like a celestial harmony. And when we get up and are putting on our gowns or washing our faces or gargling our mouths or sipping the morning tea, we see their gorgeous plumes flitting about. Before we have time to look at one, we are attracted by another. This is a pleasure that far exceeds that of keeping one bird in a cage. Generally the enjoyment of life should come from a view regarding the universe as a park, and the rivers and streams as a pond, so that all beings can live in accordance with their nature. Great indeed is such happiness! How shall the keeping of a bird in a cage or a fish in a jar be compared with it in generosity of spirit and in kindness?

26. Some Chinese Proverbs

Money sometimes prevents trouble; too much money breeds it.

Endure a small insult and be safe from a big insult; suffer some small loss and be safe from a big loss. Where you miss an advantage in a deal, you gain an advantage.

The silkworm weaves its cocoon and stays inside, therefore it is imprisoned; the spider weaves its web and stays outside, therefore it is free.

Talk not of your personal success to one who has failed; forget not your failures in your moment of success.

Avoid the mean person, but do not make him your personal enemy; get close to the cultivated person, but do not always say yes to him.

All the universe is an inn; search not specially for a retreat of peace: all the people are your relatives; expect therefore troubles from them.

To see through fame and wealth is to gain a little rest; to see through life and death is to gain a big rest.

To be elated at success and disappointed at failure is to be the child of circumstances; how can such a one be called master of himself?

Who is narrow of vision cannot be big-hearted; who is narrow of spirit cannot take long, easy strides.

Who gives me goods hurts my spirit; who gives me fame injures my life.

Be firm in your acts, but easy in your heart; be strict with yourself, but gentle with your fellowmen.

Who does evil and is afraid of letting it be known has still a seed of good in his evil; who does good and is anxious to have it known has still a root of evil in his good.

One should not miss the flavor of being sick, nor miss the experience of being destitute.

Virtue in a rich person is the ability to give, in a poor man it is the refusal to beg, in a man of high position it is a humble attitude toward fellowmen, and in a man of low position it is the ability to see through life.

Of the things that are purely good without accompanying evil are: study, the love of mountains and rivers, taking pleasure in the moon, the breeze, flowers and bamboos, and sitting in upright posture in silence.

There are four rules for living in the mountains: let there be no formation in trees, no arrangement of rocks, no sumptuousness in the living house, and no contrivance in the human heart.

To stay up in the mountains is a fine thing, but the slightest attachment turns it into a market; the appreciation of old paintings is a refined hobby, but the slightest greed of possession turns one into a merchant; wine and poetry provide occasions of pleasure, but the slightest loss of freedom turns them into hell.

To go to see the prune flowers after snow, pay a visit to the chrysanthemums during frost, tend the orchid during rain, or listen to the swaying bamboos before the breeze—such are the joys of leisure of a rustic fellow, but they are also moments of the greatest meaning to the scholar.

When the tea is well-brewed and the incense has a pure fragrance, it's a delight if friends drop in; when birds twitter and flowers drop their petals, even solitude is contentment for the soul.

You are reading when incense is burning and all your human obligations are fulfilled, while outside the screen the flower petals are dripping and the moon has come up to the top of the pine trees, and you suddenly hear the temple bell and push open the window and see the Milky Way—such a moment is superior to daytime.

If a person's face does not show a little sadness his thoughts are not deep.

Whenever you do a thing, act so that it will give your friends no occasion for regret and your foes no cause for joy.

Look at beauty as you look at beautiful clouds, and your mortal passions will be milder; listen to the song of lutes as you listen to the flowing water, what harm is there?

CHAPTER FOUR

Taoism

*T*he Chinese mind has long beheld the universe as a living
*process governed by the interplay of opposites. We live, China testifies,
amid a dynamic dance of complementary forces—*yin *and* yang*—manifest in the mysterious cooperation of light and dark, heat and cold,
male and female, willfulness and receptivity: life's countless contrary
pairs. It is nothing short of cosmically fitting, then, that Chinese philosophy has also been shaped by an interplay: between Confucianism, with
its emphases on will and rationality, and Taoism, with its preference for
intelligent instinctiveness, intuition, and creative letting-be. For philosophy no less than for flavors in food, the art of living has in China always been a question of balance.*

*Taoism and Confucianism grew up together, entering Chinese his-
tory around the sixth century* B.C.E. *Taoism's beginnings are linked to
the legendary figure of Lao Tzu, senior to Confucius by about fifty
years and credited with writing Taoism's Bible, the Tao Te Ching or
The Book of the Way and Its Power. Because this tiny text has proven
an inexhaustible well of inspiration for thinkers of all stripes, it claims
the lion's share of attention in this chapter. Selections from the writings*

of Chuang Tzu, a Taoist sage who lived some two centuries after Lao Tzu, complete the chapter's main sections.

In its long life, Taoism has come to stand for much more than the subtle outlooks proffered by these two sages. There are, in fact, at least three extant strains of Taoism: philosophical Taoism, yogic and vitalist Taoism, and popular or religious Taoism.[1] Only the first has consistently claimed worldwide attention, however, and we will limit our attention exclusively to it.

THE TAO TE CHING

Wise with years but dismayed by the folly of his fellow human beings, Lao Tzu—the story goes—retired from his archivist post, seeking solitude. Climbing on a water buffalo, he rode west, toward the high country now known as Tibet. At the Hankao Pass a prescient gatekeeper implored him to record his views for posterity before disappearing into the mountain fastness. Obligingly, Lao-tzu hunkered down for three days, then emerged with a slim sheaf of five thousand Chinese characters arranged in eighty-one brief chapters. The Tao Te Ching has been translated more times and into more languages than any book in history except the Bible. "A testament to humanity's at-home-ness in the universe," writes Huston Smith, "it can be read in half an hour or a lifetime, and remains to this day the basic text of Taoist thought."[2] There are but two central topics in the Tao Te Ching, the Tao itself, and the power or fulfillment that results from living in harmony with it.

Original verse numbers are given above each selection.

1. The Tao Itself

1

The tao that can be told
is not the eternal Tao.

---

1. Cf. Huston Smith, *The World's Religions* (San Francisco: HarperSanFrancisco, 1991), 199–206.
2. Smith, *The World's Religions*, 197.

The name that can be named
is not the eternal Name.

The unnameable is the eternally real.
Naming is the origin
of all particular things.

Free from desire, you realize the mystery.
Caught in desire, you see only the manifestations . . .

2

The Tao is like a well:
used but never used up.
It is like the eternal void:
filled with infinite possibilities.

It is hidden but always present.
I don't know who gave birth to it.
It is older than God.

4

The Tao is called the Great Mother:
empty yet inexhaustible,
it gives birth to infinite worlds.

It is always present within you.
You can use it any way you want.

7

The Tao is infinite, eternal.
Why is it eternal?
It was never born;
thus it can never die.
Why is it infinite?
It has no desires for itself;
thus it is present for all beings . . .

25

There was something formless and perfect
before the universe was born.

It is serene. Empty.
Solitary. Unchanging.
Infinite. Eternally present.
It is the mother of the universe.
For lack of a better name,
I call it the Tao.

It flows through all things,
inside and outside, and returns
to the origin of all things.

The Tao is great.
The universe is great.
Earth is great.
Man is great.
These are the four great powers.

Man follows the Earth.
Earth follows the universe.
The universe follows Tao.
The Tao follows only itself.

34

The great Tao flows everywhere.
All things are born from it,
yet it doesn't create them.
It pours itself into its work,
yet it makes no claim.
It nourishes infinite worlds,
yet it doesn't hold on to them.
Since it is merged with all things
and hidden in their hearts,
it can be called humble.
Since all things vanish into it
and it alone endures,
it can be called great.
It isn't aware of its greatness;
thus it is truly great.

51

Every being in the universe
is an expression of the Tao.
It springs into existence,
unconscious, perfect, free,
takes on a physical body,
lets circumstances complete it.
That is why every being
spontaneously honors the Tao.

The Tao gives birth to all beings,
nourishes them, maintains them,
cares for them, comforts them, protects them,
takes them back to itself,
creating without possessing,
acting without expecting,
guiding without interfering.
That is why love of the Tao
is in the very nature of things.

41

When a superior man hears of the Tao,
he immediately begins to embody it.
When an average man hears of the Tao,
he half believes it, half doubts it.
When a foolish man hears of the Tao,
he laughs out loud.
If he didn't laugh,
it wouldn't be the Tao.

2. Living in Harmony with the Tao: *The Quiet Mind*

16

Empty your mind of all thoughts.
Let your heart be at peace.
Watch the turmoil of beings,
but contemplate their return.

Each separate being in the universe
returns to the common source.
Returning to the source is serenity.

If you don't realize the source,
you stumble in confusion and sorrow.
When you realize where you come from,
you naturally become tolerant,
disinterested, amused,
kindhearted as a grandmother,
dignified as a king.
Immersed in the wonder of the Tao,
you can deal with whatever life brings you,
and when death comes, you are ready.

12

Colors blind the eye.
Sounds deafen the ear,
Flavors numb the taste.
Thoughts weaken the mind.
Desires wither the heart.

The Master observes the world
but trusts his inner vision.
He allows things to come and go.
His heart is open as the sky.

15

The ancient Masters were profound and subtle.
Their wisdom was unfathomable.
There is no way to describe it;
all we can describe is their appearance.

They were careful
as someone crossing an iced-over stream.
Alert as a warrior in enemy territory.
Courteous as a guest.
Fluid as melting ice.
Shapable as a block of wood.

Receptive as a valley.
Clear as a glass of water.

Do you have the patience to wait
till your mud settles and the water is clear?
Can you remain unmoving
till the right action arises by itself?

The Master doesn't seek fulfillment.
Not seeking, not expecting,
she is present, and can welcome all things.

23

Express yourself completely,
then keep quiet.
Be like the forces of nature:
when it blows, there is only wind;
when it rains, there is only rain;
when the clouds pass, the sun shines through.

If you open yourself to the Tao,
you are at one with the Tao
and you can embody it completely.
If you open yourself to insight,
you are at one with insight
and you can use it completely.
If you open yourself to loss,
you are at one with loss
and you can accept it completely.

Open yourself to the Tao,
then trust your natural responses;
and everything will fall into place.

50

The Master gives himself up
to whatever the moment brings.
He knows that he is going to die,
and he has nothing left to hold on to:
no illusions in his mind,

no resistances in his body.
He doesn't think about his actions;
they flow from the core of his being.
He holds nothing back from life;
therefore he is ready for death,
as a man is ready for sleep
after a good day's work.

56

Those who know don't talk.
Those who talk don't know.

Close your mouth,
block off your senses,
blunt your sharpness,
untie your knots,
soften your glare,
settle your dust.
This is the primal identity . . .

3. Harmony with the Tao: *Creative Letting-Be* (Wei Wu Wei) *in Personal Life*

The Taoist phrase here rendered "creative letting-be" is wei wu wei, literally, the action of non-action. It is Taoism's key principle of practical living. It encourages going with the flow, cutting with the grain, and certainly not spitting against the wind. It is not a counsel of passivity or torpor; rather it warns against aggressive, ego-laden action that seeks to shape life in one's own image. It has also been translated as "creative quietude" and "actionless activity."

2

. . . Therefore the Master
acts without doing anything
and teaches without saying anything.
Things arise and she lets them come;
things disappear and she lets them go.
She has but doesn't possess,

acts but doesn't expect.
When her work is done, she forgets it.
That is why it lasts forever.

3

. . . Practice not-doing,
and everything with fall into place.

9

Fill your bowl to the brim
and it will spill.
Keep sharpening your knife
and it will blunt.
Chase after money and security
and your heart will never unclench.
Care about people's approval
and you will be their prisoner.

Do your work, then step back.
The only path to serenity.

22

. . . the Master by residing in the Tao,
sets an example for all beings.
Because he doesn't display himself,
people can see his light.
Because he has nothing to prove,
people can trust his words.
Because he doesn't know who he is,
people recognize themselves in him.
Because he has no goal in mind,
everything he does succeeds.

When the ancient Masters said,
"If you want to be given everything,
give everything up,"
they weren't using empty phrases.
Only in being lived by the Tao
can you be truly yourself.

24

He who stands on tiptoe
doesn't stand firm.
He who rushes ahead
doesn't go far.
He who tries to shine
dims his own light.
He who defines himself
can't know who he really is.
He who has power over others
can't empower himself.
He who clings to his work
will create nothing that endures.

If you want to accord with the Tao,
just do your job, then let go.

27

A good traveler has no fixed plans
and is not intent upon arriving . . .

43

The gentlest thing in the world
overcomes the hardest thing in the world.
That which has no substance
enters where there is no space.
This shows the value of non-action.

Teaching without words,
performing without actions:
that is the Master's way.

47

Without opening your door,
you can open your heart to the world.
Without looking out your window,
you can see the essence of the Tao.

The more you know,
the less you understand.

The master arrives without leaving,
sees the light without looking,
achieves without doing a thing.

48

In pursuit of knowledge,
every day something is added.
In the practice of the Tao,
every day something is dropped.
Less and less do you need to force things,
until finally you arrive at non action.
When nothing is done,
nothing is left undone.

True mastery can be gained
by letting things go their own way.
It can't be gained by interfering.

64

. . . The journey of a thousand miles
starts from beneath your feet.

Rushing into action, you fail.
Trying to grasp things, you lose them.
Forcing a project to completion,
you ruin what was almost ripe.

Therefore the Master takes action
by letting things take their course.
He remains as calm
at the end as at the beginning.
He has nothing,
thus has nothing to lose.
What he desires is non–desire;
what he learns is to unlearn.
He simply reminds people
of who they have always been.
He cares about nothing but the Tao.
Thus he can care for all things.

76

Men are born soft and supple;
dead, they are stiff and hard.
Plants are born tender and pliant;
dead, they are brittle and dry.

Thus whoever is stiff and inflexible
is a disciple of death.
Whoever is soft and yielding
is a disciple of life.

The hard and stiff will be broken.
The soft and supple will prevail.

4. Harmony with the Tao: *Creative Letting-Be in Political Life*

17

When the Master governs, the people
are hardly aware that he exists.
Next best is a leader who is loved.
Next, one who is feared.
The worst is one who is despised.

If you don't trust the people,
you make them untrustworthy.

The Master doesn't talk, he acts.
When his work is done,
the people say, "Amazing:
we did it, all by ourselves!"

29

Do you want to improve the world?
I don't think it can be done.

The world is sacred.
It can't be improved.
If you tamper with it, you'll ruin it.
If you treat it like an object, you'll lose it . . .

The Master sees things as they are,
without trying to control them.
She lets them go their own way,
and resides at the center of the circle.

31

Weapons are tools of violence;
all decent men detest them.

Weapons are tools of fear;
a decent man will avoid them
except in the direst necessity
and, if compelled, will use them
only with the utmost restraint.
Peace is his highest value.
If the peace has been shattered,
how can he be content?
His enemies are not demons,
but human beings like himself.
He doesn't wish them personal harm.
Nor does he rejoice in victory.
How could he rejoice in victory
and delight in the slaughter of men?

He enters a battle gravely,
with sorrow and with great compassion,
as if he were attending a funeral.

37

The Tao never does anything,
yet through it all things are done.

If powerful men and women
could center themselves in it,
the whole world would be transformed
by itself, in its natural rhythms.
People would be content
with their simple, everyday lives,
in harmony, and free of desire.

When there is no desire,
all things are at peace.

57

If you want to be a great leader,
you must learn to follow the Tao.
Stop trying to control.
Let go of fixed plans and concepts,
and the world will govern itself.

The more prohibitions you have,
the less virtuous people will be.
The more weapons you have,
the less secure people will be.
The more subsidies you have,
the less self-reliant people will be.

Therefore the Master says:
I let go of the law,
and people become honest.
I let go of economics,
and people become prosperous.
I let go of religion,
and people become serene.
I let go of all desire for the common good,
and the good becomes common as grass.

58

If a country is governed with tolerance,
the people are comfortable and honest.
If a country is governed with repression,
the people are depressed and crafty.

When the will to power is in charge,
the higher the ideals, the lower the results.
Try to make people happy,
and you lay the groundwork for misery.

Try to make people moral,
and you lay the groundwork for vice.

Thus the Master is content
to serve as an example
and not to impose her will.
She is pointed, but doesn't pierce.
Straightforward, but supple.
Radiant, but easy on the eyes.

59

For governing a country well
there is nothing better than moderation.

The mark of a moderate man
is freedom from his own ideas.
Tolerant like the sky,
all-pervading like sunlight,
firm like a mountain,
supple like a tree in the wind,
he has no destination in view
and makes use of anything
life happens to bring his way.

Nothing is impossible for him.
Because he has let go,
he can care for the people's welfare
as a mother cares for her child.

60

Governing a large country
is like frying a small fish.
You spoil it with too much poking.

Center your country in the Tao
and evil will have no power.
Not that it isn't there,
but you'll be able to step out of its way.

Give evil nothing to oppose
and it will disappear by itself.

61

. . . A great nation is like a great man:
When he makes a mistake, he realizes it.
Having realized it, he admits it.
Having admitted it, he corrects it.
He considers those who point out his faults
as his most benevolent teachers.
He thinks of his enemy
as the shadow that he himself casts . . .

66

All streams flow to the sea
because it is lower than they are.
Humility gives it its power.

If you want to govern the people,
you must place yourself below them.
If you want to lead the people,
you must learn how to follow them.

The Master is above the people,
and no one feels oppressed.
She goes ahead of the people,
and no one feels manipulated.
The whole world is grateful to her.
Because she competes with no one,
no one can compete with her.

5. Water

Water is perhaps the Taoist's favorite image not only of the Tao itself but of the "actionless activity" of the sage who is in harmony with the Tao.

8

The supreme good is like water,
which nourishes all things without trying to.

It is content with the low places that people disdain.
Thus it is like the Tao . . .

78

Nothing in the world
is as soft and yielding as water.
Yet for dissolving the hard and inflexible,
nothing can surpass it.

The soft overcomes the hard;
the gentle overcomes the rigid.
Everyone knows this is true,
but few can put it into practice.

6. The Coinherence of Opposites

*Seeing the world as a ceaseless interaction of complementary forces
(yin and yang) is a Chinese talent that predates Taoism. Taoists, however, seem especially adept at seeing this mysterious collusion of opposites and at pointing out how our failure to understand it leads to a host
of problems.*

2

When people see some things as beautiful,
other things become ugly.
When people see some things as good,
other things become bad.

Being and non-being create each other.
Difficult and easy support each other.
Long and short define each other.
High and low depend on each other.
Before and after follow each other . . .

3

If you overesteem great men,
people become powerless.
If you overvalue possessions,
people begin to steal . . .

5

The Tao doesn't take sides;
it gives birth to both good and evil . . .

11

We join spokes together in a wheel,
but it is the center hole
that makes the wagon move.

We shape clay into a pot,
but it is the emptiness inside
that holds whatever we want.

We hammer wood for a house,
but it is the inner space
that makes it livable.

We work with being,
but non-being is what we use.

18

When the great Tao is forgotten,
goodness and piety appear.
When the body's intelligence declines,
cleverness and knowledge step forth.
When there is no peace in the family,
filial piety begins.
When the country falls into chaos,
patriotism is born.

19

Throw away holiness and wisdom
and people will be a hundred times happier.
Throw away morality and justice,
and people will do the right thing.
Throw away industry and profit,
and there won't be any thieves . . .

36

If you want to shrink something,
you must first allow it to expand.

If you want to get rid of something,
you must first allow it to flourish.
If you want to take something,
you must first allow it to be given.
This is called the subtle perception
of the way things are.

The soft overcomes the hard.
The slow overcomes the fast.
Let your workings remain a mystery.
Just show people the results.

7. Self-Knowledge

33

Knowing others is intelligence;
knowing yourself is true wisdom.
Mastering others is strength;
mastering yourself is true power.

If you realize that you have enough,
you are truly rich . . .

8. Contentment

44

Fame or integrity: which is more important?
Money or happiness: which is more valuable?
Success or failure: which is more destructive?

If you look to others for fulfillment,
you will never truly be fulfilled.
If your happiness depends on money
you will never be happy with yourself.

Be content with what you have;
rejoice in the way things are.

When you realize there is nothing lacking,
the whole world belongs to you.

9. Simplicity, Patience, Compassion

67

Some say that my teaching is nonsense.
Other call it lofty but impractical.
But to those who have looked inside themselves,
this nonsense makes perfect sense.
And to those who put it into practice,
this loftiness has roots that go deep.

I have just three things to teach:
simplicity, patience, compassion.
These three are your greatest treasures.
Simple in actions and in thoughts,
you return to the source of being.
Patient with both friends and enemies,
you accord with the way thing are.
Compassionate toward yourself,
you reconcile all beings in the world.

CHUANG TZU: Roaming Beyond the Limits of This Dusty World

Somewhere in the writings of Chuang Tzu, an aged Confucius hears a description of sagehood that puzzles him: "The true sage pays no heed to mundane affairs. . . . He adheres, without questioning, to the Tao. Without speaking he can speak; and he can speak and yet say nothing. And so he roams beyond the limits of this dusty world." Shocked, Confucius sputters: "These are wild words."[3]

Wild they may be, but they are very likely the self-description of Chuang Tzu, who lived about two hundred years after the author of the Tao Te Ching. Rambunctious, irreverent, paradoxical, and, many say,

---

3. R. O. Ballou, *The Portable World Bible* (New York: Penguin, 1944), 555.

exceedingly subtle, his writings are the second most important source for philosophical Taoism.

10. The Unfathomable Source of Existence

If there was a beginning, then there was a time before that beginning. And a time before the time which was before the time of that beginning.

If there is existence, there must have been non-existence. And if there was a time when nothing existed, then there must have been a time before that—when even nothing did not exist. Suddenly, when nothing came into existence, could one really say whether it belonged to the category of existence or of non existence? Even the very words I have just now uttered,—I cannot say whether they have really been uttered or not.

11. The Unfathomable Source of Mind

Joy and anger, sorrow and happiness, caution and remorse, come upon us by turns, with ever-changing mood. They come like music from hollowness, like mushrooms from damp. Daily and nightly they alternate within us, but we cannot tell whence they spring. Can we then hope in a moment to lay our finger upon their very cause?

But for these emotions I should not be. But for me, they would have no scope. So far we can go; but we do not know what it is that brings them into play.

12. The Hidden Unity of Opposites and the Dumb Monkeys

Viewed from the standpoint of Tao, a beam and a pillar are identical. So are ugliness and beauty, greatness, wickedness, perverseness and strangeness. . . . Nothing is subject either to construction or to destruction, for these conditions are brought together into one.

Only the truly intelligent understand this principle of the identity of all things. They do not view things as apprehended by themselves, subjectively; but transfer themselves into the position of the things viewed. . . . So it is that to place oneself in subjective relation with externals, without consciousness of their objectivity—this is Tao. But to wear out one's intellect in an obstinate adherence to the individuality of things, not recognizing the fact that all things are one—this is called Three in the Morning.

"What is Three in the Morning?" asked Tze Yu.

A keeper of monkeys . . . said with regard to their rations of chestnuts that each monkey was to have three in the morning and four at night. But at this the monkeys were very angry, so the keeper said they might have four in the morning and three at night, with which arrangement they were all well pleased.

13. Relativity

a. Chuang Tzu and the Butterfly

Once upon a time, I, Chuang Tzu, dreamt I was a butterfly, fluttering hither and thither, to all intents and purposes a butterfly. I was conscious only of following my fancies as a butterfly, and was unconscious of my individuality as a man. Suddenly, I awoke, and there I lay, myself again. Now I do not know whether I was then a man dreaming I was a butterfly, or whether I am now a butterfly dreaming I am a man.

b. Can We Know the Good?

If a man sleeps in a damp place, he gets lumbago and dies. But how about an eel? And living up in a tree is precarious and trying to the nerves—but how about monkeys? Of the man, the eel, and the monkey, whose habitat is the right one, absolutely? Human beings feed on flesh, deer on grass, centipedes on snakes, owls and crows on mice. Of these four, whose is the right taste, absolutely? Monkey mates with monkey, the buck with the doe, eels consort with fishes, while men admire Mao Ch'iang and Li Chi, at the sight of whom fishes plunge deep down in the water, birds soar high in the air, and deer hurry away. Yet who shall say which is the correct standard of beauty? In my opinion, the standard of human virtue, and of positive and negative, is so obscured that it is impossible to actually know it as such.

14. Civilization and the Violation of Instinct

Horses have hoofs to carry them over frost and snow; hair, to protect them from wind and cold. They eat grass and drink water. . . . Such is the real nature of horses. Palatial dwellings are of no use to them.

One day Poh Loh appeared, saying, "I understand the management of horses."

So he branded them, and clipped them, and pared their hoofs, and put halters on them . . . with the result that two or three in every ten died. Then he kept them hungry and thirsty, trotting them and galloping them, and grooming, and trimming . . . until more than half of them were dead. Nevertheless, every age extols Poh Loh for his skill in managing horses. . . .

The people have certain natural instincts—to weave and clothe themselves, to till and feed themselves. These are common to all humanity, and all are agreed thereon. Such instincts are called "Heaven-sent."

And so in the days when natural instincts prevailed, men moved quietly and gazed steadily. At that time, there were no roads over mountains, nor boats, nor bridges over water. . . . You could climb up and peep into the raven's nest. For then man dwelt with birds and beasts, and all creation was one. There were no distinctions of good and bad men. Being all equally without knowledge, their virtue could not go astray. Being all equally without evil desires, they were in a state of natural integrity, the perfection of human existence.

But when sages appeared, tripping people over charity and fettering [them] with duty to one's neighbor, doubt found its way into the world. And then with their gushing over music and fussing over ceremony, the empire became divided against itself.

Horses live on dry land, eat grass and drink water. . . . Thus far only do their natural dispositions carry them. But bridled and bitted, with a plate of metal on their foreheads, they learn to cast vicious looks, to turn the head to bite, to resist, to get the bit out of the mouth or the bridle into it. And thus their natures become depraved,—the fault of Poh Loh.

In the days of Ho Hsu the people did nothing particular when at rest, and went nowhere in particular when they moved. Having food, they rejoiced; having full bellies, they strolled about. Such were the capacities of the people. But when the sages came to worry them with ceremonies and music in order to rectify the form of government, and dangled charity and duty to one's neighbor before them in order to satisfy their hearts—then the people began to develop a taste for knowledge and to struggle one with the other in their desire for gain. This was the error of the sages.

15. Creative Letting-Be and the Quiet Mind

The repose of the sage is not what the world calls repose. His repose is the result of his mental attitude. All creation could not disturb his equilibrium: hence his repose.

When water is still, it is like a mirror, reflecting the beard and the eyebrows. . . . And if water thus derives lucidity from stillness, how much more the faculties of the mind? The mind of the sage being in repose becomes the mirror of the universe, the speculum of all creation.

Repose, tranquility, stillness, inaction—these were the levels of the universe, the ultimate perfection of Tao. Therefore wise rulers and sages rest therein.

Repose, tranquility, stillness, inaction—these were the source of all things. Keep to this when coming forward to pacify a troubled world, and your merit shall be great and your name illustrious, and the empire united into one. In your repose you will be wise; in your movements, powerful. By inaction you will gain honour; and by confining yourself to the pure and simple, you will hinder the whole world from struggling with you for show.

16. Against the Promotion of Virtue

Confucius visited Lao Tze, and spoke of charity and duty to one's neighbor.

Lao Tzu said: "The chaff from winnowing will blind a man's eyes so that he cannot tell the points of the compass. Mosquitoes will keep a man awake all night with their biting. And just in the same way this talk of charity and duty to one's neighbor drives me nearly crazy. Sir! strive to keep the world to its own original simplicity. And as the wind bloweth where it listeth, so let virtue establish itself. Wherefore such undue energy, as though searching for a fugitive with a big drum?"

17. The Natural Life

Chuang Tzu was fishing in the P'u when the prince of Ch'u sent two high officials to ask him to take charge of the administration of the Ch'u State. Chuang Tzu went on fishing, and without turning his head said, "I have heard that in Ch'u there is a sacred tortoise which has been dead now some three thousand years. And that the prince keeps this tortoise carefully enclosed in a chest on the altar of his ancestral people. Now would this tortoise rather be dead and have its remains venerated, or be alive and wagging its tail in the mud?"

"It would rather be alive," replied the two officials. . . .

"Begone!" cried Chuang Tzu. "I too will wag my tail in the mud."

GRACE NOTES

18. Hua Hu Ching

The Hua Hu Ching is said to be Lao Tzu's other book—a collection of his oral teachings on wisdom and mastery. It is, at the very least, a contemporary poet's experiment with the Taoist spirit. Of the Hua Hu Ching's eighty-one chapters, excerpts of eleven are represented here.

a. Living in the Tao

6

. . . If you attempt to fix a picture of [the Tao] in your mind,
you will lose it.
This is like pinning a butterfly: the husk is captured,
but the flying is lost.

22

How can the divine Oneness be seen?
In beautiful forms, breathtaking wonders, awe-
inspiring miracles?
The Tao is not obliged to present itself in this way.

If you are willing to be lived by it, you will see it
everywhere, even in the most ordinary things.

75

Would you like to liberate yourself from the lower
realms of life?
Would you like to save the world from the degradation
and destruction it seems destined for?
Then step away from shallow mass movements and
quietly go to work on your own self-awareness.

If you want to awaken all of humanity, then awaken
all of yourself.
. . . Truly, the greatest gift you have to give is that of your
own self-transformation.

So find a teacher . . .
who extends his light and virtue with equal ease to
those who appreciate him and those who don't.
Shape yourself in his mold, bathe in his nourishing
radiance, and reflect it out to the rest of the world.

You will come to understand an eternal truth: there is
always a peaceful home for a virtuous being.

b. Balance

43

In ancient times, people lived holistic lives.
They didn't overemphasize the intellect, but
   integrated mind, body and spirit in all things.

. . . If you want to stop being confused, then emulate these
   ancient folk: join your body, mind and spirit in all
   you do.
Choose food, clothing and shelter that accords with
   nature.
Rely on your own body for transportation.
Allow your work and your recreation to be one and the same.
Do exercise that develops your whole being and not
   just your body.
. . . Serve others and cultivate yourself simultaneously.

Understand that true growth comes from meeting and
   solving the problems of life in a way that is
   harmonizing to yourself and to others.
If you can follow these simple old ways, you will be
   continually renewed.

58

Unless the mind, body and spirit are equally
   developed and fully integrated, no [wisdom] . . .
   can be sustained.
This is why extremist religions and ideologies do not
   bear fruit.

When the mind and spirit are forced into unnatural
   austerities or adherence to external dogmas, the
   body grows sick and weak and becomes a traitor to the
   whole being.
When the body is emphasized to the exclusion of the
   mind and spirit, they become like trapped snakes:
   frantic, explosive, poisonous to one's person.

All such imbalances inevitably lead to exhaustion and
expiration of the life force.

c. The Quiet Mind

5

Do you imagine the universe is agitated?
Go into the desert at night and look out at the stars.
This practice should answer the question.

44

This is the nature of the unenlightened mind:
The sense organs, which are limited in scope and
ability, randomly gather information.
This partial information is arranged into judgements,
which are based on previous judgements,
which are usually based on someone's else's foolish
ideas.
These false concepts and ideas are then stored in a
highly selective memory system.

Distortion upon distortion: the mental energy flows
constantly through contorted and inappropriate
channels, and the more one uses the mind, the more
confused one becomes.

To eliminate the vexation of the mind, it doesn't help
to *do* something; this only reinforces the mind's
mechanics.
Dissolving the mind is instead a matter of not-doing:
Simply avoid becoming attached to what you see and
think.
Relinquish the notion that you are separated from the
all-knowing mind of the universe.
Then you can recover your original pure insight and
see through all illusions.
Knowing nothing, you will be aware of everything.

Remember: because clarity and enlightenment are
within your own nature, they are regained without
moving an inch.

d. Truth

38

Why scurry about looking for the truth?
. . . Can you be still and see it in the mountain? the pine
tree? yourself?

Don't imagine that you'll discover it by accumulating
more knowledge.
Knowledge creates doubt, and doubt makes you
ravenous for more knowledge.
You can't get full eating this way.
The wise person dines on something more subtle:
He eats the understanding that the named was born
from the unnamed, that all being flows from non-
being, that the describable world emanates from an
indescribable source.
He finds this subtle truth inside his own self, and
becomes completely content.

So who can be still and watch the chess game of the
world?
The foolish are always making impulsive moves, but
the wise know that victory and defeat are decided by
something more subtle.
They see that something perfect exists before any move
is made.

59

Greed for enlightenment and immortality is no
different than greed for material wealth . . .

e. True Teachers

80

The world is full of half-enlightened masters.
Overly clever, too "sensitive" to live in the real world,
they surround themselves with selfish pleasures and
bestow their grandiose teachings upon the unwary.
Prematurely publicizing themselves, intent upon

reaching some spiritual climax, they constantly
sacrifice the truth and deviate from the Tao.
What they really offer the world is their own
confusion.

The true master understands that enlightenment is not
the end but the means.
Realizing that virtue is her goal, she accepts the long
and often arduous cultivation that is necessary to
attain it.
She doesn't scheme to become a leader, but quietly
shoulders whatever responsibilities fall to her.

Unattached to her accomplishments, taking credit for
nothing at all, she guides the whole world by
guiding the individuals who come to her.
She shares her divine energy with her students,
encouraging them, creating trials to strengthen
them, scolding them to awaken them, directing the
streams of their lives toward the infinite ocean of
the Tao.

23

The highest truth cannot be put into words.
Therefore the greatest teacher has nothing to say.
He simply gives himself in service, and never worries.

CHAPTER FIVE

Judaism

*A*mong the world's major extant historical religions, *Judaism may well be the oldest. If we date its origin to the Exodus from Egypt some 3200 years ago, only certain aspects of Hinduism can claim equal antiquity. Across this sea of time, through triumph and catastrophe, the lifeline of the Jewish people has remained their Book.*

The Jewish Bible is properly called the Tanakh, *a word derived from the three consonants T, N, and K, standing for* Torah, Nevi'im, *and* Ketuvim, *respectively.* Torah *means "law" or "teaching"; broadly it refers to the whole of the Jewish Bible, more narrowly to its first five books—Genesis, Exodus, Leviticus, Numbers, and Deuteronomy.* Nevi'im, *or "prophets," refers to the twenty-one books that record the sayings and doings of those whose task it was to remind Israel of its relationship to God when it was in danger of forgetting it.* Ketuvim, *or "other writings," refers to the thirteen books that make up the Bible's balance. These three terms serve as section headings in this chapter and properly so, for most of the selections are biblical. It must never be forgotten, however, that in the Jewish view, God did not cease to speak to human beings when the last page of biblical ink was dry. In addition to the "written Torah" there is also the "oral Torah" or Talmud, a record of the ongoing task of study, commentary, and interpretation through which God's continuing communication to human partners is discerned.*

Judaism can be viewed as the evolution of a people in the grip of two toweringly great ideas. The first is the idea of One God—imageless, primordially creative, and utterly transcendent—who, nevertheless, cares for the creation. The second is the idea of human dignity: men and women become fully human only by responding to the moral intuitions divinely etched in their hearts. God calls us, Judaism says, into a sacred agreement or covenant in which respect for life and the promotion of justice are paramount concerns. Life's purpose is to be found in the healing of the world so that the world may then reflect, for the good of all, the radiance of its creative source.

The melding of these two ideas is sometimes called ethical monotheism. Through it Jews have found meaning in life and have helped others to do the same. Judaism is the parent tradition from which both Christianity and Islam spring.

TORAH: The Teaching

1. Creation

The Bible opens with an account of the creation of the world. Implicit in its opening line is the foundational Jewish belief in God as the ultimate source of all being. Judaism was perhaps five or six centuries old when priestly editors, drawing on other Near Eastern literature, composed this account as a prologue to the rest of the first five books.

a. The First Days of Creation

In the beginning God created heaven and earth—the earth being unformed and void, with darkness over the surface of the deep and a wind from God sweeping over the water—God said, "Let there be light"; and there was light. God saw that the light was good, and God separated the light from the darkness. God called the light Day, and the darkness He called Night. And there was evening and there was morning, a first day.

On successive days, sky and earth, vegetation, the sun and moon, creatures of sea and air, and creatures of land are brought into being. Then:

b. The Sixth Day: Humankind

The essential biblical doctrine of humanity and human dignity is found in the following text. To be "created in the image of God" is to be called to cocreate a just and merciful world.

And God created humankind in His image; . . . male and female He created them. God blessed them and said to them, "Be fertile and increase, fill the earth and master it. . . ."

God said, "See, I give you every seed-bearing plant that is upon all the earth, and every tree that has seed-bearing fruit; they shall be yours for food. And to all the animals on land, to all the birds of the sky, and to everything that creeps on earth, in which there is the breath of life, I give all the green plants for food." And it was so. And God saw all that He had made, and found it very good. And there was evening and there was morning, the sixth day.

c. The Seventh Day: Rest

Basic to Jewish faith is the observance of the Sabbath (see no. 38, below). Here ancient writers record its divine archetype.

The heaven and the earth were finished, and all their array. On the seventh day, God finished the work that He had been doing. . . . And God blessed the seventh day and declared it holy, because on it God ceased from all the work of creation that He had done.

2. The Garden of Eden and the Expulsion

Chapter 2 of Genesis contains a second account of the creation of humanity. It ponders the origins of human awareness, of moral responsibility, and of suffering and death.

a. The Garden, the Two Trees, and the Innocent Partners

The LORD God planted a garden in Eden. . . . And from the ground the LORD God caused to grow every tree that was pleasing to the sight and good for food, with the tree of life in the middle of the garden, and the tree of knowledge of good and bad.

. . . The LORD God took the man and placed him in the garden of Eden, to till it and tend it. And the LORD God commanded the man, saying, "Of every tree of the garden you are free to eat, but as for the tree of knowledge of good and bad, you must not eat of it; for as soon as you eat of it, you shall die."

The LORD God said, "It is not good for man to be alone; I will make a fitting helper for him.". . . So the LORD God cast a deep sleep upon the man; and while he slept, He took one of his ribs and closed up the flesh at that spot. And the LORD God fashioned the rib that He had taken from the man into a woman; and He brought her to the man. . . . The two of them were naked, the man and his wife, yet they felt no shame.

b. The Cost of Consciousness: The Expulsion

Now the serpent was the shrewdest of all the wild beasts that the LORD God had made. He said to the woman, "Did God really say: You shall not eat of any tree of the garden?" The woman replied to the serpent, "God said: 'You shall not eat of it or touch it, lest you die.'" And the serpent said, . . . "You are not going to die, but God knows that as soon as you eat of it your eyes will be opened and you will be like divine beings who know good and bad." When the woman saw that the tree was good for eating and . . . desirable as a source of wisdom, she took of its fruit and ate. She also gave some to her husband and he ate. Then the eyes of both of them were opened and they perceived that they were naked. . . .

They heard the sound of the LORD God moving about in the garden at the breezy time of day; and the man and his wife hid from the LORD God. . . . The LORD God called out to the man and said to him, "Where are you?" He replied, "I heard the sound of You in the garden, and I was afraid because I was naked, so I hid." Then He asked, "Who told you that you were naked? Did you eat of the tree from which I had forbidden you to eat?"

. . . And to the woman He said,

". . . In pain shall you bear children.

Yet your urge shall be for your husband,
And he shall rule over you."

To Adam He said,

". . . By the sweat of your brow shall you get bread to eat,
Until you return to the ground—
For from it you were taken.
For dust you are,
And to dust you shall return."

. . . And the LORD God said, "Now that the man has become like one of us, knowing good and bad, what if he should stretch out his hand and take also from the tree of life and eat, and live forever!" So the LORD God banished him from the garden of Eden, to till the soil from which he was taken.

3. The Universal Covenant with Noah

A key biblical theme is the tension between what ought to be and what is, between God's invitation to the moral life and the human failure to respond adequately thereto. Using the already ancient flood legend to make this moral point, the Noah story also introduces the idea of the covenant, *made here between God and all creatures. This is the first of three covenants that figure prominently in the Torah (see 4a, 4b, 10, and 10a).*

The LORD saw how great was man's wickedness on earth. . . . But Noah found favor with the LORD. . . .

. . . And when the waters had swelled on the earth one hundred and fifty days, God remembered Noah and . . . the waters subsided.

. . . And God said to Noah . . . "I now establish My covenant with you and your offspring to come, and with every living thing that is with you . . . : never again shall all flesh be cut off by the waters of a flood, and never again shall there be a flood to destroy the earth."

God further said, "This is the sign that I set for the covenant between Me and you, and every living creature with you, for all ages to come. I have set My bow in the clouds, and it shall serve as a sign of the covenant between Me and the earth."

4. The Origin of the Israelites: *The Story of Abraham*

Scholars refer to the first eleven chapters of Genesis as "primeval history," mythic accounts of cosmic and human origins. In chapter 12 the narrative shifts to the origins of the Israelites as a people. The story of Abraham is important for a number of reasons. First, as the original monotheist, he is considered the progenitor not only of Judaism, but of Christianity and Islam as well. Indeed, these three are sometimes called the Abrahamic religions.

Second, it is to Abraham that God promises many descendants and, just as importantly, land. "The notion of the Promised Land is peculiar to the Israelite religion and for the Israelites and Jews later, it was the most important single element in it. . . . No race has maintained over so long a period so emotional an attachment to a particular corner of the Earth's surface."[1] An understanding of the significance of the Promised Land[2] begins with these biblical passages.

Third, Abraham's story reveals the religious origins of the practice of circumcision.

Fourth, the story of Abraham's debate with God over the destruction of Sodom and Gomorrah reflects the Jewish conviction that human beings are cocreators of the moral universe. The human capacity for compassion and justice is special. Even God may have something to learn from it!

a. The Covenant with Abraham: The Promise of a Nation and a Land

The LORD said to Abram, "Go forth from your native land and from your father's house to the land that I will show you.

> I will make of you a great nation,
> And I will bless you."

. . . Abram passed through the land as far as the site of Shechem. . . . The Canaanites were then in the land. The LORD

---

1. Paul Johnson, *A History of the Jews* (New York: Harper & Row, 1987), 9, 4.
2. This land has had a number of names over three millennia: Canaan, Judah/Israel, and Palestine. Today, and since 1947, its name is Israel.

appeared to Abram and said, "I will assign this land to your off-spring." And he built an altar there to the LORD. . . .

. . . When Abram was ninety-nine years old, the LORD appeared to Abram and said to him, "I am El Shaddai. Walk in My ways and be blameless. I will establish My covenant between Me and you, and I will make you exceedingly numerous."

Abram threw himself on his face; and God spoke to him further. . . . "I will maintain My covenant between Me and you, and your offspring to come, as an everlasting covenant throughout the ages, to be God to you and to your offspring to come. I assign the land you sojourn in to you and your offspring to come, all the land of Canaan, as an everlasting holding. I will be their God."

b. Circumcision

"Such shall be the covenant between Me and you and your off-spring to follow which you shall keep: every male among you shall be circumcised. You shall circumcise the flesh of your foreskin, and that shall be the sign of the covenant between Me and you. And throughout the generations, every male among you shall be circumcised at the age of eight days. As for the homeborn slave and the one bought from an outsider who is not of your offspring, they must be circumcised, homeborn, and purchased alike. Thus shall My covenant be marked in your flesh as an everlasting pact."

. . . Then Abraham took his son Ishmael, and . . . every male in Abraham's household, and he circumcised the flesh of their fore-skins. . . . Abraham was ninety-nine years old when he circumcised the flesh of his foreskin, and his son Ishmael was thirteen years old. . . .

c. Abraham Softens God's Heart

Now the LORD had said, "Shall I hide from Abraham what I am about to do? . . ."

God is about to destroy the entire city of Sodom due to the wickedness of its inhabitants.

. . . Abraham came forward and said . . . "What if there should be fifty innocent within the city; will You then wipe out the place and not forgive it for the sake of the innocent fifty who are in it? Far be it from You to do such a thing, to bring death upon the innocent as well as the guilty, so that innocent and guilty fare alike. Far be it from You! Shall not the Judge of all the earth deal justly?" And the LORD answered, "If I find within the city of Sodom fifty innocent ones, I will forgive the whole place for their sake." Abraham spoke up, saying . . . "What if forty . . . What if thirty . . . What if twenty . . . What if ten should be found there?" And He answered, "I will not destroy, for the sake of the ten."

d. God Tests Abraham's Faith

Some time afterward, God put Abraham to the test. He said . . . "Take your son, your favored one, Isaac, whom you love, and go to the land of Moriah, and offer him there as a burnt offering on one of the heights that I will point out to you." So early next morning, Abraham . . . set out for the place of which God had told him. . . .

Then Isaac said to his father Abraham, "Father!" And he answered, "Yes, my son." And he said, "Here are the firestone and the wood; but where is the sheep for the burnt offering?" And Abraham said, "God will see to the sheep for His burnt offering, my son.". . . Abraham built an altar there; . . . he bound his son Isaac; he laid him on the altar, on top of the wood. And Abraham picked up the knife to slay his son. Then an angel of the LORD called to him from heaven: "Abraham! Abraham! . . . Do not raise your hand against the boy, or do anything to him. For now I know that you fear God, since you have not withheld your son, your favored one, from Me." When Abraham looked up, his eye fell upon a ram, caught in the thicket by its horns. So Abraham went and took the ram and offered it up as a burnt offering in place of his son.

5. Jacob Is Named Israel

Of Abraham's two sons, Ishmael and Isaac, Muslims claim descent through the former, Jews through the latter. Isaac's son, Jacob, is a pivotal figure, for it is his twelve sons who become the patriarchs of the twelve tribes of Israel. The word Israel *has its biblical origins in the fol-*

*lowing story, wherein Jacob is given it as a new name. One night, while
Jacob was alone in his encampment . . .*

. . . a man wrestled with him until the break of dawn. When he
saw that he had not prevailed against him, he wrenched Jacob's hip
at its socket. . . . Then he said, "Let me go, for dawn is breaking."
But he answered, "I will not let you go, unless you bless me." Said
the other, "What is your name?" He replied, "Jacob." Said he,
"Your name shall no longer be Jacob, but Israel, for you have
striven with beings divine and human and have prevailed."

6. The Israelites in Egypt

*One of Jacob's sons, Joseph, is sold into Egyptian slavery by his jealous
brothers. But Joseph prospers in Egypt, impressing the pharaoh with his
skill at interpreting dreams. When famine befalls the brothers, Joseph
ungrudgingly invites them and their clans to share in his prosperity.
Time passes, however, and regimes change. Joseph dies and new, less
sympathetic pharaohs come to power. In the course of four hundred
years, prosperity gives way to oppression. Enter Moses, the liberator
and arch-prophet of the Israelites.*

7. Moses Is Called

The king of Egypt [had] died. The Israelites were groaning under
the bondage and cried out; . . . God heard their moaning, and God
remembered His covenant with Abraham and Isaac and Jacob.
Now Moses, tending the flock of his father-in-law Jethro . . . came
to Horeb, the mountain of God. An angel of the LORD appeared to
him in a blazing fire out of a bush. He gazed, and there was a bush
all aflame, yet the bush was not consumed. . . . God called to him
out of the bush: "Moses! Moses!" He answered, "Here I am." And
He said, "Do not come closer. Remove your sandals from your feet,
for the place on which you stand is holy ground. I am," He said,
"the God of your father, the God of Abraham, the God of Isaac,
and the God of Jacob." And Moses hid his face, for he was afraid to
look at God.

And the LORD continued, "I have marked well the plight of My people in Egypt. . . . Yes, I am mindful of their sufferings. I have come down to rescue them from the Egyptians and to bring them out of that land to a . . . land flowing with milk and honey, the region of the Canaanites, the Hittites, the Amorites, the Perizzites, the Hivites, and the Jebusites. . . . Come, therefore, I will send you to Pharaoh, and you shall free My people, the Israelites, from Egypt."

8. God Identifies Himself

Moses said to God, "When I come to the Israelites and say to them 'The God of your fathers has sent me to you,' and they ask me, 'What is His name?' what shall I say to them?" And God said to Moses, "Ehyeh-Asher-Ehyeh." He continued, "Thus shall you say to the Israelites, 'Ehyeh[3] sent me to you.'" And God said further to Moses, "Thus shall you speak to the Israelites: The LORD, the God of your fathers, the God of Abraham, the God of Isaac, and the God of Jacob, has sent me to you:

This shall be My name forever,
This My appellation for all eternity."

9. Passover and Exodus

The pharaoh rejects Moses' demands for emancipation even though calamities befall his land as a result. However, a final calamity—the sudden death of all of Egypt's firstborn—proves too much for him. The Israelites, in order to ensure that death harmlessly passes over their own firstborn, are instructed in certain observances, including a special meal (seder) *on the eve of their exodus from Egypt.*

Every year Jews the world over gather for a seder in commemoration of this pivotal moment in their history. One of the texts recited at this time asks: "Why is this night different from all other nights?" The reply is: "Because we were slaves unto the pharaoh in Egypt, and the

---

3. This word has sometimes been translated as "I AM."

Eternal our God brought us forth thence with a mighty hand and an outstretched arm." What the Passover Seder celebrates, it may be suggested, is not only the historical liberation of a people but also the perennial longing of the human soul for spiritual freedom.

a. Passover Instructions

The LORD said to Moses and Aaron in the land of Egypt: This month shall mark for you the beginning of the months; it shall be the first of the months of the year for you. Speak to the whole community of Israel and say that on the tenth of this month each of them shall take a lamb to a family, a lamb to a household . . . and all the assembled congregation of the Israelites shall slaughter it at twilight. They shall take some of the blood and put it on the two doorposts and the lintel of the houses in which they are to eat it. They shall eat the flesh that same night; they shall eat it roasted over the fire, with unleavened bread and with bitter herbs. . . .

This is how you shall eat it: your loins girded, your sandals on your feet, and your staff in your hand; and you shall eat it hurriedly: it is a passover offering to the LORD. For that night I will go through the land of Egypt and strike down every first-born in the land of Egypt, both man and beast; and I will mete out punishments to all the gods of Egypt, I the LORD. And the blood on the houses where you are staying shall be a sign for you: when I see the blood I will pass over you, so that no plague will destroy you when I strike the land of Egypt.

This day shall be to you one of remembrance: you shall celebrate it as a festival to the LORD throughout the ages; you shall celebrate it as an institution for all time. Seven days you shall eat unleavened bread; on the very first day you shall remove leaven from your houses, for whoever eats leavened bread from the first day to the seventh day, that person shall be cut off from Israel.

. . . The Israelites journeyed from Raamses to Succoth, about six hundred thousand men [and women] on foot, aside from children. . . . The length of time that the Israelites lived in Egypt was four hundred and thirty years; at the end of the four hundred and thirtieth year, to the very day, all the ranks of the LORD departed from the land of Egypt. . . . That same night is the LORD's, one of vigil for all the children of Israel throughout the ages.

b. Deliverance

The LORD stiffened the heart of the Pharaoh king of Egypt, and he gave chase to the Israelites. [He] overtook them encamped by the sea. . . .

. . . Then Moses held out his arm over the sea and the LORD drove back the sea with a strong east wind all that night and turned the sea into dry ground. The waters were split, and the Israelites went into the sea on dry ground, the waters forming a wall for them on their right and on their left. The Egyptians came in pursuit of them into the sea. . . .

Then the LORD said to Moses, "Hold out your arm over the sea, that the waters may come back upon the Egyptians and upon their chariots and upon their horsemen." Moses held out his arm over the sea, and at daybreak the sea returned to its normal state. . . . The Pharaoh's entire army that followed them into the sea; not one of them remained. . . . Thus the LORD delivered Israel that day from the Egyptians.

10. The Covenant at Sinai

Three months out of Egypt, in the wilderness of Sinai, Israel pitches camp. Through Moses God proposes to Israel a final covenant whose terms are fundamentally moral: I will be your God if you will be a righteous people. It is, by any measure, one of the greatest moments in all of Jewish history. In the words of Nobel laureate Elie Wiesel:

> *Think about it. God decided for the first and last time . . . to reveal himself. . . . You would expect God to give you a lecture on theology at least. After all it's his domain. . . . Instead . . . He gave you all kind of commands about human relations: Thou shall not kill; Thou shall not lie; . . . Why did he do that? It was so simple. But* this *was the lesson: God can take care of himself. What he had to give man was the dignity of man.*[4]

---

4. From the film *The Chosen People,* in the British Broadcasting System's educational series *The Long Search.*

a. The Ten Commandments

And Moses went up to God. The LORD called to him from the mountain, saying, "Thus shall you say to the house of Jacob and declare to the children of Israel: 'You have seen what I did to the Egyptians, how I bore you on eagles' wings and brought you to Me. Now then, if you will obey Me faithfully and keep My covenant, you shall be My treasured possession among all the peoples. Indeed, all the earth is Mine, but you shall be to Me a kingdom of priests and a holy nation.' These are the words that you shall speak to the children of Israel."

. . . God spoke all these words, saying:

I the LORD am your God who brought you out of the land of Egypt, the house of bondage: You shall have no other gods beside Me.

You shall not make for yourself a sculptured image, or any likeness of what is in the heavens above, or on the earth below, on in the waters under the earth. You shall not bow down to them or serve them. For I the LORD your God am an impassioned God, visiting the guilt of the parents upon the children, upon the third and upon the fourth generations of those who reject Me, but showing kindness to the thousandth generation of those who love Me and keep My commandments.

You shall not swear falsely by the name of the LORD your God; for the LORD will not clear one who swears falsely by His name.

Remember the sabbath day and keep it holy. Six days you shall labor and do all your work, but the seventh day is a sabbath of the LORD your God: you shall not do any work—you, your son or daughter, your male or female slave, or your cattle, or the stranger who is within your settlements. For in six days the LORD made heaven and earth and sea, and all that is in them, and He rested on the seventh day; therefore the LORD blessed the sabbath day and hallowed it.

Honor your father and your mother, that you may long endure on the land that the LORD your God is assigning you.

You shall not murder.

You shall not commit adultery.

You shall not steal.

You shall not bear false witness against your neighbor.

You shall not covet your neighbor's house; you shall not covet your neighbor's wife, or . . . anything that is your neighbor's.

b. The Promise

Know, therefore, that only the LORD your God is God, the stead-fast God who keeps His covenant faithfully to the thousandth generation of those who love Him and keep His commandments. . . . And if you obey these rules and observe them carefully, the LORD your God will maintain faithfully for you the covenant that He made on oath with your fathers: He will favor you and bless you and multiply you; He will bless the issue of your womb and the produce of your soil . . . in the land that He swore to your fathers to assign to you.

11. Other Laws

The terms of the covenant at Sinai consist not only of the Ten Commandments but of some six hundred and thirteen other laws governing various phases of life. Jews differ on the matter of how many of these laws remain relevant, but the following verses from Exodus, Leviticus, and Deuteronomy suggest some of the perennially relevant moral attitudes of Judaism. (For a separate note on Jewish dietary practices see this chapter's Grace Notes, selection 35.)

a. Concern for the Unfortunate

You shall not ill-treat any widow or orphan. If you do mistreat them, I will heed their outcry as soon as they cry out to Me.

If you lend money to My people, to the poor among you, do not act toward them as a creditor: exact no interest from them.

You shall not oppress a stranger, for you know the feelings of the stranger, having yourselves been strangers in the land of Egypt.

When you reap the harvest of your land, you shall not reap all the way to the edges of your field, or gather the gleanings of your harvest. You shall not pick your vineyard bare, or gather the fallen fruit of your vineyard; you shall leave them for the poor and the stranger: I the LORD am your God.

For the LORD your God . . . shows no favor and takes no bribe, but upholds the cause of the fatherless and the widow, and befriends the stranger, providing him with food and clothing. You too must befriend the stranger, for you were strangers in the land of Egypt.

You shall not insult the deaf, or place a stumbling block before the blind. You shall fear your God: I am the LORD.

If . . . there is a needy person among you . . . do not harden your heart and shut your hand against your needy kinsman. Rather, you must open your hand and lend him sufficient for whatever he needs. For there will never cease to be needy ones in your land, which is why I command you: open your hand to the poor and needy. . . .

When you reap the harvest in your field and overlook a sheaf in the field, do not turn back to get it; . . . When you beat down the fruit of your olive trees, do not go over them again; . . . When you gather the grapes of your vineyard, do not pick it over again; [all of] that shall go to the stranger, the fatherless and the widow.

Six years you shall sow your land and gather in its yield; but in the seventh you shall let it rest and lie fallow. Let the needy among your people eat of it, and what they leave let the wild beasts eat. You shall do the same with your vineyards and your olive groves.

b. The Sacredness of Lifeblood

For the life of all flesh— its blood is its life. Therefore I say to the Israelite people: You shall not partake of the blood of any flesh. . . . And if any Israelite or any stranger who resides among them hunts down an animal or a bird that may be eaten, he shall pour out its blood and cover it with earth.

Do not deal basely with your countrymen. Do not profit by the blood of your fellow: I am the LORD.

One who kills a beast shall make restitution for it; but one who kills a human being shall be put to death.

c. Stewardship of the Earth

The LORD spoke to Moses on Mount Sinai: Speak to the Israelite people and say to them:

. . . Six years you may sow your field and six years you may prune your vineyard and gather in the yield. But in the seventh year the land shall have a sabbath of complete rest, a sabbath of the LORD: . . . it shall be a year of complete rest for the land.

When you enter the land and plant any tree for food, you shall regard its fruit as forbidden. [For] three years it shall be forbidden. . . . In the fourth year all its fruit shall be set aside for jubilation before the LORD; and only in the fifth year may you use its fruit—that its yield to you may be increased: I the LORD am your God.

d. Social Relations

When you encounter your enemy's ox . . . wandering, you must take it back to him. When you see the [donkey] of your enemy lying under its burden and would refrain from raising it, you must nevertheless raise it with him.

You shall not defraud your fellow. You shall not commit robbery. The wages of a laborer shall not remain with you until morning.

You shall not render an unfair decision: do not favor the poor or show deference to the rich; judge your kinsman fairly.

You shall not hate your kinsfolk in your heart. Reprove your kinsman but incur no guilt because of him. You shall not take vengeance or bear a grudge against your countrymen. Love your fellow as yourself: I am the LORD.

12. The Death of Moses

It was common for ancient cultures to deify their human heroes. It is therefore a testament to the monotheism and consequent iconoclasm of the Jewish tradition that the temptation to deify Moses, the great liberator and prophet of prophets, was resisted.

As if to preclude a cult in his name, Moses dies before entering the Promised Land, away from his people, in an unknown grave.

Moses went up from the steppes of Moab to Mount Nebo . . . and the LORD showed him the whole land. . . . The LORD said to him, "This is the land of which I swore to Abraham, Isaac, and Jacob, 'I will assign it to your offspring.' I have let you see it with your own eyes, but you shall not cross there." So Moses the servant of the LORD died there. . . at the command of the LORD. He buried him in the valley in the land of Moab, near Beth-peor; and no one knows his burial place to this day. . . . Never again did there arise in Israel a prophet like Moses—whom the LORD singled out, face to face.

NEVI'IM: The Prophets

It has been said that "the overall theme of the biblical narrative is Israel's successes and failures—mainly failures—in fulfilling the divine demands," and that the unblinking candor with which Israel exposes its own shortcomings makes the Bible a "national epic of self-criticism."[5] As such the Bible stands without peer in the literature of the world. In taking Israel to task for its failings, in measuring its realities against sacred ideals, the prophets initiated the tradition of moral critique that we now recognize as the soul of a just society.

The prophets were the spiritual antennae of Israel, monitoring its fidelity to the covenant. They castigated Israel not only for its repeated lapses into idolatry, but still more for its neglect of social justice and

---

5. Robert Seltzer, *Jewish People, Jewish Thought* (New York: Macmillan, 1980), 10, 108.

charity. For the prophets, the heart of religion is moral action, not ritual or lip-service. "No other sacred scripture contains books that speak out against social injustice as eloquently, unequivocally and sensitively."⁶ The prophets are one in their conviction that "every human being, simply by virtue of his or her humanity, is a child of God and therefore in possession of rights that even kings must respect."⁷

13. Visions and Callings

a. Isaiah's Vision

In the year that King Uzziah died, I beheld my Lord seated on a high and lofty throne; and the skirts of His robe filled the Temple. Seraphs stood in attendance on Him. Each of them had six wings: with two he covered his face, with two he covered his legs, and with two he would fly.

And one would call to the other,

> "Holy, holy, holy! The LORD of Hosts!
> His presence fills all the earth!"
> . . . I cried, "Woe is me; I am lost!
> For I am a man of unclean lips
> And I live among a people of unclean lips;
> Yet my own eyes have beheld the King LORD of Hosts."

b. Isaiah's Calling

Then one of the seraphs flew over to me with a live coal, which he had taken from the altar with a pair of tongs. He touched it to my lips and declared,

> "Now that this has touched your lips,
> Your guilt shall depart
> And your sin be purged away."

---

6. Walter Kaufmann, *Religions in Four Dimensions* (New York: Reader's Digest Press, 1976), 42.
7. Huston Smith, *The World's Religions* (San Francisco: HarperSanFrancisco, 1991), 292.

Then I heard the voice of my Lord saying, "Whom shall I send? Who will go for us?" And I said, "Here am I; send me."

c. Ezekiel's Vision

In the thirtieth year, on the fifth day of the fourth month, when I was in the community of exiles by the Chebar Canal, the heavens opened and I saw visions of God. . . . I looked, and lo, a stormy wind came sweeping out of the north—a huge cloud and flashing fire, surrounded by a radiance; and . . . in the center of the fire, a gleam as of amber. In the center of it were also the figures of four creatures. And this was their appearance:

They had the figures of human beings. However, each had four faces, and each of them had four wings. . . .

They had human hands below their wings. . . . Each one's wings touched those of the other. They did not turn when they moved; each could move in the direction of any of its faces.

Each of them had a human face [at the front] . . . the face of a lion on the right . . . the face of an ox on the left . . . and the face of an eagle [at the back]. . . . They went wherever the spirit impelled them to go. . . .

. . . With them was something that looked like burning coals of fire . . . and lightning issued from the fire.

. . . Above the heads of the creatures was a form: an expanse, with an awe-inspiring gleam as of crystal. . . . Above the expanse . . . was the semblance of a throne, in appearance like sapphire; and on top, upon this semblance of a throne, there was the semblance of a human form.

d. Ezekiel's Calling

Like the appearance of the bow which shines in the clouds on a day of rain, such was the . . . surrounding radiance. That was the . . . semblance of the Presence of the LORD. When I beheld it, I flung myself down on my face. And I heard the voice of someone speaking.

And He said to me, "O mortal, stand up on your feet that I may speak to you." As He spoke to me, a spirit entered into me and set me upon my feet; and I heard what was being spoken to me. He said to me, "O mortal, I am sending you to the people of Israel, that nation of rebels, who have rebelled against Me.—They as well as their fathers have defied Me to this very day; for the sons are brazen of face and stubborn of heart. I send you to them, and you shall say to them: 'Thus said the Lord GOD'. . . that they may know that there was a prophet among them.

"And you, mortal, do not fear them and do not fear their words, though thistles and thorns press against you, and you sit upon scorpions. Do not be . . . dismayed by them, though they are a rebellious breed; but speak My words to them, whether they listen or not, for they are rebellious."

14. Isaiah Chastises Israel for Ignoring the Covenant

Isaiah prophesied in Jerusalem between 742 and 701 B.C.E. During this time the Israelite kingdoms were victims of Assyrian might. Isaiah interprets this misfortune as the result of Israel's immorality and lack of fidelity to the covenant.

Hear, O heavens, and give ear, O earth,
For the LORD has spoken:
"I reared children and brought them up—
And they have rebelled against Me!
An ox knows its owner,
An ass its master's crib:
Israel does not know,
My people take no thought."

Ah, sinful nation!
People laden with iniquity!
Brood of evildoers!
Depraved children!
They have forsaken the LORD,
Spurned the Holy One of Israel,
Turned their backs.

. . . Your land is a waste,
Your cities burnt down;
Before your eyes, the yield of your soil

Is consumed by strangers—
A wasteland as overthrown by strangers!

15. Kings Are Not Above the Moral Law: *The Prophet Nathan Chastises King David*

After King David has Uriah the Hittite killed so that he can sleep with Uriah's wife, Bathsheba, Nathan visits David and tells him about a rich man who, rather than select one of his own many sheep to feed a guest, steals and butchers the sole, beloved sheep of a poor neighbor.

David flew into a rage against the [rich] man, and said to Nathan, "As the LORD lives, the man who did this deserves to die! He shall pay for the lamb four times over, because he did such a thing and showed no pity." And Nathan said to David, "That man is you! Thus said the LORD, the God of Israel: 'It was I who anointed you king over Israel. . . . I gave you your master's house and possession of your master's wives; and I gave you the House of Israel and Judah. . . . Why then have you flouted the command of the LORD and done what displeases Him? . . .'"

16. Hosea: *Against Idolatry*

Hosea lived a generation before Isaiah in the first half of the eighth century B.C.E. and was a contemporary of Isaiah's father, the prophet Amos. Here Hosea decries idolatry, the chronic human tendency to make gods out of things that are not God.

a. My People Obey Their Lusts

Hear the word of the LORD,
O people of Israel!
For the LORD has a case
Against the inhabitants of this land,
Because there is no honesty and no goodness
And no obedience to God in the land.

. . . My people . . .
consults its stick,

Its rod directs it!
A lecherous impulse has made them go wrong,
And they have strayed from submission to their God.
They sacrifice on the mountaintops
And offer on the hills,
Under oaks, poplars, and terebinths
Whose shade is so pleasant . . .

b. Sow the Wind, Reap the Whirlwind

They have made kings,
But not with My sanction;
They have made officers,
But not of My choice.
Of their silver and gold
They have made themselves images,
To their own undoing.

. . . They sow wind,
And they shall reap whirlwind—
. . . Israel is bewildered;
They have now become among the nations
Like an unwanted vessel . . .

17. Against Empty Ritual: *True Religion Is Righteousness and Justice*

a. Hosea

For I desire goodness, not sacrifice;
Obedience to God, rather than burnt offerings.

b. Isaiah

"What need have I of all your sacrifices?"
Says the LORD.

"I am sated with burnt offerings of rams,
And suet of fatlings,
And blood of bulls;
. . . Your new moons and fixed seasons
Fill Me with loathing;
They are become a burden to Me,
I cannot endure them.
And when you lift up your hands,
I will turn My eyes away from you;
Though you pray at length,
I will not listen.
Your hands are stained with crime—
Wash yourselves clean;
Put your evil doings
Away from My sight.
Cease to do evil;
Learn to do good.
Devote yourselves to justice;
Aid the wronged.
Uphold the rights of the orphan;
Defend the cause of the widow."

c. Isaiah

The LORD will bring this charge
Against the elders and officers of his people:
. . . "It is you who have ravaged the vineyard;
That which was robbed from the poor is in your houses.
How dare you crush My people
And grind the faces of the poor?"

d. Amos

Spare me the sound of your songs,
I cannot endure the music of your lutes.
But let justice roll on like a river,
And righteousness like an ever-flowing stream.

e. Micah

With what shall I approach the LORD . . . ?
Shall I approach Him with burnt offerings,
With calves a year old?

. . . He has told you, O man, what is good,
And what the LORD requires of you:
Only to do justice
And to love goodness,
And to walk modestly with your God.

18. Awaiting the Messiah

The prophets did not only look down in righteous indignation; they looked forward in hope for a time when peace and justice would reign and people would live in full cognizance of their sacred birthright. Hope was sometimes personified in the figure of a coming Messiah, and sometimes it was linked to the dawning of a messianic age, alternately conceived as either continuous with present history or as an apocalyptic end of the world resulting in a new order of things. If any themes can be said to be persistent in the long and complex history of messianic expectation, they are Israel's hope for its own spiritual restoration and, sometimes, for a more universal transformation "in which there would be political freedom, moral perfection and earthly bliss for [both] the people of Israel in their own land and also for the entire human race."[8]

a. Isaiah: The Messiah Will Usher In Universal Peace

Thus He will judge among the nations
And arbitrate for the many people,
And they shall beat their swords into plowshares
And their spears into pruning hooks:
Nation shall not take up

---

8. Joseph Klausner, *The Messianic Idea in Israel* (New York: Macmillan, 1955), 9.

Sword against nation;
They shall never again know war.

b. Isaiah: The Messiah Will Bring Order, Justice, and Peace

But a shoot shall grow out of the stump of Jesse,
A twig shall sprout from his stock.
The spirit of the LORD shall alight upon him:
A spirit of wisdom and insight,
A spirit of counsel and valor,
A spirit of devotion and reverence for the LORD.
. . . Integrity is the loincloth round his waist,
Faithfulness the belt about his hips.
The wolf shall dwell with the lamb,
The leopard lie down with the kid;
The calf, the beast of prey, and the fatling together,
With a little boy to herd them.
. . . A babe shall play
Over a viper's hole,
And an infant pass his hand over an adder's den.
In all of My sacred mount
Nothing evil or vile shall be done;
For the land shall be filled with devotion to the LORD
As water covers the sea.

c. Isaiah: An Image of the Dawning of the Messianic Age and the Restoration of Israel

A voice rings out:
"Clear in the desert
A road for the LORD!
Level in the wilderness
A highway for our God!
Let every valley be raised,
Every hill and mount made low.
Let the rugged ground become level
And the ridges become a plain.

The Presence of the LORD shall appear,
And all flesh, as one, shall behold—
For the LORD Himself has spoken.

. . . But you, Israel, My servant,
. . . Fear not, for I am with you,
Be not frightened, for I am your God;
I strengthen you and I help you,
I uphold you with My victorious right hand.

. . . Fear not, for I will redeem you;
I have singled you out by name,
You are Mine.
. . . I will bring your folk from the East,
Will gather you out of the West;
I will say to the North, "Give back!"
And to the South, "Do not withhold!
Bring My sons from afar,
And My daughters from the end of the earth. . . ."

d. Ezekiel: Suffering and Dispersion Will One Day End in Restoration

So I poured out My wrath on them for the blood which they shed upon their land, and for the fetishes with which they defiled it. I scattered them among the nations, and they were dispersed through the countries: I punished them in accordance with their ways and their deeds.

. . . But you, O mountains of Israel, shall yield your produce and bear your fruit for My people Israel, for their return is near. For I will care for you: I will turn to you, and you shall be tilled and sown. I will settle a large population on you, the whole House of Israel; the towns shall be resettled, and the ruined sites rebuilt. I will multiply men and beasts upon you, and they shall increase and be fertile, and I will resettle you as you were formerly, and will make you more prosperous than you were at first. And you shall know that I am the LORD.

. . . I will take you from among the nations and gather you from all the countries, and I will bring you back to your own land. I will

sprinkle clean water upon you, and you shall be clean: I will cleanse
you from all your uncleanness and from all your fetishes. And I will
give you a new heart and put a new spirit into you: I will remove
the heart of stone from your body and give you a heart of flesh; and
I will put My spirit into you. Thus I will cause you to follow My
laws and faithfully to observe My rules. Then you shall dwell in the
land which I gave to your fathers, and you shall be My people and
I will be your God.

KETUVIM: Other Writings

*The third category of the Tanakh contains a wide variety of literary
works from different periods of early Jewish history. Below are selections from four: Psalms, Proverbs, Job, and Ecclesiastes.*

19. Psalms

*The book of Psalms is the principal collection of religious lyrical poetry
in the Bible. Selections from Psalms figure prominently in Jewish
prayer books. Unlike the prophetic books, the psalms do not protest social justice or interpret Israel's defeats as consequences of faithlessness to
the covenant. The psalms are concerned, rather, with the expression of
religious emotion. Traditionally, psalms have been categorized either as
hymns, laments, or thanksgiving songs. The headings used below are
Lament, Celebration, and Contemplative Gratitude.*

Lament

a. How Long, O Lord?

How long, O LORD; will You ignore me forever?
How long will You hide Your face from me?
. . . Look at me, answer me, O LORD, my God!

b. Why Have You Forsaken Me?

My God, my God, why have You deserted me?
How far from saving me, the words I groan!

c. My Soul Thirsts for God

As a doe longs
    for running streams,
So longs my soul
    for you, my God
My soul thirsts for God,
    the God of life;
When shall I go to see
    the face of God?

d. How Can We Sing in a Strange Land?

By the rivers of Babylon—,
    there we sat down and there we wept,
    when we remembered Zion.
On the willows there
    we hung up our harps.
For there our captors asked us for songs,
    and our tormentors asked for mirth, saying,
"Sing us one of the songs of Zion!"
How could we sing the LORD's song in a foreign land?

Celebration

e. Happy Are the Good

Happy is the man
    who does not take the wicked for his guide,
    nor walk the road that sinners tread,
    nor take his seat among the scornful;
    the law of the LORD is his delight,
    the law his meditation night and day.
      He is like a tree
        planted beside a watercourse,
        which yields its fruit in season,
        and its leaf never withers . . .
Wicked men are not like this;
    they are like chaff driven by the wind.

f. The Silent Eloquence of the World

The heavens declare the glory of God,
   the sky proclaims His handiwork.
Day to day makes utterance,
   night to night speaks out.
There is no utterance,
   there are no words,
[Yet] their voice carries throughout the earth . . .

g. The Joyful Noise

Make a joyful noise to God, all the earth;
   sing the glory of his name . . .

h. This Is the Day the Lord Has Made

This is the day that the LORD has made—
   let us rejoice and be glad . . .

i. How Good It Is to Be Together!

How good and how pleasant it is
   that kindred dwell together.
It is like fine oil on the head
   running down onto the beard,
   the beard of Aaron,
   that comes down over the collar of his robe.

Contemplative Gratitude

j. Those Who Worship Things Become like Them

Why should the nations say: "Where is their God?"
Our God is in heaven; He does whatever He wills.

Their idols are silver and gold, made by human hands.
They have a mouth and cannot speak, eyes and cannot see.
They have ears and cannot hear, a nose and cannot smell.
They have hands and cannot feel, feet and cannot walk.
They cannot make a sound in their throat.

Their makers shall become like them; [and] all who trust in
them.

k. A Little Lower than God

. . . what are human beings that You have been mindful of
them,
mortals that You have taken note of them,
that You have made them little less than divine,
and adorned them with glory and majesty?

l. If I Lift Up My Eyes to the Hills

If I lift up my eyes to the hills,
where shall I find help?
Help comes only from the LORD,
maker of heaven and earth.

m. We Are but a Moment Here

O Lord, You have been our refuge in every generation.
Before the mountains came into being,
before You brought forth the earth and the world,
from eternity to eternity You are God.

You return man to dust;
You decreed, "Return you mortals!"
For in Your sight a thousand years
are like yesterday that has past,
like a watch of the night.
You engulf men in sleep;
at daybreak they are like grass that renews itself;
at daybreak it flourishes anew;
by dusk it withers and dries up.

n. You Are Always with Me

O LORD, You have examined me and know me.
When I sit down or stand up You know it;
You discern my thoughts from afar.

You observe my walking and reclining,
 and are familiar with all my ways,
There is not a word on my tongue
 but that You, O LORD, know it well.
. . . It is beyond my knowledge;
 it is a mystery; I cannot fathom it,
Where can I escape from Your spirit?
Where can I flee from Your presence?
If I ascend to heaven, You are there;
 if I descend to Sheol, You are there too.
If I take wing with the dawn
 to come to rest on the western horizon,
 even there Your hand will be guiding me,
 Your right hand will be holding me fast.
If I say, "Surely darkness will conceal me,
 night will provide me with cover,"
 darkness is not dark for You;
 night is as light as day;
 darkness and light are the same.
It was You who created my conscience,
 You fashioned me in my mother's womb.
I praise You,
 for I am awesomely, wondrously made . . .

o. The Lord Is My Shepherd, I Shall Not Want

The LORD is my shepherd, I shall not want.
He makes me lie down in green pastures;
 He leads me to water in places of repose;
 he renews my life;
He guides me in right paths
 as befits His name.

Though I walk through a valley of deepest darkness,
 I fear no harm, for You are with me;
 Your rod and Your staff—they comfort me.

You spread a table for me in full view of my enemies;
 You anoint my head with oil;
 my cup overflows.

Surely goodness and mercy shall follow me
    all the days of my life,
and I shall dwell in the house of the LORD
    my whole life long.

20. Proverbs

For the biblical sages, truth is disclosed not only in divine revelation but also in the regularities of daily life. Skill in negotiating the ways of the world is the concern of Proverbs. References to the larger Jewish story are absent here; instead we confront maxims and aphorisms aimed at social harmony and a happy life. A brief sampling:

The beginning of wisdom is this: get wisdom;
With all your getting, get insight.

Go to the ant, you sluggard,
Study its ways and learn.

A gentle response allays wrath;
A harsh word provokes anger.

He who satisfies others shall himself be sated.

He who loves discipline loves knowledge;
stupid is the person who hates correction.

The wise are grateful for a rebuke.

Pride goes before ruin,
Arrogance, before failure.

A base fellow gives away secrets,
But a trustworthy soul keeps a confidence.

As a dog returns to his vomit,
So a fool repeats his folly.

21. The Book of Job

An acknowledged masterpiece of world literature, the book of Job is a sustained reflection on the nature of genuine religious faith. It squarely faces the possibility that in the grand scheme of things God neither re-

wards persons for their faith and virtue nor punishes them for lack thereof. At the heart of the inquiry lies the problem of evil: if God is all-good and all-powerful, why do bad things happen to good people? Will the apparent injustices of this life ultimately be balanced by a cosmic justice? The answer that the book of Job gives to these questions— or whether it can be said to give an answer at all—remains a matter of controversy. (See editorial comment preceding selection 21c.) At the outset of the book, the virtuous Job suffers the death of his ten children and the devastation of his property. Faithfully humble at first, Job cries out in resignation:

a. Naked Came I

Naked came I out of my mother's womb, and naked shall I return there; the LORD has given, and the LORD has taken away; blessed be the name of the LORD.

But the limits of Job's patience are soon exceeded. When he further suffers the ravages of a debilitating disease, he curses the day of his birth. Three of his friends arrive to comfort him, but in effect, they rebuke Job for a lack of faith. Surely God's justice is supreme, surely Job must have done something to deserve this, they tell him. But Job insists—and the book's omniscient author verifies—that Job is blameless. Job challenges God to provide a justification for a good person's undeserved suffering and defiantly asks how it is that evil people can prosper:

b. Why Do the Wicked Live On?

Why should I not lose my patience?
Look at me and be appalled,
And clap your hand to your mouth.
When I think of it I am terrified;
My body is seized with shuddering.

Why do the wicked live on,
Prosper and grow wealthy?
Their children are with them always,
And they see their children's children.
Their homes are secure, without fear;
They do not feel the rod of God.

Their bull breeds and does not fail;
Their cow calves and never miscarries;
They let their infants run loose like sheep,
And their children skip about.
They sing to the music of timbrel and lute,
And revel to the tune of the pipe;
They spend their days in happiness,
And go down to Sheol in peace.
They say to God, "Leave us alone,
We do not want to learn Your ways;
. . . What will we gain by praying to Him?"
. . . How seldom does the lamp of the wicked fail,
Does the calamity they deserve befall them,
Does He apportion [their] lot in anger! . . .

The contest between Job's friends' traditional pieties and his own despair ends in a deadlock. Toward the book's end, God speaks to Job out of a whirlwind. Are Job's misgivings answered? Because God does not respond directly to them, some commentators believe that the answer is, in effect, that God's ways are flatly incomprehensible to human beings. Rational understanding thereof is impossible. Others believe that Job gets his answer precisely in the direct experience *of God; only experience, not explanation, can resolve Job's questions. In this view, mystical experience doesn't answer questions, it* swallows *them. Still others believe that God's words imply that there is no divine system of justice, and that authentic religious faith requires human righteousness in spite of this fact.*

c. God Responds to Job: Where Were You When I Laid the Foundations of the Earth?

Then the LORD replied to Job out of the tempest and said:

Who is this who darkens counsel,
Speaking without knowledge?
Gird your loins like a man;
I will ask and you will inform Me.

Where were you when I laid the earth's foundations?
Speak if you have understanding.

Do you know who fixed its dimensions
Or who measured it with a line?
Onto what were its bases sunk?
Who set its cornerstone
When the morning stars sang together
And all the divine beings shouted for joy?

. . . Have you ever commanded the day to break,
Assigned the dawn its place . . . ?

. . . Have you penetrated to the sources of the sea,
Or walked in the recesses of the deep?
Have the gates of death been disclosed to you?
. . . Have you surveyed the expanses of the earth?
If you know of these—tell Me.

. . . Who cut a channel for the torrents
And a path for the thunderstorms,
To rain down on uninhabited land,
. . . And make the crop of grass sprout forth?
. . . Who begot the dewdrops?

. . . Can you tie cords to Pleiades
Or undo the reins of Orion?

. . . Can you dispatch the lightning on a mission
And have it answer you, "I am ready"?
Who put wisdom in the hidden parts?
Who gave understanding to the mind?
Who is wise enough to give an account of the heavens?

. . . Who provides food for the raven
When his young cry out to God
And wander about without food?

. . . Do you know the season when the mountain goats give
    birth?
. . . Is it by your wisdom that the hawk grows pinions,
Spreads his wings to the south?
Does the eagle soar at your command,
Building his nest high,
. . . Lodging upon the fastness of a jutting rock?

d. Job's Closing Response

Job said in reply to the LORD:

> I know that You can do everything,
> That nothing you propose is impossible for You.
> . . . Indeed, I spoke without understanding
> Of things beyond me, which I did not know.
> . . . I had heard You with my ears,
> But now I see You with my eyes;
> Therefore, I recant and relent,
> Being but dust and ashes.

22. Ecclesiastes

It is a testament to the breadth of Jewish religious sensibility that the book of Ecclesiastes is given its place in the Bible. Its skepticism and pessimism stand in sharp contrast to much of the biblical message. Conspicuously absent are a sense of humanity's high moral calling, the experience of repentance and reconciliation, and the attitude of unquestioned or rediscovered trust in God. "There is nothing new under the sun," says the wealthy, world-weary author who lived around 300 B.C.E. And what there is amounts only to "emptiness and a chasing of wind."

a. All Things Are Wearisome

> Generations come and generations go,
>   while the earth endures forever.
> The sun rises and the sun goes down;
>   back again it returns to its place and rises there again.
> The wind blows south, the wind blows north,
>   round and round it goes and returns full circle.
> All streams run into the sea, yet the sea never overflows;
>   back to the place from which the streams ran
>   they return to run again.
> All things are wearisome; no man can speak of them all.

What has happened will happen again,
    and what has been done will be done again,
And there is nothing new under the sun.

Is there anything of which one can say, "Look, this is new"? No, it has already existed, long ago before our time. The people of old are not remembered, and those who follow will not be remembered by those who follow them. . . . It is a sorry business that God has given men to busy themselves with. I have seen all the deeds that are done here under the sun; they are all emptiness and a chasing of wind.

b. Hedonism Is No Solution

I said to myself, "Come, I will plunge into pleasures and enjoy myself"; but this too was emptiness. . . . I undertook great works; I built myself houses and planted vineyards; I made myself gardens and parks and planted all kinds of fruit trees in them; . . . I bought slaves, male and female. . . . I had . . . more cattle and flocks than any of my predecessors in Jerusalem; I amassed silver and gold also. . . . Whatever my eyes coveted, I refused them nothing, nor did I deny myself any pleasure.

. . . Then I turned and reviewed all my handiwork . . . and I saw that everything was emptiness and chasing the wind. . . .

c. You Can't Take It with You

Alas, the wise man and the fool die the same death! . . . So I came to hate all my labour and toil here under the sun, since I should have to leave its fruits to my successor. . . . Who knows whether he will be a wise man or a fool? Yet he will be a master of all the fruits of my labor and skill here under the sun. This too is emptiness.

d. For Everything There Is a Season

It is rarely realized that the oft-quoted "there is a time for every purpose under heaven" is not the sanguine benediction it is usually thought to be, but a melancholy ode to life's tiresome round.

For everything its season, and for every activity under heaven its time:

a time to be born and a time to die;
a time to plant and a time to uproot;
a time to kill and a time to heal;
a time to pull down and a time to build up;
a time to weep and a time to laugh;
a time for mourning and a time for dancing;
a time to scatter stones and a time to gather them;
a time to embrace and a time to refrain from embracing;
a time to seek and a time to lose;
a time to keep and a time to throw away;
a time to tear and a time to mend;
a time for silence and a time for speech;
a time to love and a time to hate;
a time for war and a time for peace.

e. Death Is the End

For man is a creature of chance and the beasts are creatures of chance, and one mischance awaits them all: death comes to both alike. . . . Men have no advantage over beasts. . . . All go to the same place: all came from the dust, and to the dust all return.

f. Better Not to Have Been Born

Again, I considered all the acts of oppression here under the sun; I saw the tears of the oppressed, and I saw that there was no one to comfort them. Strength was on the side of their oppressors, and there was no one to avenge them. I counted the dead happy because they were dead, happier than the living who are still in life. More fortunate than either I reckoned the man yet unborn who had not witnessed the wicked deeds done here under the sun.

g. Chance, Not Justice, Governs All

One more thing I have observed here under the sun: Speed does not win the race, nor strength the battle. Bread does not belong to the wise, nor wealth to the intelligent, nor success to the skilful; time and chance govern all. Moreover, no man knows when his hour will come; like fish caught in a net, like a bird taken in a snare, so men are trapped when bad times come suddenly.

h. Enjoy Your Lot

What I have seen is this: that it is good and proper for a man to eat and drink and enjoy himself in return for his labours here under the sun, throughout the brief span of life which God has allotted him.

. . . I perceived that God has so ordered it that man should not be able to discover what is happening here under the sun. However hard a man may try, he will not find out; the wise man may think that he knows, but he will be unable to find the truth of it.

. . . Go to it then, eat your food and enjoy it, and drink your wine with a cheerful heart; for already God has accepted what you have done.

ORAL TORAH: The Talmud

Jewish tradition holds that God gave the Israelites two teachings, written and oral. The record of the oral teaching as it was transmitted and debated by Jewish scholars from ancient times to the beginning of the Middle Ages is called the Talmud. The Talmud, then, is nothing less than a sacred repository of two thousand years of Jewish reflection, a great conglomerate of law, legend, and philosophy. There is no way to summarize the Talmud's encyclopedic content, but it is possible perhaps to reveal something of its essential spirit, its recognition of study as a holy act, its faith in the profound importance of human interpretive response to the divine. For in Judaism, human beings have never been seen as passive recipients of God's word. Study and interpretation of the scriptures are understood as sacred acts through which God's will continues to be revealed. Talmudic passages may also be found in selections 31, 32, 33, and 34 in the next section.

23. Rabbi Eliezer Debates His Fellow Sages

On that day, Rabbi Eliezer used all the arguments in the world. He produced powerful arguments to justify his position. . . . But the Sages did not accept his arguments. . . .

After Rabbi Eliezer saw that he was not able to persuade his ten colleagues with logical arguments, he said to them: "If I am right . . . let this carob tree prove it by uprooting itself and moving one hundred cubits away." The carob tree immediately uprooted itself and moved one hundred cubits. . . .

The Sages were unimpressed and said: "Proof cannot be had from a carob tree."

Rabbi Eliezer then said to the ten: "If I am right let the river prove it by flowing in the opposite direction." The river immediately flowed backward, against the direction in which it usually flowed.

The Sages sniffed and said: "Proof cannot be had from a river either."

. . . Rabbi Eliezer then said to the ten Sages: "If I am right let it be proved directly from Heaven." Suddenly the divine voice thundered forth and said to the Sages: "Why are you disputing with Rabbi Eliezer? He is right in all circumstances!"

Rabbi Yehoshua slowly rose to his feet and said: "Okay, Eliezer, ten to *two!*"

24. The Inestimable Value of Studying Torah

Turn [the Torah] over and over, for it contains everything. Keep your eyes riveted to it. Spend yourself in study. Never budge from it, for there is no better life than that.

If you study Torah in order to learn and do God's will . . . the whole world is indebted to you. You will be cherished as a friend, a lover of God and people. [Torah study] clothes you with humility and reverence [and] you benefit humanity with counsel and knowledge, wisdom and strength.

Once I was on a journey and I encountered a man. We greeted one another. Then he said to me: "Rabbi, where are you from?" I replied to him: "I come from a great city of sages and scribes." He then said: "Rabbi, if you are willing to dwell in our place, I will give you a thousand gold dinars and gems and pearls." I replied to him: "Were you to give me all the world's silver and gold and gems and pearls, I would not live save in a place of Torah. . . . When we die it is neither silver nor gold nor gems nor pearls that accompany us, but Torah and good deeds only."

25. The Primacy of Deeds

a. Growing Roots

When our learning exceeds our deeds we are like trees whose branches are many but whose roots are few: the wind comes and uproots them. . . . But when our deeds exceed our learning we are like trees whose branches are few but whose roots are many, so that even if all the winds of the world were to come and blow against them, they would be unable to move them.

b. A Parable

A man came to the shopkeeper to buy a measure of wine.
The shopkeeper said to him: Bring me your vessel.
But the man opened his bag.
. . . Said the shopkeeper to him: How can you buy wine . . . if you have no vessel at hand?
Similarly:
God says to the wicked:
You have no good deeds with you—how then do you wish to learn Torah?

26. Rabbi Hillel

Hillel (ca. 60 B.C.E. to ca. 10 C.E.) was an early and great Talmudic master whose teachings, it is said, could be boiled down to one word: loving-kindness.

a. The Rest Is Commentary

A certain heathen came to [Hillel] and said to him:
Convert me provided that you teach me the entire Torah

while I stand on one foot.
. . . Hillel . . . said to him:
What is hateful to you, do not do to your neighbor:
that is the entire Torah;
the rest is commentary;
go and learn it.

b. If Not Now, When?

If I am not for myself, who then will be for me? If I am only for my-self, what am I? And if not now, when?

27. Prayer

Regular prayer is crucial for an observant Jew. The Torah exhorts its students to "love the Lord your God, and to serve God with all your heart. . . ."

[And] what is the service of the heart? It is prayer.

The Holy One, praised be He, longs for the prayers of the righteous.

Rabbi Eliezer said: Prayer is greater than the offering of sacrifices. . . .

GRACE NOTES: *LA CHAIM!* (TO LIFE!)

28. The *Shema*

Shema *literally means "hear." The* Shema *is the core declaration of Judaic spirituality:*

Hear, O Israel, the LORD is our God, the LORD alone.

29. Choose Life

I have put before you life and death, blessing and curse. Choose life . . . by loving the LORD your God. . . .

30. All Life Is Linked in God

Everything is linked with everything else down to the lowest ring on the chain, and the true essence of God is above as well as below, in the heavens and on the earth, and nothing exists outside Him.

31. Do Not Corrupt or Destroy My World

Consider the work of God; who can make straight what He has made crooked? When the Holy One, praised be He, created Adam, he showed him all of the trees in the Garden of Eden, telling him "Behold, My works are beautiful and glorious; yet everything which I have created is for your sake. Take care that you do not corrupt or destroy My world."

32. Why Were We Created on the Sixth Day?

Why was man created on the sixth day? So that, should he become overbearing, he can be told: "The gnat was created before you were."

33. On the Sanctity of Individual Life

. . . Therefore was a single person [first] created to teach thee that if anyone destroy a single soul . . . Scripture charges him as though he had destroyed a whole world, and whosoever rescues a single soul . . . Scripture credits him as though he had saved a whole world. . . . The Holy One has stamped all mankind with the die of the first man and yet not one of them is like to his fellow. Therefore, everyone is bound to say, "For my sake was the universe created."

34. Enjoy

At Judgment Day everyone will have to give an account for every good thing which he [or she] might have enjoyed and did not enjoy.

35. Albert Einstein on Judaism: *The Sanctification of Life*

There is, in my opinion, no Jewish view of life in the philosophic sense. Judaism appears to me to be almost exclusively concerned with the moral attitude in and toward life.

. . . The essence of the Jewish concept of life seems to me to be the affirmation of life for all creatures. For the life of the individual has meaning only in the service of enhancing and ennobling the life of every living thing. Life is holy; i.e., it is the highest worth on which all other values depend . . .

Judaism is not a faith. The Jewish God is but a negation of superstition and an imaginative result of its elimination. He also represents an attempt to ground morality in fear—a deplorable, discreditable attempt. Yet it seems to me that the powerful moral tradition in the Jewish people has, in great measure, released itself from this fear. Moreover, it is clear that "to serve God" is equivalent to serving "every living thing." It is for this that the best among the Jewish people, especially the Prophets including Jesus, ceaselessly battled. Thus Judaism is not a transcendental religion. It is concerned only with the tangible experiences of life, and with nothing else. Therefore, it seems to me to be questionable whether it may be termed a "religion" in the customary sense of the word, especially since no "creed" is demanded of Jews, but only the sanctification of life in its all-inclusive sense.

There remains, however, something more in the Jewish tradition, so gloriously revealed in certain of the psalms; namely a kind of drunken joy and surprise at the beauty and incomprehensible sublimity of this world, of which man can attain but a faint intimation. It is the feeling from which genuine research draws its intellectual strength, but which also seems to manifest itself in the song of birds. . . .

Is this, then, characteristic of Judaism? And does it exist elsewhere under other names? In *pure form* it exists nowhere, not even in Judaism where too much literalism obscures the pure doctrine. But, nevertheless, I see in Judaism one of its most vital and pure realizations. This is especially true of its fundamental principle of the sanctification of life.

36. Herman Wouk on Dietary Laws: *Respect for Life*

Herman Wouk is a noted contemporary novelist who grew up in an Orthodox Jewish household. Here he provides a lucid commentary on traditional dietary practices.

People may neglect work, play, prayer, and love-making, but they seldom forget to eat. All religions include grace over food. Many religions go farther and set a mark on what one eats and how one eats. Often such austerities are reserved for the monk, the nun, the priest, the ascetic, the lama. Judaism's disciplines are relatively mild, but they are for everybody. . . .

There is no limit on food that grows from the ground; the disciplines deal only with sentient life. The Bible gives us physical tokens of the creatures that may be eaten.

For animals, the two marks are a split hoof and cud-chewing. In effect this admits a small class of beasts that live on grass and leaves, and shuts out the rest of animal life. . . .

Of creatures in the sea, Jews eat those with fins and scales. . . .

There are no specific marks for birds. The Torah lists a large number of proscribed ones, all birds of prey or carrion. . . .

"Kosher" is a late Hebrew word that does not occur in the Books of Moses. Perhaps the nearest English word is "fit," in the sense of proper or suitable. . . .

The Torah has four main rules for preparing meat. . . . Breaking any one of the four renders the meat "torn" [*trefe*] and inedible under Hebrew law.

The first rule, the only law of diet in the Bible for all mankind, is clearly human in intent. It bars the eating of flesh cut from a live creature—"the limb of the living." If the reader shrinks from horror at the thought, he is not familiar with ancient killing and cooking practices that still survive in primitive communities, and in some not considered primitive.

The second law forbids the drinking of blood, on the ground that "the blood is the life." The use of blood in sophisticated cookery is common, especially for sauces. Jewish law not only bans this, but it excludes the meat itself unless most of the circulatory blood is removed. . . .

The third rule stems from the bizarre prohibition repeated three times in the Torah in identical words: "You shall not boil a kid in the milk of its mother. . . ." [This] led long ago to complete separation of flesh and dairy food in the Hebrew diet. . . . Meat and milk, or their products, never appear together on the table. In observant homes, there are separate utensils and crockery for the two types of meals. . . .

The fourth rule bans suet, the hard fat formed below the diaphragm. The regulations separating suet from edible fat are complex and help make butchery of kosher meat a work for skilled and learned men. . . .

The bans against drinking blood and against the "limb of the living" determine the rigid, indeed sacred, method of taking animal life under Hebrew law. There is only one way: a single, instantaneous severance of the carotid arteries in the neck. The blood pours out; the supply to the brain is at once cut off; the animal's consciousness vanishes. The rest is muscular reflexes, to which the beast is as oblivious as a man in a coma.

. . . Scientific testimony, gathered when this mode of slaughter has been under attack, shows that it is a death as merciful as any that humans can visit on animals, and far more merciful than most.

Stringent conditions to endure a painless death are part of our law. If one of these precautions is omitted, the meat is called torn, and we cannot eat it. The death stroke must be a single slash. Even one sawing motion disqualifies, let alone a second stroke, a stunning blow, or any other inflicting of pain. The edge of the knife must be ground razor-sharp and smooth; one detectable nick causes rejection of the meat. The animal must be motionless at the instant of the death strike, so that the knife may cut true. Skilled professional slaughterers, who undergo qualifying examinations for dexterity and technical knowledge, do this work. Equally knowledgeable inspectors watch each move.

37. A God Who Feels

Abraham Joshua Heschel (1907–1972) was a noted Jewish scholar, theologian, and mystic. Selections 37 and 38b are from his work.

. . . *Pathos* is the central category of the prophetic understanding of God.

To the prophet, God does not reveal himself in an abstract absoluteness, but in a specific and unique way—in a personal and intimate relation to the world. . . . Events and human actions arouse in Him joy or sorrow, pleasure or wrath. He is not conceived as judging facts, so to speak, "objectively," in detached impassibility. He reacts in an intimate and subjective manner, and thus determines the value of events.

. . . The category of divine *pathos* leads to the basic affirmation that God is interested in human history, that every deed and event in the world concerns Him and arouses His reaction. What is characteristic of the prophets is not foreknowledge of the future but insight into the present *pathos* of God.

The idea of divine *pathos* has also its anthropological significance. Man has his relation to God. A religion without man is as impossible as a religion without God. That God takes man seriously is shown by his concern for human existence. It finds its deepest expression in the fact that God can actually suffer. At the heart of the prophetic affirmation is the certainty that God is concerned about the world to the point of suffering.

38. The Meaning of Shabbat (Sabbath)

It is often said that more than the Jew has preserved the Sabbath, the Sabbath has preserved the Jew. This weekly, twenty-four-hour contemplative pause, in which human beings cease doing in order to enjoy being, to cease creating in order to remember the creator, is the only one of all the Jewish holidays and festivals that is mentioned in the Ten Commandments. It is considered the most important of all holy days, regularly reminding Jews of the larger scheme of things and of their inherent freedom from servitude to human designs.

a. The Sabbath as Freedom

By desisting from all work on the seventh day, we testify that the world is not ours; that, not we, but God is the Lord and creator of the Universe. . . .

If the Sabbath on the one hand emphasizes our servitude to God, it also stresses our *freedom from servitude to human masters*. . . . [For] slavery doesn't only consist of doing forced labor for which one doesn't get paid. . . . Have you ever stopped to think that you yourself can be your own cruelest taskmaster, that you are capable of driving yourself in a manner that no slavemaster ever drove his slaves?

You've got to finish the job. You can't stop. There are deadlines, . . . obligations, . . . commitments, . . . house cleaning, . . . shopping, the need to get ready for an evening out . . . and we think we are *free!*

Even when contemporary man doesn't actually go to his job, what does he do? He plays just as hard. He transfers the same tension . . . the same frenzy and the same pressure on his nervous system . . . from the business office to the ball field, the golf course, the highways of our land, to mowing the lawn, and fixing the house. . . . He may even be having a good time . . . but the mental and emotional and physical rest, the tranquility of mind and soul—this he doesn't have.

b. The Sanctification of Time

The higher goal of spiritual living is not to amass a wealth of information, but to face sacred moments. . . . Spiritual life begins to decay when we fail to sense the grandeur of what is eternal in time.

. . . Judaism is a *religion of time* aiming at *the sanctification of time*. . . . Judaism teaches us to be attached to *holiness in time*, to be attached to sacred events, to learn how to consecrate sanctuaries that emerge from the magnificent stream of a year. . . . Jewish ritual may be characterized as [an] *architecture of time.*

. . . One of the most distinguished words in the Bible is the word *qadosh*, holy; a word which more than any other is representative of the mystery and majesty of the divine. Now what was the first holy object in the history of the world? Was it a mountain? Was it an altar?

It is, indeed, a unique occasion at which the distinguished word *qadosh* is used for the first time . . . at the end of the story of creation. How extremely significant is the fact that it is applied to time: "And God blessed the seventh *day* and made it *holy.*"

. . . The meaning of the Sabbath is to celebrate time rather than space. Six days a week we live under the tyranny of things of space; on the Sabbath we try to become attuned to *holiness in time.* It is a day on which we are called upon to share in what is eternal in time, to turn from the results of creation to the mystery of creation; from the world of creation to the creation of the world.

. . . To set apart one day a week for freedom, a day on which we would not use the instruments which have been so easily turned into weapons of destruction, a day for being with ourselves, a day of detachment from the vulgar, of independence of external obligations, a day on which we stop worshipping the idols of technical civilization, a day on which we use no money, a day of armistice in the economic struggle with our fellow men and the forces of nature—is there any institution that holds out a greater hope for man's progress than the Sabbath?

The solution of mankind's most vexing problem will not be found in renouncing technical civilization, but in attaining some degree of independence of it.

39. The Holocaust: *Elie Wiesel on the Trial of God*

Elie Wiesel is an internationally known Jewish novelist and Nobel laureate. Sent to Auschwitz as a young boy, he was the only member of his family to escape extermination. In a film interview he tells the following story:

During the war, in one of the camps one evening, three Jews, who before the war were heads of academies, sages, learned men, and who all knew the Talmud by heart, decided that the time had come to do something about it, to indict God. And they conducted a trial. I was very young then. But I remember I was there. They sat on the bed one evening and they began the trial, the trial of God, with all the arguments for and against. And it lasted a couple of days. It was very serious, very dramatic. There was a certain gravity, a certain solemnity in every word they uttered because they knew that whatever they say has an impact, whatever they say is being heard. And I remember that after many days the verdict came. And the verdict was: "Guilty."

But, then, the head of the tribunal simply said: "Now let's go and pray."

Mr. Wiesel now comments:

I would like to do a story on that one day . . . but I will introduce a new character, a character who defends God, the only one who defends God, the only one who says that God's ways are justified even there, even in Auschwitz. And I would say that that character is Satan.

. . . For a Jew to believe in God is good. For a Jew to protest against God is still good. But simply to ignore God—that is not good. Anger, yes. Protest, yes. Affirmation, yes. But indifference? No. You can be a Jew with God. You can be a Jew against God. But not without God.

40. Martin Luther King, Jr.: *Free at Last*

Dr. Martin Luther King, Jr., was a Christian minister and leader of the nonviolent struggle against racial discrimination in America. Excerpts from his "I Have a Dream" speech[9] are included in this chapter because they powerfully echo the Jewish prophets' cry for social justice and the great Exodus theme of liberation, illustrating the universal reach of these ideas.

---

9. Delivered at the Lincoln Memorial, Washington, D.C., August 28, 1963.

I am happy to join with you today in what will go down in history as the greatest demonstration for freedom in the history of our nation.

Five score years ago, a great American, in whose symbolic shadow we stand, signed the Emancipation Proclamation. This momentous decree came as a great beacon light of hope to millions of Negro slaves who had been seared in the flames of withering injustice. It came as a joyous daybreak to end the long night of captivity.

But one hundred years later, we must face the tragic fact that the Negro is still not free. One hundred years later, the life of the Negro is still sadly crippled by the manacles of segregation and the chains of discrimination. . . .

I have a dream that one day this nation will rise up and live out the true meaning of its creed: "We hold these truths to be self-evident; that all men are created equal."

I have a dream that one day on the red hills of Georgia the sons of former slaves and the sons of former slave owners will be able to sit down together at the table of brotherhood.

. . . I have a dream that my four little children will one day live in a nation where they will not be judged by the color of their skin but by the content of their character.

. . . I have a dream that one day every valley shall be exalted, every hill and mountain shall be made low, the rough places will be made plains, and the crooked places will be made straight, and the glory of the Lord shall be revealed, and all flesh shall see it together.[10]

. . . This will be the day when all of God's children will be able to sing with new meaning "My country 'tis of thee, sweet land of liberty, of thee I sing. Land where my fathers died, land of the pilgrim's pride, from every mountainside, let freedom ring."

And if America is to be a great nation this must become true. So let freedom ring from the prodigious hilltops of New Hampshire. Let freedom ring from the mighty mountains of New York.

---

10. Isaiah 40:4–5.

Let freedom ring from the heightening Alleghenies of Pennsylvania! . . .

But not only that; let freedom ring from Stone Mountain of Georgia!

Let freedom ring from Lookout Mountain of Tennessee!

Let freedom ring from every hill and molehill of Mississippi. From every mountainside, let freedom ring.

When we let freedom ring, when we let it ring from every village and every hamlet, from every state and every city, we will be able to speed up that day when all of God's children, black men and white men, Jews and Gentiles, Protestants and Catholics, will be able to join hands and sing in the words of the old Negro spiritual, "Free at last! Free at last! Thank God Almighty, we are free at last!"

CHAPTER SIX

Christianity

*T*he term Christ *is the English rendering of the Greek* Kristos, *a word used by early, Greek-speaking Christians to translate the Hebrew word* mashiah *or* messiah. *To call Jesus of Nazareth the "Christ," which is precisely what a small number of his Jewish brothers and sisters did, was to claim that Jesus was the messiah long awaited in the Jewish tradition. Other Jews, of course, did not see it that way; and therein lies the story of how a small, fringe sect of Judaism eventually became a vast new religion. For as that small community of Jewish messiah-ists (that is, Christ-ians) spread Jesus' good news throughout the Roman Empire, non-Jews responded enthusiastically. Within three hundred years, Christianity had become the dominant religion of the Roman Empire, and in the intervening two thousand years it has become the world's most populous religion, albeit divided into many denominations.*

Christians everywhere look to the New Testament as a continual source of revelation, inspiration, and renewal, for within its covers is contained what is commonly referred to by Christians as "the greatest story ever told," the story of Jesus of Nazareth. The New Testament records Jesus' life and ministry, his deeds and sayings. It also witnesses the faith and activity of the earliest Christians.

THE LIFE OF JESUS[1]

1. The Annunciation

. . . The angel Gabriel was sent by God to a town in Galilee called Nazareth, to a virgin engaged to a man whose name was Joseph, of the house of David. The virgin's name was Mary. And he came to her and said, "Greetings, favored one! The Lord is with you. . . . Do not be afraid Mary for you have found favor with God. And now, you will conceive in your womb and bear a son, and you will name him Jesus. He will be great and will be called the Son of the Most High . . . and of his kingdom there will be no end."

. . . And Mary said,

My soul magnifies the Lord,
And my spirit rejoices in God my Savior. . . .

2. The Birth of Jesus

Now the birth of Jesus the Messiah took place in this way. When his mother Mary had been engaged to Joseph, but before they lived together, she was found to be with child from the Holy Spirit. Her husband Joseph, being a righteous man and unwilling to expose her to public disgrace, planned to dismiss her quietly. But just when he had resolved to do this, an angel of the Lord appeared to him in a dream and said, "Joseph, son of David, do not be afraid to

---

1. No attempt has been made here to reflect the scholarly debate about what parts of the Gospels reflect historical fact and what parts comprise symbolic discourse and mythic amplification.

take Mary as your wife, for the child conceived in her is from the Holy Spirit. She will bear a son, and you are to name him Jesus, for he will save his people from their sins.". . . When Joseph awoke from sleep, he did as the angel of the Lord commanded him; he took her as his wife, but had no marital relations with her until she had borne a son; and he named him Jesus.

And she gave birth to her firstborn son and wrapped him in bands of cloth, and laid him in a manger, for there was no room at the inn. In that region there were shepherds living the fields, keeping watch over their flock by night. Then an angel of the Lord stood before them, and the glory of the Lord shone around them, and they were terrified. But the angel said to them, "Do not be afraid; for see—I am bringing you good news of great joy for all the people: to you is born this day in the city of David a Savior, who is the Messiah, the Lord."

3. The Growing Boy in His Father's House

Now every year his parents went to Jerusalem for the festival of the Passover. And when he was twelve years old, they went up as usual for the festival. When the festival was ended and they started to return, the boy Jesus stayed behind in Jerusalem, but his parents did not know it. . . . After three days they found him in the temple, sitting among the teachers, listening to them and asking them questions. And all who heard him were amazed at his understanding and his answers. When his parents saw him they were astonished; . . . He said to them, "Why were you searching for me? Did you not know that I must be in my Father's house?"

4. Baptism and the Beginning of His Ministry

In those days John the Baptist appeared in the wilderness of Judea, proclaiming, "Repent, for the kingdom of heaven has come near.". . . Then the people of Jerusalem and all Judea were going out to him . . . and they were baptized by him in the river Jordan, confessing their sins.

Then Jesus came from Galilee to John at the Jordan, to be baptized by him. . . . And when Jesus had been baptized, just as he came up from the water, suddenly the heavens opened to him and he saw the Spirit of God descending like a dove and alighting on him. And a voice from heaven said, "This is my Son, the Beloved, with whom I am well pleased."

5. The Three Temptations

Then Jesus was led up by the Spirit into the wilderness to be tempted by the devil. He fasted forty days and forty nights, and afterwards he was famished. The tempter came and said to him, "If you are the Son of God, command these stones to become loaves of bread." But he answered, "It is written,

'One does not live by bread alone,
But by every word that comes from the mouth of God.'"

Then the devil took him to the holy city and placed him on the pinnacle of the temple, saying to him, "If you are the Son of God, throw yourself down; for it is written,

'He will command his angels concerning you,' and 'On
their hands they will bear you up, so that you will not
dash your foot against a stone.'"

Jesus said to him, "Again it is written, 'Do not put the Lord your God to the test.'"

Again the devil took him to a very high mountain and showed him all the kingdoms of the world and their splendor; and he said to him, "All these will I give you, if you will fall down and worship me." Jesus said to him, "Away with you, Satan! for it is written,

'Worship the Lord your God, and serve only him.'"

6. Calling the First Disciples

As he walked by the Sea of Galilee, he saw two brothers, Simon, who is called Peter, and Andrew his brother, casting a net into the sea—for they were fishermen. And he said to them, "Follow me, and I will make you fish for people."

7. Deeds of Power

A conduit for the power of the Spirit, Jesus healed many. In so doing he challenged traditional notions of ill people as unclean or outcast, and he signaled the depth of God's love. The Gospels abound in reports of miraculous healings; here are but a few.

a. Exorcism

He went down to Capernaum, a city in Galilee, and was teaching them on the sabbath. . . . In the synagogue there was a man who had the spirit of an unclean demon, and he cried out with a loud voice, "Let us alone! What have you to do with us, Jesus of Nazareth? Have you come to destroy us? I know who you are, the Holy One of God." But Jesus rebuked him, saying, "Be silent, and come out of him!" When the demon had thrown him down before them, he came out of him without having done him any harm. They were all amazed and kept saying to one another, "What kind of utterance is this? For with authority and power he commands the unclean spirits, and out they come!" And a report about him began to reach every place in the region.

b. Healing a Paralyzed Man: "Stand Up and Walk"

One day, while he was teaching, Pharisees and teachers of the law were sitting near by. . . . Just then some men came, carrying a paralyzed man on a bed. They were trying to bring him in and lay him before Jesus; but finding no way to bring him in because of the crowd, they went up on the roof and let him down with his bed through the tiles into the middle of the crowd in front of Jesus. When he saw their faith, he said, "Friend, your sins are forgiven you." Then the scribes and the Pharisees[2] began to question, "Who is this who is speaking blasphemies? Who can forgive sins but God alone?" When Jesus perceived their questionings, he answered them, "Why do you raise such questions in your hearts? Which is easier, to say, 'Your sins are forgiven you,' or to say, 'Stand up and walk'? But so that you may know that the Son of Man has authority on earth to forgive sins"—he said to the one who was paralyzed—"I say to you, stand up and take your bed and go to your home." Immediately he stood up before them, took what he had been lying on, and went to his home, glorifying God.

c. Healing a Hemorrhaging Woman: "Your Faith Has Made You Well"

Then suddenly a woman who had been suffering from hemorrhages for twelve years came up behind him and touched the fringe of his cloak, for she said to herself, "If I only touch his cloak, I will be made well." Jesus turned, and seeing her he said, "Take heart, daughter; your faith has made you well." And instantly, the woman was made well.

d. Giving Sight to a Blind Man: "Your Faith Has Saved You"

As he approached Jericho, a blind man was sitting by the roadside begging. When he heard a crowd going by, he asked what was happening.

They told him, "Jesus of Nazareth is passing by." Then he shouted, "Jesus, Son of David, have mercy on me!" Those who were in front sternly ordered him to be quiet; but he shouted even more loudly, "Son of David, have mercy on me!" Jesus stood still and ordered the man to be brought to him; and when he came near, he asked him, "What do you want me to do for you?" He said, "Lord, let me see again." Jesus said to him, "Receive your sight; your faith has saved you." Immediately he regained his sight and followed him, glorifying God; and all the people, when they saw it, praised God.

---

2. Jewish religious scholars and authorities.

8. Amid Growing Fame. . .

Jesus went throughout Galilee, teaching in their synagogues and proclaiming the good news of the kingdom and curing every disease and every sickness among the people. So his fame spread throughout all Syria. . . . And great crowds followed him from Galilee, the Decapolis, Jerusalem, Judea, and from beyond the Jordan.

9. . . . Rejection in Nazareth

He came to his hometown and began to teach the people in their synagogue, so that they were astounded and said, "Where did this man get this wisdom and these deeds of power? Is not this the carpenter's son? Is not his mother called Mary? And are not his brothers James and Joseph and Simon and Judas? And are not all his sisters with us?" And they took offense at him. But Jesus said to them, "Prophets are not without honor except in their own country and in their own house." And he did not do many deeds of power there, because of their unbelief.

10. An Ill Omen for Jesus: *The Death of the Baptist*

Herod was the Roman-appointed king of Judea, and part of his job was to prevent Jewish revolt against Roman rule. The Baptist had been drawing enthusiastic crowds, and Herod knew that the line between religious fervor and political agitation was thin. Herod's motive for executing John might, therefore, be only partly explained in the following selection. In any case, Jesus surely knew that many saw him as John's successor.

For Herod had arrested John . . . because John had been telling him, "It is not lawful for you to have [your sister-in-law]."

. . . The king . . . had John beheaded in the prison. . . .

. . . [Jesus'] disciples came and took the body and buried it; then they went and told Jesus.

Now when Jesus heard this, he withdrew from there in a boat to a deserted place by himself.

11. The Beginning of the End

From that time on, Jesus began to show his disciples that he must go to Jerusalem and undergo great suffering at the hands of the elders and chief priests and scribes, and be killed, and on the third day be raised.

12. Jesus' Conspicuous Arrival in Jerusalem

a. The Triumphal Entry

And after throwing their cloaks on the colt, they set Jesus on it. As he rode along, people kept spreading their cloaks on the road. As he was now approaching the path down from the Mount of Olives, the whole multitude of the disciples began to praise God joyfully with a loud voice for all the deeds of power that they had seen, saying,

> "Blessed is the king who comes in the name of the Lord!
> Peace in heaven, and glory in the highest heaven!"

b. Cleansing the Temple

Then he entered the temple and began to drive out those who were selling things there; and he said, "It is written,

> 'My house shall be a house of prayer';
> but you have made it a den of robbers."

13. The Last Supper: *Jesus Celebrates Passover a Final Time*

a. Jesus Washes the Feet of His Disciples

Now before the festival of the Passover, Jesus knew that his hour had come to depart from this world and go to the Father. [And during supper he] got up from the table, took off his outer robe, and tied a towel around himself. Then he poured water into a basin and began to wash the disciples' feet and to wipe them with the towel that was tied around him. . . .

After he had washed their feet, had put on his robe, and had returned to the table, he said to them, "Do you know what I have done to you? You call me Teacher and Lord—and you are right, for that is what I am. So if I, your Lord and Teacher, have washed your feet, you also ought to wash one another's feet. For I have set you an example, that you also should do as I have done to you."

b. "This Is My Body"

Then he took a loaf of bread, and when he had given thanks, he broke it and gave it to them, saying, "This is my body, which is given for you. Do this in remembrance of me." And he did the same with the cup after supper, saying, "This cup that is poured out for you is the new covenant in my blood."

14. "Not My Will, But Thine"

[On the Mount of Olives] he withdrew from them about a stone's throw, knelt down and prayed, "Father, if you are willing, remove this cup from me; yet, not my will but yours be done."

15. The Trial

Now Jesus stood before the governor; and the governor asked him, "Are you the King of the Jews?" Jesus said, "You say so." But when he was accused by the chief priests and elders, he did not answer. Then Pilate said to him, "Do you not hear how many accusations they make against you?" But he gave him no answer, not even to a single charge, so that the governor was greatly amazed.

Now at the festival the governor was accustomed to release a prisoner for the crowd, anyone whom they wanted. . . . The chief priests and the elders persuaded the crowds to ask for Barabbas and to have Jesus killed. The governor again said to them, "Which of the two do you want me to release for you?" And they said, "Barabbas." Pilate said to them, "Then what should I do with Jesus who is called the Messiah?" All of them said, "Let him be crucified!" Then he asked, "Why, what evil has he done?" But they shouted all the more, "Let him be crucified!"

16. The Outrage

The soldiers of the governor took Jesus into the governor's headquarters, and they gathered the whole cohort around him. They stripped him and put a scarlet robe on him, and after twisting some thorns into a crown, they put it on his head. They put a reed in his right hand and knelt before him and mocked him, saying, "Hail, King of the Jews!" They spat on him, and took the reed and struck him on the head. After mocking him, they stripped him of the robe and put his own clothes on him. They then led him away to crucify him.

17. The Crucifixion

a. Golgotha

So they took Jesus; and carrying the cross by himself, he went out to what is called The Place of the Skull, which in Hebrew is called Golgotha. There they crucified him, and with him two others, one on either side, with Jesus between them. Pilate also had an inscription written and put on the cross. It read, "Jesus of Nazareth, the King of the Jews."

b. "Forgive Them"

Then Jesus said, "Father, forgive them; for they do not know what they are doing."

c. "You Will Be with Me in Paradise"

One of the criminals who were hanged there kept deriding him and saying, "Are you not the Messiah? Save yourself and us!" But the other rebuked him, saying, "Do you not fear God, since you are under the same sentence of condemnation? And we indeed have been condemned justly, for we are getting what we deserve for our deeds, but this man has done nothing wrong." Then he said, "Jesus, remember me when you come into your kingdom." He replied, "Truly, I tell you, today you will be with me in Paradise."

d. Mother and Son

Meanwhile, standing near the cross of Jesus were his mother, and his mother's sister, Mary, . . . and Mary Magdalene. When Jesus saw his mother and the disciple whom he loved standing beside her, he said to his mother, "Woman, here is your son." Then he said to the disciple, "Here is your mother." And from that hour the disciple took her into his own home.

e. "Why Have You Forsaken Me?"

From noon on, darkness came over the whole land until three in the afternoon. And about three o'clock Jesus cried with a loud voice, "Eli, Eli, lema sabachthani?" that is, "My God, my God, why have you forsaken me?". . . Then Jesus cried again with a loud voice and breathed his last.

18. The Resurrection: *Two Accounts*

a. Mark

When the sabbath was over, Mary Magdalene, and Mary the mother of James, and Salome bought spices, so that they might go and anoint him. And very early on the first day of the week, when the sun had risen, they went to the tomb. . . . When they looked up, they saw that the stone, which was very large, had already been rolled back. As they entered the tomb, they saw a young man, dressed in a white robe, sitting on the right side; and they were alarmed. But he said to them, "Do not be alarmed; you are looking for Jesus of Nazareth, who was crucified. He has been raised; he is not here. Look, there is the place they laid him. But go, tell his disciples and Peter that he is going ahead of you to Galilee; there you will see him just as he told you."

b. John

[Now] Mary stood weeping outside the tomb. As she wept, she bent over to look into the tomb; and she saw two angels in white, sitting where the body of Jesus had been lying, one at the head and the other at the feet. They said to her, "Woman, why are you weeping?" She said to them, "They have taken away my Lord, and I do not know where they have laid him." When she had said this, she turned around and saw Jesus standing there, but she did not know that it was Jesus. Jesus said to her, "Woman, why are you weeping? Whom are you looking for?" Supposing him to be the gardener, she said to him, "Sir, if you have carried him away, tell me where you have laid him, and I will take him away." Jesus said to her, "Mary!" She turned and said to him in Hebrew "Rabbouni!" (which means Teacher). Jesus said to her, "Do not hold on to me, because I have not yet ascended to the Father. But go to my brothers and say to them, 'I am ascending to my Father and your Father, to my God and your God.'" Mary Magdalene went and announced to the disciples, "I have seen the Lord"; and she told them that he had said these things to her.

19. Postresurrection Appearances[3]

a. Luke

Now on that same day [as the resurrection] two of them were going to a village called Emmaus, about seven miles from Jerusalem, and talking with each other about all these things that had happened. While they were talking Jesus himself came near and went with them, but their eyes were kept from recognizing him.

. . . When he was at table with them, he took bread, blessed and broke it, and gave it to them. Then their eyes were opened, and they recognized him; and he vanished from their sight.

. . . That same hour they got up and returned to Jerusalem; and they found the eleven and their companions gathered together. They were saying, "The Lord has risen indeed, and he has appeared to Simon!" They then told what had happened on the road, and how he had been made known to them in the breaking of the bread.

---

3. See also selection 32, below.

While they were talking about this, Jesus himself stood among them and said to them, "Peace be with you." They were startled and terrified, and thought that they were seeing a ghost. He said to them, "Why are you frightened, and why do doubts arise in your hearts? Look at my hands and my feet: see that it is I myself. Touch me and see; for a ghost does not have flesh and bones as you see that I have." And when he had said this, he showed them his hands and his feet. While in their joy they were disbelieving and still considering, he said to them, "Have you anything here to eat?" They gave him a piece of broiled fish, and he took it and ate it in their presence.

b. John

A week later his disciples were again in the house, and Thomas [a disciple who doubted Jesus had risen] was with them. Although the doors were shut, Jesus came and stood among them and said, "Peace be with you." Then he said to Thomas, "Put your finger here and see my hands. Reach out your hand and put it in my side. Do not doubt but believe." Thomas answered him, "My Lord and My God!" Jesus said to him, "Have you believed because you have seen me? Blessed are those who have not seen and yet have come to believe."

THE SAYINGS OF JESUS: "Never Has Anyone Spoken like This!"[4]

Scholars continue to debate which of Jesus' sayings may confidently be attributed to him and which were likely to have been placed in his mouth by his faith-inspired followers. No attempt has been made to reflect this complex and unresolved controversy. Instead, I have selected aspects of the Good News that have for nearly two thousand years resonated most deeply in the hearts of believers.

---

4. John 7:46.

20. On the Mystery of Himself

a. The Bread of Life

I am the bread of life. . . . Whoever eats of this bread will live forever.

b. The Light of the World

I am the light of the world. Whoever follows me will never walk in darkness but will have the light of life.

c. The Resurrection and the Life

I am the resurrection and the life. Those who believe in me, even though they die, will live, and everyone who lives and believes in me will never die.

d. Come to Me, You Who Are Weary

Come to me, all you that are weary and are carrying heavy burdens, and I will give you rest. Take my yoke upon you, and learn from me; for I am gentle and humble in heart, and you will find rest for your souls. For my yoke is easy, and my burden is light.

e. I Came to Save the Lost

For the Son of Man came to save the lost. What do you think? If a shepherd has a hundred sheep, and one of them has gone astray, does he not leave the ninety-nine on the mountains and go in search of the one that went astray? And if he finds it, truly I tell you, he rejoices over it more than over the ninety-nine that never went astray.

f. I Am Among You

Again, truly I tell you, if two of you agree on earth about anything you ask, it will be done for you by my Father in heaven. For where two or three are gathered in my name, I am there among them.

g. I Am the True Vine, Abide in Me

I am the true vine, and my Father is the vinegrower. . . . Abide in me as I abide in you. Just as the branch cannot bear fruit by itself unless it abides in the vine, neither can you unless you abide in me. I am the vine, you are the branches.

h. My Peace I Give You

Peace I leave with you; my peace I give to you. I do not give to you as the world gives. Do not let your hearts be troubled, and do not let them be afraid.

i. I Will Come Again

In my Father's house there are many dwelling places. . . . And if I go and prepare a place for you, I will come again and will take you to myself, so that where I am, there you may be also.

j. The Way, the Truth, and the Life

I am the way, and the truth, and the life. No one comes to the Father except through me.

k. Who Do People Say That I Am?

Jesus . . . asked his disciples, "Who do people say that the Son of Man is?" And they said, "Some say John the Baptist, but others Elijah, and still others Jeremiah or one of the prophets." He said to them, "But who do you say that I am?" Simon Peter answered, "You are the Messiah, the Son of the living God." And Jesus answered him, "Blessed are you, Simon son of Jonah! For flesh and blood has not revealed this to you, but my Father in heaven."

21. Love and Its Expression in Forgiveness

It has been said that "everything that came from [Jesus'] lips . . . focus[ed] human awareness on the two most important facts about life: God's overwhelming love for humanity, and the need for people to accept that love and let it flow through them to others."[5] The following utterances help us to understand the extraordinary fellowship of the early Christians.

a. Love One Another

I give you a new commandment, that you love one another. Just as I have loved you, you also should love one another. By this everyone will know that you are my disciples, if you have love for one another.

b. Turn the Other Cheek

You have heard that it was said, "An eye for an eye and a tooth for a tooth." But I say to you . . . if anyone strikes you on the right cheek, turn the other also; . . . and if anyone forces you to go one mile, go also the second mile.

c. Love Your Enemies

You have heard that it was said, "You shall love your neighbor and hate your enemy." But I say to you, Love your enemies and pray for those who persecute you so that you may be children of your Father in heaven; for he makes his sun rise on the evil and on the good, and sends rain on the righteous and on the unrighteous.

d. The Golden Rule

In everything do to others as you would have them do to you; for this is the law and the prophets.

e. I Was Hungry and You Gave Me Food

Come, you that are blessed by my Father, inherit the kingdom prepared for you from the foundation of the world, for I was hungry and you gave me food, I was thirsty and you gave me something to drink, I was a stranger and you welcomed me, I was naked and you

---

5. Huston Smith, *The World's Religions* (San Francisco: HarperSanFrancisco, 1991), 326–27.

gave me clothing, I was sick and you took care of me, I was in prison and you visited me. . . . Truly I tell you, just as you did it to one of the least of these who are members of my family, you did it to me.

f. Before All Else, Be Reconciled

So when you are offering your gift at the altar, if you remember that your brother or sister has something against you, leave your gift there at the altar and go; first be reconciled to your brother or sister, and then come and offer your gift.

g. Forgive Seventy-Seven Times

Then Peter came and said to him, "Lord, if another member of the church sins against me, how often should I forgive? As many as seven times?" Jesus said to him, "Not seven times, but I tell you, seventy-seven times."

h. Let the Sinless Cast the First Stone

. . . They said to him, "Teacher, this woman was caught in the very act of committing adultery. Now in the law Moses commanded us to stone such women. Now what do you say?". . . Jesus bent down and wrote with his finger on the ground. When they kept on questioning him, he straightened up and said to them, "Let anyone among you who is without sin be the first to throw a stone at her.". . . When they heard it, they went away. . . . Jesus . . . said to her, "Woman, where are they? Has no one condemned you?" She said, "No one, sir." And Jesus said, "Neither do I condemn you. Go your way, and from now on do not sin again."

22. The Kingdom of God

Often upon Jesus' lips, the phrase "kingdom of God," alternately rendered as "reign of God" or "kingdom of heaven," was central to his teaching.

He sometimes spoke of it as a near-future apocalyptic event (see selections 26a and 26b, below), but he often implied that the kingdom was here and now, dawning as a present fact (see 22j and 22k, below). As to what he meant by the kingdom of God, there is no better or more intriguing guide than the sayings and parables of the master.

a. The Beatitudes

When he saw the crowds he went up the hill. There he took his seat, and when his disciples had gathered round him he began to address them. And this is the teaching he gave:

> How blest are these who know their need of God;
>> the kingdom of heaven is theirs.
> How blest are the sorrowful;
>> they shall find consolation.
> How blest are those of a gentle spirit;
>> they shall have the earth for their possession.
> How blest are those who hunger and thirst to see right prevail;
>> they shall be satisfied.
> How blest are those who show mercy;
>> mercy shall be shown to them.
> How blest are those whose hearts are pure;
>> they shall see God.
> How blest are the peacemakers;
>> God shall call them his sons.
> How blest are those who have suffered persecution for the
>> cause of right;
>> the kingdom of heaven is theirs.

b. Become as Little Children

At that time the disciples came to Jesus and asked, "Who is the greatest in the kingdom of heaven?" He called a child, whom he put among them, and said, "Truly I tell you, unless you change and become like children, you will never enter the kingdom of heaven."

c. You Must Be Born Again

Very truly, I tell you, no one can see the kingdom of God without being born from above. . . . The wind blows where it chooses, and you hear the sound of it, but you do not know where it comes from or where it goes. So it is with everyone who is born of the Spirit.

d. The Parable of the Mustard Seed

And this is another parable that he put before them: "The kingdom of Heaven is like a mustard-seed, which a man took and sowed in his field; As a seed, mustard is smaller than any other; but when it has grown it is bigger than any garden plant; it becomes a tree, big enough for the birds to come and roost among its branches."

e. The Parable of the Treasure

The kingdom of Heaven is like treasure lying buried in a field. The man who found it, buried it again; and for sheer joy went and sold everything he had, and bought that field.

f. The Parable of the Vineyard Laborers

The kingdom of Heaven is like this. There was once a landowner who went out early one morning to hire labourers for his vineyard; and after agreeing to pay them the usual day's wage he sent them off to work. Going out three hours later he saw some more men standing idle in the market-place. "Go and join the others in the vineyard," he said, "and I will pay you a fair wage"; so off they went. At midday he went out again, and at three in the afternoon, and made the same arrangement as before. An hour before sunset he went out and found another group standing there; so he said to them, "Why are you standing about like this all day with nothing to do?" "Because no one has hired us," they replied; so he told them, "Go and join the others in the vineyard." When evening fell, the owner of the vineyard said to his steward, "Call the labourers and give them their pay, beginning with those who came last and ending with the first." Those who had started work an hour before sunset came forward, and were paid the full day's wage. When it was the turn of the men who had come first, they expected something extra, but were paid the same amount as the others. As they took it, they grumbled at their employer: "These late-comers have done only one hour's work, yet you have put them on a level with us, who have sweated the whole day long in the blazing sun!" The owner turned to one of them and said, "My friend, I am not being unfair to you. You agreed on the usual wage for the day, did you not? Take your pay and go home. I choose to pay the last man the same as you. Surely I am free to do what I like with my own money. Why be jealous because I am kind?"

g. The Parable of the Wedding Feast

The kingdom of Heaven is like this. There was a king who prepared a feast for his son's wedding; but when he sent his servants to summon the guests he had invited, they would not come. He sent others again, telling them to say to the guests, "See now! I have prepared this feast for you. I have had my bullocks slaughtered; everything is ready; come to the wedding at once." But they took no notice; one went off to his farm, another to his business, and the others seized the servants, attacked them brutally, and killed them. The king was furious; he sent troops to kill those murderers and set their town on fire. Then he said to his servants, "The wedding feast is ready; but the guests I invited did not deserve the honour. Go out to the main thoroughfares, and invite everyone you can find to the wedding." The servants went out into the streets, and collected all they could find, good and bad alike. So the hall was packed with guests.

When the king came in to see the company at the table, he observed one man who was not dressed for a wedding. "My friend," said the king, "how do you come to be here without your wedding clothes?" He had nothing to say. The king then said to his attendants, "Bind him hand and foot; turn him out into the dark, the place of wailing and grinding of teeth." For though many are invited, few are chosen.

h. The Parable of the Prodigal Son

There was once a man who had two sons; and the younger said to his father, "Father, give me my share of the property." So he divided his estate between them. A few days later the younger son turned the whole of his share into cash and left home for a distant country, where he squandered it in reckless living. He had spent it all, when a severe famine fell upon that country and he began to feel the pinch. So he went and attached himself to one of the local landowners, who sent him on to his farm to mind the pigs. He would have been glad to fill his belly with the pods that the pigs were eating; and no one gave him anything. Then he came to his senses and said, "How many of my father's paid servants have more food than they can eat, and here am I, starving to death! I will set off and go to my father, and say to him, 'Father, I have sinned, against God and against you; I am no longer fit to be called your son; treat me as one of your paid servants.'" So he set out for his father's house. But while he was still a long way off his father saw him, and his heart went out to him. He ran to meet him, flung his arms round him, and kissed him. The son said, "Father, I have sinned, against God and against you; I am no longer fit to be called your son." But the father said to his servants, "Quick! fetch a robe, my best one, and put it on him; put a ring on his finger and shoes on his feet. Bring the fatted calf and kill it, and let us have a feast to celebrate the day. For this son of mine was dead and has come back to life; he was lost and is found." And the festivities began.

Now the elder son was out on the farm; and on his way back, as he approached the house, he heard music and dancing. He called one of the servants and asked what it meant. The servant told him, "Your brother has come home, and your father has killed the fatted calf because he has him back safe and sound." But he was angry and refused to go in. His father came out and pleaded with him; but he retorted, "You know how I have slaved for you all these years; I never once disobeyed your orders; and you never gave me so much as a kid, for a feast with my friends. But now that this son of yours turns up, after running through your money with his women, you kill the fatted calf for him." "My boy," said the father, "you are always with me, and everything I have is yours. How could we help celebrating this happy day? Your brother was dead and has come back to life, was lost and is found."

i. The Parable of the Good Samaritan

As non-Jews, Samaritans (persons from Samaria) would have been considered heathens by many in Jesus' audience. In casting a

Samaritan as the spiritual hero of this story, Jesus underscored the un-conditionality of God's love, the universality of the kingdom, and the importance of the spirit, rather than merely the letter, of religious faith.

Just then a lawyer stood up to test Jesus. "Teacher," he said, "what must I do to inherit eternal life?" He said to him, "What is written in the law? What do you read there?" He answered, "You shall love the Lord your God with all your heart, and with all your soul, and with all your strength, and with all your mind; and your neighbor as yourself." And he said to him, "You have given the right answer; do this and you will live."

But wanting to justify himself, he asked Jesus, "And who is my neighbor?" Jesus replied, "A man was going down from Jerusalem to Jericho, and fell into the hands of robbers, who stripped him, beat him, and went away leaving him half dead. Now by chance a priest was going down that road; and when he saw him, he passed by on the other side. So likewise a Levite, when he came to the place and saw him, passed by on the other side. But a Samaritan while traveling came near him; and when he saw him, he was moved with pity. He went to him and bandaged his wounds, having poured oil and wine on them. Then he put him on his own animal, brought him to an inn, and took care of him. The next day he took out two denarii, gave them to the innkeeper, and said, 'Take care of him; and when I come back, I will repay you whatever more you spend.' Which of these three, do you think, was a neighbor to the man who fell into the hands of the robbers?" He said, "The one who showed him mercy." Jesus said to him, "Go and do likewise."

j. The Immanence of the Kingdom: Many Have Longed to See What You See

But blessed are your eyes, for they see, and your ears, for they hear. Truly I tell you, many prophets and righteous people longed to see what you see, but did not see it, and to hear what you hear, but did not hear it.

k. The Kingdom of God Is Among You

Once Jesus was asked by the Pharisees when the kingdom of God was coming, and he answered, "The kingdom of God is not coming with things that can be observed; nor will they say, 'Look, here it is!' or 'There it is!' For, in fact, the kingdom of God is among you."[6]

23. Putting the Pursuit of Wealth in Perspective

a. Store Treasures Where Moths and Rust Do Not Corrupt

Do not store up for yourselves treasures on earth, where moth and rust consume and where thieves break in and steal; but store up for yourselves treasures in heaven, where neither moth nor rust consumes and where thieves do not break in and steal. For where your treasure is, there your heart will be also.

b. You Cannot Serve Two Masters

No one can serve two masters; for a slave will either hate the one and love the other, or be devoted to the one and despise the other. You cannot serve God and wealth.

c. Consider the Lilies

Therefore I tell you, do not worry about your life, what you will eat or what you will drink, or about your body, what you will wear. Is not life more than food, and the body more than clothing? Look at the birds of the air; they neither sow nor reap nor gather into barns, and yet your heavenly Father feeds them. Are you not of more value than they? And can any of you by worrying add a single hour to your span of life? And why do you worry about clothing? Consider the lilies of the field, how they grow; they neither toil nor spin, yet I tell you, even Solomon in all his glory was not clothed like one of these. But if God so clothes the grass of the field, which is alive today and tomorrow is thrown into the oven, will he not much more clothe you—you of little faith?

---

6. See selection 37f, below.

d. The Eye of the Needle

Then Jesus said to his disciples, "Truly I tell you, it will be hard for a rich person to enter the kingdom of heaven. Again I tell you it is easier for a camel to go through the eye of a needle than for someone who is rich to enter the kingdom of God." When the disciples heard this, they were greatly astounded and said, "Then who can be saved?" But Jesus looked at them and said, "For mortals it is impossible, but for God all things are possible."

e. What Profit?

For what will it profit them if they gain the whole world but forfeit their life?

f. Give to the Poor and Come Follow Me

Then someone came to him and said, "Teacher, what good deed must I do to have eternal life?" And [Jesus] said to him. . . "Keep the commandments." The young man said . . . "I have kept all these; what do I still lack?" Jesus said to him, "If you wish to be perfect, go, sell your possessions, and give the money to the poor, and you will have treasure in heaven; then come, follow me."

24. Against Hypocrisy

a. The Log in Your Own Eye

Why do you see the speck in your neighbor's eye, but do not notice the log in your own eye?

b. Straining Out a Gnat While Swallowing a Camel

Woe to you, scribes and Pharisees, hypocrites! For you tithe mint, dill, and cumin, and have neglected the weightier matters of the law: justice and mercy and faith. It is these you ought to have practiced without neglecting the others. You blind guides! You strain out a gnat but swallow a camel!

c. One Is Corrupted by What One Says, Not by What One Eats

Then he called the crowd to him and said to them, "Listen and understand; it is not what goes into the mouth that defiles a person, but it is what comes out of the mouth that defiles."

25. Other Exhortations

a. The Conditions of Discipleship: Take Up Your Cross

If any want to become my followers, let them take up their cross and follow me. For those who want to save their life will lose it, and those who lose their life for my sake will find it.

b. Ask and You Will Receive

Ask, and it will be given you; search, and you will find; knock, and the door will be opened for you.

c. Let Your Light Shine

You are the light of the world. A city built on a hill cannot be hid. No one after lighting a lamp puts it under the bushel basket, but on the lampstand, and it gives light to all in the house. In the same way, let your light shine before others, so that they may see your good works and give glory to your Father in heaven.

d. The One Thing Needful

[Jesus] entered a certain village, where a woman named Martha welcomed him into her home. She had a sister named Mary, who sat at the Lord's feet and listened to what he was saying. But

Martha was distracted by her many tasks; so she came to him and asked, "Lord, do you not care that my sister has left me to do all the work by myself? Tell her then to help me." But the Lord answered her, "Martha, Martha, you are worried and distracted by many things; there is need of only one thing. Mary has chosen the better part, which will not be taken away from her."

e. Do Not Throw Pearls Before Swine

Do not give what is holy to dogs; and do not throw your pearls before swine. . . .

f. By Their Fruits You Will Know Them

Beware of false prophets, who come to you in sheep's clothing but inwardly are ravenous wolves. You will know them by their fruits.

g. Pray in This Way

Pray then in this way:

> Our Father in heaven,
> hallowed be your name. Your kingdom come.
> Your will be done, on earth as it is in heaven.
> Give us this day our daily bread.
> And forgive us our debts,
> as we also have forgiven our debtors.
> And do not bring us to the time of trial,
> but rescue us from the evil one.

26. The End of the World

a. Its Signs

For at that time there will be great suffering. . . . Immediately after the suffering of those days, the sun will be darkened and the moon will not give its light, the stars will fall from heaven, and the powers of heaven will be shaken. . . . Then . . . they will see "the Son of Man coming on the clouds of heaven" and with power and great glory. And he will send out his angels with a loud trumpet call, and they will gather his elect from the four winds, from one end of heaven to the other.

b. Its Time

Truly I tell you, this generation will not pass away until all these things have taken place.

THE LIFE OF THE EARLY CHURCH

27. The Keys of the Kingdom

[Jesus said,] "You are Peter and on this rock I will build my Church. And the gates of the underworld can never hold out against it. I will give you the keys of the kingdom of heaven: whatever you bind on earth shall be considered bound in heaven; whatever you loose on earth shall be considered loosed in heaven."

28. The Mission

[After Jesus' death] the eleven disciples set out for Galilee, to the mountain where Jesus had arranged to meet them. When they saw him they fell down before him, though some hesitated. Jesus came up and spoke to them. He said, "All authority in heaven and on earth has been given to me. Go, therefore, make disciples of all the nations; baptize them in the name of the Father and of the Son and of the Holy Spirit, and teach them to observe all the commands I gave you. And know that I am with you always; yes, to the end of time."

29. The Ascension of Jesus

[And Jesus said to them:] you will receive power when the Holy Spirit has come upon you; and you will be my witnesses in all Judea and Samaria, and to the ends of the earth." When he had said this, as they were watching, he was lifted up, and a cloud took him out of their sight. While he was going and they were gazing up toward heaven, suddenly two men in white robes stood by them. They said, "Men of Galilee, why do you stand looking up toward heaven? This Jesus, who has been taken up from you into heaven, will come in the same way as you saw him go into heaven."

30. The Descent of the Spirit

When the day of Pentecost had come, they were all together in one place. And suddenly from heaven there came a sound like the rush of a violent wind, and it filled the entire house where they were sitting. Divided tongues, as of fire, appeared among them, and a tongue rested on each of them. All of them were filled with the Holy Spirit and began to speak in other languages, as the Spirit gave them ability.

Now there were devout Jews from every nation under heaven living in Jerusalem. . . . Amazed and astonished, they asked, "Are not all these who are speaking Galileans? And how is it that we hear, each of us, in our own native language? Parthians, Medes, Elamites, and residents of Mesopotamia, Judea and Cappadocia, Pontus and Asia . . . visitors from Rome, . . . Cretans and Arabs— in our own languages we hear them speaking about God's deeds of power." All were amazed and perplexed. . . .

31. The Early Christian Commune

a. Possessions in Common

They devoted themselves to the apostles' teaching and fellowship, to the breaking of bread and the prayers. . . . All who believed were together and had all things in common; they would sell their possessions and goods and distribute the proceeds to all, as any had need. Day by day, as they spent much time together in the temple, they broke bread at home and ate their food with glad and generous hearts, praising God and having the goodwill of all the people. And day by day the Lord added to their number those who were being saved.

b. One in Christ Jesus

And you are, all of you, sons of God through faith in Jesus Christ. . . . And there are no more distinctions between Jew and Greek, slave and free, male and female, but all of you are one in Christ Jesus.

c. Life Anew

So if anyone is in Christ, there is a new creation: everything old has passed away; see, everything has become new!

32. The Mind of the Early Church

a. In Him We Live

God. . . is not far from each of us. For in him we live and move and have our being.

b. Incarnation

In the beginning was the Word, and the Word was with God, and the Word was God. He was in the beginning with God. All things came into being through him, and without him not one thing came into being. What has come into being in him was life, and the life was the light of all people. The light shines in the darkness, and the darkness did not overcome it. . . . To all who received him, who believed in his name, he gave the power to become children of God, who were born, not of blood or of the will of the flesh or of the will of man, but of God.

And the Word became flesh and lived among us, and we have seen his glory, the glory as of a father's only son, full of grace and truth.

Then they said to him, "Where is your Father?" Jesus answered, ". . . If you knew me you would know my Father also."

Believe me that I am in the Father and the Father is in me.

The Father and I are one.

c. Atonement

Here is the lamb of God, who takes away the sins of the world.

For God so loved the world that he gave his only Son, so that everyone who believes in him may not perish but may have eternal life.

For since death came through a human being, the resurrection of the dead has also come through a human being; for as all die in Adam, so all will be made alive in Christ.

For there is one God; there is one mediator between God and humankind, Christ Jesus, himself human, who gave himself a ransom for all. . . .

Since, therefore, the children share in flesh and blood, he himself likewise shared the same things, so that through death he might destroy the one who has the power of death, that is, the devil, and free those who all their lives were held in slavery by the fear of death.

Do you not know that all of us who have been baptized into Christ Jesus were baptized into his death? . . . But if we have died with Christ, we believe that we will also live with him. We know that Christ, being raised from the dead, will never die again; death no longer has dominion over him. The death he died, he died to sin, once for all; but the life he lives, he lives to God. So you must also consider yourselves dead to sin and alive to God in Christ Jesus.

d. Trinity[7]

And I will ask the Father, and he will give you another Helper to be with you forever. This is the Spirit of truth, whom the world cannot receive, because it neither sees him nor knows him. You know him, because he abides with you and he will be in you.

The grace of the Lord Jesus Christ and the love of God and the fellowship of the Holy Spirit be with you all.

---

7. See also selection 28, above.

e. The Good News of Grace

But life to me is not a thing to waste words on, provided that when I finish my race I have carried out the mission the Lord Jesus gave me—and that was to bear witness to the Good News of God's grace.

f. The Centrality of the Resurrection: If Christ Has Not Been Raised Your Faith Is in Vain

I would remind you, brothers and sisters, of the good news that I proclaimed to you. . . . Now if Christ is proclaimed as raised from the dead, how can some of you say there is no resurrection of the dead? If there is no resurrection of the dead, then Christ has not been raised; and if Christ has not been raised, then our proclamation has been in vain and your faith has been in vain. . . . Then those also who have died in Christ have perished. If for this life only we have hoped in Christ, we are of all people most to be pitied.

g. Death, Where Is Thy Sting?

Listen, I will tell you a mystery! We will not all die, but we will all be changed, in a moment, in the twinkling of an eye, at the last trumpet. For the trumpet will sound, and the dead will be raised imperishable, and we will be changed. For this perishable body must put on imperishability, and this mortal body must put on immortality. When this perishable body puts on imperishability, and this mortal body puts on immortality, then the saying that is written will be fulfilled:

> "Death has been swallowed up in victory.
> Where O death, is your victory?
> Where, O death, is your sting?"

h. The Depth of God's Love

Nothing. . . can come between us and the love of Christ, even if we are troubled or worried, or being persecuted, or lacking food or clothes, or being threatened or even attacked. . . . For I am certain of this: neither death nor life, no angel, no prince, nothing that exists, nothing still to come, not any power, or height or depth, nor any created thing, can ever come between us and the love of God made visible in Christ Jesus our Lord.

i. The Centrality of Love

If I speak in the tongues of mortals and of angels, but do not have love, I am a noisy gong or a clanging cymbal. And if I have prophetic powers, and understand all mysteries and all knowledge, and if I have all faith, so as to remove mountains, but do not have love, I am nothing. If I give away all my possessions, and if I hand over my body so that I may boast, but do not have love, I gain nothing.

Love is patient; love is kind. . . . It does not insist on its own way. . . . It bears all things, . . . hopes all things, endures all things. . . .

. . . When I was a child, I spoke like a child, I thought like a child, I reasoned like a child; when I became an adult, I put an end to childish ways. For now we see in a mirror, dimly, but then we will see face to face. Now I know only in part; then I will know fully, even as I have been fully known. And now faith, hope, and love abide, these three; and the greatest of these is love.

j. "Let This Mind Be in You"

Let each of you look not to your own interests but to the interests of others. Let the same mind be in you that was in Christ Jesus,

> who, though he was in the form of God,
> . . . emptied himself, taking the form of a slave
>   being born in human likeness.
> And being found in human form,
>   he humbled himself and became obedient to the point of
>   death—even death on a cross.
> Therefore God also highly exalted him
>   and gave him a name that is above every name,
> so that at the name of Jesus
>   every knee should bend,
>   in heaven and on earth and under the earth,
> and every tongue should confess
>   that Jesus Christ is the Lord,
>   to the glory of God the Father.

k. Salvation by Faith

Fifteen hundred years later, Martin Luther's interpretation of the following words of Paul will spark the Protestant Reformation.

For I am not ashamed of the gospel; it is the power of God for salvation to everyone who has faith, to the Jew first and also to the Greek. For in it the righteousness of God is revealed through faith for faith; as it is written, "The one who is righteous will live by faith."

l. Faith Must Be Proven by Works

What good is it, my brothers and sisters, if you say you have faith but do not have works? Can faith save you? If a brother or sister is naked and lacks daily food, and one of you says to them, "Go in peace; keep warm and eat your fill," and yet you do not supply their bodily needs, what is the good of that? So faith by itself, if it has no works, is dead.

33. Persecution

a. Tension Between the Jewish Authorities and the New Jewish Christians

The high priest questioned them, saying, "We gave you strict orders not to teach in this name, yet you have filled Jerusalem with your teaching. . . ." But Peter and the apostles answered, "We must obey God rather than any human authority. The God of our ancestors raised up Jesus, whom you had killed by hanging him on a tree. . . ." When they heard this they were enraged and wanted to kill them. But a Pharisee in the council named Gamaliel [said]: " . . . Keep away from these men and let them alone; because if this plan is of human origin, it will fail; but if it is of God, you will not be able to overthrow them—in that case you may even be found fighting against God!"

They were convinced by him, and when they had called in the apostles, they had them flogged. Then they ordered them not to speak in the name of Jesus, and let them go. As they left the council, they rejoiced that they were considered worthy to suffer dishonour for the sake of the name. And every day in the temple and at home they did not cease to teach and proclaim Jesus as the Messiah.

b. Stephen, the First Martyr

[Stephen rebukes the Sanhedrin[8]:] "You stiff-necked people, un-circumcised in heart and ears, you are forever opposing the Holy Spirit, just as your ancestors used to do. . . ." When they heard these things, they became enraged and ground their teeth at Stephen. . . . Then they dragged him out of the city and began to stone him; and the witnesses laid their coats at the feet of a young man named Saul. While they were stoning Stephen, he prayed, "Lord Jesus, receive my spirit." Then he knelt down and cried out in a loud voice, "Lord, do not hold this sin against them." When he had said this, he died.

c. Saul the Persecutor

And Saul was among those who approved of [Stephen's] murder. This was the beginning of a time of violent persecution for the church of Jerusalem. . . . Saul, meanwhile, was harrying the church; he entered house after house, seizing men and women, and sending them to prison.

34. Saul Becomes Paul: Conversion on the Road to Damascus

Meanwhile Saul, still breathing threats and murder against the disciples of the Lord, went to the high priest and asked him for letters to the synagogues at Damascus, so that if he found any who belonged to the Way, men or women, he might bring them bound to Jerusalem. Now as he was going along and approaching Damascus, suddenly a light from heaven flashed around him. He fell to the ground and heard a voice saying to him, "Saul, Saul, why do you persecute me?" He asked, "Who are you, Lord?" The reply came,

---

8. The Sanhedrin was the supreme Jewish legislative-judicial assembly, headquartered in Jerusalem.

"I am Jesus, whom you are persecuting. But get up and enter the city and you will be told what you are to do.". . . Saul got up from the ground, and though his eyes were open, he could see nothing; so they led him by the hand and brought him into Damascus. For three days he was without sight and neither ate nor drank.

Now there was a disciple in Damascus named Ananias. [He] went and entered the house. He laid his hands on Saul and said, "Brother Saul, the Lord Jesus, who appeared to you on your way here, has sent me so that you may regain your sight and be filled with the Holy Spirit." And immediately something like scales fell from his eyes, and his sight was restored. Then he got up and was baptized, and after taking some food, he regained his strength.

35. Opening the Jesus-Community to the Gentiles

Jesus said he came "not to abolish but to fulfill" the Jewish Torah (Matt. 5:17). His early followers, themselves all Jews, assumed that the normal requirements of Jewish religious practice—circumcision for males, Sabbath observance, dietary laws—remained in force. So radical was Paul's conversion, however, that he insisted the gospel be preached universally, beyond the bounds and requirements of Jewish tradition. Life in the early church witnessed a tension between the Hebraists or Torah-loyalists and the Hellenists who, like Paul, wished to universalize the Good News.

a. The Council at Jerusalem

But some believers . . . stood up and said, "It is necessary for them [that is, new non-Jews] to be circumcised and ordered to keep the law of Moses."

The apostles and the elders met together to consider this matter. After there had been much debate, Peter stood up and said to them, ". . . God, who knows the human heart, testified to them by giving them the Holy Spirit, just as he did to us; and in cleansing their hearts by faith he has made no distinction between them and us. . . . We believe that we will be saved through the grace of the Lord Jesus, just as they will."

The whole assembly kept silence, and listened to Barnabas and Paul as they told of all the signs and wonders that God had done through them among the Gentiles. After they finished speaking, James replied, "My brothers, listen to me. . . . I have reached the decision that we should not trouble those Gentiles who are turning to God, but we should write to them to abstain only from [certain] things. . . ."

Then the apostles and the elders, with the consent of the whole church, decided to choose men from among their members and to send them to Antioch . . . with the following letter: ". . . To the believers of Gentile origin in Antioch and Syria and Cilicia, greetings. Since we have heard that certain persons who have gone out from us . . . have said things to disturb you and have unsettled your minds, we have decided unanimously . . . to impose on you no further burden than these essentials: that you abstain from what has been sacrificed to idols and from blood and from what is strangled and from fornication. If you keep yourselves from these, you will do well. Farewell."

b. The Handshake That Universalized Christianity

Then after fourteen years I went up again to Jerusalem with Barnabas. . . . Then I laid before them (though only in a private meeting with the acknowledged leaders) the gospel that I proclaim among the Gentiles, in order to make sure that I was not running, or had not run, in vain. . . . When they saw that I had been entrusted with the gospel for the uncircumcised, just as Peter had been entrusted with the gospel for the circumcised . . . and when James and Cephas and John, who were acknowledged pillars, recognized the grace that had been given to me, they gave to Barnabas and me the right hand of fellowship, agreeing that we should go to the Gentiles and they to the circumcised.

36. The Creeds

Those who wished to enter the Christian fold were asked to formally state their beliefs at the time of their baptism. These doctrinal affirmations were the precursors of the creeds, the formal statements of Christian faith. As Christianity spread throughout the Roman Empire,

*variations in the interpretation and practice of the faith began to de-
velop, threatening the unity of the Church. In response to these diver-
gences, particularly with regard to beliefs as to whether Jesus was
purely divine, purely human, or somehow both, the emperor Con-
stantine called the first great Christian Council at Nicaea in 325 C.E.
Out of that council came the Nicene Creed, a nuanced and doctrinally
precise statement of Christian orthodoxy.*

a. The Nicene Creed

We believe in one God,
    the Father, the Almighty,
    maker of heaven and earth,
    of all that is, seen and unseen.
We believe in one Lord, Jesus Christ,
    the only son of God,
    eternally begotten of the Father,
    God from God, Light from Light,
    true God from true God,
    begotten, not made,
    of one Being with the Father;
    through him all things were made.
    For us and for our salvation
    he came down from heaven,
    was incarnate of the Holy Spirit and the Virgin Mary
    and became truly human.
    For our sake he was crucified under Pontius Pilate;
    he suffered death and was buried.
    On the third day he rose again
    in accordance with the Scriptures;
    he ascended into heaven
    and is seated at the right hand of the Father.
    He will come again in glory to judge the living and the dead,
    and his kingdom will have no end.
We believe in the Holy Spirit, the Lord, the giver of life,
    who proceeds from the Father [and the Son],
    who with the Father and the Son is worshiped and glorified,
    who has spoken through the prophets.

We believe in one holy catholic and apostolic Church.
We acknowledge one baptism for the forgiveness of sins.
We look for the resurrection of the dead,
and the life of the world to come. Amen.

GRACE NOTES

37. The Gospel of Thomas

The Gospel of Thomas surfaced in the archaeological discovery of the Nag Hammadi Library around 1945. Unlike the Gospels of Matthew, Mark, Luke, and John, it does not narrate Jesus' life but is solely a collection of one hundred and fourteen of his sayings. Many echo the canonical Gospels, but some do not. With the exception of number f below, I have chosen those that are largely unique to the Gospel of Thomas and that have a mystical flavor. My selections are not meant to be representative of the Gospel of Thomas as a whole.

a. Inside You

Jesus said, "If your leaders say to you, 'Look, the kingdom is in heaven,' then the birds of heaven will precede you. If they say to you, 'It is in the sea,' then the fish will precede you. Rather, the kingdom is inside you and it is outside you."

b. Know Yourselves

[Jesus said,] "When you know yourselves, then you will be known, and you will understand that you are children of the living father. But if you do not know yourselves, then you dwell in poverty, and you are poverty."

c. Wholeness

Jesus said, ". . . If one is [whole][9], one will be filled with light, but if one is divided, one will be filled with darkness."

---

9. Translator's indication of a correction of a scribal error or omission.

d. I Am There

Jesus said, "I am the light that is over all things. I am all: From me all has come forth, and to me all has reached. Split a piece of wood; I am there. Lift up the stone, and you will find me there."

e. Presence

They said to him, "Tell us who you are so that we may believe in you."

He said to them, "You examine the face of heaven and earth, but you have not come to know the one who is in your presence, and you do not know how to examine this moment."

f. The Kingdom

His followers said to him, "When will the kingdom come?"
"It will not come by watching for it, It will not be said, 'Look, here it is,' or 'Look, there it is.' Rather, the father's kingdom is spread out upon the earth, and people do not see it."

38. Clement of Alexandria (150?–220?)

An early Christian thinker, Church Father, and head of the catechetical school at Alexandria.

God became a person, so that persons might become God.

39. St. Augustine (ca. 354–430)

Bishop of Hippo, philosopher, theologian, and inestimably important shaper of the Christian mind.

a. Our Hearts Are Restless

For Thou hast made us for Thyself, and our hearts are restless till they rest in Thee.

b. Late Have I Loved Thee!

Late have I loved Thee, O Beauty so ancient and so new; late have I loved Thee! For behold Thou wert within me, and I outside; and I sought Thee outside and in my unloveliness fell upon those lovely things that Thou hast made. Thou wert within me and I was not with Thee. I was kept from Thee by those things, yet had they not been in Thee, they would not have been at all. Thou didst call and cry to me and break open my deafness: and Thou didst send forth Thy beams and shine upon me and chase away my blindness: Thou didst breathe fragrance upon me, and I drew in my breath and do now pant for Thee: I tasted Thee, and now hunger and thirst for Thee: Thou didst touch me, and I have burned for Thy peace.

c. A Real Life

When once I shall be united to Thee . . . my life shall be a real life, being wholly full of Thee.

40. St. Hildegard of Bingen (1098–1179)

Medieval German abbess, contemplative, and mystic.

a. The Fiery Light

In the year 1141 of the incarnation of Jesus Christ the Son of God, when I was forty-two years and seven months of age, a fiery light, flashing intensely, came from the open vault of heaven and poured through my whole brain. Like a flame that is hot without burning it kindled all my heart and all my breast. . . . And suddenly I could understand what such books as the . . . Old and New Testament actually set forth. . . .

b. God Speaks Through Hildegard

I, the highest and fiery power, have kindled every living spark and I have breathed out nothing that can die. . . . I flame above the beauty of the fields, I shine in the waters; in the sun, the moon and the stars, I burn. . . . All living things take their radiance from me;

and I am the life which remains the same through eternity, having neither beginning nor end;

c. God as Mother

The faithful . . . thirst for God's Justice and they suck holiness from her breasts. . . .

41. St. Francis of Assisi (1182–1226)

Beloved Italian saint, founder of the Franciscan order, dedicated to serving the needy.

a. The Canticle of Brother Sun

All praise be yours, my Lord, through all that you have made,
    And first my lord Brother Sun,
      Who brings the day; and light you give to us through him.

How beautiful he is, how radiant in all his splendour!
    Of you, Most High, he bears the likeness.

All praise be yours, my Lord, through Sister Moon and Stars;
    In the heavens you have made them, bright
    And precious and fair.

All praise be yours, my Lord, through Brothers Wind and Air,
    And fair and stormy, all the weather's moods,
    By which you cherish all that you have made.

All praise be yours, my Lord, through Sister Water,
    So useful, lowly, precious and pure.

All praise be yours, my Lord, through Brother Fire,
    Through whom you brighten up the night.
    How beautiful he is, how gay! Full of power and strength.

All praise be yours, my Lord, thought Sister Earth, our mother,
    Who feeds us in her sovereignty and produces
    Various fruits and colored flowers and herbs.

All praise be yours, my Lord, through Sister Death,
    From whose embrace no mortal can escape.

Woe to those who die in mortal sin!
Happy those She finds doing your will!
The second death[10] can do no harm to them.

Praise and bless my Lord, and give him thanks,
And serve him with great humility.

b. An Instrument of Thy Peace[11]

Lord make me an instrument of Thy peace.
Where there is hatred, let me sow love,
Where there is offence, pardon,
Where there is discord, unity,
Where there is doubt, faith,
Where there is error, truth,
Where there is despair, hope,
Where there is sadness, joy,
Where there is darkness, light.
O Divine Master, grant that I may not so much seek
To be consoled as to console,
To be understood as to understand,
To be loved as to love.
For:
It is in giving that we receive.
It is in pardoning that we are pardoned.
It is in dying that we are born to eternal life.

42. Mechthild of Magdeburg (1210–1297)

German visionary and poet, member of the Beguine order of lay sisters.

a. Two Lovers

That prayer has great power
which a person makes with all his might . . .
It draws down the great God into the little heart,

---

10. That is, the end of our natural life. The first death (and rebirth) is baptism.
11. Commonly ascribed to St. Francis, this poem was written by an unknown twentieth-century author.

It drives the hungry soul up into the fullness of God.
It brings together two lovers,
God and the soul,
In a wondrous place where they speak much of love.

b. See and Taste the Flowing Godhead

Wouldst thou know my meaning?
Lie down in the Fire
See and taste the Flowing
Godhead through thy being;
Feel the Holy Spirit
Moving and compelling
Thee within the Flowing
Fire and Light of God.

c. The Overflow

Great is the overflow of Divine Love which is never still but
ever ceaselessly and tirelessly pours forth, so that our little vessel
is filled to the brim and overflows. If we do not choke the
channel with self-will, God's gifts continue to flow and overflow,
Lord!

43. St. Bonaventure (1221–1274)

*Called the "Seraphic Doctor," Bonaventure was an eminent medieval
writer and contemplative.*

God is a sphere whose center is everywhere and whose circumference is nowhere.

44. St. Thomas Aquinas (1225?–1274)

*Called the "Angelic Doctor," Thomas's profound and lasting influence
stems from his formidable synthesis of Catholic theology and Greek
philosophical ideas.*

a. Knower and Known

A thing is known according to the state of consciousness of the
knower.

b. The Way of Negation

The chief way to consider God is the way of negation, for by its immensity the divine essence transcends every form attained by our intellect; . . . By *knowing what it is not* we get some knowledge of it, and the more things we are able to deny of it, the nearer we come to knowing it.

45. Meister Eckhart (1260–1327)

German priest and one of the greatest Christian mystics.

a. God's Eye

The eye by which I see God is the same as the eye by which God sees me. My eye and God's eye are one and the same.

b. The Birth of Christ

Christ's birth is always happening. And yet if it doesn't happen in me, how can it help me? Everything depends on that.

c. The Way It Is

God *must* act and pour himself into you the moment he finds you ready. Don't imagine that God can be compared to an earthly carpenter, who acts or doesn't act, as he wishes; who can will to do something or leave it undone, according to his pleasure. It is *not* that way with God: where and when God finds you ready, he *must* act and overflow into you, just as when the air is clear and pure, the sun must overflow into it and cannot refrain from doing that.

d. The Eternal Now

The Now in which God created the first man and the Now in which the last man will disappear and the Now in which I am speaking—all are the same in God, and there is only one Now.

e. Be the Son

Scripture says, "No one knows the Father but the Son." Therefore, if you want to know God, you must not only be like the Son, you must *be* the Son.

46. Julian of Norwich (1342?–1420?)

English anchoress and contemplative.

a. God Suffices

God, of your goodness, give me yourself; for you are sufficient for me, and I cannot properly ask anything less, to be worthy of you. If I were to ask less, I should always be in want. In you alone do I have all.

b. True Rest

This is the reason why we have no ease of heart or soul, for we are seeking our rest in trivial things which cannot satisfy. . . .

He [alone] is true rest. . . . Nothing less will satisfy us.

c. Body and Soul in God

For [God] does not despise what he made, nor does he disdain to serve us in the simplest function that belongs to our body. . . . For as the body is clad in the cloth, and the flesh in the skin, and the bones in the flesh, and the heart in the trunk, so are we, soul and body, clad and enclosed in the goodness of God. Yes, and more intimately, for all these vanish and waste away; but the goodness of God is ever whole and nearer to us, beyond any comparison.

d. God as Mother

This fair lovely word "mother" is so sweet and so kind in itself that it cannot truly be said of anyone or to anyone except of him and to him who is the true Mother of life and of all things. To the property of motherhood belong nature, love, wisdom and knowledge, and this is God.

47. St. Thomas à Kempis (1380–1471)

The author of The Imitation of Christ, *possibly the most published book in Christendom after the Bible.*

He who is thus a spiritual lover knows well what that voice means which says: You, Lord God, are my whole love and desire. You are all mine, and I all Yours. Dissolve my heart into Your love so that I may know how sweet it is to serve You and how joyful it is to praise You, and to be as though I were all melded into Your love. . . . I shall sing to you the song of love. . . and my soul will never be weary in praising You with the joyful songs of unconditional love.

48. Teresa of Avila (1515–1582)

Spanish mystic and cofounder with St. John of the Cross of the Order of Discalced Carmelites.

LINES WRITTEN IN HER BREVIARY

Let nothing disturb you,
Let nothing frighten you;
All things are passing;
God never changes;
Patient endurance
Obtains all things;
Who God possess
In nothing is wanting;
God alone suffices.

49. St. John of the Cross (1542–1591)

Spanish poet and one of the Catholic tradition's greatest mystics.

THE DARK NIGHT

One dark night,
Fired with love's urgent longings
—Ah, the sheer grace!—

I went out unseen,
My house being now all stilled;

. . . With no other light or guide
Than the one that burned in my heart;

This guided me
More surely than the light of noon
To where He waited for me
—Him I knew so well—
In a place where no one else appeared.

O guiding night!
O night more lovely than the dawn!
O night that has united
The Lover with His beloved,
Transforming the beloved in her Lover.

. . . I abandoned and forgot myself,
Laying my face on my Beloved;
All things ceased; I went out from myself,
Leaving my cares
Forgotten among the lilies.

50. St. Ignatius Loyola (1491–1556)

Founder of the Society of Jesus.

ANIMA CHRISTI (SOUL OF CHRIST)

Soul of Christ, sanctify me
Body of Christ, save me
Blood of Christ, inebriate me
Water from the side of Christ, wash me
Passion of Christ, strengthen me

O Good Jesus, hear me
Within thy wounds, hide me
Permit me not to be separated from Thee
From the wicked foe defend me
At the hour of my death call me And bid me to come to Thee
That with Thy saints I may praise Thee
For ever and ever. Amen.

51. Jean Pierre de Caussade (1675–1751)

French priest and contemplative.

Abandonment to Divine Providence

But what is the secret of finding this treasure?—There isn't one. This treasure is everywhere. It is offered to us all the time and wherever we are. All creatures, friends or foes, pour it out in abundance, and it flows through every fiber of our body and soul until it reaches the very core of our being. . . . God's activity runs through the universe. It wells up around and penetrates every created being. Where they are, there it is also. It goes ahead of them, it is with them, and it follows them. All they have to do is let its waves sweep them onward, fulfill the simple duties of their religion and state, cheerfully accept all the troubles they meet, and submit to God's will in all they have to do. . . . This is true spirituality, which is valid for all times and for everyone. We cannot become truly good in a better, more marvelous, and yet easier way than by the simple use of the means offered us by God: the ready acceptance of all that comes to us at each moment of our lives.

52. The Russian Pilgrim (ca. 1850)

Here an anonymous Eastern Orthodox Christian reports the extraordinary effects of the "prayer of the heart" or "Jesus prayer," the practice of silently repeating "Lord Jesus Christ, Son of God, have mercy upon me" in one's every waking moment.

By the grace of God, I am a Christian man, by my actions a great sinner, and by calling a homeless wanderer of the humblest birth who roams from place to place. My worldly goods are a knapsack with some dried bread in it on my back, and in my breast-pocket a Bible. And that is all.

And when . . . I prayed with my heart, everything around me seemed delightful and marvelous. The trees, the grass, the birds, the earth, the air, the light seemed to be telling me that they existed for man's sake, that they witnessed to the love of God for man, that everything proved the love of God for man, that all things prayed to God and sang His praise.

. . . Sometimes my heart would feel as though it were bubbling with joy, such lightness, freedom and consolation were in it. Sometimes I felt a burning love for Jesus Christ and for all God's creatures. Sometimes my eyes brimmed over with tears of thankfulness to God who was so merciful to me, a wretched sinner. Sometimes my understanding, which had been so stupid before, was given so much light that I could easily grasp and dwell upon matters of which up to now I had not been able even to think at all. Sometimes that sense of a warm gladness in my heart spread throughout my whole being and I was deeply moved as the fact of the presence of God everywhere was brought home to me. Sometimes by calling upon the Name of Jesus I was overwhelmed with bliss, and now I knew the meaning of the words "The Kingdom of God is within you."

. . . The prayer of the heart gave me such consolation that I felt there was no happier person on earth than I, and I doubted if there could be greater and fuller happiness in the kingdom of Heaven. Not only did I feel this in my own soul, but the whole outside world also seemed to me full of charm and delight. Everything drew me to love and thank God: people, trees, plants, animals. I saw them all as my kinsfolk. I found on all of them the magic of the name of Jesus. Sometimes I felt as light as though I had no body and was floating happily through the air instead of walking. Sometimes when I withdrew into myself I . . . was filled with wonder at the wisdom with which the human body is made. . . . And at all such times of happiness, I wished that God would . . . let me pour out my heart in thankfulness at His feet. . . .

53. Thomas Merton (1915–1968)

Trappist monk and widely influential twentieth-century Catholic writer.

a. What Is Contemplation?

Contemplation is spontaneous awe at the sacredness of life. . . . It is gratitude for life, for awareness and for being. It is a vivid realization of the fact that life and being proceed from an invisible, transcendent and infinitely abundant Source.

b. The True Joy

The only true joy on earth is to escape from the prison of our own false self, and enter by love into union with the Life Who dwells and sings within the essence of every creature and in the core of our own souls.

c. One Problem

There is only one problem on which all my existence, my peace and my happiness depend: to discover myself in discovering God.

d. The Difference Between Pleasure and Joy

Do not look for rest in any pleasure, because you were not created for pleasure: you were created for JOY. And if you do not know the difference between pleasure and spiritual joy you have not yet begun to live.

e. Grace

So keep still, and let Him do some work.

54. Reinhold Niebuhr (1892–1971)

An influential Protestant theologian.

THE SERENITY PRAYER

God
Grant me
Serenity
To accept the things I cannot change
Courage
To change the things I can and
Wisdom to know the difference.

55. Martin Luther King, Jr. (1929–1968): *Letter from the Birmingham City Jail*

Dr. King was the leading spokesman for the American civil rights movement and was awarded the Nobel Peace Prize in 1964. In 1963, some of his fellow clergymen had issued a statement that, while sympathizing with his civil rights goals, criticized his tactic of civil disobedience. In jail for that offense, King, with a smuggled pen and on scraps of paper, defended his actions in a letter that was to become the most famous document of the movement. Only a brief portion is excerpted here.

My fellow clergymen. . .

You express a great deal of anxiety over our willingness to break laws. . . . One may well ask, "How can you advocate breaking some laws and obeying others?" The answer is found in the fact that there are two types of laws: There are *just* laws and there are *unjust* laws. I would agree with St. Augustine that "An unjust law is no law at all."

Now what is the difference between the two? How does one determine when a law is just or unjust? A just law is a man-made code which squares with the moral law or the law of God. An unjust law is a code that is out of harmony with the moral law. To put it in the term of St. Thomas Aquinas, an unjust law is a human law that is not rooted in eternal and natural law. Any law that uplifts human personality is just. Any law that degrades human personality is unjust. All segregation statutes are unjust because segregation distorts the soul and damages the personality. . . . To use the words of Martin Buber, the great Jewish philosopher, segregation substitutes an "I-it" relationship for the "I-thou" relationship, and ends up relegating persons to the status of things. . . . So I can urge men to disobey segregation ordinances because they are morally wrong. . . .

You spoke of our activity in Birmingham as extreme. At first I was rather disappointed that fellow clergymen would see my nonviolent efforts as those of the extremist. . . .

But as I continued to think about the matter I gradually gained a bit of satisfaction from being considered an extremist. Was not Jesus an extremist in love—"Love your enemies, bless them that curse you, pray for them that despitefully use you." Was not Amos an extremist for justice—"Let justice roll down like waters and righteousness like a mighty stream." Was not Paul an extremist for the gospel of Jesus Christ—"I bear in my body the marks of the Lord Jesus." Was not Martin Luther an extremist—"Here I stand; I can do no other so help me God." Was not John Bunyan an extremist—"I will stay in jail to the end of my days before I make a butchery of my conscience." Was not Abraham Lincoln an extremist—"This nation cannot survive half slave and half free." Was not Thomas Jefferson an extremist—"We hold these truths to be self-evident, that all men are created equal." So the question is not whether we will be extremist but what kind of extremist will we be.

. . . Let us hope that the dark clouds of racial prejudice will soon pass away and the deep fog of misunderstanding will be lifted from our fear-drenched communities and in some not too distant tomorrow the radiant stars of love and brotherhood will shine over our great nation with all of their scintillating beauty.

Yours for the cause of Peace and Brotherhood,
Martin Luther King, Jr.

56. Amazing Grace

A renowned Christian hymn.

Amazing grace! how sweet the sound
That saved a wretch like me!
I once was lost, but now am found,
Was blind, but now I see.

'Twas grace that taught my heart to fear,
And grace my fears relieved;
How precious did that grace appear
The hour I first believed.

Through many dangers, toils and snares,
I have already come;
'Tis grace hath brought me safe thus far,
And grace will lead me home.

When we've been there ten thousand years,
Bright shining as the sun,
We've no less days to sing God's praise
Than when we first begun.

CHAPTER SEVEN

Islam

*T*he first of Islam's two central affirmations is "There is no god but God" (La ilaha illa'llah). *The God referred to here is none other than the One God of the Jews and the Christians, the God who created the universe, revealed his will to Abraham, Moses, and the Jewish prophets, and the God whom Jesus called Father. The problem, Muslims say, is that over the Jewish and Christian centuries, God's message was sometimes lost in human static. God therefore resolved to disclose his will for humankind once again—fully, unambiguously, and finally—through a devout Arab of the sixth century C.E. His name was Muhammad, and the sum of the revelation he received over the relatively short span of twenty-three years is the Qur'an, the holy book of Islam. For Muslims there is nothing holier on earth. The Qur'an is for them, like Christ for Christians, the living Word of God, God's presence on earth. Muhammad's role in conveying the Qur'an is honored in the second of Islam's great affirmations: "Muhammad is the Prophet of God"* (Muhammadan rasulu'llah).

Though Islam is the youngest (and fastest growing) of the world's religions, it does not think of itself as a new tradition, but rather as the culmination of a very old one. Nor does it think of itself as a "religion," if by that word we mean a set of beliefs and actions sealed off from the rest of our worldly business. Rather, Islam sees itself as an all-embracing way of life. Contained within its teaching of the path to God is guidance for the entire range of human life—social, political, and economic.

The two basic sources for the Islamic tradition are the Qur'an[1] itself and the hadiths *or "traditions" of Muhammad. The latter are reports of the sayings and deeds of the Prophet by those who knew him. Accordingly, most of the selections below belong either to the Qur'an or to the* hadiths, *with a final section of Grace Notes paying tribute to the spirit of Islamic mysticism or Sufism.*

THE QUR'AN: Suras of Mecca and Medina

Over the twenty-three-year period in which the Qur'an was revealed to Muhammad, he resided first at Mecca as the embattled Prophet of embryonic Islam, and then at Medina as the respected leader of an established Islamic community. The suras, or chapters, of the Qur'an are often classified according to these two loci of revelation. The earlier Meccan suras are highly oracular utterances concerning the unity, glory, and power of God, the moral responsibility of human beings, and the coming end of the world and judgment of humankind. The later Medinan suras, while including these themes, are more prosaic dictates regarding legal and social matters and the general conduct of life. Unlike its cousins, the Hebrew Bible and the Christian New Testament, the holy Qur'an contains little narrative. There is no story of a people's movement across time and space as there is in the Hebrew Bible, no story of God's incarnation as we find in the New Testament.

The reader should note that in the Qur'an God refers to himself interchangeably as "We," "He," and "I." All of the verses of the Qur'an

---

1. Throughout this book I have tried to select passages that edify as well as instruct. One feels that nowhere is this task more difficult than in the case of the Qur'an. Its power resides not only in the meanings of its words but in the untranslatable lyrical beauty of its Arabic original. Anyone trying to get a feel for Islam is well advised to hear the Qur'an recited.

are to be understood as the direct speech of God, not of Muhammad. Muhammad was the Qur'an's conduit, not its author.

1. Suras of Mecca

Of the headings in this section only numbers a and h reflect the actual titles of the suras in the Qur'an. The other headings are mine, used for descriptive purposes.

a. The *Fatihah* (Opening)

This sura has been called the very essence of the Qur'an.

> In the Name of God, the merciful Lord of mercy.
> Praise be to God, the Lord of all being,
> The merciful Lord of mercy,
> Master of the Day of Judgment.
> You alone we serve and to You alone we come for aid.
> Guide us in the straight path,
> The path of those whom You have blessed,
> Not of those against whom there is displeasure,
> Nor of those who have gone astray.

b. The First Verses Revealed to Muhammad

> RECITE, in the Name of your Lord who created,
> Created man from a sperm-cell.
> Recite, how altogether gracious is your Lord,
> who taught by the pen, taught man what he knows not.

c. God Celebrates the Night of His First Revelation to Muhammad

> Truly we revealed the Qur'an on the night of authority.
> Would that you knew what the night of authority means!
> Better than a thousand months is the night of authority.
> Thereon come the angels and the Spirit down,
> By leave of their Lord, for every behest.
> It is a night of peace until the breaking of the day.

d. God Begets Not, Nor Is He Begotten

In the name of the merciful Lord of mercy. Say:
"He is God, One, God the ever self-sufficing,
He begets not, nor is begotten.
None is like unto Him."

e. Say: I Take Refuge in God

In the name of the merciful Lord of mercy. Say:
"I take refuge with the Lord of men,
The King of men, the God of men,
From the evil of the whispering insinuator
Who whispers in the hearts of men,
From jinn[2] and men."

f. God, the Creator, Knows All

Praise the Name of your Lord most high, He who created and
fashioned, He who measured and guided, who caused the pasture
to spring forth and then turned its green to decay. We will cause
you to recite: so forget not, except as God wills. For He knows what
is uttered and what is concealed. . . .

g. Death and Judgment

. . . Death to man! how thankless he is! From what did God create
him? From a drop of sperm He made him and ordered his being,
facilitating his course, and then of God comes his dying and his
being laid in the grave. Then, when he wills, He brings him forth
to life again.

. . . When the resurrection trump is heard, on a day when a man
shall flee from his brother, his mother, and his father, from his wife
and children—on that day every human living will have more than
enough on his hands. On that day there will be shining faces, blithe

---

2. Invisible demons and spirits, mainly malevolent but sometimes helpful to
human beings. The English word *genie* originates here.

with joy, and there will be faces blackened with dust—the faces of the faithless and the graceless.

h. The Earthquake

When Earth is rocked in her last convulsion; when Earth shakes off her burdens and man asks, "What may this mean?"—on that day she will proclaim her tidings, for your Lord will have inspired her.

On that day mankind will come in broken bands to be shown their labours. Whoever does an atom's weight of good shall see it, and whoever does an atom's weight of evil will see it also.

2. A Sura of Medina

Medinan suras tend to be much longer than Meccan suras. Below are selections from the longest Medinan sura, Sura 2, with my own sub headings. Other examples of the content of Medinan suras may be found in selection 10, "Social Matters."

a. On Eating

Believers! Eat of the good things with which We have provided you and give thanks to God—if indeed it is His worshippers you are! However, carrion, blood, and the meat of swine are prohibited to you as well as that over which any other name than God's has been invoked. But if anyone is driven by necessity, without deliberate intent and not going beyond his need, there will be no sin incurred by him. God is forgiving and merciful.

b. On Wills

. . . It is decreed that when death approaches, those of you that leave property shall bequeath it equitably to parents and kindred. This is a duty incumbent upon the righteous. He that alters a will after hearing it shall be accountable for his crime. God hears all and knows all.

He that suspects an error or an injustice on the part of a testator and brings about a settlement among the parties incurs no guilt. God is forgiving and merciful.

c. On Fasting

You who have believed, fasting is decreed for you as it was for those who came before you, with a view to a deep sense among you of devotion to God. . . . When anyone, of his own free will, outdoes what is enjoined that is certainly to his own good. For when you fast, you do good to yourselves, did you but realise it.

d. On Almsgiving

Whatever alms you give shall rebound to your own advantage, provided that you give them for the love of God. And whatever alms you give shall be paid back to you in full: you shall not be wronged.

As for those needy men who, being wholly preoccupied with fighting for the cause of God, cannot travel the land in quest of trading ventures: the ignorant take them for men of wealth on account of their modest behavior. But you can recognize them by their look—they never importune men for alms. Whatever alms you give are known to God.

Those who give alms by day and by night, in private and in public, shall be rewarded by their Lord. They shall have nothing to fear or to regret.

e. On Debts and Transactions

Those that live on usury shall rise up before God like men whom Satan has demented by his touch; for they claim that trading is no different from usury. But God has permitted trading and made usury unlawful. . . .

God has laid His curse on usury and blessed almsgiving with increase. God bears no love for the impious and the sinful.

. . . If your debtor be in straits, grant him a delay until he can discharge his debt; but if you waive the sum as alms it will be better for you, if you but knew it.

. . . Believers, when you contract a debt for a fixed period, put it in writing. Let a scribe write it down for you with fairness; no scribe should refuse to write as God has taught him. Therefore, let him write; and let the debtor dictate, fearing God his Lord and not diminishing the sum he owes. If the debtor be a feeble-minded or ignorant person, or one who cannot dictate, let his guardian dictate for him in fairness. Call in two male witnesses from among you, but if two men cannot be found, then one man and two women whom you judge fit to act as witnesses; so that if either of them commit an error, the other will remember. Witnesses must not refuse to give evidence if called upon to do so. So do not fail to put your debts in writing, be they small or big, together with the date of payment. This is more just in the sight of God; it ensures accuracy in testifying and is the best way to remove all doubt. But if the transaction in hand be a bargain concluded on the spot, it is no offence for you if you do not commit it to writing.

See that witnesses are present when you barter with one another, and let no harm be done to either scribe or witness. If you harm them you shall commit a transgression. Have fear of God, who teaches you: God has knowledge of all things.

If you are travelling the road and a scribe cannot be found, then let pledges be taken. If any one of you entrusts another with a pledge, let the trustee restore the pledge to its owner; and let him fear God, his Lord.

You shall not withhold testimony. He that withholds it is a transgressor. God has knowledge of all your actions.

THE QUR'AN: Selections Thematically Arranged

3. The Unimpeachability of the Qur'an

This Book is not to be doubted. It is a guide for the righteous, who have faith in the unseen and are steadfast in prayer.

People of the Book! Our apostle has come to reveal to you much of what you have hidden in the Scriptures, and to forgive you much. A light has come to you from God and a glorious Book, with which He will guide to the paths of peace those that seek to please Him; He will lead them by His will from darkness to the light; He will guide them to a straight path.

And to you [Muslims] We have revealed the Book with the truth. It confirms the Scriptures which came before it and stands as a guardian over them.

4. The Inimitability of the Qur'an

Muslims emphasize that the Qur'an came through Muhammad, not from him. God alone is its author.

If you are in doubt of what We have revealed to Our Servant, produce one chapter comparable to it.

If they say: "He [Muhammad] invented it himself," say: "Bring me one chapter like it. Call on whom you may besides Allah to help you, if what you say be true!"

5. The Five Elements of Islamic Faith (*Iman*)

Islamic faith affirms and celebrates five holy realities: The Godhead Itself and Its Unity; Angels; Scriptures, and Messengers; the Last Day; and the Divine Will and Providence.[3]

Believers, have faith in God and His apostle, in the Book He has revealed to His Apostle, and in the Scriptures He formerly revealed. He that denies God, His angels, His scriptures, His apostles, and the Last Day, has gone far astray.

a. The Nature of God

One and Infinitely Aware

Say: "God is One, the Eternal God. He begot none, nor was He begotten. None is equal to Him."

Say: "Praise be to God who has never begotten a son; who has no partner in His Kingdom; who needs none to defend Him from humiliation." Proclaim His greatness.

Are sundry gods better than God, the One who conquers all? Those whom you serve besides Him are nothing but names which you and your fathers have devised and for which God has revealed no sanction. Judgement rests only with God. He has commanded you to worship none but Him. That is the true faith: yet most men do not know it.

---

3. The Arabic is *al-qada wa'l-qadar,* "divine decree and predestination."

God, there is none but He, the alive, the ever real. Slumber takes Him not, nor sleep. Everything in the heavens and earth is his, and who—His leave apart—shall intercede with Him? He knows everything that mankind have presently in hand and everything about them that is yet to be. Of a knowledge like His they are entirely uncomprehending—unless he gives them leave to know. In the vastness of the heavens and the earth His Throne is established. Tirelessly He preserves them. So great is His majesty.

God is his own witness that there is no God but He. Angels bear witness also and those of discerning mind. He is the arbiter of justice. There is no god but He, infinite in power and wisdom.

Such is God your Lord. There is no God but He, Creator of all things. Then worship Him who is guardian over all there is. No human perception comprehends Him, while He comprehends all perception. He is beyond all conceiving, the One who is infinitely aware.

All that is in the heavens and in the earth magnifies God. He is the all-strong, the all-wise. To Him belongs the kingdom of the heavens and of the earth. He gives life and He brings on death and He is omnipotent over all things. He is the first and the last, the manifest and the hidden, and has knowledge over all things. It is He who created the heavens and the earth in six days and then assumed his Throne. He knows all that permeates the ground and all that issues from it, what comes down from the heaven and what ascends thither. He is with you wherever you are. God is aware of all you do.

His is the kingdom of the heavens and of the earth and to Him all things return. He makes the night to give way to the day and the day to the night and He knows the innermost heart.

Closer than Our Jugular Vein

We created man. We know the promptings of his soul, and are closer to him than his jugular vein.

God's Glorious Names

God has the Most Excellent Names. Call on Him by His names and keep away from those that pervert them.

Say: "It is the same whether you call on God or on the Merciful: His are the most gracious names."

He is God, the Creator, the Originator, the Modeller.... All that is in heaven and earth gives glory to Him. He is the Mighty, the Wise One.

From the Traditional Ninety-nine Names of Allah:

Al-Qabid *(The Constrictor)*
Al-Khafid *(The Abaser)*
Al-Hadi *(The Guide)*
Al-Muntaqim *(The Avenger)*
Al-Mumit *(The Creator of Death)*
Al-Mujib *(The Responsive)*
Al-Wakil *(The Trustee)*
Al-Wali *(The Protecting Friend)*
Al-Muhsi *(The Reckoner)*
Al-Awwal *(The First)*
Az-Zahir *(The Manifest)*
Al-Khaliq *(The Creator)*
Ar-Rahman *(The Beneficent)*

Al-Basit *(The Expander)*
Ar-Rafi' *(The Exalter)*
As-Sabur *(The Patient)*
Al-'Afuw *(The Pardoner)*
As-Samad *(The Eternal)*
Al-Wadud *(The Loving)*
Al-Ghafur *(The All-Forgiving)*
Al-Muhyi *(The Giver of Life)*
Al-Mubdi *(The Originator)*
Al-Akhir *(The Last)*
Al-Batin *(The Hidden)*
Al-Bari' *(The Evolver)*
Ar-Rahim *(The Merciful)*

Bismi'llah and Insha'llah

Every sura of the Qur'an begins, "In the name of God [Allah], The Compassionate, the Merciful"; likewise, Muslims undertake many daily actions with the invocation "bismi'llah," "In the name of Allah." When speaking about their intentions for the near or distant future Muslims often append the phrase "insha'llah" or "If Allah wills it."

Bismi'llah Ar-Rahman Ar-Rahim (In the Name of Allah, the Compassionate, the Merciful)

Do not say of anything: "I will do it tomorrow," without adding: "If Allah wills" [*insha'llah*]. When you forget, remember your Lord and say: "May Allah guide me and bring me nearer to the Truth."

b. Angels

Whoever is an enemy of God, His angels, or His apostles, or of Gabriel or Michael, will surely find that God is the enemy of the unbelievers.

The Apostle believes in what has been revealed to him by his Lord, and so do the faithful. They all believe in God and His angels. . . .

c. God Reveals Scripture and Sends Messengers and Prophets

Scriptures

We have revealed the Torah, in which there is guidance and light. By it the prophets who surrendered themselves judged the Jews . . . according to God's Book which had been committed to their keeping and to which they themselves were witnesses.

. . . After them We sent forth Jesus, the son of Mary, confirming the Torah already revealed, and gave him the Gospel, in which there is guidance and light, corroborating what was revealed before it in the Torah, a guide and an admonition to the righteous. . . .

. . . And to you [Muslims] We have revealed the Book with the truth. It confirms the Scriptures which came before it and stands as a guardian over them.

A Prophet for Each Nation

An apostle is sent to every nation. When their apostle comes, justice is done among them; they are not wronged.

We raised an apostle in every nation, saying: "Serve [the One] God and keep away from false gods."

Islam's Continuity with the Prophetic Traditions of Judaism and Christianity

Say: "We believe in God and that which is revealed to us; in what was revealed to Abraham, Ishmael, Isaac, Jacob, and the tribes; to Moses and Jesus and the other prophets by their Lord.

We make no distinction among any of them, and to Allah we have surrendered ourselves."

God Recognizes the Righteous Irrespective of Sect

There are among the People of the Book some upright persons who all night long recite the revelations of God and worship Him; who believe in God and the Last Day; who enjoin justice and forbid evil and vie with each other in good works. These are righteous people: whatever good they do, its reward shall not be denied them. God knows the righteous.

d. The Last Day and Final Judgment

There are well over one hundred mentions of the Judgment Day in the Qur'an. They underscore Muslims' profound belief in a divine and universal justice that weighs every human act.

Every soul shall taste death, and in the end you shall return to Us.

The day will surely come when each soul will be confronted with whatever good it has done. As for its evil deeds, it will wish they were a long way off.

God will wrong none by an atom's weight. A good deed He will repay twofold.

They ask you about the Hour of Doom and when it will come. Say: "None knows except my Lord. He alone will reveal it—at the appointed time. A fateful hour it shall be, both in the heavens and on earth. It will overtake you without warning."

They will put questions to you as though you had full knowledge of it. Say: "None but God has knowledge of it, though most men are unaware of this."

To God belong the secrets of the heavens and the earth. The business of the Final Hour shall be accomplished in the twinkling of an eye, or in a shorter time. God has power over all things.

The fate of each man We have bound about his neck. On the Day of Resurrection, We shall confront him with a book spread wide open, saying: "Here is your book: read it. Enough for you this day that your own soul should call you to account."

Tell of the day when We shall blot out the mountains and make the earth a barren waste; when We shall gather all mankind together, leaving not a soul behind.

They shall be ranged before your Lord, and He will say to them: "You have returned to Us as We created you at first. Yet you supposed We had not set for you a predestined time."

Their book will be laid down, and you shall see the sinners dismayed at the content. They will say: "Woe to us! What can this book mean? It omits nothing small or great: all is noted down!" and they shall find their deeds recorded there. Your Lord will wrong none.

. . . But on the Day of Resurrection He will hold the entire earth in his grasp and fold up the heavens in His right hand. Glory be to Him! Exalted be He above their idols!

The Trumpet shall be sounded, and all who are in heaven and earth shall fall down fainting, except those that shall be spared by God. Then the Trumpet will be blown again and they shall rise and gaze around them. The earth will shine with the light of her Lord, and the Book will be laid open. The prophets and witnesses shall be brought in, and all shall be judged with fairness: none shall be wronged. Every soul shall be paid back according to its deeds, for He best knows all that they did.

When the sky is rent asunder; when the stars scatter and the oceans roll together; when the graves are hurled about; each soul shall know what it has done and what it has failed to do.

It is We who will resurrect the dead. We record the deeds of men and the marks they leave behind. We note all things in a glorious book.

For the Believers: Paradise

These shall have a blissful end. They shall enter the gardens of Eden, together with the righteous. . . . From every gate the angels will come to them, saying: "Peace be to you for all that you have steadfastly endured. Blessed is the reward of Paradise."

Every ellipsis in the following passage marks a place in the original where the question "Which of your Lord's blessings would you deny?" is repeated.

But for those that fear the majesty of their Lord there are two gardens. . . . They shall recline on couches lined with thick brocade, and within reach will hang the fruits of both gardens. . . . Therein are bashful virgins whom neither man nor jinnee [spirits] will have touched before. . . . Virgins as fair as corals and rubies. . . . Shall the reward of goodness be anything but good? . . . And beside these there shall be two other gardens . . . of darkest green. . . . A gushing fountain shall flow in each. . . . Each planted with fruit-trees, the palm and the pomegranate. . . . In each there shall be virgins chaste and fair. . . . Dark-eyed virgins sheltered in their tents . . . whom neither man nor jinnee will have touched before. . . . They shall recline on green cushions and fine carpets. Which of your Lord's blessings would you deny?

God will deliver [the righteous] from the evil of that day, and make their faces shine with joy. He will reward them for their steadfastness with robes of silk and the delights of Paradise. Reclining there upon soft couches, they shall feel neither the scorching heat nor the biting cold.

. . . They shall be served with silver dishes, and beakers as large as goblets; silver goblets which they themselves shall measure: and cups brim-full with ginger-flavored water from a fount called Salsabil. They shall be attended by boys graced with eternal youth, who to the beholder's eyes will seem like sprinkled pearls. When you gaze upon that scene, you will behold a kingdom blissful and glorious.

For the Faithless: Hell

Those who have denied the Book and the message We sent through Our apostles shall realize the truth hereafter: when with chains and shackles round their necks, they shall be dragged through scalding water and burnt in the fire of Hell.

They will be asked: "Where are the gods whom you have served besides God?"

"They have forsaken us," they will reply. "Indeed, they were nothing, those gods to whom we prayed." Thus God confounds the unbelievers.

And they will be told: "That is because on earth you took delight in falsehoods, and led a wanton life. Enter the gates of Hell and stay therein for ever. Evil is the home of the arrogant."

Those that deny Our revelations We will burn in fire. No sooner will their skins be consumed than We shall give them other skins, so that they may truly taste the scourge.

. . . Scalding water shall be poured upon their heads, melting their skins and that which is in their bellies.

. . . Whenever in their anguish, they try to escape from Hell, back they shall be dragged, and will be told: "Taste the torment of the Conflagration!"

e. The Divine Will and Providence

Creator of the heavens and the earth! When He decrees a thing, He need only say "Be," and it is.

Say: "Grace is in the hands of God: He bestows it on whom He will. God is munificent and all-knowing. . . . God's grace is infinite."

If God afflicts you with a misfortune none can remove it but He; and if He bestows on you a favour, none can withhold His bounty. He is bountiful to whom He will. He is the Forgiving One, the Merciful.

We charge no soul with more than it can bear. Our Book records the truth; none shall be wronged.

If you reckoned up God's favors you could not count them.

God alone has knowledge of the Hour of Doom. He sends down the abundant rain and knows what every womb contains.

No mortal knows what he will earn tomorrow; no mortal knows where he will breathe his last. God alone is wise and all-knowing.

Have they never observed sky above them, and marked how We built it up and furnished it with ornaments, leaving no crack in its expanse?

We spread out the earth and set upon it immovable mountains. We brought forth from it all kinds of delectable plants. A lesson and an admonition to penitent men.

We send down blessed water from the sky with which We bring forth gardens and the harvest grain, and tall palm trees laden with clusters of dates, a sustenance for men; thereby giving new life to some dead land. Such shall be the Resurrection.

6. The Five Pillars of Islam

These are the five religious practices enjoined upon all Muslims.

a. Recitation of the *Shahadah* (Testimony)

La ilaha illa'llah (There is no god but God)
  Muhammadan rasulu'llah (Muhammad is His Messenger)

b. *Zakat* or Alms-Levy: The Compulsory Annual Giving of a Portion of One's Holdings to Those in Need

The alms-levy, an annual duty, is different from ordinary charity (sadaqah), *which the Muslim is enjoined to give generously and often. Compare with selections 10b and 23 below.*

Attend to your prayers and render the alms-levy. Whatever good you do shall be rewarded by Allah. God is watching over all your actions.

Alms shall be only for the poor and the helpless, for those that are engaged in the management of alms and those who hearts are sympathetic to the Faith, for the freeing of slaves and debtors, for the advancement of God's cause, and for the traveller in need. That is a duty enjoined by God. God is all-knowing and wise.

To be charitable in public is good, but to give alms to the poor in private is better and will atone for some of your sins. God has knowledge of all your actions.

Believers, give in alms of the wealth you have lawfully earned and of that which We have brought out of the earth for you; not worthless things which you yourselves would but reluctantly accept.

c. *Salat* or Daily Prayer

Exhortations to Prayer

Fortify yourselves with patience and prayer. This may indeed be an exacting discipline, but not to the devout, who know that they will meet their Lord and that to Him they will return.

Glory be to God in the evening and morning of your days. His be the praise in the heavens and in the earth, alike in the day's decline and when high noon is upon you.

Remember your Lord deep in your soul with humility and reverence, and without ostentation: in the morning and in the evening; and do not be negligent.

Praise him day and night, so that you may find comfort.

The Call to Prayer (Adhan)[4]

Allahu akbar (God is most great) (four times)
Ashhadu an la ilaha illa Allah (I testify that there is no god but God) (twice)
Ashhadu anna Muhammadan rasul Allah (I testify that Muhammad is the Messenger of God) (twice)
Hayya 'ala al-salat (Hurry to prayer) (twice)
Hayya 'ala al-falah (Hurry to betterment) (twice)
Allahu akbar (God is most great) (twice)
La ilaha illa Allah (I testify that there is no god but God)

The Prayer Itself

In the course of the day some prayers are said silently, some aloud. During each prayer time the Muslim moves through the postures of standing, bowing, prostrating, and sitting on one's heels, while reciting one or more rak'a *or units of prayer. These* rak'a *center in the Fatihah; the introductions and conclusions that bracket it can vary from the one given here.*

God is Most Great.
Recitation of the Fatihah or opening sura of the Qur'an (see 1a).

---

4. This is a basic *adhan*. There are variations according to whether one is a Sunni or Shi'i Muslim.

Recitation of another short passage or sura from the Qur'an.

God is most great (aloud)
Glory be to my Lord, the Almighty (three times silently)
God hears those who call upon him (aloud)
Our Lord, praise be to Thee (silently)
God is most great (aloud)
Glory be to my Lord, the Most High (silently, three times,
   while prostrating)
God is most great (aloud) (lifting to a sitting position)
Glory be to my Lord, the Most High (silently, three times,
   while prostrating)

The Direction of Mecca

Many a time we have seen you [Muhammad] turn your face to-wards heaven. We will make you turn towards a *qiblah* [direction] that will please you. Turn your face towards the Holy Mosque; wherever you [the faithful] be, turn your faces towards it.

Dhikr: *Repeated Invocation of God's Name*

Perhaps the important practice of Muslim contemplatives, or Sufis, is the continuous invocation of Allah's name. (See number 19.) Verses of the Qur'an that mention "remembrance of God" authorize this practice.

Believers, be ever mindful of God. . . .

Surely in remembrance of God are all hearts comforted.

When you forget, remember your Lord and say: "May God guide me and bring me nearer to the Truth."

Remember Me, then, and I will remember you.

d. *Sawm*, or Fasting, During the Month of Ramadan

The month of Ramadan was the time in which the Qur'an was sent down as guidance for mankind. . . . So then, any of you, ob-serving the incidence of the month, let him take up the fast throughout it. . . .

. . . The fast proceeds through a set period of days. Any of your number who is sick or on a journey must observe a like sequence of other days and, in the event of their being able to undertake the feeding of some needy person, that may be for them a way of making it good.

e. *Hajj:* Pilgrimage to Mecca and the Ka'ba

The Founding of the Ka'ba

For Muslims the holiest place in creation is a cubical building, the Ka'ba, in the center of the Great Mosque at Mecca. Islamic tradition attributes the founding of the Ka'ba to the biblical Abraham and his son Ishmael. The culmination of the pilgrimage to Mecca is a ritual circumambulation of the Ka'ba.

We made a House [Ka'ba], a resort and a sanctuary for mankind, saying: "Make the place where Abraham stood a house of worship." We enjoined Abraham and Ishmael to cleanse our House for those who walk round it, who meditate in it, and who kneel and prostrate themselves. . . .

Abraham and Ishmael built the House and dedicated it, saying: "Accept this from us, Lord. You are the One that hears all and knows all. . . ."

Injunctions to Perform the Hajj

Make the pilgrimage and visit the sacred House for His sake.

Exhort all [people] to make the pilgrimage. They will come to you on foot and on the backs of swift camels from every distant quarter; they will come to avail themselves of many a benefit, and to pronounce on the appointed days the name of God over the cattle which He has given them for food. Eat of their flesh, and feed the poor and the unfortunate.

Then let the pilgrims spruce themselves, make their vows, and circle the Ancient House. Such is God's commandment.

7. *Shirk* (Idolatry): *The Cardinal Error*

Islam, like Judaism and Christianity, condemns idolatry, a condemnation that at its deepest level is a warning not to enslave oneself to anything less than God.

God will not forgive those who serve other gods besides Him; but He will forgive whom He will for other sins. He that serves other gods besides Him is guilty of a heinous sin.

God has said: "You shall not serve two gods, for He is but one God. Fear none but Me."

Set up no other deity besides God. I come from him to warn you plainly.

Say: "I will pray to my Lord and worship none besides Him."

8. *Jihad* (Exertion, Struggle, Holy War)

Muslims are commanded not to be aggressors. Moreover, a well-known saying attributed to Muhammad states that the lesser jihad *is the struggle with an external enemy, while the* true or greater jihad *is the struggle with oneself. See no. 21j.*

Fight for the sake of God those that fight against you, but do not attack them first. God does not love the aggressors.

Permission to take up arms is hereby given to those who are attacked, because they have been wronged.

[But if they attack you] slay them wherever you find them. Drive them out of the places from which they drove you. Idolatry is worse than carnage. . . . Thus shall the unbelievers be rewarded: but if they mend their ways, know that God is Forgiving and Merciful.

Fighting is obligatory for you, much as you dislike it. But you may hate a thing although it is good for you, and love a thing although it is bad for you. God knows, but you do not.

They ask you about the sacred month. Say: "To fight in this month is a grave offence, but to debar others from the path of God, to deny Him, and to expel His worshippers from the Holy Mosque, is far more grave in His sight. Idolatry is worse than carnage."

God's Promise to Martyrs

As for those who are slain in the cause of God, He will not allow their works to perish. He will vouchsafe them guidance and ennoble their state; He will admit them to the Paradise he has made known to them.

9. There Shall Be No Compulsion in Religion

The following verse is often cited to correct the mistaken impression that Islam has a mandate to convert by force. The historical record of Islam's tolerance of other faiths is uneven, but the religious freedoms of Jews and Christians, for example, have on balance fared well under Islamic rule.

There shall be no compulsion in religion. True guidance is now distinct from error. He that renounces idol-worship and puts his faith in God shall grasp a firm handle that will never break. God hears all and knows all.

10. Social Matters

a. Believers Are a Single Community

Your [community] is but one [community], and I am Your only Lord. Therefore serve Me. People have divided themselves into factions, but to Us they shall all return.

b. Supererogatory Charity (*Sadaqah*)[5]

Your wealth and your children are but a temptation. God's reward is great. Therefore fear God with all your hearts, and be attentive, obedient and charitable. That will be best for you.

Those that preserve themselves from their own greed will surely prosper.

If the debtor be in straits, grant him a delay until he can discharge his debt; but if you waive the sum as alms it will be better for you, if you but knew it.

---

5. Compare with nos. 21 and 23.

Show kindness to parents and kindred, to orphans and to the helpless, to near and distant neighbors, to those that keep company with you, to the traveller in need . . . . God does not love the arrogant and boastful men, who are themselves niggardly and enjoin others to be niggardly; who conceal the riches which God of His bounty has bestowed upon them . . . and who spend their wealth for the sake of ostentation. . . .

. . . The righteous . . . give sustenance to the poor man, the orphan, and the captive, saying: "We feed you for God's sake only; we seek of you neither recompense nor thanks."

c. Kindness to Parents

Your Lord has enjoined you. . . to show kindness to your parents. If either or both of them attain old age in your dwelling, show them no sign of impatience, nor rebuke them; but speak to them kind words. Treat them with humility and tenderness and say: "Lord, be merciful to them. They nursed me when I was an infant."

d. Rights of Women

The Qur'an improved the situation of women in the ancient Arabian world. Girl-child infanticide was outlawed (see 10m[7] and 28), protections including divorce rights were sanctioned (see 10f[1]), and women were given inheritance rights for the first time (see 10i).

It would be wrong to say that Muslim feminists see the Qur'an as unproblematic. Nevertheless, many see it as an ally rather than an enemy: "Muslim thinkers, and especially feminists . . . have found [the Qur'an] often to be at odds with the frankly male chauvinist institutions and customs of Islamic societies since early times."[6] The Qur'an

---

6. Frederick M. Denny, *An Introduction to Islam*, 2d ed. (New York: Macmillan, 1994), 352. Professor Denny rightly adds, "The emancipation of women in Western countries is a relatively recent development and is still unfolding. So when Westerners heap criticism on Islam and Muslims for their sex and gender customs and practices, they often forget that their own histories have contained similarly unjust and abusive assumptions and practices that do not reflect the highest aspirations of their faiths' teachings" (352).

explicitly asserts that men and women *are equal before God and enjoy the same religious duties and privileges, as per the first selection below.*

For Muslim men and women—
For believing men and women,
For devout men and women,
For truthful men and women,
For men and women who are
Patient and constant, for men
And women who humble themselves,
For men and women who give
In charity, for men and women
Who fast (and deny themselves),
For men and women who
Engage much in Allah's praise—
For them has Allah prepared
Forgiveness and great reward.

Believers, it is unlawful for you to inherit the women of your deceased kinsmen against their will, or to bar them from remarrying. . . . Treat them with kindness. . . .

Lodge them in your own homes, according to your means. You shall not harass them so as to make life intolerable for them. If they are with child, maintain them until the end of their confinement; and if, after that, they give suck to the infants they bore you, give them their pay and consult together in all reasonableness.

Believers, if you marry believing women and divorce them before the marriage is consummated, you have no right to require them to observe a waiting period. Provide well for them and release them honourably.

Widows shall wait, keeping themselves apart from men for four months and ten days after their husband's death. When they have reached the end of their waiting period, it shall be no offence for you to let them do whatever they choose for themselves, provided that it is decent.

The following selection will seem out of place under "Rights of Women." It is cited to avoid misrepresenting the complexity of this issue and also to lead the reader to its footnote, a fine example of contemporary Qur'anic commentary.

Men have authority over women because Allah has made the one superior to the other, and because they spend their wealth to maintain them. Good women are obedient. They guard their unseen parts because Allah has guarded them. As for those from whom you fear disobedience, admonish them and send them to beds apart and beat them.[7] Then if they obey you, take no further action against them.

e. Marriage Restrictions on Men

You shall not marry the women whom your fathers married: all previous such marriages excepted. That was an evil practice, indecent and abominable.

Forbidden to you are your mothers, your daughters, your sisters, your paternal and maternal aunts, the daughters of your brothers and sisters, your foster-mothers, your foster-sisters, the mothers of your wives, your step-daughters who are in your charge, born of the wives with whom you have lain (it is no offence for you to marry your step-daughters if you have not consummated your marriage with their mothers), and the wives of your own begotten sons. You are also forbidden to take in marriage two sisters at one and the same time: all previous such marriages excepted. God is Forgiving and Merciful.

[Forbidden also are] married women. . . . Such is the decree of Allah. All women other than these are lawful to you, provided you seek them with your wealth, in modest conduct, not in fornication.

---

7. Many Traditions (*hadith*) suggest that the Prophet himself detested the idea of husbands beating their wives. According to the Qur'an scholar M. Asad: "He forbade the beating of *any* woman with the words, 'Never beat God's handmaidens.'. . . On the basis of these Traditions, all the authorities stress that this 'beating,' if resorted to at all, should be more or less symbolic—'with a toothbrush or some such thing'. . . or even 'with a folded handkerchief'. . . and some of the greatest Muslim scholars . . . are of the opinion that it is just barely permissible, and should preferably be avoided: and they justify this opinion by the Prophet's personal feelings with regard to this position." See Muhammad Asad, *The Message of the Qur'an* (Gibralter: Dar Al-Andalus, 1980), 109–10.

Give them their dowry for the enjoyment you have had of them as a duty; but it shall be no offence for you to make any other agreement among yourselves after you have fulfilled your duty. God is all-knowing and wise.

Polygamy

If you fear that you cannot treat orphans [girls] with fairness, then you may marry such women as seem good to you: two, three, or four of them. But if you fear that you cannot maintain equality among them, marry one only. . . . This will make it easier for you to avoid injustice.

Try as you may, you cannot treat all your wives impartially. Do not set yourself altogether against any of them, leaving her, as it were, in suspense.

f. Divorce

The Prophet said, "The thing which is lawful but disliked by God is divorce."[8]

Provisions Protecting Women

Women shall with justice have rights similar to those exercised against them, although men have a status above women.

When you have renounced your wives and they have reached the end of their waiting period, either retain them in honour or let them go with kindness. But you shall not retain them in order to harm them or wrong them. Whoever does this wrongs his own soul. . . . It is unlawful for husbands to take from them anything they have given them. . . .

You shall bequeath your widows a year's maintenance without causing them to leave their homes. . . . Reasonable provision shall also be made for divorced women. That is incumbent on righteous men.

---

8. Allama Sir Abdullah and Al-Mamum Al-Suhrawardy, *The Sayings of Muhammad* (New York: Citadel Press, 1990), 69.

g. Modesty in Women

Enjoin believing women to turn their eyes away from temptation and to preserve their chastity; to cover their adornments (except such as are normally displayed); to draw their veils over their bosoms and not to reveal their finery except [to members of the household]. . . . And let them not stamp their feet when walking so as to reveal their hidden trinkets.

Prophet, enjoin your wives, your daughters, and the wives of true believers to draw their veils close round them. That is more proper, so that they may be recognized and not be molested.

Women who are past child-bearing and those who have ceased to anticipate marriage incur no blame if they leave off their garments, provided they are not flaunting charms. Yet to refrain from doing so is better.

h. Modesty in Men

Enjoin believing men to turn their eyes away from temptation and to restrain their carnal desires. This will make their lives purer. Allah has knowledge of all their actions.

i. Inheritance

Men shall have a share in what their parents and kinsmen leave; and women shall have a share in what their parents and kinsmen leave: whether it be little or much, they shall be legally entitled to their share.

A male shall inherit twice as much as a female. If there be more than two girls, they shall have two-thirds of the inheritance; but if there be one only she shall inherit the half. . . .

You shall inherit the half of your wives' estate if they die childless. If they leave children, a quarter of their estate shall be yours after payment of any legacy they may have bequeathed for any debt they may have owed.

Your wives shall inherit one quarter of your estate if you die childless. If you leave children, they shall inherit one-eighth, after payment of any legacy you may have bequeathed or any debt you may have owed.

j. Economic Justice

Do not devour one another's property by unjust means, nor bribe with it the judges in order that you may wrongfully and knowingly usurp the possessions of other men.

Do not interfere with the property of orphans except with the best of motives, until they reach maturity.

God commands you to hand back your trusts to their rightful owners, and, when you pass judgment among men, to judge with fairness. Noble is that to which God exhorts you. God hears and observes all.

Believers, do not live on usury, doubling your wealth many times over.

k. The Status of Animals

All the beasts that roam the earth and all the birds that wing their flight are but communities like your own. . . . They shall all be gathered before their Lord.[9]

l. Other Social Virtues Enjoined by Islam

Right Speech

God does not love harsh words, except when uttered by a man who is truly wronged.

There is no virtue in much of their counsel: only in him who enjoins charity, kindness, and peace among men. He who does this to please God shall be richly rewarded.

Do not confound the truth with falsehood, nor knowingly conceal the truth.

A kind word with forgiveness is better than charity followed by an insult.

---

9. Compare with selection no. 30, below.

Integrity and Circumspection

Believers, if an evil-doer brings you a piece of news inquire first into its truth, lest you should wrong others unwittingly and then regret your action.

Do not follow what you do not know. Human eyes, ears, and heart—each of these senses can be closely questioned.

Earnestness

God is watching over His servants . . . who are steadfast, sincere, obedient, and charitable.

. . . Be steadfast in prayer, enjoin justice, and forbid evil. Endure with fortitude whatever befalls you. That is a duty incumbent upon all.

Forgiveness

. . . The righteous . . . curb their anger and forgive their fellow men.

That which you have been given is but the fleeting comfort of this life. Better and more enduring is God's reward to those who . . . when angered, are willing to forgive . . . and conduct their affairs by mutual consent.

Humility

Do not treat men with scorn, nor walk proudly on the earth: God does not love the arrogant and the vainglorious. Rather let your gait be modest and your voice low: the harshest of voices is the braying of the ass.

Do not walk proudly on the earth. You cannot cleave the earth, nor can you rival the mountains in stature.

Fairness

Give full measure, when you measure, and weigh with even scales. That is fair, and better in the end.

m. Acts Forbidden in Islam

Social mores are everywhere in flux. Yet since almost one-fifth of the world's population are Muslims, it is appropriate to note some of the Qur'an's specific proscriptions.

Adultery

You shall not commit adultery for it is foul and indecent.

The adulterer and the adulteress shall each be given a hundred lashes. Let no pity for them cause you to disobey God . . . and let their punishment be witnessed by a number of believers.

The adulterer may marry only an adulteress or an idolatress; and the adulteress may marry only an adulterer or an idolator. True believers are forbidden such marriages.

Homosexual Acts

If two men among you commit indecency, punish them both. If they repent and mend their ways, let them be. God is forgiving and merciful.

Will you fornicate with males and abandon your wives, whom God has created for you? Surely you are great transgressors.

Fornication

Blessed are the believers . . . who restrain their carnal desires (except with their wives . . . for these are lawful to them) and do not transgress through lusting after other women. . . .

If any of your women commit fornication, call in four witnesses from among yourselves against them; if they testify to their guilt confine them to their houses till death overtakes them or till God finds another way for them.

Infanticide

Losers are those that in their ignorance have wantonly slain their own children and made unlawful what God has given them, inventing falsehoods about God. They have gone astray and are not guided.

You shall not kill your children for fear of want. We will provide for them and for you. To kill them is a great sin.

Suicide

Do not destroy yourselves. God is merciful to you, but he that does that through wickedness and injustice shall be burned in fire. That is easy enough for God.

Murder

You shall not kill any man whom God has forbidden you to kill except for a just cause. If a man is slain unjustly, his heir shall be entitled to satisfaction. But let him not carry his vengeance too far, for his victim will in turn be assisted and avenged.

Pilferage

As for the man or woman who is guilty of theft, cut off their hands to punish them for their crimes. That is the punishment enjoined by God. God is mighty and wise. But whoever repents after committing evil, and mends his ways, shall be pardoned by God. God is forgiving and merciful.

Drinking and Gambling

They ask about drinking and gambling. Say: "There is great harm in both, although they have some benefit for men; but their harm is far greater than their benefit."

11. Objections to Christianity

The Qur'an pays special respect to Jesus:

Of these messengers We have exalted some above others. To some Allah spoke directly; others He raised to a lofty status. We gave Jesus, the son of Mary, veritable signs and strengthened him with the Holy Spirit.

But Jesus is said to be an apostle, not God:

The Messiah, Jesus the son of Mary, was no more than God's Apostle.

Muslims therefore decry the notions that God has a son or that Jesus is God:

Say: "God is One, the Eternal God. He begot none, nor was He begotten. None is equal to Him."

Say: "Praise be to God who has never begotten a son; who has no partner in His Kingdom; who needs none to defend Him from humiliation." Proclaim His greatness.

Unbelievers are those that say: "God is . . . the son of Mary."
For the Messiah himself said: "Children of Israel, serve God, my
Lord and your Lord."

*For Muslims, then, the Christian doctrine of the trinity smacks of
polytheism:*

So believe in God and His Apostles and do not say: "Three."
Forbear, and it shall be better for you. God is but one God. God
forbid that He should have a son!

The Qur'an also asserts that it was not Jesus who died on the cross.

They denied the truth and uttered a monstrous falsehood
against Mary. They declared: "We have put to death the Messiah,
Jesus the son of Mary, the Apostle of God." They did not kill him,
nor did they crucify him, but they thought they did.

12. Objections to Judaism

*Though the Qur'an affirms Islam's profound connection to Judaism,
saying, "We believe in the faith of Abraham" (2:136), it charges
Judaism with having corrupted its own scriptures, broken its covenant,
and erroneously claimed exclusivity.*

God made a covenant with the Israelites and raised among them
twelve chieftains.
. . . But because they broke their covenant We laid on them our
curse and hardened their hearts. They have tampered with words
out of their context and forgotten much of what they were enjoined. . . . But pardon them and bear with them.

Those to whom the burden of the Torah was entrusted and yet
refused to bear it are like a donkey laden with books. Wretched is
the example of those who deny God's revelations. . . .
Say to the Jews: "If you claim that of all men you alone are
God's friends, then you should wish for death, if what you say is
true!" But, because of what their hands have done, they will never
wish for death. God knows the wrongdoers.

HADITH: Sayings and Traditional Accounts of the Prophet

13. 'A'ishah's Description of How Muhammad Began to Receive Revelation

'A'ishah [Muhammad's second wife] said: The first revelation that was granted to the Messenger of Allah, peace and blessings of Allah be upon him, was the true dream in a state of sleep. . . . Then solitude became dear to him and he used to seclude himself in the cave of Hira, and therein he devoted himself to Divine worship . . . until the Truth came to him while he was in the cave of Hira; so the angel (Gabriel) came to him and said, "Read." He (the prophet) said, ". . . I am not one who can read." And he continued: "Then he (the angel) took hold of me and he pressed me so hard that I could not bear it any more, and then he let me go and said, 'Read.' I said, 'I am not one who can read.' Then he took hold of me and pressed me a second time so hard that I could not bear it any more, then he let me go again and said, 'Read.' I said, 'I am not one who can read.'. . . Then he took hold of me and pressed me hard for a third time, then he let me go and said, 'Read in the name of thy Lord Who created—He created man from a clot—Read and thy Lord is most Honourable.'"

The Messenger of Allah, peace and blessings of Allah be upon him, returned with this (message) while his heart trembled and he came to Khadijah [his first wife] and said, "Wrap me up, wrap me up." And she wrapped him up until the awe left him. Then he said to Khadijah while he related to her what happened: "I fear for myself." Khadijah said, "Nay, by Allah, Allah will never bring thee to disgrace. . . ."

14. The Prophet Recalls How Revelation Resumed After Having Stopped

While I was walking along, I heard a voice from heaven and I raised up my eyes and lo! the Angel that had appeared to me in Hira was sitting on a throne between heaven and earth and I was struck with awe on account of him and returned (home) and said, "Wrap me up, wrap me up." Then Allah revealed: "O thou who art clothed! Arise and warn, And thy Lord do magnify, And thy garments do purify, And uncleanness do shun."

The revelation became brisk and in succession.

15. The Prophet's Manner of Receiving Revelation

Ibn 'Abbas . . . said, The Messenger of Allah . . . used to exert himself hard in receiving Divine revelation and would on this account move his lips. . . . So Allah revealed: "Move not thy tongue with it to make haste with it. Surely on Us devolves the collecting of it and the reciting of it.". . . So after this, when Gabriel came to him, [he] would listen attentively, and when Gabriel departed, the Prophet . . . recited it as he (Gabriel) recited it.

'A'ishah reported that [someone] asked [Muhammad], "O Messenger of Allah! How does revelation come to thee?" The Messenger of Allah . . . said:

"Sometimes it comes to me like the ringing of a bell and that is the hardest on me, then he departs from me and I retain in memory from him what he says; and sometimes the Angel comes to me in the likeness of a man and speaks to me and I retain in memory what he says."

'A'ishah said, "And I saw him when revelation came down upon him on a severely cold day, then it departed from him and his forehead dripped with sweat."

16. "If Someone Walks Toward Me, I Run Toward Him"

In certain hadith, *called* hadith qudsi, *Allah speaks in the first person outside the Qur'an. Selections 16–18a are hadith qudsi.*

God says: "I fulfill My servant's expectation of Me, and I am with him when he remembers Me. If he remembers Me in his heart, I remember him in my heart; and if he remembers Me in public, I remember him before a public [far] better than that. And if he draws nearer to Me by a handsbreadth, I draw nearer to Him by an armslength; and if he draws nearer to Me by an armslength, I draw nearer to him by a fathom; and if he comes to Me walking, I come to him running."

17. "I Loved That I Be Known"

I was a hidden treasure, and I loved that I be known, so I created the world.

18. "My Mercy Exceeds My Wrath"

a. Mercy Uppermost

Verily My mercy taketh precedence over my Wrath.

b. Mercy's Extent

If the unbeliever knew of the extent of the Lord's mercy, even he would not despair of Paradise.

19. Remembering God

a. Moistening the Tongue

A man said: O prophet of God, truly the laws of Islam are numerous. Tell me of one thing throughout with which I can obtain reward. The prophet replied: Let thy tongue always be moist in remembrance of Allah.

b. Polishing the Heart

There is a means of polishing all things whereby rust may be removed; that which polishes the heart is the invocation of Allah and there is no act which removes the punishment of Allah further from you than this invocation.

20. God Sees Thee

You should serve God as though you could see Him, for if you cannot see Him, know that He sees you.

21. True Islam Is Kindness

a. Golden Rule

No one is a true believer unless he desireth for his brother that which he desireth for himself.

b. Fellow-Beings

Do you love your Creator? Love your fellow-beings first.

c. The Mark of Faith

Kindness is a mark of faith: and whoever hath not kindness hath not faith.

d. Good to God's Creatures

All God's creatures are His family; and he is the most beloved of God who doeth most good to God's creatures.

e. Actions Most Excellent

What actions are most excellent? To gladden the heart of a human being, to feed the hungry, to help the afflicted, to lighten the sorrow of the sorrowful, and to remove the wrongs of the injured.

f. The Needy

Feed the hungry and visit the sick, and free the captive, if he be unjustly confined. Assist any person oppressed, whether Muslim or non-Muslim.

g. The Perfect Muslim

That person is not a perfect Muslim who eateth his fill, and leaveth his neighbors hungry.

h. The Aged

Verily to honour an old person is showing respect to God.

i. Goodness

Follow up an evil deed by a good one which will wipe [the former] out, and behave good-naturedly to people.

j. Ultimate Jihad

The most excellent Jihad is that for the conquest of self.

22. The Importance of Intention

Actions will be judged according to intentions.

23. There Are Many Ways to Give

a. An Open Countenance

Every good act is charity; and verily it is a good act to meet your brother with an open countenance, and to pour water from your own water-bag into his vessel.

b. The Best Alms

The best of all alms is that which the right hand giveth and the left hand knoweth not of.

c. The Faces of Charity

If you straighten out [some trouble] between two individuals, that is an alms. If you help a lame man with his beast, mounting him thereon, or hoisting up on to it his baggage, that is an alms. A good word is an alms. In every step you take while walking to prayers there is an alms.

Your smiling in your brother's face, is charity; and your exhorting mankind to virtuous deeds, is charity; and your prohibiting the forbidden, is charity; and your showing men the road, in the land in which they lose it, is charity; and your assisting the blind, is charity.

24. Right Speech

a. Minding the Mouth

[In the midst of responding to questions about how to live a good life, Muhammad said:] "And shall I not tell you how to possess all this?". . . So he took hold of his tongue and said: "Keep this under control."

b. No Backbiting

Let whosoever believes in Allah and in the Last Day either speak good or be silent.

Abuse nobody, and if a man abuse thee, and lay open a vice which he knoweth in thee; then do not disclose one which thou knowest in him.

c. The Truth

Appropriate yourselves to the truth. Avoid lying.

Say what is true, although it may be bitter and displeasing to people.

25. Nonviolence

a. Better than Prayer

Shall I not inform you of a better act than fasting, alms and prayers? Making peace between one another: enmity and malice tear up heavenly rewards by the roots.

b. The Greatest Enemies

The greatest enemies of God are those who are entered into Islam, and do acts of infidelity, and who, without cause, shed the blood of man.

26. Conception and Destiny

. . . Verily the creation of any one of you takes place when he is assembled in his mother's womb; for forty days [he is] as a drop, then he becomes a clot . . . and then in the same way as a mass. Then an angel is sent to him, who breathes the spirit into him. Four words of command are given [to this angel], viz. that he write down his fortune (*rizq*), his life-span, his works, and whether [at Judgment] he will be among the wretched or the happy. . . .

27. Marriage

Marriage is half the tradition. [The other half is patience].

There is no monasticism in Islam.

28. Women

a. The Prophet's Delight

There are two things in this world that delight me: women and perfumes. These two things rejoice my eyes, and render me more fervent in devotion.

b. The Rights of Women

The rights of women are sacred. See that women are maintained in the rights assigned to them.

Allah enjoins you to treat women well, for they are your mothers, daughters and aunts.

Whoever hath a daughter, and doth not bury her alive,[10] or scold her, or prefer his male children to her, may God bring him into Paradise.

29. Abstinence

a. The Middle Path

Kill not your hearts with excess of eating and drinking.

Torment not yourselves, lest God should punish you.

b. When in Doubt

That which is lawful is clear, and that which is unlawful likewise, but there are certain doubtful things between the two from which it is well to abstain.

30. Kindness to Animals

Fear God, in treating dumb animals and ride them when they are fit to be ridden and get off them when they are tired.

An adulteress passed by a dog at a well; and the dog was holding out his tongue from thirst, which was near killing him, and the woman drew off her boot, and tied it to the end of her garment, and drew water for the dog, and gave him to drink; and she was forgiven for that act.

"Are there rewards for doing good to quadrupeds, and giving them water to drink?" Muhammad said, "Verily there are heavenly rewards for any act of kindness to a live animal."

---

10. This refers to the pre-Islamic practice of infanticide, which Muhammad abolished.

31. On the Qur'an and Himself

a. The Prophet's Miracle

The other messengers of God had their miracles, mine is the Qur'an and will remain for ever.

b. Only a Servant and Messenger

Do not exceed the bounds in praising me, as the Christians do in praising Jesus, the son of Mary, by calling Him God, and the Son of God; I am only the Lord's servant; then call me the servant of God, and His messenger.

32. Of Contentment

a. Overlooked Treasures

There are two benefits, of which the generality of men are losers, and of which they do not know the value, health and leisure.

b. The Fire of Envy

Keep yourselves away from envy; because it eateth up and taketh away good actions, like as fire eateth up and burneth wood.

c. True Wealth

Riches are not from abundance of worldly goods, but from a contented mind.

God loveth those who are content.

33. Of Learning

a. A Duty

The acquisition of knowledge is a duty incumbent upon every Muslim, male and female.

b. Seek!

Seek knowledge from the cradle to the grave.

Go in quest of knowledge even unto China.

c. The Value of a Learned Person

One learned man is harder on the devil than a thousand ignorant worshippers.

That person who shall pursue the path of knowledge, God will direct him to the path of Paradise; and verily the superiority of a learned man over an ignorant worshipper is like that of the full moon over all the stars.

To spend more time in learning is better than spending more time in praying. . . .

Acquire knowledge. It enableth its possessor to distinguish right from wrong; it lighteth the way to Heaven; it is our friend in the desert, our society in solitude, our companion when friendless; it guideth us to happiness; it sustaineth us in misery; it is an ornament amongst friends, and an armour against enemies.

The ink of the scholar is more holy than the blood of the martyr.

Who are the learned? They who practice what they know.

d. The Beauty of Reason

God hath not created anything better than Reason, or anything more perfect, or more beautiful than Reason; the benefits which God giveth are on its account. . . .

e. Self-Knowledge

Learn to know thyself.

Who knows himself, knows his Lord.[11]

---

11. A traditional Islamic saying; it may be doubted whether it is a *hadith*.

34. Miscellaneous Hadith

Be in this world as though you were a stranger or a traveller.

Men are asleep and when they die they wake.

Die before ye die.

I was a prophet when Adam was still between water and clay.

Whoever loveth to meet God, God loveth to meet him.

God is beautiful and loves beauty.

When someone has no Teacher, the devil becomes his Teacher.

Haste is of the devil, slowness of God.[12]

First tie your camel's knee, then trust in Allah.

GRACE NOTES

Sufis are the mystics of Islam. Whereas for Muslims and other monotheists, there is one God, for Sufis and other mystics there is only God. Apart from the Real, Sufis tell us in a host of ways, there is nothing at all. All but the final selection in this section are sayings of the Sufis.

35. Four Mystical Verses from the Qur'an

Wheresoe'er ye turn, there is the Face of God.

There is no refuge from God but in Him.

It is not their eyes that are blind, but their hearts.

Verily we are God's and unto Him we shall return.

---

12. A traditional Islamic saying; it may be doubted whether it is a *hadith*.

36. Abu-Yazid Al-Bistami (died ca. 874)

An early Persian Sufi from northwestern Iran.

a. The Great Paradox

God can never be found by seeking, yet only seekers find Him.

b. I Am He

I sloughed off my self as a snake sloughs off its skin. Then I looked into myself and saw that I am He.

c. Not Two

For thirty years God was my mirror, now I am my own mirror. What I was I no longer am, for "I" and "God" are a denial of God's unity. Since I no longer am, God is his own mirror. He speaks with my tongue, and I have vanished.

d. Self and God

Forgetfulness of self is remembrance of God.

37. Al-Hallaj (888–922)

Al-Hallaj, a Sufi of Baghdad, once declared that he and God (literally, al-Haqq, *the Real), were One. According to Sufi tradition, he was crucified for this.[13] Before his crucifixion he said:*

a. Forgive Them

And these Thy servants who are gathered to slay me, in zeal for Thy Religion, longing to win Thy favor, forgive them, Lord. Have mercy on them. Surely if Thou hadst shown them what Thou has shown me, they would never have done what they have done; and

---

13. Scholars like C. Ernst argue that the real reason for Hallaj's execution was political. See *Words of Ecstasy in Sufism* (Albany: State Univ. of New York Press, 1985).

hadst Thou kept from me what Thou hadst kept from them, I should not have suffered this tribulation. Whatsoever Thou wilt do, I praise Thee! Whatsoever Thou dost will, I praise Thee!

b. The One

I have meditated on the different religions, endeavoring to understand them, and I have found that they stem from a single principle with numerous ramifications. Do not therefore ask a man to adopt a particular religion (rather than another), for this would separate him from the fundamental principle. It is this principle itself which must come to seek him. . . .

c. The Eye of the Heart

I saw my Lord with the eye of the heart. I said: Who art Thou? He answered: Thou.

38. Firdausi (949?–1020?)

A Sufi poet from Khurasan in northwest Iran.

> If on earth there be
> a Paradise of Bliss,
> It is this,
> It is this,
> It is this.

39. Abu Sa'id Ibn Abi'l Khayr (967–1049)

Persian mystic and poet.

a. Even on the Path to God, All Is God

You are freed from your own desires only when God frees you. This is not effected by your own exertion, but by the grace of God. First he brings forth in you the desire to attain this goal. Then he opens to you the gate of repentance. Then . . . you continue to strive and . . . pride yourself upon your efforts, thinking that you are advancing or achieving something; but afterward you fall into despair and feel no joy. Then you know your work is not pure but tainted, you repent of acts of devotion which you had thought were your own, and perceive that they were done by God's grace and that you were guilty of polytheism in attributing them to your own exertion. When this becomes manifest, a feeling of joy enters your heart. . . . God opens to you the gate of love. . . .

But still you think "I love" and find no rest until you perceive that it is God who loves you and keeps you in the state of loving, and that this is the result of divine love and grace, not of your own endeavor. Then God opens to you the gate of unity, and causes you to know that all action depends on God Almighty. Hereupon you perceive that all is God, and all is by him, and all is his [even] this self conceit. . . . Then you entirely recognize that you do not have the right to say "I" or "mine." At this stage you behold your help-lessness; desires fall away from you and you become free and calm. You desire what God desires; your own desires are gone, you are emancipated from your wants, and have gained peace and joy in both worlds.

First, action is necessary, then knowledge, in order that you may know that you know nothing and are no one. This is not easy to know. It is a thing that cannot be rightly learned by instruction, nor sewed on with needle nor tied on with thread. It is the gift of God.

b. Remembrance of God

The true man of God sits in the midst of his fellow-men, and rises and eats and sleeps and marries and buys and sells and gives and takes in the bazaars and spends the days with other people, and yet never forgets God even for a single moment.

40. Ibn 'Arabi (1165–1240)

Spanish-born Sufi and one of Sufism's greatest teachers.

My heart has opened unto every form: it is a pasture for gazelles, a cloister for Christian monks, a temple for idols, the Ka'ba of the pilgrim, the tablets of the Torah and the book of the Qur'an. I practice the religion of Love. . . .

41. Jelaluddin Rumi (1207–1273)

a. The Reed

In the opening verses of his epic work, the Mathnawi, *Rumi likens the human soul to a reed torn from its "rushy bed." Now a reed flute, its music is but a plaintive longing for its divine source.*

> Hearken to this Reed forlorn,
> > breathing even since 'twas torn
> From its rushy bed, a strain of impassioned love and pain.
>
> "The secret of my song, though near,
> > none can see and none can hear.
> Oh, for a friend to know the sign
> > and mingle all his soul with mine!
>
> 'Tis the flame of Love fired me,
> > 'Tis the wine of love inspired me.
> Wouldst thou know how lovers bleed,
> > hearken, hearken to the Reed!"

b. Wean Yourself

Little by little, wean yourself. This is the gist of what I have to say. From an embryo, whose nourishment comes in the blood, move to an infant drinking milk, to a child on solid food, to a searcher after wisdom, to a hunter of more invisible game.

Think how it is to have a conversation with an embryo. You might say, "The world outside is vast and intricate. There are wheat fields and mountain passes, and orchards in bloom. At night there are millions of galaxies, and in sunlight the beauty of friends dancing at a wedding."

You ask the embryo why he, or she, stays cooped up in the dark with eyes closed. Listen to the answer.

There is no "other world." I only know what I've experienced. You must be hallucinating.

c. Completely Cooked

A certain person came to the Friend's door and knocked.

"Who's there?"

"It's me."

The Friend answered, "Go away. There's no place for raw meat at this table."

The individual went wandering for a year. Nothing but the thirst of separation can change hypocrisy and ego. The person returned completely cooked, walked up and down in front of the Friend's house, gently knocked.

"Who is it?"

"You."

"Please come in, my Self. There's no place in this house for two."

d. God Sees Beneath the Forms

In the following story, the great prophet Moses has just scolded an ordinary person for addressing God in simple, human terms. Mortified, the person shrinks away. God then appears to Moses and says:

You have separated Me from one of My own. Did you come as a Prophet to unite, or to sever? I have given each being a separate and unique way of seeing and knowing and saying that knowledge. What seems wrong to you is right for him. What is poison to one is honey to someone else. Purity and impurity, sloth and diligence in worship, these mean nothing to Me. I am apart from all that. Ways of worshipping are not to be ranked as better or worse than one another. Hindus do Hindu things. The Dravidian Muslims in India do what they do. It's all praise, it's all right. It's not Me that's glorified in acts of worship. It's the worshippers! I don't hear the words they say. I look inside at the humility. That broken-open lowliness is the Reality, not the language! Forget phraseology. I want burning, *burning*. . . . Burn up your thinking and forms of expression! Moses, those who pay attention to ways of behaving and speaking are one sort. Lovers who burn are another.

e. The Field of Unity

Out beyond ideas of wrongdoing and rightdoing,
there is a field. I'll meet you there.

When the soul lies down in that grass,
the world is too full to talk about.

Ideas, language, even the phrase *each other*
doesn't make sense.

f. The Caravan of Joy

Come, come, whoever you are,
Wanderer, worshipper, lover of leaving,
    it doesn't matter.
Ours is a caravan of endless joy.
Even if you've broken your vows a hundred times—
Come, come, yet again come!

g. Seek That

There is a force within that gives you life—
    Seek that.
In your body there lies a priceless jewel—
    Seek that.
Oh, wandering Sufi,
    if you are in search of the greatest treasure,
    don't look outside,
Look within, and seek That.

h. Sleep No More

If you want great wealth,
    and that which lasts forever,
Wake up!
If you want to shine
    with the love of the Beloved,
Wake up!
You've slept a hundred nights,
And what has it brought you?
For your Self, for your God,
Wake up! Wake up!
Sleep no more.

i. The Long Journey

I died as a mineral and became a plant,
I died as a plant and rose to animal,

I died as an animal and I was man.
Why should I fear? When was I less by dying?
Yet once more I shall die as a man, to soar
With angels blest; but even from angelhood
I must pass on: all except God doth perish.
When I have sacrificed my angel soul,
I shall become what no mind e'er conceived.
Oh, let me not exist! for Non-existence
Proclaims in organ tones, "To Him we shall return."

j. The Lover

Kings lick the earth whereof the fair are made.
For God hath mingled in the dusty earth
A draught of Beauty from his choicest cup.
'Tis *that*, fond lover—not these lips of clay—
Thou art kissing with a hundred ecstasies.
Think, then, what it must be when undefiled!

k. God's Proof

The proof of the sun is the sun; if thou require the proof, do not
avert thy face!

42. Fakhruddin 'Iraqi (1213–1289)

Persian Sufi connected to the Suhrawardiyya order.

a. Love

Every word of every tongue is
    Love telling a story to her own ears.

Every thought in every mind,
    She whispers a secret to her own Self.

Every vision in every eye,
    She shows her beauty to her own sight.

Every smile on every face,
    She reveals her own joy for herself to enjoy.

Love courses through everything,
No, Love is everything.
How can you say, *there is no love,*
   when nothing but Love exists?
All that you see has appeared because of Love.
   All shines from Love,
   All pulses with Love,
   All flows from Love—
No, once again, all *is* Love!

b. It Is God You Love

. . . Although you may not know it,
If you love anyone, it is Him you love;
If you turn your head in any direction,
   it is toward Him you turn.

. . . In the light I praised you
   and never knew it.
In the dark I slept with you
   and never knew it.
I always thought that I was me,
But no, I was you
   and never knew it.

43. Ghalib (1797–1869)

A leading mystic in Rumi's lineage at Istanbul.

a. The Veil

. . . My yearning has loosened
   the veil hiding Beauty.
She is now mine—but alas,
   My own sight is there
   blocking the view.

The beat of my own heart
   sounds in my ear.

The wish to live as others do
    has long been silenced.
What does their world have to offer?—
Nothing but the echo of voices
yelling, "more, more."

b. What We Are

This world is nothing more than
    Beauty's chance to show Herself.
And what are we?—
Nothing more than Beauty's chance to see Herself.
For if Beauty were not seeking Herself
    we would not exist.

44. Eyes to See

When a pickpocket sees a saint, all he sees are his pockets.

45. Malcolm X (1925–1965): *Letter from Mecca*

Once a thief, drug pusher, and pimp, Malcolm X discovered a new life with the Black Muslims of the Nation of Islam and rose to prominence as an African American leader. Deeply repulsed by white racism, Malcolm nevertheless grew increasingly uncomfortable with the black separatist stance of the Nation. When he converted to orthodox Islam, he undertook the pilgrimage to Mecca. His autobiography includes the text of a letter written in 1964 from Mecca, where his experience of color-blind Muslim solidarity came as a revelation:

Never have I witnessed such sincere hospitality and the overwhelming spirit of true brotherhood as is practiced by people of all colors and races here in this Ancient Holy Land, the home of Abraham, Muhammad, and all the other prophets of the Holy Scriptures. For the past week, I have been utterly speechless and spellbound by the graciousness I see displayed all around me by people *of all colors.*

    I have been blessed to visit the Holy City of Mecca. . . .

There were tens of thousands of pilgrims, from all over the world. They were of all colors, from blue-eyed blonds to black-skinned Africans. But we were all participating in the same ritual, displaying a spirit of unity and brotherhood that my experiences in America had led me to believe never could exist between the white and the non-white.

America needs to understand Islam, because this is the one religion that erases from its society the race problem. . . .

During the past eleven days here in the Muslim world, I have eaten from the same plate, drunk from the same glass, and slept in the same bed (or on the same rug)—while praying to the *same God*—with fellow Muslims, whose eyes were the bluest of blue, whose hair was the blondest of blond, and whose skin was the whitest of white. And in the *words* and in the *actions* and in the *deeds* of the "white" Muslims, I felt the same sincerity that I felt among the black African Muslims of Nigeria, Sudan, and Ghana.

We were *truly* all the same (brothers)—because their belief in one God had removed the "white" from their *minds*, the "white" from their *behavior*, and the "white" from their *attitude*.

. . . Each hour here in the Holy Land enables me to have greater spiritual insights into what is happening in America between black and white. The American Negro never can be blamed for his racial animosities—he is only reacting to four hundred years of the conscious racism of the American whites. But as racism leads America up the suicide path, I do believe, from the experiences that I have had with them, that the whites of the younger generation, in the colleges and universities, will see the handwriting on the wall and many of them will turn to the *spiritual* path of *truth*—the *only* way left to America to ward off the disaster that racism inevitably must lead to.

. . . All praise is due to Allah, the Lord of all the Worlds.
Sincerely,
El-Hajj Malik El-Shabazz
(Malcolm X)

CHAPTER EIGHT

Primal Religions

*I*t has been estimated that since the
dawn of humankind our planet
has hosted nearly 100,000 religions.[1] Very few of these have been the
widely influential, scriptural traditions such as those treated in earlier
chapters. Rather, they have been the traditions of small-scale, preliter-
ate communities who transmitted their sacred lore orally from generation to generation. We call these religions primal because they came
first, long before the advent of the great written traditions. Most are
long dead; those that survive—in Africa, Australia, Southeast Asia,
the Pacific Islands, Siberia, and in the Indian cultures of North and
South America—do so precariously on the borders of global technologi-
cal civilization. Taken collectively, however, they represent an important dimension of human religious experience.

Oral traditions have no written texts, but anthropologists have
recorded their myths and legends. These accounts will serve as ana-
logues to the scriptures of the historical traditions.

---

1. A. F. C. Wallace, *Religion: An Anthropological View* (New York: Random House,
1966), 4.

BEGINNINGS

Prevalent in primal lore are stories of beginnings. Sacred myths and cherished legends narrate the origins of the cosmos itself, the earth and its life, and human beings and their purposes. Only if we know how things began, the primal mind seems to say, do we know how to continue. Creation stories grapple with the fundamental mysteries of creation and destruction, chaos and meaning, power and impotence, and good and evil, while locating human beings in their encompassing spiritual milieu.

1. The Supreme Io and the Creation of the World (Maori, New Zealand)

Io dwelt within the breathing-space of immensity.
The Universe was in darkness with water everywhere.
There was no glimmer of dawn, no clearness, no light.
And he began by saying these words,—
. . . "Darkness become a light possessing darkness."
And at once light appeared.
(He) then repeated those self-same words in this manner . . .
    "Light, become a darkness-possessing light."
And again an intense darkness supervened.
Then a third time He spake saying:
    "Let there be one darkness above,
    Let there be one darkness below . . .
    Let there be one light above,
    Let there be one light below, . . .
    A dominion of light,
    A bright light."
And now a great light prevailed.
(Io) then looked to the waters which compassed him about,
    and spake a fourth time, saying:
    "Ye waters of Tai-kama, be ye separate.
    Heaven be formed." Then the sky became suspended.
    "Bring forth thou Tupua-horo-nuku."
    And at once the moving earth lay stretched abroad.

Those words (of Io) became impressed on the minds of our ancestors, and by them were they transmitted down through generations, our priest joyously referred to them as being:

The ancient and original sayings.
The ancient and original words.
The ancient and original cosmological wisdom (*wananga*).
Which caused growth from the void,
As witness the tidal waters,
The evolved heaven,
The birth-given evolved earth.

It is a Maori practice to reenact Io's original creation in their own human acts of creation as an attempt to bring light where there was darkness. In so doing human beings are in harmony with Io:

And now, my friends, there are . . . very important applications of those original sayings, as used in our sacred rituals. . . . The words by which Io fashioned the Universe . . . are used in the ritual for implanting a child in a barren womb. The next [use] occurs in the ritual for enlightening both the mind and the body. The words by which Io caused light to shine in the darkness are used in the rituals for cheering a gloomy and despondent heart, [and for] shedding light into secret places and matters, for inspiration in song-composing, and in many other affairs. . . . For all such the ritual to enlighten and cheer includes the words (used by Io) to overcome and dispel darkness.

2. The World Was in God's Mind (Omaha, North America)

At the beginning all things were in the mind of Wakonda. All creatures including man were spirits. They moved about in space between the earth and the stars. They were seeking a place where they could come into bodily existence. They ascended to the sun, but the sun was not fitted for their abode. They moved on to the moon and found that it also was not good for their home. They descended to the earth. They saw it was covered with water. They floated through the air to the north, the east, the south, and the west, and found no dry land. They were sorely grieved. Suddenly from the midst of the water uprose a great rock. It burst into flames and the waters floated into the air in clouds. Dry land appeared; the grasses and the trees grew. The hosts of spirits descended and became flesh and blood. They fed on the seeds of the grasses and the fruits of the trees, and the land vibrated with their expressions of joy and gratitude to Wakonda, the maker of all things.

3. The Brotherhood of Beast and Man (Bushongo, Central Africa)

In an interesting variation, here the world is created not by a majestic fiat but by a divine regurgitation.

In the beginning, in the dark, there was nothing but water. And Bumba was alone.

One day Bumba was in terrible pain. He retched and strained and vomited up the sun. After that light spread over everything. The heat of the sun dried up the water until the black edges of the world began to show. Black sandbanks and reefs could be seen. But there were not living things.

Bumba vomited up the moon and then the stars, and after that the night had its own light also.

Still Bumba was in pain. He strained again and nine living creatures came forth: the leopard named Koy Bumba, and Pongo Bumba the crested eagle, the crocodile . . . and one little fish named Yo; next . . . the tortoise, and Tsetse, the lightning . . . then the white heron [and] also one beetle, and the goat named Budi.

Last of all came forth men. There were many men, but only one was white like Bumba. His name was Loko Yima.

The creatures themselves then created all the creatures. The heron made all the birds of the air. . . . The crocodile made serpents and the iguana. The goat produced every beast with horns. Yo, the small fish, brought forth all the fish of all the seas and waters. The beetle created insects. . . .

Of all the creatures, Tsetse, lightning, was the only trouble-maker. She stirred up so much trouble that Bumba chased her into the sky. Then mankind was without fire until Bumba showed the people how to draw fire out of trees. "There is fire in every tree," he told them, and showed them how to make the firedrill and liberate it. Sometimes today Tsetse still leaps down and strikes the earth and causes damage.

When at last the work of creation was finished, Bumba walked through the peaceful villages and said to the people, "Behold these wonders. They belong to you." Thus from Bumba, the Creator, the First Ancestor, came forth all the wonders that we see and hold and use, and all the brotherhood of beast and man.

4. The Origins of Night and Sleep (People of the Banks Islands, Melanesia)

Here the Creator, Qat, seeks to create darkness as a respite from relentless light.

When the Melanesian people in the Banks Islands see the shadow of a cloud moving swiftly over the face of the sea, they say "There flies Qat." Qat created men and pigs and food, they say, and if a pig runs into the house, they drive it out with the words "Qat says stay outside."

Qat himself was born on Vanna Lava, the very center of the world, and of what happened before that there is no tale.

Qat was born from the bursting of a stone. His mother was a great stone that split in two and Qat came forth and named himself. He had no father; but he had eleven brothers . . .

Qat began to make things right away; men and pigs and plants and stones—or whatever he thought up. . . .

But he did not know how to make darkness. It was light in the world all the time, without dimness or dark or rest.

The eleven brothers did not like the world this way.

"Look here, Qat! It's too light," they said, or "There's nothing but light all the time, Qat!", or "Qat, can't you do something?"

Qat searched around and one day he heard that there was something called *night* over at Vava in the Torres Islands. . . . There he bought (in exchange for a pig) a piece of night from Qong, Night, who dwelt in that place. . . .

At any rate, Qat returned to Vanna Lava bearing night and bringing also various birds and fowls to make a clamor when it was time for day.

Qat showed the brothers how to construct beds of coca fronds and spread them on the floor and how to lie down for rest.

The brothers looked out and saw the sun moving down the west.

"It is departing," they cried to Qat. "Will it come back?"

"What is happening is called *night*," Qat told them.

Then he let loose the night.

"What is spreading and covering the sky?" cried the brothers.

"This is night," said Qat. "Lie down and keep quiet."

The brothers lay down, and in the dark they felt strange and dreamy; their eyes grew heavy and closed.

"Are we dying?" said the brothers.

"This is sleep," said Qat.

Only the birds knew how long the night should last; so when the night had lasted as long as the night should last, the cock crowed and the birds began to call and answer.

Qat then took a piece of red obsidian for a knife and cut a hole in the night. The first light that showed through was red, and soon all the light the night had covered shone through once again. The brothers opened their eyes and started the work of the day.

This is the way mankind lives now: day—sleep—day.

5. Mother Corn Grows the First Human Beings from the Earth (Pawnee, North America)

The preceding creation stories feature male divinities. Primal traditions often recognize the Mother Goddess as life's creative source, as in the following accounts.

Before the World was we were all within the Earth.

Mother Corn caused movement. She gave life.

Life being given we moved towards the surface:

We shall stand erect as men!

The being is become human! He is a person!

To personal form is added strength:

Form and intelligence united, we are ready to come forth—

But Mother Corn warns us that the Earth is still in flood.

Now Mother Corn proclaims that the flood is gone, and the Earth [is] now green.

Mother Corn commands that the people ascend to the surface.

Mother Corn has gathered them together, they move half way to the surface;

Mother Corn leads them near to the surface of the Earth;

Mother Corn brings them to the surface. The first light appears!

Mother Corn leads them forth. They have emerged to the waist.

They step forth to the surface of the Earth.
Now all have come forth; and Mother Corn leads them from
    the East towards the West.
Mother Corn leads them to the place of their habitation . . .
All is completed! All is perfect!

6. The Universal Mother (Kagaba, South America)

The mother of our songs, the mother of all our seed, bore us in the beginning of things and so she is the mother of all types of men, the mother of all nations. She is the mother of the thunder, the mother of the streams, the mother of the trees and all things. She is the mother of the world and of the older brothers, the stone-people. She is the mother of the fruits of the earth and of all things. She is the mother of our youngest brothers, the French and the strangers. She is the mother of our dance paraphernalia, of all our temples and she is the only mother we possess. She alone is the mother of the fire and the Sun and the Milky Way. . . . She is the mother of the rain and the only mother we possess. And she has left us a token in all temples . . . a token in the form of songs and dances.

She has no cult, and no prayers are really directed to her, but when the fields are sown and the priests chant their incantations the Kagaba say, "And then we think of the one and only mother of the growing things, of the mother of all things." One prayer was recorded. "Our mother of the growing fields, our mother of the streams, will [you] have pity upon us? For [to] whom do we belong? Whose seeds are we? To our mother alone do we belong."

7. Kuma, the Mother (Yaruro, South America)

Everything sprang from Kuma, and everything that the Yaruros do was established by her. She is dressed like a shaman, only her ornaments are of gold and much more beautiful.

With Kuma sprang Puana and Itciai; Hatchawa is her grandson and Puana made a bow and arrow for him. Puana taught Hatchawa to hunt and fish. When Hatchawa saw the people at the bottom of a hole and wished to bring them to the top, Puana made him a rope and a hook.

Another figure that sprang with Kuma was Kiberoh. She carried fire in her breast and at Kuma's request gave it to the boy Hatchawa. But when the boy wanted to give it to the people, Juma refused and cleverly threw live fish in the fire, spreading coals all about. The people seized the hot coals and ran away to start fires of their own. Everything was at first made and given to the boy and he passed it on to the people. Everybody sprang from Kuma, but she was not made pregnant in the ordinary way. It was not necessary.

8. The Androgynous Nana-Buluku (Fon, West Africa)

Some origin stories explicitly recognize the coinherence of female and male principles in creative activity, as in 8, 9, and 10 below.

The World was created by one god, who is at the same time both male and female. This Creator is neither Mawu or Lisa, but is named Nana-Buluku. In time, Nana-Buluku gave birth to twins, who were named Mawu and Lisa, and to whom eventually dominion over the real thus created was ceded. To Mawu, the woman, was given command of the night; to Lisa, the man, command of the day. Mawu, therefore, is the moon and inhabits the west, while Lisa, who is the sun, inhabits the east. At the time their respective domains were assigned to them, no children had as yet been born to this pair, though at night the man was in the habit of giving a "rendezvous" to the woman, and eventually she bore him offspring. This is why, when there is an eclipse of the moon, it is said the celestial couple are engaged in love-making; when there is an eclipse of the sun, Mawu is believed to be having intercourse with Lisa.

9. Ta'aroa, the Creator; Hina, the Mitigator (Tahiti, Polynesia)

Three of several different versions of the Tahitian creation story are excerpted here.

a. Ta'aroa Becomes the Universe

He existed, Ta'aroa was his name.
In the immensity [of space]

There was no earth, there was no sky.
There was no sea, there was no man.
Above, Ta'aroa calls.
Existing alone, he became the universe.
Ta'aroa is the origin, the rocks.
Ta'aroa is the sands,
　　It is thus that he is named.
Ta'aroa is the light;
　　Ta'aroa is within;
　　Ta'aroa is the germ.
Ta'aroa is beneath;
　　Ta'aroa is firm;
　　Ta'aroa is wise.
He created the land of Hawaii,
　　Hawaii the great and sacred,
　　As a body of shell for Ta'aroa . . .

b. But Who Is Ta'aroa's Shell?

As Ta'aroa had crusts, that is, shells, so has everything a shell

The sky is a shell, that is, endless space in which the gods placed the sun, the moon, the Sporades, and the constellations of the gods.

The earth is a shell to the stones, the water, and plants that spring from it.

Man's shell is woman because it is by her that he comes into the world; and woman's shell is a woman because she is born of woman.

One cannot enumerate the shells of all the things that this world produces.

c. Hina the Mediatrix, Mitigator of Many Things

After the creation peace and harmony everywhere existed for a long time. But at last, discontentment arose and there was war among the gods in their different regions, and among men, so Ta'aroa and Tu [male divinities] uttered curses to punish them.

They cursed the stars, which made them blink; and they cursed the moon, which caused it to wane and go out. But Hina [the First Woman], the mitigator of many things, saved their lives since which the host of stars are ever bright, but keep on twinkling; and the moon always returns after it disappears.

They cursed the sea, which caused low tide; but Hina preserved the sea, which produced high tide; and so these tides have followed each other ever since.

They cursed the rivers, which frightened away the waters, so that they hid beneath the soil; but Hina reproduced the shy waters, which formed springs, and so they continue to thus exist.

. . . According to Tahitians, the man and not the woman caused people to lose eternal life. . . .

10. The Potent and Fertile Ancestors (Wulamba, Australia)

This much-abbreviated story recounts the origins of the aboriginal Wulamba people through the cosmic sexuality of the Djanggawul, a brother and his two sisters, denizens of the spiritual continuum known as the Dreamtime. "The great and easy fertility of the Djanggawul is celebrated by the entire people annually: Women and children of the tribe wriggle under the mat in imitation of unborn babies, while the men dance around and poke it with their rangga *poles; finally the women and children emerge, just as their ancestors did from the wombs of the Djanggawul sisters."[2] Thus do the Wulamba reenter the sacred ancestral world and make sacred their own.*

In the beginning there were land and sky, animals and birds, foliage and trees. There was sea, too, in the waters of which were fish and other creatures; and upon the land were beings of totemic origin . . . but man, as we know him today, was not among them.

Far out to sea . . . was an island known as Bralgu, the land of Eternal Beings. . . .

It was here . . . that the Djanggawul were living. . . .

There were three of them: Djanggawul himself, his elder Sister . . . and his younger Sister. [All three] were nearly always known as Djanggawul. Djanggawul himself had an elongated

2. Barbara C. Sproul, *Primal Myths: Creation Myths Around the World* (San Francisco: Harper & Row, 1979), 315.

penis, and each of the Two Sisters had a long clitoris; these were so long that they dragged upon the ground as they walked . . .

At Bralgu, as they walked around with these, they left grooves in the ground from their dragging. And when the Djanggawul Brother had coitus with his Sisters, he lifted aside their clitorises, entering them in the usual way. . . . They lived at Bralgu for some little time, putting people there, and leaving "Dreamings" in the form of totemic origins, sacred emblems and body paintings. They also instituted their rituals and ceremonies. The Brother's penis and the Sisters' clitorises were sacred emblems, like *rangga* poles.

. . . Then they paddled out to sea, leaving the island of Bralgu far behind. . . .

[After long journeyings] the Djanggawul reached Nganma-ruwi. . . . While they were living there, [the Brother] said to [his sister]: "I want to copulate with you, Sister."

But the elder Sister was shy. "Why?" she asked him.

"I want to put a few people in this place," the Brother replied.

So he lifted her clitoris and put in his long penis. He did the same with [the younger].

After some time, [the elder Sister] became pregnant, and her brother said to her, "Sister, may I have a look at you?". . .

"All right," she replied. She opened her legs a little, resting her clitoris on her left leg. The Brother sat before his Sister and placed his index finger into her vagina, up to the first joint. Then he pulled it away, and at the same time a baby boy came out. [She] was careful to open her legs only a little; if she had spread them out, children would have flowed from her, for she kept many people stored away in her uterus. . . .

She continued giving birth to children of both sexes; when she had finished she closed her legs, and the Djanggawul Brother said to her:

"Sister, these little boys we will put in the grass, so that later, when they group up, they will have whiskers. . . . We will always do that when we remove male children. And these little girls we have put under the *ngainmara* mat, hiding them there. That is because they must be smooth and soft and have no body hair, and because girls are really sacred. . . . We will always do that when we remove female children."

The Djanggawul then left this place. The children they had produced grew up and married, and were the progenitors of the present Aborigines of those parts.

11. Why God Is Remote

a. Mulungu Flees the Cruelty of Humankind (Yao, East Africa)

Some primal stories tell why God, once near, is now distant.

At first there were no people. Only Mulungu and the decent peaceful beasts were in the world.

One day Chameleon sat weaving a fish trap, and when he had finished he set it in the river. In the morning he pulled the trap and it was full of fish, which he took home and ate.

He set the trap again. In the morning he pulled it out and it was empty: no fish.

"Bad luck," he said, and set the trap again.

The next morning when he pulled the trap he found a little man and woman in it. He had never seen creatures like this.

"What can they be?" he said. "Today I behold the unknown." And he picked up the fish trap and took the two creatures to Mulungu.

"Father," said Chameleon, "see what I have brought."

Mulungu looked. "Take them out of the trap," he said. "Put them down on the earth and they will grow."

Chameleon did this. And the man and woman grew. They grew until they became as tall as men and women are today.

All the animals watched to see what people would do. They made fire. They rubbed two sticks together in a special way and thus made fire. The fire caught in the bush and roared through the forest and the animals had to run to escape the flames.

The people caught a buffalo and killed it and roasted it in the fire and ate it. Then next day they did the same thing. Every day they set fires and killed some animal and ate it.

"They are burning up everything!" said Mulungu. "They are killing my people!"

All the beasts ran into the forest as far away from mankind as they could get. Chameleon went into the high trees.

"I'm leaving!" said Mulungu.

He called to Spider. "How do you climb on high?" he said.

"Very nicely," said Spider. And Spider spun a rope for Mulungu and Mulungu climbed the rope and went to live in the sky.

Thus the gods were driven off the face of the earth by the cruelty of man.

b. No One Has Seen Him Since (Ngombe, Central Africa)

Akongo was not always as he is now. In the beginning the creator lived among men; but men were quarrelsome. One day they had a big quarrel and Akongo left them to themselves. He went and hid in the forest and nobody has seen him since. People today can't tell what he is like.

12. The Devolution of the World (Hopi, North America)

Although the following myth of the Hopi ("peaceful ones") presents our current world as the result of a long devolution due to human folly, it is nevertheless infused with faith and hope in our sacred nature and high calling. The subheadings are not in the original.

The Infinite Conceives the Finite

But first, they say, there was only the Creator, Taiowa. All else was endless space. There was no beginning and no end, no time, no shape, no life. Just an immeasurable void that had its beginning and end, time, shape and life in the mind of Taiowa the Creator.

Then he, the infinite, conceived the finite. First he created Sotuknang to make it manifest, saying to him, "I have created you, the first power and instrument as a person, to carry out my plan for life in endless space. I am your Uncle. You are my Nephew. Go now and lay out these universes in proper order so they may work harmoniously with one another according to my plan."

Sotuknang did as he was commanded. . . .

Taiowa was pleased.

The Creation of Life and Vibration

Sotuknang . . . created her who was to remain on earth and be his helper. Her name was Kokyangwuti, Spider Woman.

When she awoke to life and received her name, she asked, "Why am I here?"

"Look about you," answered Sotuknang. "Here is the earth we have created . . . but there is no life upon it. We see no joyful movement. We hear no joyful sound. What is life without sound and movement? So you have been given the power to help us create this life. You have been given the knowledge, wisdom, and love to bless all the beings you create. That is why you are here."

The Ancestors and Sotuknang's Request

[After Spider Woman created many living things] Sotuknang was happy, seeing how beautiful it all was—the land, the plants, the birds, the animals, and the power working through them all. Joyfully he said to Taiowa, "Come see what our world looks like now!"

"It is very good," said Taiowa. "It is ready now for human life. . . ."

[Spider woman created four males in Sotuknang's image and four females in her own. Allowing them to behold their first sunrise she said:] "That is the Sun. . . . You are meeting your Father, the Creator for the first time. . . ."

Then [Sotuknang] said to them, "With all these I have given you this world to live on and to be happy. There is only one thing I ask of you. To respect the Creator at all times. Wisdom, harmony, and respect for the love of the Creator who made you. May it grow and never be forgotten among you as long as you live."

So the First People went their directions, were happy, and began to multiply.

The Primal Way

With the pristine wisdom granted them, they understood that the earth was a living entity like themselves. She was their mother; they were made from her flesh; they suckled at her breast. For her milk was the grass upon which all animals grazed and the corn which had been created specially to supply food for mankind. But the corn plant was also a living entity with a body similar to man's in many respects, and the people built its flesh into their own. Hence corn was also their mother. Thus they knew their mother in two aspects which were often synonymous—as Mother Earth and Corn Mother.

[When a child was born in that First Community,] for seven or eight years he led the normal earthly life of a child. Then came his first initiation into a religious society, and he began to learn that, although he had human parents, his real parents were the universal entities who had created him through them—his Mother Earth, from whose flesh all are born, and His Father Sun, the solar god who gives life to all the universe. He began to learn in brief, that he had two aspects. He was a member of an earthly family and a tribal clan, and he was a citizen of the great universe, to which he owed a growing allegiance as his understanding developed.

The Vibratory Centers

The First People, then, understood the mystery of their parenthood. In their pristine wisdom they also understood their own structure and functions—the nature of man himself.

The living body of man and the living body of the earth were constructed in the same way. Through each ran an axis, man's axis being the backbone, the vertebral column, which controlled the equilibrium of his movements and his functions. Along this axis were several vibratory centers which echoed the primordial sound of life throughout the universe or sounded a warning if anything went wrong.

The first of these . . . lay at the top of the head. Here . . . was . . . the "open door" through which he received his life and communicated with his Creator. . . .

Just below it was the second center . . . the brain. Its earthly function enabled man to think about his actions and work on this earth. But the more he understood that his work and actions should conform to the plan of the Creator, the more clearly he understood that the real function of the thinking organ called the brain was carrying out the plan of all Creation.

The third center lay in the throat. It tied together those openings in his nose and mouth through which he received the breath of life and the vibratory organs that enabled him to give back his breath in sound. This primordial sound, as that coming from the vibratory centers of the body of earth, was attuned to the universal vibration of all Creation. New and diverse sounds were given forth by these vocal organs in the forms of speech and song, their secondary function for man on this earth. But as he came to understand its primary function, he used this center to speak and sing praises to the Creator.

The fourth center was the heart. It too was a vibrating organ, pulsing with the vibration of life itself. In his heart man felt the good of life, its sincere purpose. He was of One Heart. But there were those who permitted evil feelings to enter. They were said to be of Two Hearts.

The last of man's important centers lay under his navel, the organ some people now call the solar plexus. As this name signifies, it was the throne in man of the Creator himself. From it he directed all the functions of man. . . .

The Erosion of Wisdom

So the First People kept multiplying and spreading over the face of the land and were happy. Although they were of different colors and spoke different languages, they felt as one and understood one another without talking. It was the same with the birds and animals. They all suckled at the breast of their Mother Earth who gave them her milk of grass, seeds, fruits and corn, and they all felt as one, people and animals.

But gradually there were those who forgot the commands of Sotuknang and the Spider Woman to respect their Creator. More and more they used the vibratory centers of their bodies solely for earthly purposes, forgetting that their primary purpose was to carry out the plan of Creation.

There then came among them Lavaihoya, the Talker . . . and the more he kept talking the more he convinced them of the differences between them: the differences between people and animals, and the differences between the people themselves by reason of the colors of their skins, their speech, and belief in the plan of the Creator.

It was then that animals drew away from people. . . .

[After further decline, the First World was destroyed by fire. A remnant of virtuous humanity embarked upon a Second World, then a Third, but each of these declined, and Sotuknang and Taiowa destroyed them by ice and water respectively. Finally, a virtuous remnant of humanity stood poised to enter the Fourth World:]

"I have something more to say before I leave you," Sotuknang told the people as they stood at their Place of Emergence on the shore of the present Fourth World. This is what he said:

"The name of this Fourth World is Tuwaqzchi, World Complete. You will find out why. It is not all beautiful and easy like the previous ones. It has height and depth, heat and cold, beauty and barrenness; it has everything for you to choose from. What you choose will determine if this time you can carry out the plan of Creation on it or whether it must in time be destroyed too. Now you will separate and go different ways to claim all the earth for the Creator. . . . Now I must go, But you will have help from the proper deities, from your good spirits. Just keep you own doors open and always remember what I have told you. This is what I say."

Then he disappeared.

13. Who Can Make an Image of God? (Pygmy, Africa)

In the beginning was God,
   Today is God
   Tomorrow will be God.
Who can make an image of God?
He has no body.
He is as a word
   which comes out of your mouth.
That word! It is no more,

It is past, and still it lives!
So is God.

RETURNING TO THE SACRED REALM

Nothing living escapes the relentless passage of time. Yet for many primal peoples time has a stable backdrop, a timeless sacred dimension from which time issues. It is spoken of, as in the previous section, as a long-ago Beginning when the gods and ancestors originated the world, established its rhythms, and provided models for human action. But it is also here and now, an "Everywhen," entered through the retelling of myths and the performance of sacred rituals. To primal peoples, events in time acquire meaning—become sacred—only to the extent that they are reflections of actions performed by the heroes and gods in that Sacred Realm of origins. We have already seen examples of this dynamic in selections 1 and 10 above. Here are three others.

14. Making Life Sacred (Dayak, Borneo)

All ceremonies of transition, such as birth . . . marriage and death correspond very closely with each other in that on every occasion they repeat the drama of primeval creation. . . .

Marriage. . . . To be married means to enter a new stage of sacred life. It means that something old is irrevocably past and something new comes about, it is death and life, passing away and coming into being. It is the same kind of event as birth, initiation, and death. The young couple die. The death is undergone through a representative, viz., the head, taken either from a raid or from a sacrificial slave, in which the spear, the stem of the Tree of Life, is stuck. . . . Today the coconut is used as a surrogate. . . . The couple are thus returned to mythical, primeval time. They return to the Tree of Life. This return is indicated by the clasping of the Tree of Life by the bridal pair. To clasp it means to be in the Tree of Life, to form a unity with it. . . . The wedding is the re-enactment of the creation, and the re-enactment of the creation of the first human couple from the Tree of Life. The bridal pair are the first human couple, and in their marital union, with its functions, duties and rights, they are also the total godhead. . . .

Birth. . . . There is also the ritual bath of the infant, which takes place either in a river or in the house, a few days or weeks after its birth. The child is taken to the middle of the river in a sacred boat shaped like the Watersnake, splendidly decorated with cloths and flags, and there, at the entrance to the Underworld, it is immersed. The meaning of the rite is clear. . . . The sacred bath means here (and wherever and whenever it is performed) a return to the godhead and a renewal of life in and through the godhead. . . .

Death. The most important and the concluding stage in the life of a man is death. It does not mean passing away and extinction of life, but returning home to the divine world and being taken up again into the social and divine unity of mythical primeval time. Death is a passage into a new existence, the transition to a new and true life. It is thus an event of the same kind as birth, initiation, and marriage, and it is not only the most important of all these stages of life, but receives the fullest and the most detailed ceremonial expression. all the other stages reach their culmination and final conclusion in this.

. . . Man originated from the godhead. The godhead has guided him through the various stages of life until his death, until he returns to the godhead and is given new life and a new existence in the Upperworld from which he once departed and from which there will be no more separation.

15. The Annual Cycle and the Sacred Realm (Dayak, Borneo)

The sacred era of this world, created and given by the godhead, has a beginning and also an end. The beginning was the creation, the end will be brought about by the passage of time. Strictly speaking, this era lasts only one year. The beginning occurs with . . . the beginning of work in the fields. . . .

... The sacred year (and with it the world-era) ends with the harvest. The two or three months between the harvest and the resumption of work in the fields are called *helat nyelo,* the time between the years. For a few weeks in this period, the so-called harvest feast or new year's feast is held. But the ceremonies which are performed show that this feast has a far deeper significance. It is not only that another harvest has been brought in, or that another year is passed: there is much more to it than this, for a whole era in the existence of the world has elapsed, a period of creation is ended, and the people return not only from their fields to the village but they return also to the primeval time of myth and the beginning of everything. People return to the Tree of Life and the divine totality, and live and act in it. This is most clear in the lifting of all secular regulations and in the submission to the commandments of mythical antiquity and the total ... godhead.

... This is a joyful and sublime period, in which the major sacrifices are offered, and after the expiry of the world-era (the old year) the creation is re-enacted and the entire cosmos renovated. ... During this sacred period there is a return to cosmic/divine, social and sexual unity and wholeness. ... When the feast reaches its climax, there is sexual exchange and intercourse between the participants. The total and mass sexual intercourse is not adulterous or contrary to *hadat* [law, custom, right behavior] and does not infringe or destroy the cosmic/divine order; it is the union of the Upperworld and the Underworld ... in a personal and social whole and unity. It takes place in accordance with the commandments of the ... godhead itself.

16. The Outbursting (Yami, Indonesia)

The following creation myth concludes with a description of the Flying-fish Festival and its rituals, through which the Yami return to the time of origins, to the time of essential discoveries and masteries, reintegrating themselves into the sacred realm.

"Good is the island of Yami," said the god, looking down at the flat world, and dropped a big stone on the spot which is now the village of Ipaptok. The village is named that because there grows the bean-bearing plant called *paptok*, which the first man used for food.

The big stone fell . . . and out of it burst a man. He was hungry when he first came out and ate the *paptok*. Then he walked down to the sea.

He saw that a bamboo was growing by the sea, and as he watched, it split and out burst another man.

"Who are we?" said one. "We are man," said the other.

The son of bamboo walked in one direction and found silver. . . .

The son of stone waked in another direction and found iron. . . . They returned to their house and beat out the hard iron and the soft silver.

One day the right knee-joint of the son of bamboo swelled and itched and a boy child burst out; from the left knee-joint came a girl child. The same thing happened to the son of stone: from his right knee burst out a boy child; from his left knee came a girl.

These children grew up and married. The daughter of the son of stone wed the son of the son of bamboo, and happy generations followed.

The people built themselves canoes. But the son of bamboo could not fell the heavy trees with his silver ax. . . . So the people learned that the silver ax was too soft for hewing wood, but because they loved the silver, they made themselves silver helmets. Today they wear silver helmets adorned with beautiful silver lead-shapes when they launch the canoes for the Flying-fish Festival and perform the fish-calling ceremony.

They built canoes and launched them with song. They were very beautiful, carved with trees and waves and painted with black and white and red. . . . When the canoe of the son of stone entered the sea, it leaked. "That's bad," he said. Quickly he looked for something to plug the leaks and chose the fiber of the *kulau* tree. When the leaks were stopped, "Mended," he said. And the people use this fiber today to plug a leak.

Thus the people learned to make canoes and become fishermen. Every year during the season of flying-fish, they hold their Flying-fish Festival. At this time no one will offend the wonderful fish by spitting in the sea or throwing stones in the water. They fish at night by torchlight with torches in the end of each canoe. They perform the sacred fish-calling ceremony, and sing this song:

> From Ipaptok, the place of the outbursting of man,
> The first one descended to the plain of the sea.
> He performed the fish-calling rite;
> The torch was lighted: and the fish
> Were dazzled by the flames.

THE SPIRIT-FILLED WORLD

The world of primal peoples is largely an inspirited world, wherein all beings and things are felt and treated as living presences. Ancestral spirits are venerated, and the good and evil spirits that inhabit the natural world are given due attention. Here is but one indication of the inspirited primal world.

17. The Web of *Wakan* (Oglala Sioux, North America)

Every object in the world has a spirit and that spirit is *wakan*. Thus the spirits of the tree or things of that kind, while not like the spirit of man, are also *wakan*. *Wakan* comes from the *wakan* beings. These *wakan* beings are greater than mankind in the same way that mankind is greater than the animals. They are never born and never die. They can do many things that mankind cannot do. Mankind can pray to the *wakan* beings for help. There are many of these beings but all are of four kinds. The word *Wakan Tanka* means all of the *wakan* beings because they are all as if one. *Wakan Tanka Kin* signifies the chief or leading *Wakan* being which is the Sun. However, the most powerful of the *Wakan* beings is *Nagi Tanka*, the Great Spirit, who is also *Taku Skanskan*. *Taku Skanskan* signifies the Blue, in other words, the Sky.

THE SHAMAN

Most religious traditions involve specialists. In the historical traditions we meet the prophet who speaks God's mind, the priest who presides over sacred ritual, and the mystic or yogi who seeks direct communion with the Real. In primal traditions we encounter the shaman. *The word itself comes from* saman, *which, in the language of the Tungus people of Siberia, means "one who is excited, moved, or raised" and, arguably, "one who knows." The shaman is a person who can by means of ecstatic states journey outside himself or herself to know other worlds and channel the knowledge gained there toward the benefit of his or her community. The shaman's soul journeys often reflect the three-tiered cosmos common among primal traditions: an upper sky-world, a middle earth-world, and an underground or undersea world.*

18. Shamanic "Lighting" (Eskimo, Siberia)

The next thing an old shaman has to do for his pupil is to procure him an anak ua, . . . i.e., the altogether special and particular element which makes this man an angákoq (shaman). It is also called . . . his "lighting" or "enlightenment.". . . The first time a young shaman experiences this light, while sitting up on the bench invoking his helping spirits, it is as if the house in which he is suddenly rises; he sees far ahead of him, through mountains, exactly as if the earth were one great plain, and his eyes could reach to the end of the earth. Nothing is hidden from him any longer; not only can he see things far, far away, but he can also discover souls, stolen souls, which are either kept concealed in far, strange lands or have been taken down to the Land of the Dead.

. . . Then I sought solitude, and here I soon became very melancholy. I would sometimes fall to weeping, and feel unhappy without knowing why. Then for no reason, all would suddenly be changed, and I felt a great, inexplicable joy, a joy so powerful that I could not restrain it, but had to break into song, a mighty song, with only room for the one word: joy, joy! And I had to use the full strength of my voice. And then in the midst of such a fit of mysterious and overwhelming delight I became a shaman. I could see and hear in a totally different way. I had gained my quameneq, my enlightenment, the shaman-light of brain and body, and this in such a manner that it was not only I who could see through the darkness of life, but the same light also shone out from me, imperceptible to human beings, but visible to all the spirits of earth and sky and sea, and these now came to me and became my helping spirits.

19. Shamanic Initiation (Unmatjera, Central Australia)

This is an account given by the shaman Ilpailurkna speaking of himself in the third person.

When he was [about to be] made into a medicine man, a very old doctor [medicine man] came one day and threw some of his *atnongara* stones[3] at him with a spear-thrower. Some hit him on the chest, others went right through his head, from ear to ear, killing him. The old man then cut out all his insides, intestines, liver, heart, lungs—everything in fact, and left him lying all night long on the ground. In the morning the old man came and looked at him and placed some *atnongara* stones inside his body and in his arms and legs, and covered his face with leaves. Then he sang over him until his body was all swollen up. When this was so he provided him with a complete set of new inside parts, placed a lot more *atnongara* stones in him, and patted him on the head, which caused him to jump up alive. The old medicine man then made him drink water and eat meat containing *atnongara* stones. When he awoke he had no idea as to where he was, and said, "Tju, tju, tju—I think I am lost." But when he looked round he saw the old medicine man standing beside him, and the old man said, "No, you are not lost; I killed you a long time ago." Ilpailurkna had completely forgotten who he was and all about his past life. After a time the old man led him back to his camp and showed it to him. . . . His coming back this way and his strange behaviour at once showed the other natives that he had been made into a medicine man.

---

3. The editor's note here is: "These *atnongara* stones are small crystalline structures which every medicine man is supposed to be able to produce at will from his body, through which it is believed that they are distributed. In fact it is the possession of these stones which gives his virtue to the medicine man." See M. Eliade, ed., *Essential Sacred Writings from Around the World* (San Francisco: Harper & Row, 1967), 429.

20. Shamanic Initiation and Journey (Wiradjuri, Southeast Australia)

The shaman's journey is often preceded by a purifying period of fasting or isolation and induced by singing, dancing, drumming, or the ingestion of psychoactive substances. The journey to the lower world usually commences at a hole, cave, or tree stump, while access to the sky world is provided by a god or creature of the air.

My father is Yibai–dthulin. When I was a small boy he took me into the bush to train me to be a Wulla-mullung. He placed two large quartz crystals against my breast, and they vanished into me. I do not know how they went, but I felt them going through me like warmth. This was to make me clever and able to bring things up. He also gave me some things like quartz crystals in water. They looked like ice and the water tasted sweet. After that I used to see things that my mother could not see. When I was out with her I would say, "What is out there like men walking?" She used to say, "Child there is nothing." These were the *jir* (ghosts) which I began to see. . . .

When I was about ten years old . . . I went into the bush for a time, and while there my old father came out to me. He said . . . "Come with me to this place." I saw him standing by a hole in the ground, leading to a grave. I went inside and saw a dead man, who rubbed me all over to make me clever, and who gave me some Wallung [quartz crystals]. When we came out, my father pointed to a Gunr (tiger-snake) saying, "That is your *budjan* [secret personal totem]; it is mine also." There was a string tied to the tail of the snake, and extending to us. . . .

He took hold of it saying, "Let us follow him." The tiger-snake went through several tree trunks, and let us through. Then we came to a great Currajong tree, and went through it, and after that to a tree with a great swelling around its roots. It is in such places that Daramulun [a deity] lives. Here the Gunr went down into the ground, and we followed him, and came up inside the tree, which was hollow. There I saw a lot of little Daramuluns, the sons of Baiame [a deity]. After we came out again the snake took us into a great hole in the ground in which were a number of snakes, which

rubbed themselves against me, but did not hurt me. . . . They did
this to make me a clever man. . . . My father then said to me, "We
will go up to Baiame's camp." He got astride of a Mauir (thread)
and put me on another, and we held by each other's arms. At the
end of the thread was Wombu, the bird of Baiame. We went
through the clouds, and on the other side was the sky. We went
through the place where the Doctors go through, and it kept opening and shutting very quickly. My father said that, if it touched a
Doctor when he was going through, it would hurt his spirit, and
when he returned home he would sicken and die. On the other side
we saw Baiame sitting in his camp. He was a very great old man
with a long beard. He sat with his legs under him and from his
shoulders extended two great quartz crystals to the sky above him.

21. A Shaman's Journey to the Depths of the Sea (Eskimo, Siberia)

*Sometimes a shaman's journey is undertaken to placate angry spirits so
as to restore beneficial living conditions to the tribe. Here a shaman un-
dertakes a harrowing descent to the sea spirit Takánakapsâluk, who,
angry over the human breach of taboo, is withholding the sea animals
on which Eskimo hunters depend for life. The account closes with the
shaman's extraction of a communal confession, suggesting that one purpose of his otherworld journey was to provide a psychological catharsis
for the community.*

When a shaman wishes to visit Takánakapsâluk, he sits on the
inner part of a sleeping place behind a curtain, and must wear
nothing but his kamiks [boots] and mittens. A shaman about to
make this journey is said to be nak'a': one who drops down to the
bottom of the sea. . . .

The shaman sits for a while in silence, breathing deeply, and
then, after some time has elapsed, he begins to call upon his helping spirits, repeating over and over again: . . . "The way is made
ready for me; the way opens before me!"

Whereat all present must answer in chorus: . . . "Let it be so!"

And when the helping spirits have arrived, the earth opens
under the shaman, but often only to close up again; he has to strug-

gle for a long time with hidden forces, ere he can cry at last: "Now the way is open. . . ."

And now one hears, at first under the sleeping place: "Halala—he—he—he, halala—he—he—he!" and afterwards under the passage, below the ground, the same cry. . . . And the sound can be distinctly heard to recede farther and farther until it is lost altogether. Then all know that he is on his way to the ruler of the sea beasts. . . .

An ordinary shaman will, even though skillful, encounter many dangers in his flight down to the bottom of the sea; the most dreaded are three large rolling stones which he meets as soon as he has reached the sea floor. There is no way round; he has to pass between them, and take great care not to be crushed by these stones, which churn about, hardly leaving room for a human being to pass. Once he has passed beyond them, he comes to a broad, trodden path, the shamans' path; he follows a coastline resembling that which he knows from the earth, and entering a bay, finds himself on a great plain, and here lies the house of Takánakapsâluk, built of stone. . . . In the passage leading to the house lies Takánakapsâluk's dog stretched across the passage taking up all the room; it lies there gnawing at a bone and snarling. It is dangerous to all who fear it, and only the courageous shaman can pass by it, stepping straight over it as it lies; the dog then knows that the bold visitor is a great shaman, and does him no harm. . . .

Should a great shelter wall be built outside the house of Takánakapsâluk, it means that she is very angry and implacable in her feelings towards mankind, but the shaman must fling himself upon the wall, kick it down and level it to the ground. There are some who declare that her house has no roof, and is open at the top, so that she can better watch, from her place by the lamp, the doings of mankind. All the different kinds of game: seal, bearded seal, walrus and whale, are collected in a great pool on the right of her lamp, and there they lie puffing and blowing. When the shaman enters the house, he at once sees Takánakapsâluk, who, as a sign of anger, is sitting with her back to the lamp and with her back to all the animals in the pool. Her hair hangs down loose all over one side of her face, a tangled, untidy mass hiding her eyes, so that she cannot see. It is the misdeeds and offenses committed by men which gather in dirt and impurity over her body. All the foul emanations from the sins of mankind nearly suffocate her. . . . And he must now grasp Takánakapsâluk by one shoulder and turn her face towards the lamp and towards the animals, and stroke her hair, the hair she has been unable to comb out herself, because she has no fingers, and he must smooth it and comb it, and as soon as she is calmer, he must say: "Pik'ua qilusinEq ajulErmata": "Those up above can no longer help the seals up by grasping their foreflippers."

Then Takánakapsâluk answers in the spirit language: "The secret miscarriages of the women and breaches of taboo in eating boiled meat bar the way for the animals."

The shaman must now use all his efforts to appease her anger, and at last, when she is in a kindlier mood, she takes the animals one by one and drops them on the floor, and then it is as if a whirlpool arises in the passage, the water pours out from the pool and the animals disappear in the sea. This means rich hunting and abundance for mankind.

It is then time for the shaman to return to his fellows up above, who are waiting for him. They can hear him coming a long way off; the rush of his passage through the tube kept open for him by the spirits comes nearer and nearer, and with a mighty "Plu—a—he—he" he shoots up into his place behind the curtain: "Plu-plu," like some creature of the sea, shooting up from the deep to take breath under the pressure of mighty lungs.

Then there is silence for a moment. No one may break this silence until the shaman says: "I have something to say."

Then all present answer: "Let us hear, let us hear."

Here the anthologizer[4] interpolates: "But the shaman does not answer immediately. Rather, he uses this dramatic moment to force the audience to confess their breaches of taboo. All must acknowledge their sins, a process that produces a powerful group confession and cohesion. Only when that is complete does the shaman sigh with relief."

---

4. Roger Walsh, M.D., Ph.D., *The Spirit of Shamanism* (Los Angeles: Tarcher, 1990), 146–47.

[Now] the cause of Takánakapsâluk's anger is explained, and all are filled with joy at having escaped disaster. . . . This then was what happened when shamans went down and propitiated the great Spirit of the Sea.

22. The Journey of the First Shaman (Eskimo, Siberia)

In this fragment from an Eskimo creation myth, Raven, a spiritual intermediary with creative power, guides the primal human being on an initial journey to the upper and lower worlds.

. . . Raven continued for several days making birds, fishes, and animals, showing them to Man [and Woman], and explaining their uses. . . .

Raven remained with them a long time, teaching them how to live. He taught them how to make a fire drill and bow from a piece of dried wood. . . . He taught the men to make bows and arrows, spears, nets, and all the implements of the chase and how to use them; also how to capture the seals. . . . And he taught them how to make kaiaks, he showed them how to build houses of drift logs and bushes covered with earth. . . .

One day Raven came back and sat by Man, and they talked of many things. Man asked Raven about the land he had made in the sky. Raven said that he had made a fine land there, whereupon Man asked to be taken to see it. This was agreed to and they started toward the sky where they arrived in a short time. . . . Man looked about as they journeyed and saw many strange animals; also that the country was much finer than the one he had left. Raven told him that this land, with its people and animals, was the first he had made.

The people living here wore handsomely made fur clothing, worked in ornamental patterns, such as people now wear on earth; for Man, on his return, showed his people how to make clothes in this manner. . . .

Next they came to a round hole in the sky, around the border of which grew a ring of short grass, glowing like fire. This Raven said, was a star called the Moon-dog. . . .

Man was now told to close his eyes and he would be taken to another place. Raven took him upon his wings and dropping through the star hole, they floated down for a long time, until at last they entered something that seemed to resist their course. Finally they stopped, and Raven said they were standing at the bottom of the sea. Man breathed quite easily there, and Raven told him that the foggy appearance was caused by the water. . . . [Raven created many kinds of sea animals and other creatures and then] they passed many kinds of fish and then the shore rose before them, and overhead could be seen the ripples on the surface of the water. "Close your eyes, and hold fast to me," said Raven. As soon as he had done this, Man found himself standing on the shore near his home, and was very much astonished to see a large village where he had left only a few huts; his wife had become very old and his son was an old man. The people saw him and welcomed him back, making him their headman; he was given the place of honor . . . and there told the people what he had seen and taught the young men many things. The villagers would have given Raven a seat by the old man in the place of honor, but he refused it and chose a seat with the humble people near the entrance.

23. Inward Joy (Eskimo, Siberia)

When one night an unbeckoned, sky-borne fireball descended into her body, triggering a profound shamanic "lighting," the following song spontaneously erupted from Uvavnuk's[5] lips. Thereafter, singing it acted as a great healing force.

The great sea has set me in motion
set me adrift,
moving me like a weed in a river.

The sky and strong wind
Have moved the spirit inside me

---

5. Uvavnuk lived in the late nineteenth and early twentieth centuries.

till I am carried away
trembling with joy.

24. Is This Real, This Life I Am Living? (Pawnee, North America)

Let us see, is this real,
Let us see, is this real,
This life I am living?
You, Gods, who dwell everywhere,
Let us see, is this real,
This life I am living?

25. You Cannot Harm Me (Dakota, North America)

You cannot harm me,
    you cannot harm
    one who has dreamed a dream like mine.

THE SACRED EARTH

Primal religions are often called "ecological" because they are intimately linked to their native terrain and are therefore not usually available for export. Accordingly, primal traditions often evince a profound sense of place and display a singular reverence for the land. The land of primal peoples is holy because it is composed of ancestors' bones and pervaded by ancestors' spirits. The Earth is holy because it is, quite plainly, the ground and source of life.

26. This Newly Created World (Winnebago, North America)

Pleasant it looked,
this newly created world.
Along the entire length and breadth

of the earth, our grandmother,
extended the green reflection
of her covering
and the escaping odors
were pleasant to inhale

27. The Earth Is Beautiful (Navaho, North America)

The Earth is beautiful
The Earth is beautiful
The Earth is beautiful
Below the East, the Earth, its face toward the East, the top
    of its head is beautiful
The soles of its feet, they are beautiful
Its legs, they are beautiful
Its body, it is beautiful
Its chest, it is beautiful
Its breath, it is beautiful
Its head-feather, it is beautiful
The Earth is beautiful.

28. Its Life Am I (Navaho, North America)

In the following chant, the Navaho word hozhoni *compactly expresses
the qualities of beauty, peace, and harmony.*

Hozhoni, hozhoni, hozhoni
Hozhoni, hozhoni, hozhoni
The Earth, its life am I, hozhoni, hozhoni
The Earth, its feet are my feet, hozhoni, hozhoni
The Earth, its legs are my legs, hozhoni, hozhoni
The Earth, its body is my body, hozhoni, hozhoni
The Earth, its thoughts are my thoughts, hozhoni, hozhoni
The Earth, its speech is my speech, hozhoni, hozhoni
. . . The sky, its life am I, hozhoni, hozhoni—
The mountains, its life am I—
. . . The Sun, its life am I—

. . . White corn, its life am I—
Yellow corn, its life am I—
The corn beetle, its life am I—
Hozhoni, hozhoni, hozhoni
Hozhoni, hozhoni, hozhoni

29. The Sacred Land (Dayak, Bornco)

The area inhabited by the sacred people is the sacred land. It was given to them by the godhead, which had shaped it out of the remains of the sun and the moon. It lies among the primeval waters, between Upperworld and Underworld, and rests on the back of the Watersnake. . . . The world is thus supported and enclosed by the godhead, a man lives under its protection, in divine peace and well-being. . . .

The real native village of mankind is not in this world: it is Batu Nindan Tarong, in the Upperworld. Man dwells only for a time in this world, which is "lent" to him, and when the time has come and he is old, then he returns for ever to his original home. To die is not to become dead; it is called *buli*, to return home. This idea has nothing to do with any Christian influence; it is an ancient Dayak concept which is understandable in relation to the primeval sacred events and the mode of thought connected with them.

The Dayak loves the world into which he is born and where he grows up. His village is the largest and most beautiful place in the whole world, and he could change it for no other. If he leaves his village he takes with him sacred medicines which will guarantee his safe return, and if he himself never comes back his bones or his ashes are still brought back into the village and thereby he finds his last resting place in the sacred land. . . . There are old people who have never left their own village, not because they have never had a chance to, but because they simply never felt the need to do so. Why should one leave the village? Why roam far among strangers? Peace, safety, happiness, and the good life are to be found only in one's own world where one is protected by the godhead, surrounded by the primevally maternal Watersnake, where one rests on its body and is enclosed by its head and tail. . . .

Man lives not only in the divine land, not only in the peace of the godhead, but actually in the godhead, for the sacred land is a part of the Tree of Life, it was created from the sun and moon which flank the tree, and which issued from the Gold Mountain and the Jewel Mountain, and thus from the total godhead.

30. This Beautiful Land (Chief Seathl of the Dwamish, North America)

As in the next two selections, Native American expressions of reverence for the earth were sometimes cloaked in sorrow over the loss of their heritage. Chief Seathl spoke the following words to the Pacific Northwest territorial governor Isaac Stevens in 1854.

The son of the white chief says his father sends us greetings of friendship and good will. This is kind, for we know he has little need of our friendship in return, because his people are many. They are like the grass that covers the vast prairies while my people are few, and resemble the scattering trees of a storm-swept plain. . . .

Your God seems to us to be partial. He came to the white man. We never saw Him; never even heard His voice; He gave the white man laws but He had no word for his red children whose teeming millions filled this vast continent as the stars fill the firmament. No, we are two distinct races. . . . There is little in common between us. The ashes of our ancestors are sacred and their final resting place is hallowed ground, while you wander away from the tombs of your fathers seemingly without regret. Your religion was written on tables of stone by the iron finger of an angry God, lest you might forget it. The red man could never remember nor comprehend it.

Our religion is the traditions of our ancestors, the dreams of our old men, given them by the Great Spirit, and the visions of our sachems [chiefs], and is written in the hearts of our people.

Your dead cease to love you and the homes of their nativity as soon as they pass the portals of the tomb. They wander far off beyond the stars, are soon forgotten, and never return. Our dead never forget the beautiful world that gave them being. They still love its winding rivers, its great mountains and its sequestered vales. . . .

Every part of this country is sacred to my people. Every hillside, every valley, every plain and grove, has been hallowed by some fond memory or some sad experience of my tribe.

Even the rocks that seem to lie dumb as they swelter in the sun along the silent seashore in solemn grandeur thrill with memories of past events connected with the fate of my people, and the very dust under your feet responds more lovingly to our footsteps than to yours, because it is the ashes of our ancestors, and our bare feet are conscious of the sympathetic touch, for the soil is rich with the life of our kindred. . . .

And when the last red man shall have perished from the earth and his memory among white men shall have become a myth, these shores shall swarm with the invisible dead of my tribe, and when your children's children shall think themselves alone in the field, the store, the shop, upon the highway, or in the silence of the woods, they will not be alone. . . . At night when the streets of your cities and villages shall be silent, and you think them deserted, they will throng with the returning hosts that once filled and still love this beautiful land.

31. The Sons of the Forest (Potowatami, North America)

These words are attributed to Senachwine, a Potowatami elder, who spoke at a council fire at Indiantown, Illinois, in 1830.

For more than seventy years I have hunted in this grove and fished in this stream, and for many years I have worshipped on this ground. Through these groves and over these prairies in pursuit of game our fathers roamed, and by them this land was left unto us a heritage forever. No one is more attached to his home than myself, and none among you is so grieved to leave it. . . . In my boyhood days I have chased the buffalo across the prairies, and hunted the elk in the groves; but where are they now? Long since they have left us; the near approach of the white man has frightened them away. The deer and turkey will go next, and with them the sons of the forest.

32. Our Gods Were Here First (A Balinese Priest)

We are ready to receive Jesus Christ among our gods, and to set up a shrine for him, but we cannot allow that he supersede them and hold the only place; for our gods are the ones who own this island, and the ones who came here first.

33. The Meaning of the Sacred Pipe (Sioux, North America)

Black Elk, a noted seer of the Oglala Sioux, here recalls the instructions given by the White Buffalo Cow Woman, who in primeval times brought the calumet (sacred pipe) to human beings.

With this sacred pipe you will walk upon the Earth; for the Earth is your Grandmother and Mother, and She is sacred. Every step that is taken upon Her should be as a prayer. The bowl of this pipe is of red stone; it is the Earth. Carved in the stone and facing the center is this buffalo calf who represents all the four-leggeds who live upon your Mother. The stem of the pipe is of wood, and this represents all that grows upon the Earth. And these twelve feathers which hang here where the stem fits into the bowl . . . represent the eagle and all the wingeds of the air. All these peoples, and all the things of the universe, are joined to you who smoke the pipe—all send their voices to *Wakan-Tanka*, the Great Spirit. When you pray with this pipe, you pray for and with everything.

34. Relatives of Grandmother Earth (Sioux, North America)

We shall burn the sweet grass as an offering to *Wakan-Tanka*, and the fragrance of this will spread throughout the heaven and earth; it will make the four-leggeds, the wingeds, the star peoples of the heavens, and all things as relatives. From you, O Grandmother Earth, who are lowly, and who support us as does a mother, this fragrance will go forth; may its power be felt throughout the uni-

verse, and may it purify the feet and hands of the two-leggeds, that
they may walk forward upon the sacred earth, raising their heads
to *Wakan-Tanka!*

35. That We May Walk Fittingly (Tewa Pueblo, North America)

O our mother the Earth, O our father the sky,
Your children are we, and with tired backs
We bring you gifts that you love.
Then weave for us a garment of brightness;
May the warp be the white light of morning,
May the weft be the red light of evening,
May the fringes be the falling rain,
May the border be the standing rainbow.
Thus weave for us a garment of brightness
That we may walk fittingly where grass is green,
O our mother the earth, O our father the sky!

36. Earth Teach Me to Remember (Ute, North America)

Earth teach me stillness
    as the grasses are stilled with light.
Earth teach me suffering
    as old stones suffer with memory.
Earth teach me humility
    as blossoms are humble with beginning.
Earth teach me caring
    as the mother who secures her young.
Earth teach me courage
    as the tree which stands all alone.
Earth teach me limitation
    as the ant which crawls on the ground.
Earth teach me freedom
    as the eagle which soars in the sky.

Earth teach me resignation
as the leaves which die in the fall.
Earth teach me regeneration
as the seed which rises in the spring.
Earth teach me to forget myself
as melted snow forgets its life.
Earth teach me to remember kindness
as dry fields weep with rain.

37. With Tenderness They Have Come Up (Sioux, North America)

Grandfather Great Spirit
All over the world the faces of living ones
are alike
With tenderness they have come up out
of the ground.
. . . Give us the strength to understand,
and the eyes to see.
Teach us to walk the soft Earth as relatives
to all that live.

38. Behold Our Mother Earth (Pawnee, North America)

Behold! Our Mother Earth is lying here.
Behold! She gives of her fruitfulness.
Truly, her power she gives us.
Give thanks to Mother Earth who lies here.

Behold on Mother Earth the growing fields!
Behold the promise of her fruitfulness!
Truly, her power she gives us.
Give thanks to Mother Earth who lies here.

Behold on Mother Earth the spreading trees!
Behold the promise of her fruitfulness!

Truly, her power she gives us.
Give thanks to Mother Earth who lies here.

Behold on Mother Earth the running streams!
We see the promise of her fruitfulness.
Truly, her power she gives us.
Our thanks to Mother Earth who lies here.

39. Prayer for the Great Family (Gary Snyder, North America)

After a Mohawk prayer.

Gratitude to Mother Earth, sailing through night and day—
    and to her soil: rich, rare, and sweet
        in our minds so be it.

Gratitude to Plants, the sun-facing light-changing leaf
    and fine root-hairs; standing still through wind
    and rain; their dance is in the flowing spiral grain
        in our minds so be it.

Gratitude to Air, bearing the soaring Swift and the silent
    Owl at dawn. Breath of our song
    clear spirit breeze
        in our minds so be it.

Gratitude to Wild Beings, our brothers, teaching secrets,
    freedoms, and ways; who share with us their milk;
    self complete, brave, and aware
        in our minds so be it.

Gratitude to Water: clouds, lakes, rivers, glaciers;
    holding or releasing, streaming through all
    our bodies salty seas
        in our minds so be it.

Gratitude to the Sun: blinding pulsing light through
    trunks of trees, through mists, warming caves where

bears and snakes sleep—he who wakes us—
in our minds so be it.

Gratitude to Great Sky
who holds billions of stars—and goes yet beyond that—
beyond all powers, and thoughts
and yet is within us—
Grandfather Space
The Mind is his Wife.

so be it.

40. The Bush (Ojibwa, North America)

The Bush is sitting under a tree and
singing

GRACE NOTES

41. The Sayings of Black Elk

Black Elk (1862–1950) was a holy man of the Oglala division of the Teton Sioux.

Perhaps you have noticed that even in the very lightest breeze you can hear the voice of the cottonwood tree; this we understand is its prayer to the Great Spirit, for not only men, but all things and all beings pray to Him continually in differing ways.

For the Great Spirit is everywhere; he hears whatever is in our minds and hearts, and it is not necessary to speak to Him in a loud voice.

Since the drum is often the only instrument used in our sacred rites, I should perhaps tell you here why it is especially sacred and important to us. It is because the round form of the drum represents the whole universe, and its steady strong beat is the pulse, the heart, throbbing at the center of the universe. It is as the voice of *Wakan-Tanka*, and this sound stirs us and helps us to understand the mystery and power of all things.

42. The Story of Jumping Mouse

Jumping Mouse is a Native American "hero myth," a story of transformation and spiritual maturity.

Once there was Mouse. He was a Busy Mouse, Searching Everywhere . . . and Looking. He was Busy as all Mice are, Busy with Mice things. But Once in a while he would Hear an odd Sound. He would Lift his Head, Squinting Hard to See . . . and he would Wonder. One Day he Scurried up to a fellow Mouse and asked him, "Do you Hear a Roaring in your Ears, my Brother?"

"No, no," answered the Other Mouse, not Lifting his Busy Nose from the Ground. "I hear Nothing. I am Busy now. Talk to me Later."

He asked Another Mouse the same Question and the Mouse Looked at him Strangely. "Are you Foolish in your Head? What Sound?" he asked and Slipped into a Hole in a Fallen Cottonwood Tree.

The little Mouse shrugged his Whiskers and Busied himself again, Determined to Forget the Whole Matter. But there was that Roaring again. It was faint, very faint, but it was there! One Day he Decided to investigate the Sound just a little. Leaving the Other Busy Mice, he Scurried a little Way away and Listened again. There It was! He was Listening hard when suddenly, Someone said Hello.

"Hello, little Brother," the Voice said, and Mouse almost Jumped right Out of his Skin. He Arched his Back and Tail and was about to Run.

"Hello," again said the Voice. "It is I, Brother Raccoon." And sure enough, It was! "What are you Doing Here all by yourself, little Brother?" asked the Raccoon. The Mouse blushed, and put his Nose almost to the Ground. "I Hear a Roaring in my Ears and I am Investigating it," he answered timidly.

"A Roaring in Your Ears?" replied the Raccoon. . . . "What you Hear, little Brother, is the River."

"The River? . . . What is a River?"

"Walk with me and I will Show you the River," Raccoon said.

Little Mouse was terribly Afraid, but he was Determined to Find Out Once and for All about the Roaring. "I can Return to my Work," he thought, "after this thing is Settled, and possibly this thing may Aid me in All my Busy Examining and Collecting. And my Brothers All Said it was Nothing. I will Show them. I will Ask Raccoon to Return with me and I will have Proof."

"All Right Raccoon, my Brother," said Mouse. "Lead on to the River. I will Walk with you."

Little Mouse Walked with Raccoon. His little Heart was Pounding in his Breast. The Raccoon was taking him upon Strange Paths and little Mouse Smelled the Scent of many things that had Gone by this Way. Many times he became so Frightened he almost Turned Back. Finally, they Came to the River! It was Huge and Breathtaking, Deep and Clear in Places, and Murky in Others. Little Mouse was unable to See Across it because it was so Great. It Roared, Sang, Cried, and Thundered on its Course. . . .

"It is Powerful!" little Mouse said, Fumbling for Words.

"It is a Great thing," answered the Raccoon, "but here, let me Introduce you to a Friend."

In a . . . Shallower Place was a Lily Pad. . . . Sitting upon it was a Frog. . . .

"Hello, little Brother," said the Frog. "Welcome to the River."

"I must Leave you Now," cut in Raccoon, "but do not Fear, little Brother, for Frog will Care for you Now." And Raccoon left. . . .

Little Mouse approached the Water and looked into it. He saw a Frightened Mouse Reflected there.

"Who are you?" little Mouse asked the Reflection. "Are you not Afraid being that Far out into the Great River?"

"No," answered the Frog, "I am not Afraid. I have been Given the Gift from Birth to Live both Above and Within the River. When Winter Man Comes and Freezes This Medicine, I cannot be Seen. But all the while Thunderbird Flies, I am here. To Visit me, One must Come when the World is Green. I, my Brother, am the Keeper of the Water."

"Amazing!" little Mouse said at last, again Fumbling for Words.

"Would you like to have some Medicine Power?" Frog asked.

"Medicine Power? Me?" asked little Mouse. "Yes, Yes! If it is Possible."

"Then Crouch as Low as you Can, and then Jump as High as you are Able! You will have your Medicine!" Frog said.

Little Mouse did as he was Instructed. He crouched as Low as he Could and Jumped. And when he did, his Eyes Saw the Sacred Mountains.

Little Mouse could hardly Believe his Eyes. But there They were! But then he Fell back to Earth, and he landed in the River!

Little Mouse became Frightened and Scrambled back to the Bank. He was Wet and Frightened nearly to Death.

"You have tricked me!" little Mouse Screamed at the Frog.

"Wait," said the Frog. "You are not Harmed. Do not let your Fear and Anger Blind you. What did you See?"

"I," Mouse stammered, "I, I Saw the Sacred Mountains!"

"And you have a New Name!" Frog said. "It is Jumping Mouse."

"Thank you. Thank you," Jumping Mouse said, and Thanked him again. "I want to Return to my People and Tell them of this thing that has Happened to me."

"Go, go then," Frog said. "Return to your People. . . . Keep the Sound of the Medicine River to the Back of your Head.". . .

Jumping Mouse Returned to the World of the Mice. But he Found Disappointment. No One would Listen to him. And because he was Wet, and had no Way of explaining it because there had been no Rain, many of the other Mice were Afraid of him. They believed he had been Spat from the Mouth of Another Animal that had tried to Eat him. And they all Knew that if he had not been Food for the One who Wanted him, then he must also be Poison for them.

Jumping Mouse Lived again among his people but he could not Forget his Vision of the Sacred Mountains.

[But] the Memory Burned in the Mind and Heart of Jumping Mouse, and One Day he Went to the Edge of the . . . Place of Mice and Looked out onto the Prairie. He looked up for Eagles. The Sky was Full of many Spots, each One an Eagle. But he was Determined to Go to the Sacred Mountains. He Gathered All of his Courage and Ran just as Fast as he Could onto the Prairie. His little Heart Pounded with Excitement and Fear.

He ran until he Came to a Stand of Sage. He was Resting and trying to Catch his Breath when he saw an Old Mouse. The Patch of Sage . . . was a haven for Mice. Seeds were Plentiful and there was Nesting Material and many things to be Busy with.

"Hello," said Old Mouse. "Welcome."

Jumping Mouse was Amazed. Such a Place and such a Mouse. "You are Truly a great Mouse," Jumping Mouse said with all the Respect he could Find. "This is Truly a Wonderful Place. And the Eagles cannot See you here, either," Jumping Mouse said.

"Yes," said Old Mouse, "and One can See All the Beings of the Prairie here: the Buffalo, Antelope, Rabbit, and Coyote. One can See them All from here and Know their Names."

"That is Marvelous," Jumping Mouse said. "Can you also See the River and the Great Mountains?"

"Yes and No," Old Mouse Said with Conviction. "I Know there is the Great River. But I am Afraid that the Great Mountains are only a Myth. Forget your Passion to See Them and Stay here with me. There is Everything you Want here, and it is a Good Place to Be."

"How can he Say such a thing?" Thought Jumping Mouse. "The Medicine of the Sacred Mountains is Nothing One can Forget. Thank you very much for the Meal you have Shared with me, Old Mouse, and also for sharing your Great Home," Jumping Mouse said. "But I must Seek the Mountains."

"You are a Foolish Mouse to Leave here. There is Danger on the Prairie! . . . See all those Spots! They are Eagles, and they will Catch you!"

It was hard for Jumping Mouse to Leave, but he Gathered his Determination and Ran hard Again. The Ground Was Rough. . . . He could Feel the Shadows of the Spots upon his Back as he Ran. All those Spots! Finally he Ran into a Stand of Chokecherries. . . . It was Cool there and very Spacious. There was Water, Cherries and Seeds to Eat, Grasses to Gather for Nests, Holes to be Explored and many Other Busy Things to do. . . .

He was Investigating his New Domain when he Heard very Heavy Breathing. He quickly Investigated the Sound and Discovered its Source. It was a Great Mound of Hair with Black Horns. It was a Great Buffalo. Jumping Mouse could hardly Believe the Greatness of the Being he Saw Lying there before him. He was so large that Jumping Mouse could have Crawled into One of his Great Horns. "Such a Magnificent Being," thought Jumping Mouse, and he Crept Closer.

"Hello, my Brother," said the Buffalo. "Thank you for Visiting me."

"Hello, Great Being. . . . Why are you Lying here?"

"I am Sick and I am Dying," the Buffalo said. "And my Medicine has Told me that only the Eye of a Mouse can Heal me. But little Brother, there is no such thing as a Mouse."

Jumping Mouse was Shocked. "One of my Eyes!" he Thought, "one of my Tiny Eyes." He Scurried back into the Stand of Chokecherries. But the Breathing came Harder and Slower.

"He will Die," thought Jumping Mouse, "If I do not Give him my Eye. He is too Great a Being to Let Die."

He Went Back to where the Buffalo Lay and Spoke. "I am a Mouse," he said with a Shaky Voice. "And you, my Brother, are a Great Being. I cannot Let you Die. I have Two Eyes, so you may have One of them."

The minute he had Said it, Jumping Mouse's Eye Flew Out of his Head and the Buffalo was Made Whole. The Buffalo Jumped to his Feet, Shaking Jumping Mouse's Whole World.

"Thank you, my little Brother," said the Buffalo. "I Know of your Quest for the Sacred Mountains and of your Visit to the River. You have Given me Life so that I may Give-Away to the People. I will be your Brother Forever. Run under my Belly and I will Take you right to the Foot of the Sacred Mountains, and you need not Fear the Spots. The Eagles cannot See you while you Run under Me. All they will See will be the Back of a Buffalo. I am of the Prairie and I will Fall on you if I Try to Go up to the Mountains."

Little Mouse Ran under the Buffalo, Secure and Hidden from the Spots, but with only One Eye it was Frightening. The Buffalo's Great Hooves Shook the Whole World each time he took a Step. Finally they Came to a Place and Buffalo Stopped.

"This is Where I must Leave you, little Brother," said the Buffalo. . . .

Jumping Mouse Immediately Began to Investigate his New Surroundings. There were even more things here than in the

Other Places. Busier things, and an Abundance of Seeds and Other things Mice Like. . . . Suddenly he Ran upon a Gray Wolf who was Sitting there doing absolutely Nothing.

"Hello, Brother Wolf," Jumping Mouse said.

The Wolf's Ears Came Alert and his Eyes Shone. "Wolf! Wolf! Yes, that is what I am, I am a Wolf!" But then his mind Dimmed again and it was not long before he Sat Quietly again, completely without Memory as to who he was. Each time Jumping Mouse Reminded him who he was, he became Excited with the News, but soon would Forget again.

"Such a Great Being," thought Jumping Mouse, "but he has no Memory."

Jumping Mouse Went to the Center of this New Place and was Quiet. He listened for a very long time to the Beating of his Heart. Then Suddenly he Made up his Mind. He Scurried back to where the Wolf sat and he Spoke.

"Brother Wolf," Jumping Mouse said. . . .

"Wolf! Wolf!" said the Wolf. . . .

"Please, Brother Wolf," said Jumping Mouse, "Please Listen to me. I Know what will Heal you. It is one of my Eyes. And I want to Give it to you. You are a Greater Being than I. I am only a Mouse. Please Take it."

When Jumping Mouse Stopped Speaking his Eye Flew out of His Head and the Wolf was made Whole.

Tears Fell Down the Cheeks of Wolf, but his little Brother could not See them, for Now he was Blind.

"You are a Great Brother," said the Wolf, "for Now I have my Memory. But Now you are Blind. I am the Guide into the Sacred Mountains. I will Take you there. There is a Great Medicine Lake there. The most Beautiful Lake in the World. All the World is Reflected there. The People, the Lodges of the People, and All the Beings of the Prairies and Skies."

"Please Take me there," Jumping Mouse said.

The Wolf guided him through the Pines to the Medicine Lake. Jumping Mouse Drank the Water from the Lake. The Wolf Described the Beauty to him.

"I must Leave you here," said Wolf, "for I must Return so that I may Guide Others, but I will remain with you as long as you Like."

"Thank you, my Brother," said Jumping Mouse. "But although I am Frightened to be Alone, I Know you must Go so that you may Show Others the Way to this Place."

Jumping Mouse Sat there Trembling in Fear. It was no use Running, for he was Blind, but he Knew an Eagle would Find him Here. He Felt a Shadow on his Back and Heard the Sound that Eagles Make. He Braced himself for the Shock. And the Eagle Hit! Jumping Mouse went to Sleep.

Then he Woke Up. The Surprise of being Alive was Great, but Now he could See!

Everything was Blurry, but the Colors were Beautiful.

"I can See! I can See!" said Jumping Mouse over again and again.

A Blurry Shape Came toward Jumping Mouse. Jumping Mouse Squinted hard but the Shape Remained a Blur.

"Hello Brother," a Voice said. "Do you Want some Medicine?"

"Some Medicine for me?" asked Jumping Mouse. "Yes! Yes!"

"Then Crouch down as Low as you Can," the Voice said, "and Jump as High as you Can."

Jumping Mouse did as he was Instructed. He Crouched as Low as He Could and Jumped! The Wind Caught him and Carried him Higher.

"Do not be Afraid," the Voice called to him. "Hang on to the Wind and Trust!"

Jumping Mouse did. He Closed his Eyes and Hung on to the Wind and it Carried him Higher and Higher. Jumping Mouse Opened his Eyes and they were Clear, and the Higher He Went the Clearer they Became. Jumping Mouse Saw his Old Friend upon a Lily Pad on the Beautiful Medicine Lake. It was the Frog.

"You have a New Name," Called the Frog. "You are Eagle!"

Index of Texts

CHAPTER SIX: *Christianity*

CHAPTER SEVEN: *Islam*

Endnotes

A concluding asterisk (*) signals a passage that has been adapted for inclusive language.

CHAPTER ONE: *Hinduism*

1. Rig-Veda II:12.1–3, 5, 13 A. A. Macdonell, trans., *A Vedic Reader for Students* (Oxford: Clarendon Press, 1917), 45–54, *passim*, slightly modified; quoted in M. Eliade, ed., *Essential Sacred Writings from Around the World* (San Francisco: Harper & Row, 1967), 36.

2a–c. All selections are from R. T H. Griffith, *The Hymns of the Rigveda* (Benares, 1889–91), adapted by M. Eliade; quoted in Eliade, ed., *Essential Sacred Writings*, 280–82.

2a. Rig-Veda I:1:1, 7–9.

2b. Rig-Veda II:1:1, 14.

2c. Rig-Veda VII:15:4, 10, 13.

3. Rig-Veda VIII:48:1, 3–5, 8–9, 11. H. D. Griswold, trans., *The Religion of the Rigveda* (London, 1923), 210–11, quoted in Eliade, ed., *Essential Sacred Writings*, 246–47.

4a. Rig-Veda I:25:3, 7, 9–11. *Hymns of the Rigveda*, 42–43, quoted in Eliade, ed., *Essential Sacred Writings*, 31.

4b. Atharva-Veda IV:16:2–5. Maurice Bloomfield, trans., *Hymns of the Atharva Veda*, in *Sacred Books of the East* (Oxford, 1897), 42:88–89, quoted in Eliade, ed., *Essential Sacred Writings*, 32.

5. Rig-Veda X:129:1–4, 6–7. A. L. Basham, *The Wonder That Was India* (London, 1954), 247–48, quoted in Eliade, ed., *Essential Sacred Writings*, 109–10.

6. Rig-Veda X:90:1–3, 6, 8–14. Griffith, *Hymns of the Rigveda*, 289–93, quoted in Eliade, ed., *Essential Sacred Writings*, 227–28.

7–16. All selections are quoted from Juan Mascaro, ed. and trans., *The Upanishads* (London: Penguin, 1965). Page numbers listed below after the semicolon refer to this text.

7. Isa 1–2, 4, 6, 15; Mascaro, 49–50.
8. Kena I:4–8; 51.
9a. Katha I:20–29, II:1–9; 57–58.
9b. Katha II:19, 20, 24; 59–60.
9c. Katha III:3–15; 60–61.
9d. Katha IV:10–12, 14–15; 63.
9e. Katha V:9–13; 63–64.
9f. Katha VI:1; 65.
9g. Katha VI:10–11, 14–15, 18; 65–66.
10a. Mundaka II:1:1; 76.
10b. Mundaka II:2:2; 78.
10c. Mundaka II:2:3–7, 9–12; 78–79.
10d. Mundaka II:1:1–2; 80.
10e. Mundaka III:2:2, 9; 81.
11a. Katha II:15–17; 59.
11b. Maitri VI:22; 102.
11c. Chandogya II:23:2; 113.
11d. Mandukya 1–6, 8–12; 83–84.
12a. Svetesvatara II:8–10, 13–15; 88.
12b. Svetesvatara V:11–13; 94.
12c. Svetesvatara VI:16, 18–20; 96–97.
13. Maitri VI:24; 102–4.
14a. Taittiriya III:1–6; 110–11.
14b. Taittiriya 3:10:6; 111–12.
15. Chandogya VI:1, 12, 13; 116–18.
16. Brihadaranyaka II:4, IV:4; 132.
17–23. All selections are quoted from Swami Prabhavananda and Christopher Isherwood, trans., *The Song of God: Bhagavad Gita* (New York: New American Library, 1944). Page numbers listed below after the semicolon refer to this text.
17. Bhagavad Gita I.28–31, 35–39, 44–47; 31–34.
18a. Bhagavad Gita II:2–3; 35.
18b. Bhagavad Gita II.11–18; 36.

18c. Bhagavad Gita II:19–22, 27–28; 35–38.
19. Bhagavad Gita II:56–66, 70–72; 42–44.
20a. Bhagavad Gita II: 47–53; 40–41.
20b. Bhagavad Gita III:3–5, 9; 44–45.
20c. Bhagavad Gita III:19; 46–47.
20d. Bhagavad Gita V:7–12; 57–58.
20e. Bhagavad Gita VI:6; 64.
20f. Bhagavad Gita IV:41–42; 55–56.
21a. Bhagavad Gita VI:33–34; 68.
21b. Bhagavad Gita VI:10–12, 16–19; 65–66.
21c. Bhagavad Gita VI:27, 29, 32; 67.
22a. Bhagavad Gita XI:5–19; 91–93.
22b. Bhagavad Gita XI:28–33; 94.
22c. Bhagavad Gita XI:36–38; 95.
22d. Bhagavad Gita XI:45, 50–51; 96.
22e. Bhagavad Gita XI:50–55; 97.
23. Bhagavad Gita XII:13–20; 99–100.
24a–b. Prabhavananda and Isherwood, trans., *Crest-Jewel of Discrimination* (New York: New American Library, 1947), 114–15, 119–27.
25. All selections are quoted from Les Hixon, *Great Swan: Meetings with Ramakrishna* (Boston and London: Shambhala, 1992). Page numbers listed below refer to this text.
25a(2). 30.
25b. 15; 25b. 30; 25b. viii.
25c. 7; 25c. 29; 25c. 60; 25c. 65; 25c. 143; 25c. 141; 25c. viii–ix.
25d. 158; 25d. 158; 25d. 109; 25d. 108–9; 25d. 126.
25e. 26–27.
26a–d. Munagala S. Venkataramiah, *Talks with Sri Ramana Maharshi*, 6th ed. (Tiruvannamalai, South India: Sri Ramanashramam),

quoted in Stephen Mitchell, ed., *The Enlightened Mind* (San Francisco: HarperSanFrancisco, 1991), 193, 195, 196.

CHAPTER TWO: *Buddhism*

1. The Buddhacarita (Acts of the Buddha) of Ashvaghosha, in *Buddhist Scriptures*, trans. Edward Conze (London: Penguin, 1959), 35–36.
2. Conze, trans., *Buddhist Scriptures*, 36–37.
3. Conze, trans., *Buddhist Scriptures*, 38.
4a. Conze, trans., *Buddhist Scriptures*, 39.
4b. Edwin Arnold, *The Light of Asia* (Wheaton, Il.: Theosophical Publishing House, 1969), 39.
4c. Conze, trans., *Buddhist Scriptures*, 39–40.
5. Conze, trans., *Buddhist Scriptures*, 40–41.
6. Conze, trans., *Buddhist Scriptures*, 42–43.
7. Conze, trans., *Buddhist Scriptures*, 43.
8. Conze, trans., *Buddhist Scriptures*, 44–45.
9. Conze, trans., *Buddhist Scriptures*, 46
10. Conze, trans., *Buddhist Scriptures*, 48.
11. Conze, trans., *Buddhist Scriptures*, 48–49; adapted.
12a. Conze, trans., *Buddhist Scriptures*, 49–51.
12b. Dhammapada 153–54. Author's free rendering.
12c. Arnold, *Light of Asia*, 138.
13a. Conze, trans., *Buddhist Scriptures*, 51–52.
13b. Majjhima Nikāya 26.
14. Conze, trans., *Buddhist Scriptures*, 53–54.
15. Conze, trans., *Buddhist Scriptures*, 60–61.
16a. Mahāparinibbāna Sutta, in W. T. de Bary, ed., *The Buddhist Tradition* (New York: Random House, 1969), 28–29.
16b. Digha Nikāya 16, quoted in Nyanatiloka Mahathera, ed. and trans., *The Word of the Buddha* (Kandy, Sri Lanka: Buddhist Publication Society, 1981), 89–90.
16c. Mahāparinibbāna Sutta, in de Bary, ed., *Buddhist Tradition*, 29; adapted.
16d. Samyutta Nikāya 4.i.5 (Dutiya Marapāsa Sutta).
17. Digha Nikāya 2.99; author's free rendering. A typical, more literal, rendering would be: "All conditioned things are subject to decay. Strive onward vigilantly."
18. Soma Thera, *Kālāma Sutta* (Kandy, Sri Lanka: Buddhist Publication Society, 1965), 6. *The Wheel*, no. 8.
19a. Samyutta Nikāya 42.6, quoted in George Grimm, *The Doctrine of the Buddha* (Delhi: Motilal Barnasidass, 1958), 54.
19b. Tevijja Sutta, Digha Nikāya 13, as published in *The Wheel*, no. 57/58, trans T. W. Rhys Davids (Kandy, Sri Lanka: Buddhist Publication Society, 1963), 11.
20a. Majjhima Nikāya 63, trans. H. C. Warren, quoted in E. A. Burtt, ed., *The Teachings of the Compassionate Buddha* (New York: New American Library, 1955), 32–35.
20b. Majjhima Nikāya 2, quoted in Nyanatiloka, ed. and trans., *Word of the Buddha*, 33.

21a. Samyutta Nikāya 56.11, quoted in Nanamoli Thera, trans., *Three Cardinal Discourses of the Buddha* (Kandy, Sri Lanka: Buddhist Publication Society, 1972), 7–8. *The Wheel*, no. 17. My emphasis.

21b. Samyutta Nikāya 56.11, quoted in Nyanatiloka, ed. and trans., *Word of the Buddha*, 1.

22. Samyutta Nikāya 56.11, quoted in * Thera, trans., *Three Cardinal Discourses*, 6. *The Wheel*, no. 17.

23a. Anguttara Nikāya 6.63, quoted in Nyanatiloka, ed. and trans., *Word of the Buddha*, 19.

23b. Anguttara Nikāya 10.206, quoted in Nyanatiloka, ed. and trans., *Word of the Buddha*, 19.

23c. Majjhima–Nikāya 43, quoted in Nyanatiloka, ed. and trans., *Word of the Buddha*, 44.

24. Anguttara Nikāya 3.33, quoted in Nyanatiloka, ed. and trans., *Word of the Buddha*, 44.

25a. Samyutta Nikāya 15.3, quoted in Nyanatiloka, ed. and trans., *Word of the Buddha*, 14.

25b. Samyutta Nikāya 15.3, quoted in Nyanatiloka, ed. and trans., *Word of the Buddha*, 14–15.

26. Anguttara Nikāya 3.134, quoted in Nyanatiloka, ed. and trans., *Word of the Buddha*, 10.

27. Nyanatiloka, ed. and trans., *Word of the Buddha*, 4; adapted.

28. Samyutta Nikāya 22.95, quoted in Nyanatiloka, ed. and trans., *Word of the Buddha*, 12.

29a. Majjhima–Nikāya 1, quoted in Edward Conze et al., *Buddhist Texts Through the Ages* (New York: Harper & Row, 1964), 65. Adapted.

29b. Samyutta Nikāya 2,64–65, quoted in Conze et al., *Buddhist Texts*, 66.

29c. Vinaya Pitaka 1.1, quoted in Conze et al., *Buddhist Texts*, 67.

29d. Nancy Wilson Ross, *Buddhism: A Way of Life and Thought* (New York: Random House, 1981), 54.

30. Traditional; quoted in Nyanatiloka, ed. and trans., *Word of the Buddha*, xii.

31. Anguttara Nikāya 10.176, quoted in Nyanatiloka, ed. and trans., *Word of the Buddha*, 50–51.

32. Digha Nikāya 22*, quoted in Nyanatiloka, ed. and trans., *Word of the Buddha*, 61f.

33. "The Practice of Lovingkindness," Sutta Nipata 145–51, trans. Nanamoli Thera, quoted in *The Wheel*, no. 7 (Kandy, Sri Lanka: Buddhist Publication Society, 1964), 19.

34a. Anguttara Nikāya 3.32, quoted in Nyanatiloka, ed. and trans., *Word of the Buddha*, 24.

34b. Samyutta Nikāya 38.1, quoted in Nyanatiloka, ed. and trans., *Word of the Buddha*, 24.

34c. Majjhima Nikāya 29.

34d. Sutta Nipata 1093–94, quoted in Conze, et al., *Buddhist Texts*, 92–93.

34e. Udana 8.3, quoted in Nyanatiloka, ed. and trans., *Word of the Buddha*, 25.

35a. Samyutta Nikāya 38.1, quoted in Nyanatiloka, ed. and trans., *Word of the Buddha*, 24.

35b. Samyutta Nikāya 3.83–84, quoted in Conze, et al., *Buddhist Texts*, 42.

36. Traditional.

37. Dhammapada, 183. Author's free rendering.

38a. Santideva's Śikṣasāmuccaya 257, quoted in de Bary ed., *Buddhist Tradition*, 100–1.

38b. Conze, *Buddhist Scriptures*, 162-64.

39a. Conze, *Buddhist Scriptures*, 164–67.

39b. Santideva's Śikṣasāmuccaya 280–81, quoted in Conze et al., *Buddhist Texts*, 131–32.

39c. Pancavimsatisahasrika 40–41, quoted in Conze et al., *Buddhist Texts*, 119

40a. Sutra of the Lotus of the Wonderful Law 24, 26, 38, quoted in Conze et al., *Buddhist Texts*, 139.

40b. Taishō daizōkyō IX, quoted in de Bary, ed., *Buddhist Tradition*, 158–60.

40c. Santideva's Śikṣasāmuccaya 299–301, quoted in Conze et al., *Buddhist Texts*, 186–88.

40d. Sukhāvativyūha 15, 16, 18, 19, 21, 24, 26, 27, quoted in Conze et al., *Buddhist Texts*, 202–6.

40e. The Rev. H. H. Coates and the Rev. R. Ishizuka, trans., *Honen, The Buddhist Saint III* (Kyoto: Chionin, 1925), 371–73, quoted in M. Eliade, ed., *Essential Sacred Writings from Around the World* (San Francisco: Harper & Row, 1967), 504–5.

40f. Mahesaru Anesaki, *Nichiren, the Buddhist Prophet* (Cambridge: Harvard Univ. Press, 1916), 46–47, quoted in W. T. de Bary, ed., *Sources of Japanese Tradition* (New York: Columbia Univ. Press, 1958), 217.

41. Bardo Thödol (Tibetan Book of the Dead), Summary, quoted in Conze, *Buddhist Texts*, 227–32.

42. Aryadeva's Disquisition on the Purification of the Intellect 24, 25, 28–30, 33, 34, 37, 38, quoted in de Bary, ed., *Buddhist Tradition*, 118–20.

43. Saraha's Treasury of Songs 14, 15, 16, 19, 23, 24, 102, 103, 106, 107, and coda, quoted in Conze et al., *Buddhist Texts*, 226–27, 238–39.

44a. Walter Anderson, *Open Secrets: A Western Guide to Tibetan Buddhism* (New York and London: Penguin, 1980), 164–67.

44b. Lama Anagarika Govinda, *Foundations of Tibetan Mysticism* (York Beach, ME: Samuel Weiser, 1960), 237.

45. Heinrich Dumoulin, *A History of Zen Buddhism* (Boston: Beacon Press, 1969), 66, adapted.

46. Author's adaptation of a number of sources.

47. Dumoulin, *Zen Buddhism*, 73.

48. Takakusu XLVIII, 376, quoted in Conze et al., *Buddhist Texts*, 297-98.

49. Author's adaptation of a number of sources.

50. Dumoulin, *Zen Buddhism*, 98.

51a. Zenkei Shibayama, *Zen Comments on the Mumonkan* (New York: New American Library, 1974), 19.

51b. Shibayama, *Zen Comments*, 69.

51c. Shibayama, *Zen Comments*, 265.

51d. Shibayama, *Zen Comments*, 139.

51e. Shibayama, *Zen Comments*, 125.

51f. Shibayama, *Zen Comments*, 160.

51g. Paul Reps, *Zen Flesh, Zen Bones* (Garden City, NY: Doubleday, 1981), 92–93.

51h. Reps, *Zen Flesh, Zen Bones*, 114, adapted.

52a. Shōbō genzō zuimonki, quoted in de Bary, ed., *Buddhist Tradition*, 371.

52b. Shōbō genzō zuimonki, quoted in de Bary, ed., *Buddhist Tradition*, 373.

53. Dōgen's Bendōwa, quoted in Dumoulin, *Zen Buddhism*, 166.

54. Orategama, in Semmon hōgoshū, II, 81–85, quoted in de Bary, ed., *Buddhist Tradition*, 386–88.

55a. Irmgard Schloegl, *The Wisdom of the Zen Masters* (New York: New Directions, 1975), 49.

55b. Schloegl, *Zen Masters*, 55.

55c. Schloegl, *Zen Masters*, 68.

55d. Schloegl, *Zen Masters*, 79.

55e. Schloegl, *Zen Masters*, 55.

55f. Lines spoken by Master Kobori of Daitokuji, Kyoto, in *Land of the Disappearing Buddha*, a film in the BBC series, *The Long Search*.

56. Irving Babbitt, trans., *The Dhammapada* (New York: New Directions, 1936). Citations below refer to verse numbers.

56a. 1, 2, 21, 33, adapted; 35.

56b. 3, 4, 5, adapted; 6, 201.

56c. 28, 60, adapted; 61, 62, 64–65, 66, 347, adapted; 205.

56d. 182, adapted.

56e. 197–200.

56f. 374, adapted.

57. Yogācāra Bhūmi Sūtra, chap. 4, translated in 284 C.E., in *Taisho Issaikyo: The Tripitaka in Chinese*, ed. J. Takakusu and K. Watanaba, 85 vols. (Tokyo, 1924–32), quoted in Conze et al., *Buddhist Texts*, 274.

58. Tso-ch'an San-mei Ching, in Takakusu XV.281, quoted in Conze et al., *Buddhist Texts*, 278.

59. Schloegl, *Zen Masters*, 39.

60. Dumoulin, *Zen Buddhism*, 159.

61. E. W. Burlingame, *Buddhist Parables* (New Haven: Yale Univ. Press, 1922), 92–94, quoted in Burtt, ed., *Compassionate Buddha*, 43–45, adapted.

CHAPTER THREE:

Confucianism

Unless otherwise noted all quotations are from Arthur Waley, trans., *The Analects of Confucius* (New York: Random House), 1938. The number preceding the semicolon indicates the page number in Waley; the number after the semicolon indicates position in the original *Analects*.

1a. 83; 1.1.

1b. 88; 2.4.

1c. 126; 7.16.

2a. 123; 7.1.

2b. W. T. de Bary et al., *Sources of the Chinese Tradition* (New York, Columbia Univ. Press), 191–92; Book of Rites, sec. 9.*

3. 90; 2.11; 123; 7.2; 124; 7.7;* 124; 7.8;* 127; 7.18; 130; 7.33.

4a. 83; 1.1.

4b. 83; 1.1.*

4c. 114; 5.26.* 91; 2.17. 214; 17.19.

4d. 123; 7.3. 196; 15.15. Lin Yutang, ed., *The Wisdom of India and China* (New York: Random House), 849; The Golden Mean, sec. 13.

4e. 126; 7.15.*

4f. 124; 7.9.

4g. 155; 11.11.*

4h. 130–31; 7.34. Yutang, ed., *Wisdom of India and China*, 848; The Golden Mean, sec. 16.

5. 123; 7.4; 131; 7.37; 138; 9.4; 128; 7.26; 130; 7.31; Burton Watson, trans., in de Bary et al., *Chinese Tradition*, 20–21; Analects 11.25.

6. Yutang, ed., *Wisdom of India and China*, 845; The Golden Mean, sec. 1; Yutang, ed., *Wisdom of India and China*, 846; The Golden Mean, sec. 2;* Yutang, ed., *Wisdom of India and China*, 846; The Golden Mean, sec. 3; Yutang, ed., *Wisdom of India and China*, 847; The Golden Mean, sec. 11; 103; 4.8.

7a. James Legge, trans., *The Sacred Books of China: The Texts of Confucianism III: The Li Ki* (Oxford: Clarendon Press, 1885), 61–89; Li Ki, bk. 1.*

7b. Legge, *Sacred Books of China*, 61–89; Li Ki, bk. 1.

7c. 162; 12.1,* 132; 8.2; Yutang, ed., *Wisdom of India and China*, 852; The Golden Mean, sec. 4; 104; 4.13.

7d. Y. Mei, trans., in de Bary et al., *Chinese Tradition*, 123–124. The Hsün-Tzu, chap. 19.*

8. James Legge, *The Sacred Books of China: Texts of Confucianism* (Oxford: The Clarendon Press, 1899), 465–467; Hsiao Ching, chap. 1; Legge, *Sacred Books of China*, 481–82; Hsiao Ching, chap. 12; Legge, *Sacred Books of China*, 480; Hsiao Ching, chap. 10;* 105; 4.18; Yutang, ed., *Wisdom of India and China*, 852; The Golden Mean, sec. 19.

9. Huston Smith, *The World's Religions* (San Francisco: HarperSanFrancisco, 1991), 174–75.*

10a. Yutang, ed., *Wisdom of India and China*, 853; The Golden Mean, sec. 20.*

10b. Yutang, ed., *Wisdom of India and China*, 849; The Golden Mean, sec. 13.*

11a. 105; 4.15.

11b. 198; 15.23.

12. 102; 4.1; 102; 4.2;* 105; 4.17;* 200; 15.35; 129; 7.27; 102–3; 4.5;* 103; 4.6

13. 87; 1.16;* 90–91; 2.13;* 105; 4.16;* 106; 4.24;* 197; 15.22;* 87; 1.14;* 187; 14.29;* 91; 2.14;* 131; 7.36;* 187; 14.24;* 197; 15.18;* 197; 15.20;* 167; 12.16;* 119; 6.16;* 188; 14.30.*

14. 196; 15.12;* 88; 2.2;* 88; 2.3; 173; 13.6; 168; 12.19;* 106; 4.25; 164; 12.7.

15a. Lin Yutang, *The Wisdom of Confucius* (New York: Random House), 229–30, 232, 236–39; Li Ki, chap. 19.

15b. Legge, *Sacred Books of China*, 481–82; Hsiao Ching, chap. 12.

15c. 94; 3.3.*

16. Wing-tsit Chan, trans., *A Sourcebook in Chinese Philosophy* (Princeton, NJ: Princeton Univ. Press), 1963, 86–87; The Great Learning.

17. W. T. de Bary et al., *Chinese Tradition*, 104; Mencius, 6A:6.*

18. de Bary et al., *Chinese Tradition*, 102–3; Mencius, 6A:2.*

19. de Bary et al., *Chinese Tradition*, 105; Mencius, 2A:6.*

20. de Bary et al., *Chinese Tradition*, 102; Mencius, 6A:1.*

21. de Bary et al., *Chinese Tradition*, 107–8; Mencius, 1A:7.*

22. de Bary et al., *Chinese Tradition*, 107; Mencius, 4A:9.

23. de Bary et al., *Chinese Tradition*, 110; Mencius, 4A:5.*

24. de Bary et al., *Chinese Tradition*, 112; Mencius, 4A:26.

25a. Yutang, ed., *Wisdom of India and China*, 1070–71.

25b. Yutang, ed., *Wisdom of India and China*, 1071–72.

25c. Yutang, ed., *Wisdom of India and China*, 1073.

25d. Yutang, ed., *Wisdom of India and China*, 1073–74.

25e. Yutang, ed., *Wisdom of India and China*, 1078–79.

26. Yutang, ed., *Wisdom of India and China*, 1093–1101. The fifth and twenty-first selections are adapted.

CHAPTER FOUR: *Taoism*

1–9. All selections from the Tao Te Ching are from Stephen Mitchell, trans., *Tao Te Ching* (San Francisco: Harper & Row, 1988).

10–17. All selections from Chuang-tzu are from Herbert A. Giles, trans., *Chuang-Tzu: Mystic, Moralist and Social Reformer* (London: Bernard Quaritch, 1989), quoted in Robert O. Ballou, ed., *The Portable World Bible* (New York: Penguin, 1944). Page numbers below refer to this text.

10. 554.

11. 552–53.

12. 553–54.

13a. 556–57.

13b. 554–55.

14. 557–59.

15. 560–61.

16. 561–62.

17. 563–64.

18a–e. All selections from the Hua Hu Ching are from Brian Walker, trans., *Hua Hu Ching* (Livingston, MT: Clark City Press, 1992).

CHAPTER FIVE: *Judaism*

Unless otherwise noted, all biblical quotations are from *The Tanakh: The New JPS Translation According to the Traditional Hebrew Text* (Philadelphia: Jewish Publication Society, 1988).

NEB: *The New English Bible* (New York: Oxford Univ. Press, 1976).

JB: *The Jerusalem Bible* (Garden City, NY: Doubleday, 1966).

NRSV: *The Bible: New Revised Standard Version* (London and New York: Collins, 1989).

1a. Gen. 1:1–5.

1b. Gen. 1:27–31.*

1c. Gen. 2:1–3.

2a. Gen. 2:8–9, 15–18, 21–22, 25.

2b. 3:1–11, 16–17, 19, 22–23.

3a. Gen. 6:5, 8; 7:24; 8:1; 9:8–11.

3b. Gen. 9:12–13.

4a. Gen. 12:1–2, 6–7; 17:1–3, 7–8.

4b. Gen. 17:10–13, 23–27.

4c. Gen. 18:17, 19, 23–27, 29–32.

4d. Gen. 22:1–4, 7–13.

5. Gen. 32:25–28.

6. no quotation.

7. Exod. 2:23–24; 3:1–2, 4–8, 10.

8. Exod. 3:13–15.

9a. Exod. 12:1–3, 6–8, 11–15, 37, 40–42.

9b. Exod. 14: 21–23, 26–28, 30.

10a. Exod. 19:3–6; 20:1–14.

10b. Deut. 7:9, 12–13.

11a. Exod. 22:21–22; Exod. 22:22–24; Exod. 23:9; Lev. 19:9–10; Deut. 10:17–19; Lev. 19:14; Deut. 15:7–8, 11; Deut. 24:19–21; Exod. 23:10–11.

11b. Lev. 17:14, 13; Lev. 19:16; Lev. 24:21.

11c. Lev. 25:1, 3–5; Lev. 19:23–25.

11d. Exod. 23:4–5; Lev. 19:13; Lev. 19:15; Lev. 19:17–18.

12. Deut. 34:1, 4–6, 10.

13a. Isa. 6:1–3, 5.

13b. Isa. 6:6–8.

13c. Ezek. 1:1, 4–6, 8–10, 12–13, 22, 26.

13d. Ezek. 1:28; 2:1–7.

14. Isa. 1:2–4, 7.

15. 2 Sam. 12:5–9.

16a. Hos. 4:1, 12–13.

16b. Hos. 8:4, 7–8.

17a. Hos. 6:6.

17b. Isa. 1:11, 14–17.

17c. Isa. 3:14–15.

17d. Amos 5:23–24 NEB.

17e. Mic. 6.6, 8.

18a. Isa. 2:4.

18b. Isa. 11:1–2, 5–6, 8–9 (v. 5 is from JB).

18c. Isa. 40:3–5; 41:8, 10; 43:1, 5–6.

18d. Ezek. 36:18–19, 8–11, 24–28.

19a. Ps. 13:2, 4.

19b. Ps. 22:1–2 JB.

19c. Ps. 42:1–2 JB.

19d. Ps. 137:1–4 NRSV.

19e. Ps. 1:1–4 NEB.

19f. Ps. 19:2–5.

19g. Ps. 66:1–2 NRSV.

19h. Ps. 118:24; author's amalgam of translations.

19i. Ps. 133:1–2.*

19j. Ps. 115:2–8; *Siddur Sim Shalom*, ed. and trans. Jules Harlow (New York: The Rabbinical As-sembly and the United Syna-gogue of America, 1985), 383.

19k. Ps. 8:5–6.*

19l. Ps. 121:1–2. NEB

19m. Ps. 90:1–6.

19n. Ps. 139:1–4, 6–14.

19o. Ps. 23:1–6; author's amalgam of Tanakh and NRSV translations.

20. Prov. 4:7; author's amalgam; Prov. 6:6; author's amalgam; Prov. 15:1; Prov. 11:25; Prov. 12:1 JB;* Prov. 9:8; author's free translation; Prov. 16:18; Prov. 11:13; 26:11; author's amalgam.

21a. Job 1:21.

21b. Job 21:4–15, 17.

21c. Job 38:1–7, 12, 16–18, 25–28, 31, 35–37, 41; 39:1, 26–28.

21d. Job 42:1–3, 5–6.

22a. Eccles. 1:4–11, 13–14 NEB.

22b. Eccles. 2:1, 4–8, 10–11 NEB.

22c. Eccles. 2:16, 18–20 NEB.

22d. Eccles. 3:1–8 NEB.

22e. Eccles. 3:19–20 NEB.

22f. Eccles. 4:1–3 NEB.

22g. Eccles. 9:11–12 NEB.

22h. Eccles. 5:18; 8:17; 9:7 NEB.

23. Rabbi Adin Steinsaltz, ed., *The Talmud: Steinsaltz Edition* (Jerusalem: The Israel Institute for Talmudic Publications; New York: Random House, 1990), 59A–59B, 235–36. Adapted.

24. Chapters of the Fathers 5.25; quoted in Rabbi Jules Harlow, ed. and trans., *Prayerbook for Shabbat, Festivals and Weekdays* (New York: Rabbinical Assem-bly, United Synagogue of America, 1985), 26; Chapters of the Fathers 6.1; in Harlow, ed., *Prayerbook for Shabbat*, 27; Chapters of the Fathers 6.9; in Harlow, ed., *Prayerbook for Shabbat*, 28.

25a. Chapters of the Fathers 3.22; in Harlow, ed., *Prayerbook for Shabbat*, 22.

25b. Abot de R. Nathan, quoted in Nahum H. Glatzer, *The Judaic Tradition* (New York: Behrman House, 1969), 226.

26a. Shabbat 31a; in Glatzer, ed., *The Judaic Tradition*, 197.

26b. Charles Taylor, ed. and trans., *Sayings of the Jewish Fathers (Pirke Aboth)* (New York: KTAV Publishing House, 1969). Verse 1.14.

27. Ta'anit 2a; in Arthur Hertzberg, ed., *Judaism* (New York: Simon and Schuster, 1991), 294; Yebamot 64a; in Hertzberg, ed., *Judaism*, 294; Berakhot 32b; in Hertzberg, ed., *Judaism*, 294.

28. Deut. 6:4.

29. Deut. 30:19–20.

30. Moses de Leon, quoted in Gershom Scholem, *Major Trends in Jewish Mysticism* (New York: Schocken, 1954), 223.

31. Ecclesiastes Rabbah 7:13, quoted in Arthur Hertzberg, ed., *Judaism*, 238.

32. Sanhedrin 38a, quoted in Hertzberg, ed., *Judaism*, 238.

33. Philip Blackman, *Mishnayoth*, vol. 4, *Order Nezikin*, 2d ed. (Brooklyn: Judaica Press, 1983), Sanhedrin 4, Mishnah 5, 254–55.

34. Jerusalem Kiddushin 66d; in Hertzberg, ed., *Judaism*, 244.

35. Albert Einstein, *Opinion: A Journal of Jewish Life and Letters* 2, no. 17–18 (Sept. 26, 1932): 7, quoted in World Religions Curriculum Development Center, *The Jewish Tradition* (Allen, TX: Argus Communications, 1978), 67–68.

36. Herman Wouk, *This Is My God* (New York: Doubleday, 1959), 126–35, quoted in World Religions Curriculum Development Center, *Jewish Tradition*, 39.

37. A. Heschel, quoted in Fritz Rothschild, ed., *Between God and Man: An Interpretation of Judaism, From the Writings of A. J. Heschel* (New York: Free Press, 1959), 116, 120.

38a. Rabbi Hayin Halevy Donin, *To Be a Jew* (New York: Basic Books, 1972), 65–69, 70–88, quoted in World Religions Curriculum Development Center, *Jewish Tradition*, 71ff.

38b. A. Heschel, quoted in Rothschild, ed., *Between God and Man*, 215–18, 221–22.

39. From the film *The Chosen People*, in the BBC series, *The Long Search*.

40. M. L. King, Jr., quoted in William Safire, ed., *Lend Me Your Ears* (New York and London: W. W. Norton, 1992), 497–500.

CHAPTER SIX: *Christianity*

Unless otherwise noted all biblical quotations are from *The Holy Bible, New Revised Standard Version* (London and New York: Collins Publishers, 1989).

NEB: *The New English Bible* (New York: Oxford Univ. Press, 1976); JB: *Jerusalem Bible* (Garden City, NY: Doubleday, 1966).

1. Luke 1:26–28, 30–33, 46–47.
2. Matt. 1:18–21, 24–25; Luke 2:7–11.
3. Luke 2:41–43, 46–49.
4. Matt. 3:1–2, 5–6, 13, 16–17.
5. Matt. 4:1–10.
6. Matt. 4:18–19.
7a. Luke 4:31, 33–37.
7b. Luke 5:17–25.
7c. Matt. 9:20–22.
7d. Luke 18:35–43.
8. Matt. 4:23–25.
9. Matt. 13:54–55, 57–58.
10. Matt. 14:3–4, 9–10, 12–13.
11. Matt. 16:21.
12a. Luke 19:35–38.
12b. Luke 19:45–46.
13a. John 13:1, 4–5, 12–15.
13b. Luke 22:19–20.
14. Luke 22:41–42.
15. Matt. 27:11–15, 20–24.
16. Matt. 27:27–31.
17a. John 19:17–18.
17b. Luke 23:34.
17c. Luke 23:39–43.
17d. John 19:25–27.
17e. Matt. 27:45–46, 50.
18a. Mark 16:1–2, 4–7.
18b. John 20:11–17.
19a. Luke 24:13–16, 30–31, 33–43.
19b. John 20:26–29.
20a. John 6:48, 51.
20b. John 8:12.
20c. John 11:25.
20d. Matt. 11:28–30.
20e. Matt. 18:11–13.
20f. Matt. 18:19–20.
20g. John 15:1, 4–5.
20h. John 14:27.
20i. John 14:2–3.
20j. John 14:6.
20k. Matt. 16:13–17.
21a. John 13:34–35.
21b. Matt. 5:38–39, 41.

21c. Matt. 5:43–45.
21d. Matt. 7:12.
21e. Matt. 25:34–36, 40.
21f. Matt. 5:23–24.
21g. Matt. 21–22.
21h. John 8:4–6, 7, 9–11.
22a. Matt. 5:1–10 NEB.
22b. Matt. 18:1–3.
22c. John 3:3, 8.
22d. Matt. 13:31–32 NEB.
22e. Matt. 13:44 NEB.
22f. Matt. 20:1–15 NEB.
22g. Matt. 22:1–14 NEB.
22h. Luke 15:11–32 NEB.
22i. Luke 10:25–37.
22j. Matt. 13:16–17.
22k. Luke 17:20–21.
23a. Matt. 6:19–21.
23b. Matt. 6:24.
23c. Matt. 6:25–30.
23d. Matt. 19:23–26.
23e. Matt. 16:26.
23f. Matt. 19:21–22.
24a. Matt. 7:3.
24b. Matt. 23:23–24.
24c. Matt. 15:10–11.
25a. Matt. 16:24–25.
25b. Matt. 7:7.
25c. Matt. 5:14–16.
25d. Luke 10:38–42.
25e. Matt. 7:6.
25f. Matt. 7:15–16.
25g. Matt. 6:9–13.
26a. Matt. 24:21, 29–31.
26b. Matt. 24:34; Mark 13:30; Luke 21:32.
27. Matt. 16:18–19 JB.
28. Matt. 28:16–20 JB.
29. Acts 1:8–11.
30. Acts 2:1–5, 7–12.
31a. Acts 2:42, 44–47.
31b. Gal. 3:26, 28.
31c. 2 Cor. 5:17.
32a. Acts 17:27–28.

32b. John 1:1–5, 12–14; John 8:19; John 14:9; John 10:30.

32c. John 1:29; John 3:16; 1 Cor. 15:21–22; 1 Tim. 2:5–6; Heb. 2:14–15; Rom. 6:3, 8–11.

32d. John 14:16–17; 2 Cor. 13:14.

32e. Paul in Acts 20:24 JB.

32f. 1 Cor. 15:12–14, 18–19.

32g. 1 Cor. 15:51–55.

32h. Rom. 8:35, 38–39 JB.

32i. 1 Cor. 13:1–5, 7, 11–13.

32j. Phil. 2:4–11.

32k. Rom. 1:15–17.

32l. James 2:14–17.

33a. Acts 5:27–30, 33–34, 38–42.

33b. Acts 7:51, 54, 58–60.

33c. Acts 8:1, 3.

34. Acts 9:1–6, 8–10, 17–19.

35a. Acts 15:5–9, 11–13, 19–20, 22–25, 28–29.

35b. Gal. 2:1–2, 7, 9.

36. International Consultation on English Texts, *Prayers We Have in Common*, 2d rev. ed. (Philadelphia: Fortress Press, 1975), 6.

37a. Marvin Meyer, trans., *The Gospel of Thomas* (San Francisco: HarperSanFrancisco, 1992), 21, saying no. 3.

37b. Meyer, trans., *Gospel of Thomas*, 21, saying no. 3.

37c. Meyer, trans., *Gospel of Thomas*, 45, saying no. 61.

37d. Meyer, trans., *Gospel of Thomas*, 53, saying no. 77.

37e. Meyer, trans., *Gospel of Thomas*, 57, saying no. 91.

37f. Meyer, trans., *Gospel of Thomas*, 63, saying no. 113.

38. A paraphrase of Clement of Alexandria's *Protrepticus* 1.8, this teaching can also be found in the writings of Church Fathers Irenaeus and Athanasius and the early Christian theologians Dionysius the Areopagite and Maximus the Confessor.*

39a. F. J. Sheed, trans., *The Confessions of St. Augustine* (Kansas City: Sheed and Ward, 1942), I.1, 3.

39b. Sheed, trans., *Confessions of St. Augustine*, X.27, 192.

39c. Sheed, trans., *Confessions of St. Augustine*, X.28, 192, adapted.

40a. F. Bowie and O. Davies, trans., R. Carver, ed., *Hildegard of Bingen* (New York: Crossroad, 1992), 68.

40b. Bowie and Davies, trans., *Hildegard of Bingen*, 91–92.

40c. Bowie and Davies, trans., *Hildegard of Bingen*, 94.

41a. Marion Habig, ed., *St. Francis of Assisi: Writing and Early Biographies: English Omnibus of the Sources for the Life of St. Francis* (Chicago: Franciscan Herald Press, 1973), quoted in M. Bodo, *The Way of St. Francis* (Garden City: Doubleday, 1984), 142–143, slightly abridged.

41b. Traditional.

42a. Lucy Menzies, trans., *The Revelations of Mechthild of Magdeburg* or *The Flowing Light of the Godhead* (London: Longmans, Green, 1953), 5.13, quoted in C. L. Flinders, *Enduring Grace* (San Francisco: HarperSanFrancisco, 1993), xi.

42b. Menzies, trans., *Revelations of Mechthild*, 6.26, quoted in Flinders, *Enduring Grace*, 43.

42c. Menzies, trans., *Revelations of Mechthild*, 7.55, quoted in Flinders, *Enduring Grace*, 69.

43. *Itinerarium Mentis in Deum* 5.8.

44a. *Summa Theologica* II, II, Q.1, art. 2, adapted. The Latin is: *Cognita sunt in cognoscente secundum modum cognoscentis.*

44b. *Summa of Christian Teaching* I, 14, quoted in Mary Clark, ed., *An Aquinas Reader* (New York: Doubleday, 1972), 139.

45a. Raymond B. Blakney, trans., *Meister Eckhart* (New York: Harper Torchbooks, 1941), 206.

45b–e. Stephen Mitchell, trans., in *The Enlightened Mind* (San Francisco: HarperSanFrancisco, 1991), 114, 115.

46a. Clifton Wolters, trans., *Julian of Norwich: Revelations of Divine Love* (London: Penguin, 1966), 68–69.

46b. Wolters, trans., *Julian of Norwich*, 68.

46c. Translated by Stephen Mitchell, *Enlightened Mind*, 125, based on Wolters, trans., *Julian of Norwich*, 70.

46d. Julian of Norwich, Long Text of *Showings* 60, quoted in Flinders, *Enduring Grace*, 77.

47. Richard Whitford, trans., *The Imitation of Christ*, adapted by H. C. Gardiner (New York: Doubleday, 1955), 111, quoted in Jonathan Star, *Two Suns Rising* (New York: Bantam, 1991), 165.

48. Adapted from Arthur Symons, trans., in *Liturgy of the Hours*, vol. 1 (New York: Catholic Publishing Co., 1975), 1975.

49. "The Dark Night," verses 1, 3, 4, 5, 8; K. Kavanaugh and O. Rodriguez, trans., *The Collected Works of St. John of the Cross* (Washington, DC: ICS Publications, 1973), 711–12.

50. Louis Puhl, trans., *The Spiritual Exercises of St. Ignatius* (Chicago: Loyola Univ. Press, 1951), 1.

51. John Beevers, trans., *Abandonment to Divine Providence* (New York: Doubleday, 1975), 81–82.

52. R. M. French, trans., *The Way of a Pilgrim* (New York: Seabury, 1965), 1, 31, 41, 105–6.

53. All selections are from Thomas Merton, *New Seeds of Contemplation* (New York: New Directions, 1961). Page numbers below refer to this source.

53a. 1.

53b. 25.

53c. 36.

53d. 259.

53e. 261.

54. Quoted in William V. Pietsch, *The Serenity Prayerbook* (San Francisco: HarperSanFrancisco, 1990), 116.

55. Quoted in James Rachels, ed., *The Right Thing to Do* (New York: Random House, 1989), 242–43, 246–47, 253.

56. John Newton, quoted from the *Baptist Standard Hymnal* (Nashville: Sunday School Publishing Board, National Baptist Convention, U.S.A., 1973), 427.

CHAPTER SEVEN: *Islam*

Unless otherwise noted, all citations from the Qur'an are from *The Koran*, translated with notes by N. J. Dawood (London and New York: Penguin, 1956; reprint, 1990). Citations marked (CS) are from Kenneth Cragg and Marston Speight, *Islam from Within: Anthology of a Religion*

(Belmont, CA: Wadsworth, 1980).
Citations marked (C) are from Ken-
neth Cragg, *Readings in the Qur'an*
(London: HarperCollins, 1988).

1a. Sura 1 (C), 84.
1b. 96:1–5 (C), 177.
1c. 97 (CS), 3.
1d. 112 (CS), 2.
1e. 114 (CS), 1.
1f. 87:1–7 (CS), 3.
1g. 80:17–22, 33–42 (CS), 3–4.
1h. 99.
2a. 2:173–174 (C), 308.
2b. 2:180–182.
2c. 2:183–84 (C), 288–89.
2d. 2:272–274.
2e. 2:275–283.
2f. 2:284–286.
3. 2:2–3; 5:15–16; 5:48.
4. 2:23; 10:38.
5. 4:136.
5a 112:1–4; 17:111; 12:37–40;
   2:225 (C); 3:18 (C); 6:102–3
   (C); 57:1–6 (C); 50:16; 7:180;
   17:110; 59:24; Shems Friedlander and Al-Hajj Shaikh Muzaf-
   fereddin, *Ninety-Nine Names of
   Allah* (New York: Harper &
   Row, 1978); 1:1; 18:23–24.
5b. 2:98; 2:285.
5c. 5:44, 46, 48; 10:47; 16:36; 2:136;
   3:113–15.*
5d. 29:57; 3:30; 4:40; 7:187; 16:77;
   17:13–14; 18:47–49; 39:67–70;
   82:1–5; 36:12; 13:23–24;
   55:46–77; 76:10–13, 15–20;
   40:70–76; 4:56; 22:19–22.
5e. 2:117; 3:73–74; 10:107; 23:62;
   14:35; 31:34; 50:6–11.
6a. Traditional.
6b. 2:110; 9:60; 2:271; 2:267.
6c. 2:45–46; 30:17–18 (C), 89;
   7:205; 20:130; Traditional; Traditional; 2:144; 33:41; 13:28;
   18:25; 2:52.

6d. 2:185 (C), 289; 2:184 (C), 288.
6e. 2:125, 127; 2:196; 22:27–30.
7. 4:48; 16:51; 51:51; 72:20.
8. 2:190; 22:39; 2:191–92;
   2:216–17; 47:8.
9. 2:256.
10a. 21:92–93.*
10b. 64:15–16; 2:280; 4:36–37;
   76:8–9.
10c. 17:23–24.
10d. 33:35. A. Y. Ali, trans., *The
   Holy Qur'an* (n.p.: McGregor
   and Werner, 1946), 1116–17;
   4:19; 65:6; 33:49; 2:234; 4:34.
10e. 4:22–24; 4:3; 4:129.
10f. 2:28; 2:232, 229; 2:240–41.
10g. 24:31; 33:59; 24:60 (C), 321.
10h. 24:30.
10i. 4:7; 4:10–12.
10j. 2:188; 17:35; 4:58; 3:130.
10k. 6:38.
10l. 4:148; 4:114; 2:42; 2:263; 49:6;
   17:36;* 3:17; 31:17; 3:134;
   42:36; 31:17–19; 17:37; 17:35.
10m. 17:32; 24:2–3; 4:16; 26:166;
   23:1; 4:15; 6:140; 17:31;
   4:29–30; 17:33; 5:38–39; 2:219.
11. 2:253; 4:171; 112:14; 17:111;
   5:72; 4:171; 4:157.
12. 5:12–13; 62:5–7.
13. M. Muhammad Ali, *A Manual
   of Hadith* (London: Interlink
   Publishing Group, 1977), 3–7.
14. Ali, *Hadith*, 9–13.
15. Ali, *Hadith*, 9–13.
16. W. A. Graham, *Divine Word and
   Prophetic Word in Early Islam*
   (The Hague and Paris: Mouton,
   1977), 127.
17. Translation by Prof. Alan
   Godlas.
18a. William Stoddart, *Sufism* (New
   York: Paragon House, 1986), 80.
18b. Allama Sir Abdullah and Al-
   Mamum Al-Suhrawardy, *The*

Sayings of Muhammad (New York: Citadel Press, 1990), 83.

19a. Whithall Perry, *A Treasury of Traditional Wisdom* (San Francisco: Harper & Row, 1971), 1023.

19b. Stoddart, *Sufism*, 82.

20. Translation by Prof. Alan Godlas.

21a–h. All selections are from Abdullah and Al-Suhrawardy, *Sayings of Muhammad*, at the following page numbers:

21a. 76.

21b. 82.

21c. 90.

21d. 89.

21e. 89.

21f. 112.

21g. 78.

21h. 52.

21i. A. Jeffrey, trans., *The Forty Traditions of An-Nawawi*, quoted in *A Reader on Islam* (The Hague: Mouton, 1962), no. 18.

21j. Abdullah and Al-Suhrawardy, *Sayings of Muhammad*, 63.

22. Abdullah and Al-Suhrawardy, *Sayings of Muhammad*, 49.

23a. Abdullah and Al-Suhrawardy, *Sayings of Muhammad*, 59.

23b. Abdullah and Al-Suhrawardy, *Sayings of Muhammad*, 52.

23c. Jeffrey, trans., *An-Nawawi*, no. 26; Abdullah and Al Suhrawardy, *Sayings of Muhammad*, 59.

24a. Jeffrey, trans., *An-Nawawi*, no. 29.

24b. Jeffrey, trans., *An-Nawawi*, no. 15; Abdullah and Al-Suhrawardy, *Sayings of Muhammad*, 65.

24c. Abdullah and Al-Suhrawardy, *Sayings of Muhammad*, 114; Abdullah and Al-Suhrawardy, *Sayings of Muhammad*, 114.

25a. Perry, *Traditional Wisdom*, 699.

25b. Abdullah and Al-Suhrawardy, *Sayings of Muhammad*, 88.

26. Jeffrey, trans., *An-Nawawi*, no. 4.

27. Abu Bakr Siraj Ed-Din, *The Book of Certainty* (London: Rider Books, 1952), 41, quoted in Perry, *Traditional Wisdom*, 625; Abdullah and Al-Suhrawardy, *Sayings of Muhammad*, 51.

28a. Perry, *Traditional Wisdom*, 629.

28b. Abdullah and Al-Suhrawardy, *Sayings of Muhammad*, 118; Abdullah and Al-Suhrawardy, *Sayings of Muhammad*, 117; Abdullah and Al-Suhrawardy, *Sayings of Muhammad*, 117.

29a. Abdullah and Al-Suhrawardy, *Sayings of Muhammad*, 50; Abdullah and Al-Suhrawardy, *Sayings of Muhammad*, 51.

29b. Abdullah and Al Suhrawardy, *Sayings of Muhammad*, 49.

30. Abdullah and Al-Suhrawardy, *Sayings of Muhammad*, 55.

31a. Abdullah and Al-Suhrawardy, *Sayings of Muhammad*, 91.

31b. Abdullah and Al-Suhrawardy, *Sayings of Muhammad*, 60.

32a. Abdullah and Al-Suhrawardy, *Sayings of Muhammad*, 58.

32b. Abdullah and Al-Suhrawardy, *Sayings of Muhammad*, 79.

32c. Abdullah and Al-Suhrawardy, *Sayings of Muhammad*, 63.

33a–d. All selections are from Abdullah and Al-Suhrawardy, *Sayings of Muhammad*, at the following page numbers:

33a. 94.

33b. 93; 92.

33c. 93; 94; 93; 94–95; 94; 95.

33d. 108.

33e. Abdullah and al-Suhrawardy, *Sayings of Muhammad,* 95; Annemarie Schimmel, *Mystical Dimensions of Islam* (Chapel Hill: Univ. of North Carolina Press, 1975), 189.

34. Jeffrey, trans., *An-Nawawi,* no. 40; Schimmel, *Mystical Dimensions,* 382; Schimmel, *Mystical Dimensions,* 70; Schimmel, *Mystical Dimensions,* 215; Abdullah and Al-Suhrawardy, *Sayings of Muhammad,* 81; Schimmel, *Mystical Dimensions,* 291; Schimmel, *Mystical Dimensions,* 103, adapted; Traditional; Schimmel, *Mystical Dimensions,* 120.

35. 2:115, quoted in Stoddart, *Sufism,* 77; 9:118, quoted in Stoddart, *Sufism,* 79; 22:46, quoted in Stoddart, *Sufism,* 80; 2:156, quoted in Stoddart, *Sufism,* 80.

36a–c. Reynold A. Nicholson, *Translations of Eastern Poetry and Prose* (Cambridge Univ. Press, 1922), quoted in Stephen Mitchell, *The Enlightened Mind* (San Francisco: HarperSanFrancisco, 1991), 75–77. Selection a has been adapted by the author.

36d. Perry, *Traditional Wisdom,* 492.

37a. Eric Schroeder, *Muhammad's People: A Tale by Anthology* (Portland, ME: Bond Wheelwright, 1955), 553, quoted in F. M. Denny, *An Introduction to Islam* (New York: Macmillan, 1985), 262.

37b. Perry, *Traditional Wisdom,* 802.

37c. Stoddart, *Sufism,* 83.

38. Traditional.

39a. Reynold A. Nicholson, *Translations of Eastern Poetry and Prose* (Cambridge: Cambridge Univ. Press, 1922), quoted in Stephen Mitchell, *The Enlightened Mind* (San Francisco: HarperSanFrancisco, 1991), 83–84.

39b. Margaret Smith, *Readings from the Mystics of Islam* (London: Luzac and Co., 1950), quoted in Mitchell, *Enlightened Mind,* 85.

40. Stoddart, *Sufism,* 82.

41a. R. A. Nicholson, *Rumi: Poet and Mystic* (London: Allen and Unwin, 1950), 31.

41b. *Mathnawi,* III.49–62. Coleman Barks with R. A. Nicholson, *We Are Three: New Rumi Poems* (Putney, VT: Threshold Books, 1987), 10.

41c. *Mathnawi,* I.3065ff. Barks and Nicholson, *We Are Three,* 84.

41d. Coleman Barks with John Moyne, *This Longing* (Putney, VT: Threshold Books, 1988), quoted in Stephen Mitchell, *The Enlightened Mind* (San Francisco: HarperSanFrancisco, 1991), 104–5.

41e. Coleman Barks with John Moyne, *Open Secret* (Putney, VT: Threshold Books, 1984), 8.

41f. Traditional.

41g. Rumi, *Diwan-i Shams-i Tabriz,* trans. Jonathan Star and Shahram Shiva, in *Two Suns Rising* (New York: Bantam, 1991), 120.

41h. Rumi, trans. Star and Shiva, in *Two Suns Rising,* 121.

41i. R. A. Nicholson, *Selected Poems from the Divani Shamsi Tabriz* (London: Cambridge Univ. Press, 1898), quoted in James Kritzeck, ed., *Anthology of Islamic Literature* (New York:

New American Library, 1964),
242.

41j. Perry, *Traditional Wisdom*, 669.

41k. Perry, *Traditional Wisdom*, 750.

42a. Araqi, *La'amat (Divine Flashes)*,
trans. Star and Shiva, in *Two
Suns Rising*, 137.

42b. Araqi, *La'amat (Divine Flashes)*,
trans. Star and Shiva, in *Two
Suns Rising*, 138.

43a. Rendered by Jonathan Star, *Two
Suns Rising* (New York: Bantam,
1991), 128, from Aijaz Ahmad,
ed., *The Ghazals of Ghalib*
(New York: Columbia Univ.
Press, 1971), ghazal 1.

43b. Rendered by Star, *Two Suns Rising*, 129, from Ahmad, ed.,
Ghazals of Ghalib, ghazal 4.

44. Traditional.

45. Malcolm X with Alex Haley,
*The Autobiography of Malcolm
X* (New York: Grove Press,
1964), 339–42.

CHAPTER EIGHT: *Primal Religions*

1. Hare Hongi, "A Maori Cos-
   mogony," *Journal of the Polynesian Society* 16 (1907): 113–14,
   quoted in M. Eliade, ed., *Essential Sacred Writings from Around
   the World* (San Francisco:
   Harper & Row, 1967), 86–87.
   Final paragraph slightly rearranged.

2. Fletcher and La Flesche, "The
   Omaha Tribe," Bureau of
   American Ethnology, *Twenty-
   seventh Annual Report* (Washington, DC, 1911), 570–71,
   quoted in Eliade, ed., *Essential
   Sacred Writings*, 84.

3. Maria Leach, *The Beginning*
   (New York: Funk and Wagnalls,

1956), 145–47. Translated and
adapted from material in E.
Torday and T. A. Joyce, *Les
Boshongo, Annales du Musée de
Congo Belge, Ethnographie An-
thropologie*, Serie 4, t. 2 (Brus-
sels, 1910), 210ff., quoted in
Barbara C. Sproul, *Primal
Myths* (San Francisco: Harper
& Row, 1979), 44–45.

4. Leach, *The Beginning*, 178–181,
   rewritten from R. H. Codring-
   ton, *The Melanesians: Studies in
   Their Anthropology and Folklore*
   (Oxford, 1891), 156–158,
   quoted in Sproul, *Primal
   Myths*, 332–33.

5. From the ritual account given
   by the Pawnee Four Rings to
   Dr. Melvin Gilmore, recorded
   in H. B. Alexander, *The World's
   Rim* (Lincoln: Univ. of Nebraska Press, 1953), 89, quoted
   in Eliade, ed., *Essential Sacred
   Writings*, 137.

6. K. T. Preuss, quoted and translated by Paul Radin, *Monotheism
   Among Primitive Peoples* (New
   York: n.d.), 15, quoted in Eliade, ed., *Essential Sacred Writings*, 16.

7. Vincenzo Petrullo, "The
   Yaruros of the Capanaparo
   River, Venezuela," *U.S. Bureau
   of American Ethnology Bulletin
   123, Anthropological Papers*, no.
   11 (Washington, DC: Government Printing Office, 1939),
   238–41, quoted in Sproul, *Primal Myths*, 306.

8. Melville J. Herskovits, *Da-
   homey*, vol. 2 (New York: J. J.
   Augustin, 1958), 101, quoted in
   Sproul, *Primal Myths*, 76.

9a. E. S. Craighill Handy, *Polynesian Religion, Bernice P. Bishop*

Museum Bulletin 34 (1927), quoted in N. Smart and R. D. Hecht, eds., *Sacred Texts of the World: A Universal Anthology* (New York: Crossroad, 1982), 344.

9b. Teuira Henry, *Ancient Tahiti,* Bernice P. *Bishop Museum Bulletin* 48 (1928), 339–40, quoted in Sproul, *Primal Myths,* 350.

9c. Teuira Henry, "Tahitian Folklore," *Journal of the Polynesian Society* 37, no. 10 (1901): 51–52, quoted in Sproul, *Primal Myths,* 351.

10. Ronald M. Berndt, *Djanggawul: An Aboriginal Religious Cult of North Eastern Arnhem Land* (New York: Philosophical Library, 1953), 24–28, quoted in Sproul, *Primal Myths,* 315–16, 320.

11a. Leach, *The Beginning,* 143–44, retold from material in Duff Macdonald, *Africana: The Heart of Heathen Africa,* vol. 1 (London, 1882), 295ff., quoted in Sproul, *Primal Myths,* 36–37.

11b. Susan Feldman, ed., *African Myths and Tales* (New York: Dell Publishing, 1963), 37–39, adapted from material in E. W. Smith, *African Ideas of God* (London: Edinburgh House Press, 1950), quoted in Sproul, *Primal Myths,* 47.

12. Frank Waters, *The Book of the Hopi* (New York: Ballantine Books, 1963), 3–28, *passim,* quoted in Sproul, *Primal Myths,* 268–84, *passim.*

13. T. C. Young, *African Ways of Wisdom* (London, 1937), quoted by J. S. Mbiti, *African Religions and Philosophies* (Garden City,

NY: Anchor, 1970), quoted in Smart and Hecht, eds., *Sacred Texts,* 348.

14. Hans Schärer, *Ngaju Religion: The Conception of God Among a South Borneo People,* trans. R. Needham (The Hague: Martinus Nijhoff, 1963), 81–94, *passim,* quoted in Eliade, ed., *Essential Sacred Writings,* 165–70, *passim.*

15. Schärer, *Ngaju Religion,* 94–97, quoted in Eliade, ed., *Essential Sacred Writings,* 170–72.

16. Leach, *The Beginning,* 159–161, based on Arundel Del Re, *Creation Myths of the Formosan Natives* (Tokyo, 1951), quoted in Sproul, *Primal Myths,* 325–26.

17. The words of Sword, an Oglala Sioux, as recorded by J. R. Walker, *The Sun Dance and Other Ceremonies of the Oglala Division of the Teton Dakota,* American Museum of Natural History, Anthropological Papers 16, pt. 2 (1917): 152–53, quoted in Eliade, ed., *Essential Sacred Writings,* 11–12.

18. Knud Rasmussen, *Intellectual Culture of the Igluik Eskimos,* Report of the Fifth Thule Expedition, 1921–24, vol. 7, no. 1 (Copenhagen: Gyldendalske Boghandel, Nordisk Forlag, 1929), 112–13, quoted in Roger Walsh, *The Spirit of Shamanism* (Los Angeles: J. Tarcher, 1990), 57–58; Rasmussen, *Intellectual Culture,* 118–19, quoted in Walsh, *Spirit of Shamanism,* 52, 58.

19. B. Spencer and J. Gillen, *The Northern Tribes of Central Australia* (London, 1904), 480–81,

quoted in Eliade, ed., *Essential Sacred Writings*, 428.

20. A. W. Howitt, *The Native Tribes of South-East Australia* (London, 1904), 406–8, quoted in Eliade, ed., *Essential Sacred Writings*, 424–26.

21. Rasmussen, *Intellectual Culture*, 123–27, 129, quoted in Walsh, *Spirit of Shamanism*, 143–47.

22. E. W. Nelson, *The Eskimo About Bering Strait, 18th Annual Report of the Bureau of American Ethnology* (Washington, DC, 1899), 452–62, *passim*, quoted in Sproul, *Primal Myths*, 220–27, *passim*.

23. Rasmussen, *Intellectual Culture*, adapted by Stephen Mitchell, *The Enlightened Heart* (San Francisco: HarperSanFrancisco, 1989), 123.

24. D. G. Brinton, *Essays of an Americanist* (n.p., 1890), 292, quoted by John Bierhorst, *In the Trail of the Wind* (New York: Farrar, Straus & Giroux, 1971), 131, cited in Turner, *North American Indian Reader*, 241.

25. William Brandon, ed., *The Magic World* (New York: William Morrow, 1971), quoted in Frederick W. Turner III, *The Portable North American Indian Reader* (New York: Penguin, 1974), 239.

26. Paul Radin, *The Road of Life and Death* (1945; reprint Princeton: Princeton Univ. Press, 1991), 254.

27. Joseph Epes Brown, *The Spiritual Legacy of the American Indian* (New York: Crossroad, 1985), 90–91.

28. Brown, *Spiritual Legacy*, 92.

29. Schärer, *Ngaju Religion*, 59–62, 65, 66, quoted in Eliade, ed., *Essential Sacred Writings*, 155–58.

30. *Washington Historical Quarterly* (now the *Pacific Northwest Historical Quarterly*) 22, no. 4 (October 1931).

31. Turner, *North American Indian Reader*, 250.

32. Whithall Perry, *A Treasury of Traditional Wisdom* (San Francisco: Harper & Row, 1971), 795.

33. Joseph Epes Brown, *The Sacred Pipe* (Baltimore: Penguin, 1971), 5–7.

34. Brown, *Sacred Pipe*, 69.

35. Herbert J. Spinden, *Songs of the Tewa* (Santa Fe: Sunstone Press, 1976), quoted in Elizabeth Roberts and Elias Amidon, eds., *Earth Prayers* (San Francisco: HarperSanFrancisco, 1991), 137.

36. Quoted in Roberts and Amidon, eds., *Earth Prayers*, 176.

37. Quoted in Roberts and Amidon, eds., *Earth Prayers*, 184.

38. Quoted in Roberts and Amidon, eds., *Earth Prayers*, 240.

39. Gary Snyder, *Turtle Island* (New York: New Directions, 1969), 24–25.

40. Brandon, ed., *The Magic World*, quoted in Turner, *North American Indian Reader*, 239.

41. Brown, *Sacred Pipe*, 75; Brown, *Sacred Pipe*, 58; Brown, *Sacred Pipe*, 69.

42. Hyemeyohsts Storm, *Seven Arrows* (New York: Ballantine, 1972), 68–85.

Acknowledgments

Acknowledgment is made to the following for permission to reprint copyrighted material:

American Museum of Natural History for extracts from *The Sun Dance and Other Ceremonies of the Oglala Division of the Teton Dakota*, by J. R. Walker. Copyright © 1917.

AMS Press for extracts from *Religion and Ceremonies of the Lenape*, by M. R. Harrington. Copyright © 1921.

Walter Truett Anderson for an extract from *Open Secrets: A Western Guide to Tibetan Buddhism*. Copyright © 1979 by Walter Truett Anderson. First published in 1979 by Viking Press, New York.

Ayer Company Publishers, P.O. Box 958, Salem, NH 03079 for extracts from *A Reader on Islam*, by A. Jeffrey. Reprint copyright © 1980.

Bantam Books, a division of Bantam Doubleday Dell Publishing Group, Inc. for extracts from *Two Suns Rising*, by Jonathan Star. Translation copyright © 1991 by Jonathan Star. Used by permission of Bantam Books, a division of Bantam Doubleday Dell Publishing Group, Inc.

Beacon Press for extracts from *The Judaic Tradition*, by Nahum H. Glatzer. Copyright © 1969 by Nahum Glatzer. Reprinted with permission of Beacon Press.

Bishop Museum Press, Bishop Museum, Honolulu, Hawai'i for an extract from *Ancient Tahiti*, by Henry Teuira, copyright © 1928, and from *Polynesian Religion*, by E. S. C. Handy, copyright © 1927.

British Broadcasting System for extracts from the film *The Chosen People*, in the series *The Long Search*.

Buddhist Publication Society, Kandy, Sri Lanka, for extracts from *Word of the Buddha: An Outline of the Teaching of the Buddha in the Words of the Pali Canon*, edited by Nyanatiloka Thera, copyright © 1981. And from *Kalama Sutta: The Buddha's Charter of Free Inquiry*, translated by Soma Thera, *The Wheel*, no. 8, copyright © 1959. And from *The Tevijja Sutta*, translated by T. W. Rhys Davids, *The Wheel*, no. 57/58, copyright © 1963. And from *Three Cardinal Discourses of the Buddha*, translated by Nanamoli Thera, *The Wheel*, no. 17, copyright © 1960. And from *The Practice of Lovingkindness as Taught by the Buddha in the Pali Canon*, *The Wheel*, no. 7, copyright © 1958.

The Estate of Edwin A. Burtt for permission to quote material from *The Teachings of the Compassionate Buddha*. Copyright © 1955 by New American Library, New York.

Bruno Cassirer (Publishers) for extracts from *Buddhist Texts Through the Ages*, edited by Edward Conze. Copyright © 1964 by Harper & Row, New York.

Cambridge University Press for extracts from *Translations of Eastern Poetry and Prose*, by Reynold A. Nicholson. Copyright © 1922. Used by permission.

Carol Publishing Group for extracts from *The Sayings of Muhammad*, by Sir Abdullah and Al-Mamun Al-Suhrawardy. Copyright © 1990. Published by Citadel Press, New York.

Catholic Publishing Company for an extract from *Liturgy of the Hours*, vol. 1. Copyright © 1975.

Columbia University Press for an extract from *Sources of the Japanese Tradition*, edited by W. T. de Bary et al., copyright © 1958. And from *Sources of the Chinese Tradition*, by William T. de Bary, copyright © 1960. Reprinted with the permission of the publisher.

Crossroad Publishing Company for extracts from *Hildegard of Bingen: Mystical Writings*, translation copyright © 1990 by Robert Carver. And from *The Spiritual Legacy of the American Indian*, by Joseph Epes Brown, copyright © 1982 by Joseph Epes Brown. Both of the above reprinted by permission of The Crossroad Publishing Company.

Dell Publishing Company, a division of Bantam, Doubleday, Dell Publishing Group, for extracts from *African Myths and Tales*, edited by Susan Feldman.

Doubleday, a division of Bantam Doubleday Dell Publishing Group for extracts from *This Is My God*, by Herman Wouk, copyright © 1959 by The Abe Wouk Foundation. And from *Abandonment to Divine Providence*, translated by John Beevers, copyright © 1975. And from *An Aquinas Reader*, edited by Mary Clark, copyright © 1972. And from *The Jerusalem Bible*, copyright © 1966 by Darton, Longman & Todd. And from *The Imitation of Christ*, translated by Richard C. Whitford and adapted by H. C. Gardiner. Reprinted by permission.

Franciscan Press for extracts from *St. Francis of Assisi: Writing and Early Biographies: English Omnibus of the Sources of the Life of St. Francis*, by Marion Habig. Copyright © 1973.

Grove Press for extracts from *The Autobiography of Malcolm X*, by Malcolm X. Copyright © 1965 by Alex Haley and Betty Shabazz.

Gyldendalske Boghandel for extracts from *Intellectual Culture of the Igluik Eskimos*, by Knud Rasmussen. Copyright © 1929.

HarperCollins Publishers for extracts from *Zen Comments on the Mumonkan*, English language translation copyright © 1974 by Zenkei Shibayama. And for excerpts from *Tao Te Ching*, by Stephen Mitchell, translation copyright © 1988 by Stephen Mitchell. And for excepts from *Hua Hu Ching*, by Brian Walker, copyright © 1992 by Brian Browne Walker. And for extracts from *To Be a Jew*, by Rabbi Hayim Halevy Donin, copyright © 1972 by Hayim Halevy Donin. And for excerpts from *The Gospel of Thomas*, by Milton Meyer, copyright © 1992 by Milton Meyer. And for excerpts from *The Way of A Pilgrim*, by R. M. French, copyright © 1965 by Mrs. Eleanor French. And from *The Enlightened Mind*, by Stephen Mitchell, copyright © 1991 by Stephen Mitchell. And from *The Enlightened Heart*, by Stephen Mitchell, copyright © 1989 by Stephen Mitchell. And from *Meister Eckhart*, translated by R. B. Blakney, copyright © 1941 by Harper & Row Publishers. And from *Readings in the Qur'an*, by Kenneth Cragg, copyright © 1988 by Kenneth Cragg, published by Collins Religious Publishing. And from *Ninety-Nine Names of Allah*, by Shems Friedlander, copyright © 1978 by Shems Friedlander, published in 1978 by Harper Colophon Books. And from *Seven Arrows*, by Hyemeyohsts Storm, copyright © 1972 by Hyemeyohsts Storm. And from *A Treasury of Traditional Wisdom*, by Whithall Perry, copyright © 1971 by Whithall Perry. And from *The Beginning: Creation Myths Around the World*, by Maria Leach. All of the above reprinted by permission of HarperCollins Publishers, Inc.

The Heirs of the Estate of Martin Luther King, Jr. for extracts from "I Have a Dream," by M. L. King, Jr. Reprinted by arrangement with The Heirs to the Estate of Martin Luther King, Jr. c/o The Joan Daves agency as agent for the proprietor. Copyright © 1963 by Martin Luther King, Jr., renewed by Coretta Scott King in 1991.

Professor Arthur Hertzberg for extracts from *Judaism*, 2d ed., edited by Arthur Hertzberg. Copyright © 1991 by Arthur Hertzberg. Published in New York by Simon and Schuster.

ICS Publications, 2131 Lincoln Road, NE, Washington, DC, for an extract from *The Collected Works of St. John of the Cross*, translated by Kieran Kavanagh and Otilio Rodriguez. Copyright © 1979, 1991, by Washington Province of Discalced Carmelites.

International Consultation on English Texts for creedal extracts from *Prayers We Have in Common*. Copyright © 1975.

The Iona Community/Wild Goose Publications, Glasgow, Scotland, for extracts from *The Revelations of Mechthild of Madgeburg*, or *The Flowing Light of the Godhead*, translated by Lucy Menzies. Copyright © 1953. Used by permission.

Jewish Publication Society for extracts from *The Tanakh: The New JPS Translation According to the Traditional Hebrew Text*. Copyright © 1985. Used by permission.

Judaica Press for an extract from *Mishnayoth*, vol. 4, *Order Nezikin*, 2d ed. Copyright © 1983. Used with permission.

Kluwer Academic Publishers for extracts from *Ngaju Religion*, by Hans Schärer. Copyright © 1963. Reprinted by permission of Kluwer Academic Publishers.

Alfred A. Knopf for an extract from *Buddhism: A Way of Life and Thought*, by Nancy Wilson Ross. Copyright © 1980 by Nancy Wilson Ross.

KTAV Publishing House for extracts from *Sayings of the Jewish Fathers (Pirke Aboth)*, edited and translated by Charles Taylor. Copyright © 1969. Used by permission.

Macmillan Publishing Company for extracts from *The Analects of Confucius*, translated by Arthur Waley, copyright © 1938 by George Allen & Unwin. And from *Introduction to Islam*, 2d ed., by F. M. Denny, copyright © 1994 by Macmillan Publishing Company.

Mouton de Gruyter, a division of Walter de Gruyter and Co., for extracts from *Divine Word and Prophetic Word in Early Islam*, by W. A. Graham. Copyright © 1977 by Mouton, The Hague.

National Council of the Churches of Christ for extracts from the *New Revised Standard Version of the Bible*. Copyright © 1989 by the Division of Christian Education of the National Council of the Churches of Christ in the United States of America. Used by permission. All rights reserved.

New Directions Publishing for extracts from *The Wisdom of the Zen Masters*, by Irmgard Schloegl, copyright © 1976. And from *The Dhammapada*, translated by Edward Babbitt, copyright © 1936. And from *New Seeds of Contemplation*, by Thomas Merton, copyright © 1961 by the Abbey of Gethsemani. And from *Regarding Wave*, by Gary Snyder, copyright © 1970 by Gary Snyder. All of the above reprinted by permission of New Directions Publishing Corp.

Ohio University Press/Swallow Press for extracts from *I Have Spoken: American History Through the Voices of the Indians*, compiled by Virginia I. Armstrong. Copyright © 1971, reprinted 1992.

Opinion Magazine for an extract from "Is There a Jewish View of Life?" by Albert Einstein, vol. 2, no. 17–18 (September 26, 1932).

Oxford University Press for extracts from *A Vedic Reader For Students*, translated by A. A. Macdonell, copyright © 1917, published by Clarendon Press. And from *The Religion of the Rigveda*, translated by H. D. Griswold, copyright © 1923, by permission of Oxford University Press. And from *Documents of the Christian Church*, 2d ed., edited by Henry Bettenson, copyright © 1963, by permission of Oxford University Press. And from *The New English Bible*, copyright © 1961, 1970, 1989 by the Delegates of the Oxford University Press and the Syndics of the Cambridge University Press. Reprinted by permission

Pacific Northwest Historical Quarterly for an extract from "Chief Seattle and Angeline," by Clarence B. Bagley, *Washington Historical Quarterly* 22 (1931): 252–55.

Pantheon Books for an extract from *Major Trends in Jewish Mysticism*, by Gershom Scholem. Copyright © 1941 by Schocken Publishing House, Jerusalem. Used by permission.

Paragon House for extracts from *Sufism*, by William Stoddart. Copyright © 1986.

Paulist Press for an extract from *Julian of Norwich: Showings*, translated by Edmund Colledge, OSA, and James Walsh, SJ. Copyright © 1978.

Penguin Books for extracts from *The Upanishads*, translated and edited by Juan Mascaro, copyright © 1965 by Juan Mascaro. And for extracts from *Buddhist Scriptures*, translated by Edward Conze, copyright © 1959 by Edward Conze. And for quotations from *Revelations of Divine Love*, by Julian of Norwich, translated by Clifton Wolters, copyright © 1966 by Clifton

Wolters. And for quotations from *The Koran,* translated by N. J. Dawood, 5th rev. ed., copyright © 1990 by N. J. Dawood. All of the above reproduced by permission of Penguin Books, Ltd.

The Philosophical Library for extracts from *Djanggawul: An Aboriginal Religious Cult of North Eastern Arnhem Land,* by Ronald M. Berndt.

Princeton University Press for an extract from *A Source Book in Chinese Philosophy,* translated by Chan, Wing-Tsit. Copyright © 1963, renewed 1991. Used with permission.

Putnam Publishing Group for extracts from *The Spirit of Shamanism,* by Roger Walsh. Copyright © 1990 by Roger Walsh.

Rabbinical Assembly and the United Synagogue of America for extracts from *Siddur Sim Shalom,* edited by Rabbi Jules Harlow. Copyright © 1985. Reprinted with permission.

Sri Ramanasraman, Tiruvannamalai, 606 603, Tamil Nadu, India, for extracts from *Talks with Sri Ramana Maharshi,* by Sri Munagala S. Venkataramaiah.

Random House for extracts from *The Buddhist Tradition,* by William Theodore de Bary, copyright © 1969 by William Theodore de Bary. And from *A History of Zen Buddhism,* by Heinrich Dumoulin, SJ, copyright © 1963. And from *The Wisdom of Confucius,* edited and translated by Lin Yutang, copyright © 1938, renewed 1966. And from *The Wisdom of China and India,* by Lin Yutang, copyright © 1942. And from *The Talmud: Steinsaltz Edition,* edited by Rabbi Adin Steinsaltz, copyright © 1990, published by the Israel Institute for Talmudic Publications. And from "Letter from the Birmingham City Jail," by M. L. King, Jr., in *The Right Thing to Do,* by James Rachels, copyright © 1989 by Random House, Inc. All of the above reprinted by permission of Random House, Inc.

Rider Books for extracts from *The Book of Certainty,* by Abu-Bakr Siraj Ed-din. Copyright © 1952.

Shambhala Publications for extracts from *Great Swan: Meetings with Ramakrishna,* by Les Hixon. Copyright © 1992 by Les Hixon. Reprinted by arrangement with Shambhala Publications, 300 Massachusetts Ave., Boston, MA 02115.

Sheed & Ward for extracts from *Confessions of St. Augustine,* translated by F. J. Sheed. Copyright © 1970.

Smithsonian Institution Press for extracts from "The Yaruros of the Capanaparo River, Venezuela," by V. Petrullo, in the *U.S. Bureau of American Ethnology Bulletin 123, Anthropological Papers,* no. 11. Copyright © 1939. Reprinted by permission of the Smithsonian Institution Press.

Sunday School Publishing Board of the National Baptist Convention, U.S.A., for an extract from the *Baptist Standard Hymnal.* Copyright © 1973. Used by permission of the Sunday School Publishing Board of the National Baptist Convention, U.S.A., Incorporated.

Sunstone Press, P.O. Box 2321, Santa Fe, NM 87504–2321, for a poem from *Songs of the Tewa,* by H. J. Spinden. Copyright © 1976 by Ailes Spinden. Courtesy of Sunstone Press.

University of Oklahoma Press for extracts from *The Sacred Pipe: Black Elk's Account of the Seven Rites of the Oglala Sioux,* by Joseph Epes Brown. Copyright © 1953.

University of Nebraska Press for extracts from *The World's Rim: Great Mysteries of the North American Indians,* by H. B. Alexander. Copyright © 1953.

The Theosophical Publishing House for extracts from *The Light of Asia,* by Edwin Arnold. Copyright © 1969.

Vedanta Society of Southern California, Hollywood, CA, for extracts from *Bhagavad Gita: The Song of God,* translated by Swami Prabhavananda and Christopher Isherwood, copyright © 1951, 1972. And from *The Crest-Jewel of Discrimination,* translated by Swami Prabhavananda and Christopher Isherwood, copyright © 1947.

The Viking Press for extracts from *Book of the Hopi,* by Frank Waters. Copyright © 1963 by Frank Waters, all rights reserved. Reprinted by permission of Viking Penguin, Inc.

Wadsworth, Belmont, CA 94002, for extracts from *Islam from Within: Anthology of a Religion,* by Kenneth Cragg. Copyright © 1980.

Samuel Weiser, Inc., York Beach, ME 03910, for an extract from *Foundations of Tibetan Mysticism*, by Lama Govinda. Copyright © 1960.

Yale University Press for extracts from *Buddhist Parables*, by E. W. Burlingame. Copyright © 1922.

The author has made every effort to trace the copyright holders of every extract in this book. If he has inadvertently overlooked any, he will be pleased to make the necessary arrangements at the first opportunity.

KL
with
OW

Gerald Durrell was born in India in 1925. His family settled on Corfu when he was a boy and he spent his time studying its wildlife. He relates these experiences in the trilogy beginning with *My Family and Other Animals,* and continuing with *Birds, Beasts and Relatives* and *The Garden of the Gods.* He writes with wry humour and great perception about both the humans and the animals he meets.

On leaving Corfu, Durrell returned to England to work at Whipsnade Park as a student keeper. His adventures there are told with characteristic energy in *Beasts in My Belfry.* A few years later, he began organizing his own animal-collecting expeditions. The first, to the Cameroons, was followed by expeditions to Paraguay, Argentina and Sierra Leone. He recounts these experiences in a number of books including *The Drunken Forest.* He also visited many countries while shooting various television series.

In 1959 Durrell realized a lifelong dream when he set up the Jersey Zoological Park, followed a few years later by the Jersey Wildlife Preservation Trust, renamed the Durrell Wildlife Conservation Trust in 1999.

Whether in a factual account of an expedition or a work of non-fiction, Durrell's style is exuberant, passionate and acutely observed. Gerald Durrell died in 1995.